D1396612

*The Complete Prophecies
of Nostradamus*

The Complete Prophecies
of Nostradamus

—

Edited and introduced by
NED HALLEY

CASTLE BOOKS

This edition published in 2001 by

CASTLE BOOKS
A division of Book Sales, Inc.
114 Northfield Avenue
Edison, New Jersey 08837

Published by arrangement with and permission of

Wordsworth Editions Ltd
Cumberland House, Crib Street
Ware, Hertfordshire SG12 9 ET

Copyright © Wordsworth Editions Ltd and Ned Halley 1999
Wordsworth ® is a registered trademark of Wordsworth Editions Ltd

All rights reserved. This publication may not be reproduced, stored in a retrieval system, or transmitted, in any form or by any means, electronic, mechanical, photocopying, recording or otherwise, without the prior permission of the publishers.

ISBN: 0-7858-1472-8

Typeset by Antony Gray

Printed in the United States of America

CONTENTS

EDITOR'S NOTE vii

WHO *WAS* NOSTRADAMUS? xi

Prophecies from 1500–1599 1

    'Retrospective' Prophecies 42

Prophecies from 1600–1699 45

Prophecies from 1700–1799 69

Prophecies from 1800–1899 101

Prophecies from 1900–1999 137

Prophecies from 2000–7000 203

Prophecies Yet To Be Dated 225

    Century One 225

    Century Two 228

    Century Three 232

    Century Four 237

    Century Five 244

    Century Six 251

    Century Seven 257

    Century Eight 261

    Century Nine 266

    Century Ten 273

INDEX 279

EDITOR'S NOTE

Nostradamus in Plain English

Fascination with the prophecies of Nostradamus has endured for centuries, and at the start of a new millennium our curiosity is quite naturally sharpened. Many of his predictions focus on this great moment in the Christian calendar, and some apparently forecast nothing less than an imminent end of the world.

But Nostradamus is no mere doomsayer. His visions of Armageddon are concerned as much with humankind's spiritual fall as with our self-destruction in war. So before attempting to digest the words he wrote 450 years ago, it is crucial to accept the prophet's own warning that his oracles are coded. They are allegorical, camouflaged in references to the past, moulded into the form and rhyme of verse. Astrology plays its part. He claimed that he could date all his predictions, but chose not to – with good reason. If any event came to pass in his own lifetime, exactly as foretold, he could be indicted as a sorcerer.

Many prophecies have been attributed to Nostradamus, but this book concerns itself only with those that are known without question to be from his own pen. They were first published in 1555 as *The Centuries*. The title causes confusion, because it makes the predictions appear as if they are a chronological series, presented century by century. But this is not the case at all. Nostradamus's *Centuries* are ten volumes each consisting of a hundred (thus a century) verses, in no sort of apparent sequence.

Nostradamus wrote down his prophecies as they came to him, and there is no pattern of time, place or events in the order which he ascribes to them. But many of them can be dated, and to make these remarkable verses as accessible as possible, this book arranges them in chronological order. Those that cannot be confidently dated appear in a separate section.

In translating from the original French, I have taken care to render each verse as faithfully as possible. Some translations are more literal than others, with the common aim of making them clear. Even in modern English, many verses do look perplexing at first reading, but a glance at the interpretations should make things very much plainer.

Nostradamus was a literate writer. He knew his history and obviously had a good understanding of the complex politics of his own time. As with any educated man of his period, it was natural to him to depend on classical allusion to make himself understood. Informed readers of the subsequent centuries would have needed no help with references to the characters and events, mythological or otherwise, of the Greek and Roman worlds. I am well aware that classical allusions are now much less-widely understood, and have tried to explain these wherever necessary.

One particular difficulty modern translators face is Nostradamus's frequent use of the same word, but with many distinct variations in meaning. One such is *grand*, which the seer uses 446 times throughout his quatrains. Such a liberally interpretative use of language was commonplace in the sixteenth century and still pertains today in modern French. A modern translator must therefore enter the sixteenth-century mind-set and not be afraid to follow an instinctive, rather than a purely dogmatic course. This contributes to greater clarity and increases the chances of a successful interpretation.

Nostradamus used a vocabulary of around 8,000 words in his writing of the quatrains, but it is vital to bear in mind the exigencies of the poetical form he chose. Shakespeare used twice this number of words, including plenty he had coined when the language could not supply the right one ready-made. This roughly reflects the relative extents of the French and English vocabularies – English has twice as many words – and goes some way towards explaining the continued use of nuance in French. It's a concept for which the English have no translation.

As to the subject matter of the predictions, it is immediately obvious that most concern themselves with conflict, massacre and destruction, usually involving kings. This has earned Nostradamus a reputation as a doomsayer. But it is vital to see these expectations in context. Throughout his life, Europe was at war as emerging nations battled to establish borders, dynasties, religious supremacy. Nostradamus's world was shaped by war, and he was right to see this pattern of life continuing far into the future. Not until four hundred years after his death has France experienced a period of peace longer than 30 years. Long may it last.

Finally, just how seriously are we supposed to take the prophet's words? As a journalist, I am quite happy to admit I approached the task of writing this Plain English guide to Nostradamus with the usual scepticism. I have studied translations and interpretations of the prophecies from the sixteenth century to the present day with a mixture of awe and disbelief. But as you make the acquaintance of the man, you cannot help discovering that, whichever spin you put on the verses, some of them are the clear, incontrovertible truth.

Nostradamus's expectations of events that were to take place in his own lifetime or shortly afterwards are often astonishingly shrewd. True, he did camouflage them to keep himself out of the clutches of the Inquisition – but with hindsight, the camouflage is very thin. It was one such prediction that brought Nostradamus to the close attention of the French Court, and thus of the world.

Henri II, King of France from 1547, died on 10 July 1559 in a manner quite specifically foretold by Nostradamus four years previously. In a jousting accident, the king was mortally wounded through his visor in the eye by a young officer of his guard. The king lingered for ten agonised days before he succumbed. Nostradamus's warning had been:

> The younger lion will overcome the older
> In single combat, on the field of war
> His eyes will be pierced in their golden helm
> Two breaks made one. He subsequently dies a cruel death.

Members of the Court, including Henri's widow Catherine de Medici, were well aware that this dreadful tragedy had been anticipated in detail. Nostradamus was known to the Queen, who had invited him to Court in 1556 and consulted him about her children's futures. The prophet's acquaintance with Catherine probably saved his life, because there were calls for his arrest as a magician. On the Queen's clear instruction, Nostradamus was left alone.

Thus did the name Nostradamus find a place in history. By the time he died in 1566 many of his predictions had come palpably true, and the authenticity of his 'supernatural' powers had been proved far beyond doubt. In the hundreds of years since, the accuracy of his forecasting has continued to intrigue and amaze.

But how did he do it? Perhaps it is simple. Like his near-contemporary Leonardo da Vinci, Nostradamus might have been a savant, capable of knowing things out of his own time. As a natural scientist and a well-travelled physician in regular contact with the movers and shakers of his own time, he was certainly well placed to make shrewd guesses at how the affairs of the world might turn out in the future. Extrapolating events 250 years ahead to, say, the French Revolution (as Nostradamus did with apparent exactness) is perhaps not such an awesome achievement for a man of canny political judgement.

What is important is that Nostradamus actually committed himself to these predictions and published them for all the world to see. He was soon accustomed to accusations that he was a charlatan, a servant of the Devil, even a Protestant. But he cared enough about what he had to say to stand by his words. He was clearly sincere. If any impression is made on readers of this book, I hope that this is the one you will be left with.

NED HALLEY
May 1999

WHO *WAS* NOSTRADAMUS?

'Mediaeval mystic' is a term regularly used to describe Nostradamus. But he was no such thing. Born on 14 December 1503 at St Rémy in Provence in the south of France, Michel de Nostredame was a child of the Renaissance. His father, Jacques, was a prosperous lawyer. Michel received a liberal education, largely from his two grandfathers, Pierre de Nostradame and Jean de St Rémy, both of whom had served as physicians to the court of René, Count of Provence. René was an enlightened ruler much concerned with the arts and a believer in religious tolerance. His realm provided a merciful haven for refugees fleeing the Catholic persecutions of Spain.

The Nostradame and St Rémy families were Jews, and certainly owed their safety and prosperity to René. But the Count died without an heir, and disputes over entitlement to his domains led to the annexation of Provence by the French crown in 1486. The region did maintain a measure of self-determination but after Louis XII's accession in 1498 had to submit to his ordinance that all Jews must be baptised into the Christian faith, or face exile. The Nostradames were pragmatic, and Michel was duly christened.

As he grew up, the boy had the benefit not just of a traditional classical education, but of Jewish teachings in the natural sciences still forbidden to Christians. As well as mastering Latin, Greek and ancient history, Michel learned from his grandfather Jean de St Rémy the practices of medicine, chemistry and astronomy. These three sciences were closely linked. It is hard now to understand that five hundred years ago the ingredients of pharmacology were planted and harvested in accordance with the configurations of the stars in the sky, but this was the mainstream medical practice of the day – and Michel proved to have a natural aptitude for it.

The family were left in no doubt that medicine was the boy's *métier*, and Michel was sent to college in Avignon to study the prescribed course of grammar, rhetoric and philosophy. He distinguished himself at Avignon, in astronomy above all. Jean-Aimé de Chavigny, later a student of Nostradamus and his first biographer, records that young Michel would explain to fellow students that the Earth was like a ball and that it 'revolved each year around the Sun' each day exposing one hemisphere then the other to the Sun's light as it spun on its axis. It might be unremarkable for a sixteen-year-old to recount this to class mates now, but Michel was doing it fifty years before Galileo was even born.

Autumn 1520 brought an unexpected interruption to studies. Plague struck Avignon and felled so many students and staff that the college was closed. But Nostradamus did not return home. Instead, he seems to have taken an active decision to follow in the footsteps of a role-model, the itinerant German physician Paracelsus. Just ten years the young man's senior, Paracelsus made famous medical discoveries in his journeys through Europe and the Middle East, and became a major figure in Renaissance science.

And so Nostradamus took to the road – for eight years. Where his travels took him is unknown, but they confirmed his vocation. In October 1529 he enrolled in the medical school at Montpellier – the most distinguished faculty in France. By 1533 he had graduated and set up in practice in Agen. He married and started a family. But again, plague struck. His wife and two children, none of whose names is known, succumbed.

Nostradamus fled Agen to practise his skills wherever they were needed. In the years following, he is believed to have worked in Bordeaux, Carcassonne, Toulouse and other cities, but never to have settled for a long period in any of them.

He specialised in treating plague diseases and it is at Marseilles in 1544, amidst the outbreak there, that he returns to the light of history. He studied at Marseilles under the leading doctor Louis Serres, and soon came into demand throughout Provence in his own right for his ability to manage plague outbreaks, not only treating individual patients, but advising on prevention, hygiene, diet and disinfection.

Practising his skills in the town of Salon, Nostradamus met Anne Ponsarde, the recent widow of a wealthy lawyer. On 11 November 1547, they married and moved into a comfortable house in Salon's rue Ferreiraux – now, of course, rue Nostradamus. But this renewed domestic bliss did not interrupt the wandering physician's travels. He now set out for Italy.

His purpose was not merely to extend his now famously effective plague treatments beyond the confines of France. He wished to visit the cradle of the Renaissance, Florence, and to discover the art and science of the new enlightenment at its very fountainhead. His motive? Nostradamus had by this time in his life found his second *métier*, that of a seer. He knew that he could foretell events, and he needed to know what precedents there were for this strange power. In Renaissance Italy he would be able to devour the teachings of the classical world, of the occult, which had been so long suppressed by a monopolistic Church.

It was in Italy in 1548 that one of the first famous stories of Nostradamus's powers emerges. At Ancona in the Marches he surprised his companions when, encountering a young Franciscan friar, the great man fell to his knees. 'Because I am in the presence of the Holy Father,' came the reply to the friar's bemused enquiry. The incident was well remembered by the Franciscan, Felix Peretti, who became Pope Sixtus V in 1585.

From now, Nostradamus's fame as a physician began its gradual eclipse. He seems to have continued, certainly throughout his Italian travels, to practise medicine, but the records of his visits to cities including Venice, Milan and Naples are concerned more with his reputation as a soothsayer. To visit Naples, resting place of the poet Virgil, who predicted the coming of Christ with unearthly accuracy, must have been one of Nostradamus's most treasured ambitions.

In 1555 the first written prophecies of Nostradamus, the *Centuries*, were published. He may have embarked on them, in the special *astrologerie* room he had added as a third storey to the Salon house, as early as 1549, but had not hurried to get them into print. Jean-Aimé Chavigny, who was his pupil at that time, recorded that (in paraphrase) 'He hesitated for a long time to publish them, realising that their revelations would certainly attract harsh criticism and mockery ... but overcome by his wish to be of use to the public, he published them. Immediately, news of his words spread by word of mouth through France and beyond, with great wonderment.'

The *Centuries*, in short, caused a sensation. The initial edition, which consisted of just the first three hundred and fifty quatrains, was published on 4 May 1555 (444 years to the month before this edition) with an introduction dedicated to his baby son César – the personification of the future. 'For long I have been foretelling what will come to pass,' the seer wrote, continuing (in paraphrase) that 'I was content to hold my tongue about unhappy events in my own time and farther into the future, knowing that rulers and religions will scorn what subsequent centuries will find to be true.'

Nostradamus had no faith, in other words, that those in the future who read his *Centuries* – and only those in power, he imagined, would be literate and able to read them – would place any value on his words. But he had, understandably, an irresistible urge to publish predictions he sincerely believed to be true and significant. And that is why he chose to write the prophecies in 'abstruse and contorted phrases – even the most urgent – so that whatever the events might be, they are written down in a way that will not shock the fragile sensitivities of readers. All is written in a metaphoric cloud instead of in plain prophecy.'

Introducing the second edition of the prophecies, Nostradamus went further. He dedicated the volume to the reigning French king, Henri II, reiterating the codification of the verses, but adding that, had he wished, he could have dated every single prophecy. He forebore from doing so, he said, for fear of being branded a magician.

It is doubtful whether the King ever read the letter of dedication, but there is no question that the stir caused by the *Centuries* brought Nostradamus to the attention of the Court. Henri's Queen, Catherine de Medici, was a follower of the occult and wished to meet this new seer at the earliest opporunity. He was summoned to Paris in July 1556 and had several interviews with Catherine. He was lodged in the palace of the Archbishop of Sens, where between his encounters with the Queen he was besieged by courtiers in quest of remedies for their ailments and horoscopes for their futures.

Paris buzzed with stories of the powers of the mysterious alchemist from the South. One concerned a page in the service of the aristocratic Beauveau family who knocked, late at night, on the seer's firmly locked door. The boy had come with a message from his master but had been distracted on the way by the disappearance of a hunting hound he had been told to take along with him on the journey. Before he even opened the door to hear the boy's message Nostradamus shouted from within: 'Don't make such a fuss about the lost dog. Go and look on the Orléans road and you'll find it there tied up.' The page duly found the stray, and the story was all round Paris by the morning.

Perhaps Nostradamus's most sensitive royal assignment was his summons to Blois, private home of Henri and Catherine's seven children. The Queen wished the seer to cast their horoscopes. As history relates, although three became kings of France, six of the seven were to die tragically young after lives blighted by murder, intrigue and serial adultery. What Nostradamus revealed to Queen Catherine we do not know, but many of the verses in the *Centuries*, once unravelled, give startlingly clear presages of the princes' and princesses' fates – just as several of his verses accurately depict the destinies of their parents.

The prophet's attendance at Court was brought to a sudden conclusion by a visit from an admirer. The lady, whom Nostradamus records only as 'a very honest woman' tipped him off that the Paris Justices intended to summon him. He was to be required to explain the nature of his occupation and to satisfy them that he was neither charlatan nor miracle-worker. Nostradamus could see the witch's dilemma better than most, and on the very next day was on his way back to Salon.

He returned home a rich man. The Queen and countless members of the Court had rewarded him handsomely for his services. He and Anne settled down to a contented life. They had six children. He became involved in local politics and good works. He dispensed diagnoses, medicines and horoscopes, and perhaps revelled in some of the many fables of his own achievements.

His now-renowned prophetic powers were, inevitably, put to the test. There is an appealing story of his stay at the Château de Fains in Lorraine, where he was the guest of the sceptical Comte de Florinville. Inspecting the home farm, Florinville picked out a pair of piglets, one black and one white, and challenged Nostradamus to name the fate of each. 'You will eat the black,' replied the seer, 'and a wolf will eat the white.'

Naturally, the count promptly and secretly told his cook to prepare the white piglet for that night's supper. But as the spitted pig awaited the evening's roasting, a wolf cub kept as a pet in the castle crept into the kitchen and made off with the feast. The cook, fearing the lord's wrath, replaced the stolen white with the black. Once roasted, he was convinced the count would be none the wiser.

As he and his guest enjoyed the meal, Florinville gleefully told Nostradamus his prophecy was void, for this was the white pig. But no, the sayer replied, it is the black. The cook was summoned, and told to bring the black pig with him. History does not relate the fate of the cook.

Nostradamus's health began to fail in his sixties. He is said to have suffered painfully from arthritis and probably succumbed to heart disease symptomised by oedema and shortness of breath. He received the last rites on the evening of 1 July 1566 and was found dead the following morning. His widow lived another 16 years and was buried alongside him in the Franciscan chapel at Salon. Man and wife were reunited under the tablet she had commissioned for her husband, with this inscription:

Into Almighty God's hands I commend the bones of illustrious Michel de Nostredame, alone judged by mortal men to describe in near-divine words the events of the whole world under the influence of the stars.

1500–1599

❦ 1/1 – 1555

Etant assis, de nuit secrette étude,
Seul, repose sur la selle d'airan,
Flambe exigue, sortant de solitude,
Fait proferer qui n'est à croire vain.

Sitting at night in my private study
At rest alone on my brass stool
A tiny flame sets loneliness aside
My utterances will not be found vain.

Nostradamus embarks on his
prophecies, quiet in the writing room at
the top of his house in Salon. Seated on
the prophet's brass stool, he is ready to
receive inspiration.

❦ 1/2 – 1555

La verge en main mise au milieu de
branches
De l'Onde il mouille et le limbe et le pied:
Un peur et voix fremissent par les
manches,
Splendeur divine, Le Divin près s'assied.

With divining rod in hand at the
heart of the tree
He finds water at root and branch.
A voice makes me quake with fear
God, in divine splendour, is near.

Nostradamus uses the metaphor of the
tree of life, into which he climbs to
dowse for the water of inspiration – and
receives the message of God.

❦ 3/2 – 1555

Le divin verbe donrra à la substance,
Comprins ciel, terre, or occult au laict
mystique
Corps, ame esprit ayant toute puissance
Tant soubs ses pieds comme au siege
Celique.

The Seer will give meaning to the
substance
Comprising heaven, earth,
alchemist's gold and mystic deeds
Body, soul and spirit will be all-
powerful
In Hell, just as in Heaven's seat.

This should be read in conjunction with
quatrains 1/1 and 1/2, and taken as an
integral part of Nostradamus's articles
of faith. It describes the disembodied
and trance-like state needed to foretell
the future, and rightly emphasises the
alchemistical influences that Nostradamus kept so well hidden from the
ruling Catholic church.

❦ 6/100 – 1555

Legis Cantio Contra Ineptos Criticos

Quos legent hosce versus maturé
censunto,
Profanum vulgus, et inscium ne
attrectato
Omnesq; Astrologi Blenni, Barbari
procul sunto,
Qui alter facit, is ritè, sacer esto.

The Law Will Be Invoked Against Inept Critics

May those who read this verse
    consider it carefully
Let the profane and ignorant keep
    their distance
Astrologers, idiots and barbarians
    too, stay away
He who does not, let him be sacred.

Nostradamus is railing against ill-versed reviewers of his work in his own lifetime and thereafter. His meaning is self-evident. Whoever buys and reads this book shall be considered sacred. Debunkers beware.

☙ 10/29 – 1555

De Pol Mansol dans caverne caprine
Caché et prins extrait hors par la barbe,
Captif mené comme beste mastine
Par Begourdans amenee pres de Tarbe.

Hidden in the goat's cave at St Rémy
He is seized, extracted by his beard
Led in captivity like a mongrel dog
He is taken near Tarbes, by the
    Biggorrans.

Most commentators simply throw up their hands at this one. St Rémy was Nostradamus's birthplace, and it is conceivable that he was predicting his own arrest by the Inquisition. Perhaps he knew of a goat's cave in which he intended to hide? If so, this is a superb double-bluff, as the Inquisition would be doctrinally bound *not* to rely on one of Nostradamus's prophecies for assistance in finding him.

☙ 9/81 – 1555

Le Roi rusé entendra ses embusches
De trois quartiers ennemis affaillir
Un nombre estranges larmes de
*   coqueluches*
Viendra Lemprin du traducteur faillir.

The crafty king is a master of ambush
    strategy
Enemies threaten from three sides
The hooded ones cry many dubious
    tears
The translator's borrowing fails.

Lemprin, erroneously taken as the Greek *lempros*, meaning splendour, by many translators, stems more believably from the French word *l'emprunt*, meaning a borrowing. Once this is understood, it becomes apparent that Nostradamus is jesting. He, of course, is the crafty king – the master of trickery. The enemies threatening him from three sides are Church, Army and State. Capuchin monks weep crocodile tears, and make a great show of upbraiding him for his prophecies. His many commentators and translators, because of all their borrowings and plagiarisms, fail to understand the true import of his words.

☙ 2/11 – 1555

Le prochain fils de l'aisnier parviendra
Tant esleue jusque au regne des fors
Son apre gloire un chacun la craindra
Mais ses enfans du regne gettez dehors.

The next son of L'Aisnier will
    succeed
Raised high to great privilege
Everyone will fear his bitter fame
But his children will be ejected from
    the kingdom.

This quatrain is credibly claimed to have been one of very few written at the request of one of Nostradamus's patrons, a landowner called L'Aisnier, who asked the seer (unwisely perhaps) to tell him the fate of his children.

❦ 7/3 – 1555

Apres de France la victoire navale
Les Barchinons, Saillinons, les Phocens
Lierre d'or, l'enclume serré dedans la
  basle
Ceux de Ptolon au fraud seront consens.

After the French naval victory
People from Barcelona, Salon and
  Marseilles
The gold-robber, an anvil enclosed
  in a ball
Men from Toulon are party to the
  fraud.

An unusual mention for Salon, the town where Nostradamus spent his last years, including those dedicated to writing the *Centuries*. This prediction is probably one intended for local interest only.

❦ 8/96 – 1550–66

La synagogue sterile sans nul fruit
Sera receu entre les infideles
De Babylon la fille du porsuit
Misere et triste lui trenchera les aisles.

The sterile synagogue, bearing no
  fruit
Will be taken by the infidels
The daughter of the persecuted
  Babylonian
Miserable and sad, her wings will be
  clipped.

This may refer to one of the great paradoxes of history, the flight of the Jews to Turkey in 1550–1566. Persecuted by the Christian Church throughout most of Europe, Jews were offered hospitality in Constantinople and Salonika by Suleiman the Magnificent, Sultan of Turkey. Nostradamus was a Jew by race rather than religion, his family having converted to Catholicism in 1463, 50 years before his birth. A fervent Catholic, Nostradamus, whose very name means Our Lady, must still have cared very much what happened to his dispossessed people.

❦ 6/48 – 1555

La saincteté trop faincte et seductive,
Accompaigné d'une langue diserte
Lacité vieille et Parme trop hastive,
Florence et Sienne rendront plus desertes.

Sanctity, both faint and too seductive
Accompanied by an agile tongue
The old city and Parma are too hasty
Florence and Siena will become more
  desert-like.

Another pun on Saint Catherine and her namesake, the unsaintly Catherine de Medici. Both Florence and Siena were devastated during the pre–1555 Habsburg-Valois Wars, and Nostradamus is here predicting further depredations, which did not, fortunately, transpire.

❦ 7/26 – 1555

Fustes et galees autour de sept navires
Sera livree une mortelle guerre
Chef de Madric recevra coup de vivres
Deux eschapees et cinq menees à terre.

Sailing ships and galleys around the
   seven vessels
A deadly war will be waged
The Madrileño Captain is wounded
   by an arrow
Two escape, and five are brought to
   land.

French pirates are recorded as having
attacked a small Spanish fleet in the
English Channel in the winter of 1555.
Captured vessels were towed into
Dieppe.

❦ 1/75 – 1555

Le tyran Sienne occupera Savone,
Le fort gaigné tiendra classe marine:
Les deux armées par ta marque
   d'Ancomme,
Par effrayeur le chef s'en examine.

The tyrant of Siena will occupy
   Savona
The fort taken, the fleet will be held
   back at sea
Two armies under the colours of
   Ancona
Will cause their commander to
   examine his conscience.

When Nostradamus visited Siena in the
1540s, the tyrant of this beautiful
Tuscan city was Spain. The Habsburg
Spanish king and Holy Roman
Emperor, Charles V, had lately
occupied most of Italy, and garrisoned
strategic cities with Spanish troops.

In 1552, a group of Sienese nobles
enlisted the support of France and
successfully liberated the city. But their
triumph was brief. *Cosimo de Medici,
Duke of Florence,* infuriated at French
interference and seeing a chance to
annexe Siena to his own domain, raised
a battalion to fight alongside the
imperial forces. The two armies may

well have flown the colours of Ancona –
a Papal State providing a convenient
unifying banner. Siena was besieged
and after brave resistance capitulated
in 1555. Cosimo also seized the port of
Savona to secure it against landings by
the French fleet.

Nostradamus was writing about these
events around the time they occurred.
As to the commander and his
conscience, the seer no doubt felt that
Cosimo's alliance with Charles V
amounted to unforgivable treachery
against a neighbouring Italian city
state. As a servant of Henri II and his
consort, Catherine de Medici,
Nostradamus had every need to
camouflage his writings about the
queen's kinsman.

❦ 4/57 – 1555

Ignare envie au grand Roi supportee,
Tiendra propos deffendre les escripitz
Sa femme non femme par un autre
   tentee,
Plus double deux ne fort ne criz.

Ignorant envy is tolerated by the
   great king
He will propose a ban on writing
His wife, no wife she, will be tempted
   by another
The treacherous couple will no
   longer complain so loudly.

Nostradamus is here complaining
about his treatment by Henri II and his
mistress, Diane de Poitiers. Henri lost
his life in a joust while wearing Diane's
colours – something which must have
pleased Nostradamus, as he foretold
the tragic event in 1/35 (see page 11),
four years before it actually happened.

❦ 1/18 – 1555–6

Par la discorde negligence Gauloise,
Sera passaige á Mahommet ouvert
De sang trempé la terre et mer Senoise,
Le port phocen de voiles et nefs convert.

Due to French discord and negligence
An opportunity will be afforded the
  Mohammedans
The country and coastline of Siena
  will be soaked in blood
And the port of Marseilles will groan
  with ships.

Normally taken to imply a future Islamic
invasion of Europe, this quatrain more
likely refers to the Habsburg/Valois
Italian Wars of 1555–6. Henri II
encouraged his erstwhile ally, Suleiman
the Magnificent (1496–1566), to attack
Elba. Suleiman attacked Piombino, near
Siena, instead, much to Henri's disgust,
as the island was an ally of the French.

❦ 7/29 – 1556

Le grand Duc d'Albe se viendra rebeller
A ses grands peres fera le tradiment
Le grand de Guise le viendra debeller
Captif mené et dressé monument.

The grand Duke of Alba will rebel
Betraying his parentage
Great Guise will vanquish him
He will be captured; a monument
  will be erected.

The Dukes of Alba (Spain) and Guise
(France) were military leaders of
Nostradamus's own time. Alba (1508–
82) was the commander in chief of the
forces of Charles V's Holy Roman
Empire at the age of only 30. After
Charles V's abdication in 1556, Alba
overran the Papal States, but was
obliged by his king, Philip II of Spain, to

restore them. Nostradamus seems to
have expected Alba to rebel against
this order, but he did not. Thus he
stayed on the same side as the Duke of
Guise in the wars against Protestanism.

❦ 3/4 – 1556–7

Quand seront proches de defaut des
* lunaires,*
De l'un à l'autre ne distant grandement,
Froid, siccité, danger vers les frontieres,
Mesme ou l'oracle a prins commencement.

When the moonstruck ones are near
  defeat
They will be close, one to the other
Cold, drought and danger at the
  borders
Even at the source of the oracle.

This relates to Nostradamus himself,
and to the reaction he expected from
the publication of his prophecies, most
notably from the Huguenots. During
December 1556–7 a very severe winter
did indeed follow on from a drought-
ridden summer. Add to that the
threatened Spanish invasion of Picardy,
and the quatrain is well-dated.

❦ 3/5 – 1556–7

Pres loing defaut de deux grands
* luminaires,*
Qui surviendra entre l'Avril et Mars
O quel cherté nais deux grans
* debonnaires,*
Par terre et mer secourrant toutes pars.

The two great luminaries, after their
  long defeat
Between April and March the
  following year
Bemoan their loss. Two high-born
  sophisticates
Will help all sides, by land and sea.

This is a continuation of the previous quatrain 3/4, in which Nostradamus shows that, thanks to the influence of two benevolent stars (and possibly two benevolent patrons), the terrible drought and winter of 1556/7 (both physical and metaphorical) would prove considerably less destructive than expected.

6/58 – 1557

Entre les deux monarques esloinguez
Lors que Sol par Selin clair perdue
Simulté grande entre deux indignez
Qu'aux Isles et Sienne la liberté rendue.

Between the two distanced monarchs
When the clear sun is lost because of Selin
Great enmity between the two indignant ones
Thus liberty is restored to Siena and the Islands.

Franco-Spanish wars in Italy. The Tuscan city-state of Siena, fought over for decades, was finally incorporated into the Florentine state on 19 July 1557 under the aegis of Cosimo de Medici. The Islands refer to Corsica among others.

8/7 – 1557

Verceil, Milan donra intelligence
Dedans Tycin sera faite la paye
Courir par Siene eau, sang, feu par Florence
Unique choir d'hault en bas faisant maie.

Vercelli, Milan will break the news
The pay-off will be in Pavia
Water, blood and fire from Florence will flow past Siena
The 'one' will fall from high to low shouting for help.

Cosimo de Medici, Duke of Florence, took possession of Siena on 19 July 1557. In the preceding years, the Sienese had resisted with great bravery but were brought low by lack of help, particularly from France.

10/6 – 1557

Sardou Nemans si hault desborderont,
Qu'on cuidera Ducalion renaistre,
Dans le collosse la plus part fuiront,
Vesta sepulchre feu estaint apparoistre.

The Gardon will flood Nîmes so badly
That they will imagine Deucalion reborn
Most will flee to the amphitheatre
Vesta's sepulchral fire will seem snuffed out.

Nîmes was badly flooded by the Gardon river on 9 September 1557. Rain fell for upwards of sixteen hours, and many ancient artefacts were uncovered by the ensuing floods.

4/34 – 1557

Le grand mené captif d'estrange terre
D'or enchainé ay Roy Chyren offert
Qui dans Ausone, Milan perdra la guerre
Et tout son ost mis à feu et à fer.

The great man is captured by a strange people
Chained in gold, he is offered to King Chyren
The same man will lose the war in Milan and Ausonia
His entire army will be put to fire and the sword.

Chyren is Nostradamian code for Henri. The great man is Anne, Duke of Montmorency, who served Henri II of

France as his commanding officer in the wars against the Huguenot forces of the Prince de Condé and against the Spanish. He was taken prisoner by the Spaniards, who put his entire force to the sword at the battle of St Quentin in 1557, but was released at the request of the king.

❦ 4/8 – 1557

La grand cité d'assaut prompt et repentin
Surprins de nuict, gardes interrompus
Les excubies et vielles sainct Quintin
Trucidés gardes et les pourtails rompus.

The great city will be caught out by a
    sudden and quick
Night assault, the guards will be
    taken
The watchmen and sentinels of St
    Quintin
Will be killed, and the gates torn
    down.

The famed battle at St Quentin brought defeat for the French army of Constable Anne de Montmorency at the hands of a Spanish force under the command of the Duke of Savoy on 10 August 1557.

❦ 1/19 – 1557

Lors que serpens viendront circuir l'are,
Le sang Troyen vexé par les Espaignes
Par eux grand nombre en sera faicte tare.
Chef fruict, caché aux mares dans les
    saignes.

When coffins circle the altars
And Trojans are harried by the
    Spanish
Many of them will suffer
Their leader flees, concealed by
    marsh and swamp.

On 27 August 1557, Admiral de Coligny (1519–1572) was surrounded at Saint-Quentin by upwards of sixty thousand Spaniards. With only a thousand exhausted men under his command, Saint-Quentin fell and de Coligny was taken. His brother, Andelot, who commanded for a short time in his stead, swam through the swamps to escape capture. Trojan blood is a Nostradamian euphemism for Royal blood, in this case that of Catherine de Medici, who had changed her royal emblem to one of a serpent biting its own tail, following the death of her husband, Henri II, in a joust.

❦ 3/38 – 1557

La gent Gauloise et nation estrange,
Outre les monts, morts prins et profligez
Au mois contraire et proche de vendage,
Par les Seigneurs en accord redigez.

The French people, and a nation of
    foreigners
Are overcome and killed beyond the
    mountains
Six months later, near harvest time
Their leaders sign a peace treaty.

This probably applies to the peace treaty of September 1557, between the Pope and the Spanish. The Duke of Guise, who fought on the Pope's behalf, found himself side-lined in the agreement.

❧ 9/40 – 1557

Pres de Quintin dans la forest bourlis
Dans l'abbaye seront Flamens ranches
Les deux puisnays de coups mi estourdis
Suitte oppressee et garde tous aches.

Near St Quentin, in the Bourlis
  forest
The Flemish will be butchered in the
  Abbey
The two youngest will be stunned by
  blows
Their followers beaten, their guard
  hacked to pieces.

At quite a stretch this can be seen to
apply to the August 1557 Battle of St
Quentin. The Spaniards had seized the
Abbey of Vermandois some time
before, but the Flemish massacre still
remains a mystery.

❧ 2/20 – 1557

Freres et soeurs en divers lieux captifs,
Se trouveront passer pres du monarque
Les contempler ses rameaux ententifs,
Desplaisant voir menton, front, nez, les
    marques.

Brothers and sisters, imprisoned in
  different places
Will have the monarch pass close by
  them
His heirs will look at them attentively
He is displeased to see the marks on
  their foreheads, chin and noses.

In September 1557, Henri II went to
view some Huguenot prisoners recently
captured in a raid, taking his children
with him. He was deeply angered at the
marks of brutality visible on the
prisoner's faces, and sternly upbraided
their captors.

❧ 7/16 – 1558

Entrée profonde par la grand Roine
    faicte
Rendra le lieu puissant inaccessible
L'armee des trois lions sera deffaite,
Faisant dedans cas hideux et terrible.

A deep entry will be made by the
  great queen
The place will become inaccessible
  and powerful
The three lion army will be defeated
Causing a hideous and terrible
  occurrence within.

This may relate to the English loss of
Calais in 1558, when it was recaptured
by the Duke of Guise for France. The
three lions in line 3 refers to a device on
the English royal standard of 'bloody'
Queen Mary Tudor (1516–1558).

❧ 9/88 – 1558

Calais, Arras secours à Theroanne
Paix et semblant simulera lescoutte
Soulde d'Alabrox descendre par Roane
Destornay peuple qui deffera le routte.

Calais and Arras will help
  Thérouanne
The spy will pretend and simulate
  peace
The Savoy mercenaries descend
  through Roanne
Turning aside those who yield the
  route.

Because of the mention of Calais, most
commentators attribute this to France's
recovery of the Channel port from
English occupation on 26 January
1558.

❦ 9/29 – 1558

Lors que celui qu'à nul ne donne lieu
Abandonner vouldra lieu prins non prins
Feu nef par saignes, butiment à Charlieu
Seront Quintin Balez reprins.

When the man who has nothing
    refuses to make way
They will wish to abandon the taken,
    yet untaken, place
Fresh fire through the swamps,
    bitumen at Charlieu
St Quentin and Calais recaptured.

This seems very complicated at first
glance, but taken step by step it
applies very neatly to the capture of
Calais on 6 January 1558, when the
Duke of Guise surprised even himself
by retaking this key channel port from
the English. St Quentin was given back
a year later, in the settlement of 1559.

❦ 6/64 – 1558

On ne tiendra pache aucune arresté
Tous recevans iront par tromperie
De paix et trefve, terre et mer protesté
Par Barcelone classe prins d'industrie.

They will keep no peace treaties
All the recipients will use deceit
In truce and peace the land and sea
    protest
The fleet is taken, through hard
    work, at Barcelona.

Treaties were big news in
Nostradamus's own time – each one
bringing new hope of peace in Europe
as the principal warmonger of the day,
Charles V, king of Spain, the
Netherlands and Germany as well as
Holy Roman Emperor, sought to extend
his dominion into Italy and beyond. In
the treaty of Barcelona on 29 June

1529, Charles made his peace with
Giulio de Medici, Pope Clement VII,
after sacking Rome for making an
alliance with the French. But this, like all
treaties of Charles's long and bloody
reign (1506–1558), failed to maintain
the peace, either between warring
powers or rival Catholic and Lutheran
interests. Nostradamus predicts,
correctly, that even after Charles's
death, future European treaties will fare
no better.

❦ 5/96 – 1558

Sur le milieu du grand monde la rose
Pour nouveaux faicts sang public espandu
A dire vrai on aura bouche close
Lors au besoing viendra tard l'attendu.

There is a rose in the middle of the
    great earth
Because of new deeds, public blood is
    shed
To be honest, their mouths will be
    closed
Then, when needed, the long-
    awaited one will be late.

The rose, insignium of the Tudor
dynasty, is blamed by Nostradamus for
intrigues and crimes in the wider world.
The diplomacy of Queen Elizabeth I
(reigned 1558–1603), who was
promised in marriage to the sovereigns
of both France and Spain at different
times, was indeed successful in
manipulating continental powers to the
benefit of England. Nostradamus will
have known the Queen's reputation
well, and no doubt understood that she
would keep her suitors waiting a very
long time indeed.

6/87 – 1558

L'election faite dans Frankfort
N'aura nul lieu Milan s'opposera
Le sien plus proche semblera si grand fort
Que outre le Rhin és mareschz chassera.

The election which happened in
  Frankfurt
Will not be allowed, Milan will
  oppose it
The closest ally will seem so very
  strong
That he will drive him into the
  marshes, beyond the Rhine.

Ferdinand I (1503–1564) was crowned
Holy Roman Emperor in Frankfurt on 24
March 1558. The Pope, Paul IV, would
not recognise him, but conveniently
died in the following year and was
replaced by Pius IV, who was more
compliant. The Emperor devoted his
brief reign to trying to sort out religious
wars in Germany – with scant success.

2/78 – 1558

Le grand Neptune du profond de la mer,
De gent Punique et sang Gaulois meslé
Les isles à sang pour le tardif ramer,
Plus lui nuira que l'occult mal celé.

Great Neptune, from the depths of
  the ocean
Part Carthaginian, part French
The isles will be bloodied by those
  slow to leave
It will cause him more harm than the
  poorly hidden secret.

The island of Minorca was attacked by
the Turkish fleet in 1558. They
succeeded in taking the main port,
Ciudadela, and putting it to the sack.
Stories of bribery and equivocation on
the part of the Turks abounded,
causing problems for the French, who
were hoping for Turkish support in their
Italian ventures.

6/19 – 1558

La vraie flamme engloutira la dame
Que voudra mettre les Innocens à feu
Pres de l'assaut l'excercite s'enflamme
Quant dans Seville monstre en boeuf
sera veu.

The true flame will swallow up the
  lady
Who wishes to burn the Innocents
Before the assault the army is
  inflamed
When in Seville a monstrous ox is
  seen.

Nostradamus, never favourable
towards Queen Elizabeth I of England,
seems to have assumed that she, like
her elder sister Queen Mary I (1516–58)
whom she succeeded, would burn at
the stake hundreds of Christians
unwilling to deny the 'true' faith.
Elizabeth did no such thing. The army
mentioned could be one of any number
of invasion forces prepared against
England, and the monstrous ox an
allusion, perhaps, to the notorious beef-
eating habits of the British.

6/70 – 1558

Au chef du monde le grand Chyren sera,
Plus oultre apres aimé, craint, redoubté
Son bruit et loz les cieux surpassera,
Et du seul titre victeur fort contenté.

Great Chyren will be leader of the
  world
Loved, feared, and dreaded, after the
  'ne plus ultra'
His fame and praises will reach
  beyond the heavens
He will be satisfied with the simple
  title of 'victor'.

This was intended as a flattering quatrain to massage the ego of Henri II (1519–1558). Nostradamus needed to be in his good graces to survive the Inquisition. He implies here that Henri will become greater even than Charles V (1500–1558), Holy Roman Emperor and the 'ne plus ultra' of line 2. Might Nostradamus have been hoping that Henri, flattered into imbecility by his comparisons, would forget 1/35, which accurately predicted his death in a joust?

❦ 1/35 – 1559

Le lion jeune le vieux surmontera,
En champ bellique par singulier duelle
Dans caige d'or les yeux lui crevera,
Deux classes une, puis mourir, more
*   cruelle.*

The younger lion will overcome the
    older
In single combat, on the field of war
His eyes will be pierced in their
    golden helm
Two breaks made one. He
    subsequently dies a cruel death.

This is the famous quatrain foretelling the death of Henri II, King of France, on 10 July 1559. Despite warnings from Nostradamus and Catherine de Medici, his queen, Henri insisted on taking part in a three-day tournament to celebrate the forthcoming double marriage of his sister and his daughter to the Duke of Savoy and King Philip II of Spain, respectively. Victorious on the first two days, Henri was disappointed not to unseat Gabriel de Lorge, Count Montgomery and captain of his Scottish guard, on the third day. Against Montgomery's wishes, the king insisted on a rematch. In the ensuing clash, their two lances splintered, and entirely by accident that of Montgomery entered the king's gilt helmet, puncturing his head, just above the eye. The king died, in agony, ten days later, throwing the future of France into confusion.

❦ 7/4 – 1559

Le duc de Langres assiegé dedans Dolle
Accompaigné d'Ostun et Lyonnis
Geneve, Auspour, joinct ceux de
*   Mirandole*
Passer les monts contre les Anconnois.

The Duke of Langres is besieged in
    Dôle
Accompanied by men from Autun
    and Lyons
Geneva and Augsburg join Mirandola
Crossing the mountains against the
    Anconans.

A convoluted quatrain sometimes interpreted to concern the religious wars of the very brief reign of Francis II, King of France from 1559–60.

❦ 8/73 – 1559

Soldat barbare le grand Roi frappera,
Injustement non esloigné de mort,
L'avare mere du fait cause fera
Conjurateur et regne en grand remort.

The barbarian soldier will strike the
    king
Unjustly, bringing him near death
The greedy mother will make much
    of the deed
The conspirator and the realm will
    wallow in remorse.

Many different assassinations have been suggested for this one, but it almost certainly applies to the death of the near-ubiquitous Henri II, who was mortally injured in a joust by the commander of his Scottish Guard, on 10 July 1559.

☙ 7/10 – 1559

Par le grand Prince limitrophe du Mans
Preux et vaillant chef de grand excercite
Par mer et terre de Gallotz et Normans,
Caspre passer Barcelone pillé isle.

The great prince who borders Le
  Mans
The gallant and brave leader of the
  army
Will cross land and sea with the
  Bretons and Normans
They will pass Barcelona and
  Gibraltar to pillage the island.

This is one of Nostradamus's
'conditional', or 'retroactive' quatrains.
Here he is speculating on what would
have happened if Henri II had not been
accidentally killed in a joust. Claude de
Guise, Henri's cousin, held all the lands
around Le Mans, and Nostradamus
suggests that instead of wasting his
energies against the Protestants,
Claude would instead have led a
successful invasion against Spain and
North Africa.

☙ 9/52 – 1559

La paix s'approche d'un costé, et la guerre
Oncques ne feut la pursuitte si grande,
Plaindre homme, femme, sang innocent
* par terre*
Et ce fera de France à toute bande.

Peace comes from one side, war from
  another
Never before was it so strongly
  sought after
Pity the men and women, their
  innocent blood is shed
Throughout the whole of France.

The Treaty of Cateau-Cambrésis was
signed on 3 April 1559, effectively
ending the wars between France and
Spain. Two months later, Henri II was
killed in the famous joust predicted by
Nostradamus. The Treaty heralded a
time of much inter-religious warfare in
France, culminating in the Massacre of
the Huguenots.

☙ 10/53 – 1559

Les trois pellices de loing s'entrebatron
La plus grand moindre demeurera à
* l'escoute*
Le grand Selin n'en fera plus patron
Le nommera feu peste blanche routte.

The three harlots fight each other
  from afar
The greater will stay to hear the
  lesser
Great Selin will no longer be her
  boss
He will call her fire, plague and white
  rout.

Could this be about the three Royal
mistresses of Henri II? Henri wore
Diane de Poitier's colours during his
fatal joust with Count Montgomery on
10 July 1559. The final line could refer
to the king's feelings during his ten-
day-long death agony.

☙ 3/55 – 1559

En l'an qu'un oeil en France regnera,
La court sera en un bien dascheux trouble.
Le grand de Bloys son amy tuera,
Le regne mis en mal et doubte double.

In the year France is ruled by a one-
  eyed man
The court will be very troubled
The great one of Blois will kill his
  friend
The realm put in harm's way and
  double uncertainty.

Henry II (1519–59) lived for ten agonised days after the accident which cost him his eye. This event, which Nostradamus had accurately predicted years before, did indeed cast France into a realm of troubles.

❦ 8/54 – 1559

Soubz la colleur du traicte mariage
Fait magnanime par grand Chyren selin
Quintin, Arras recouvrez au voyage
D'espaignolz fait second banc macelin.

Under the glue of a marriage
  settlement
Great Chyren Selin does a
  magnificent act
Quintin and Arras are recovered
  during the journey
A second butcher's table is made by
  the Spanish.

Nostradamus foresees Henri II (Great Chyren Selin) turning the tables on Spain. Philip II's armies had humiliated the French at St Quentin in 1557 and held the Spanish Netherlands (in which Arras was the principal southern stronghold), where Henri was unsuccessful in an invasion bid in the same year. Henri relinquished his ambitions against Spain in a treaty of 1559 and died in the same year. An unfulfilled prediction.

❦ 9/47 – 1559–60

Les soulz signez d'indigne delivrance
Et de la multe auront contre advis
Change monarque mis en perille pence
Serrez en caige se verront vis à vis.

The signatories of the shameful
  deliverance
Will receive conflicting advice from
  the crowd

Due to change in the monarchy,
  thought becomes dangerous
They will face each other, locked in a
  cage.

This sounds rather twentieth century and Orwellian, although it probably applies to Francis II (1544–1560), the weak son of Henri II, who was so shamefully dominated by the two Guises following his sudden accession to the throne following his father's death in a joust.

❦ 1/13 – 1560

Les exilez par ire, haine intestine,
Feront au Roy grand conjuration
Secret mettront ennemis par la mine,
Et ses vieux siens contre aux sedition.

Those exiled through anger and
  internal feuds
Will hatch a great plot against the
  king
They will place enemies, in secret, by
  threats
And the king's followers will be
  undermined.

This prophecy came true five years after its publication. It tells of the 1560 Conspiracy of Amboise, in which the Bourbons and the Montmorencys conspired to kill the Duke of Guise and kidnap the king, Francis II. The plot was exposed by an informant, leading to the arrest and murder of most of the perpetrators. An outraged De Guise hung their bodies around the walls of Amboise castle.

❦ 3/41 – 1560

Bossu sera esleu par le conseil,
Plus hideux monstre en terre n'appareu,
Le coup voulant prelat crevera l'oeil,
Le trasitre au Roy pour fidelle receu.

The hunchback is elected by the
council
A more hideous monster never
appeared on earth
A direct shot will pierce his eye
This traitor whom the King received
in good faith.

The hunchback is the Prince de Condé,
arch-conspirator against the throne and
the Catholic church, and thus loathed
by Nostradamus. He was elected chief
of the Huguenot council on 19 March
1560. After many plots against his king,
for which he was forgiven more than
once, the Prince was captured at the
battle of Jarnac in 1569. He was
summarily executed with a pistol shot to
the head.

❦ 10/59 – 1560

Dedans Lyon vingt et cinq d'une haleine,
Cinq citoyens, Germains, Bressans,
*   Latins,*
Par dessous noble conduiront longue train,
Et descouverts par abois de matins.

In Lyons, 25 people with a common
purpose
Five citizens, with Germans, Bressans
and Italians
Below, nobles lay a trail of powder
And are discovered by barking guard
dogs.

The conspiracy of September 1560 in
which five Lyons citizens, including the
Prince de Condé, colluded with foreign
Protestants to blow open the gates of

the city and allow it to be seized by
Huguenots. The plot was discovered by
the night watch.

❦ 2/9 – 1560

Neuf ans le regne le maigre en paix
*   tiendra*
Puis il cherra en soif si sanguinaire
Pour lui grand peuple sans foi et loi
*   mourra*
Tué par un beaucoup plus debonnaire.

For nine years the thin man's rule
will be peaceful
Then he will fall into such a bloody
thirst
A great nation, faithless and lawless,
will die for him
Killed by a force much better than
himself.

Ivan IV, the Terrible, first Tsar of Russia
(1530–1584) was a contemporary
monster whose reputation would have
been known to Nostradamus. Ivan
succeeded as tsar of Muscovy as a
child, officially taking the reins of power
at 21 in 1551. He waged war beyond
Muscovy's borders into the wider
reaches of Russia, but maintained
peace at home until 1560 when his
beloved consort, Anastasia, died
suddenly. It was at this moment that he
became a crazed despot, submitting
his realm (which had no established
religion, and precious little civil law) to
the reign of terror for which he is
remembered. Ivan was famed for his
great height and martial figure. He was
not killed, but after an apopleptic fit,
exchanged his imperial robes for the
humble habit of a monk – thus dying as
a far better man than he had lived.

❦ 3/66 – 1560

Le grand Balif d'Orléans mis à mort
Sera par un de sang vindicatif,
De mort merite ne mourra par sort
Des pieds et mains mal le faisait captif.

The grand bailiff of Orléans
    condemned to death
By a hot-blooded man
He will not die this deserved death,
    nor any other
His bound hands and feet will not
    restrain him.

In November 1560, the grand bailiff
(chief magistrate) of Orléans, Jerome
Groslot, tried to hand over the city to
the Huguenot Prince de Condé. He
failed and was condemned to die. But
he escaped and his ultimate fate
remains unknown.

❦ 10/39 – 1560

Premier fils veufve malheureux mariage
Sans nuls enfans deux Isles en discord,
Avant dix-huit incompetent age.
De l'autre près plus bas sera l'accord.

The widow's eldest son, unhappy
    marriage
Without children two Isles in discord
Before eighteen still under age
The next eldest will be betrothed
    even younger.

It looks cryptic, but this is an
astounding forecast. The son is Francis
II of France, eldest child of Henri II (d.
1559) and Catherine de Medici.
Married to Mary Queen of Scots when
he was 14, the sickly Francis fathered
no children and died from a tumour in
his ear on 5 December 1560, aged only
16. Having mothered no heir, Mary
returned to Scotland, where she
famously did much to put the two Isles

(her own kingdom and England) into
discord. Francis's younger brother,
Charles IX (1550–74), who succeeded
him, had become engaged to Elizabeth
of Austria in 1561, aged only 11. The
couple did not marry until 1570.

❦ 9/59 – 1562

A la Ferté prendra la Vidame
Nicol tenu rouge qu'avoit produit la vie.
La grand Loisne naistra que fera clame.
Donnant Bourgongne à Bretons par
    envie.

He will seize La Ferté-Vedame
Nicol will take the red who gave him
    life
Great Louise will be born, in secret
Giving Burgundy to the Bretons,
    through envy.

Louise may be the daughter of Nicolas
de Lorraine, a kinsman of the Guise
family. She later married Henri III.
However she was neither illegitimate
nor was she known to have given birth
to a bastard child. La Ferté-Vedame
was the scene of the first major battle in
the 1562 Wars of Religion. Louise was
nine years old at the time.

❦ 9/56 – 1562

Camp pres de Noudam passera Goussan
    ville,
Et à Maiotes laissera son ensigne,
Convertira en instant plus de mille,
Cherchant les eux remettre en chaine et
    legne.

The army, near Houdan, will pass
    through Goussainville
It will cede its flag to the keen soldiers
In one instant, they will convert
    more than a thousand
Searching for the leaders, to be
    chained and burned at the stake.

This appears to describe a battle during the Wars of Religion, possibly Dreux, in 1562.

❦ 9/85 – 1562–98

Passer Guienne, Languedoc et le Rosne
D'Agen tenans de Marmande et la Roole
D'ouvrir par foi par roi Phocen tiendra
   son trosne
Conflit aupres saint Pol de Mauseole.

Passing through Guienne, the
   Languedoc and the Rhône
From the direction of Agen;
Marmande and La Réole will be held
Opening, through faith, the throne of
   Marseilles
Fighting near St Paul-de-Mausole.

An unsatisfactory quatrain that may contain a number of misprints. *Par roi*, for instance, could be taken as *parroi* or *parroy*, implying either walls or the sea-shore. *Par foi* can mean either by faith or sometimes. Given all that, this may represent any one of a dozen minor conflicts during the nine Wars of Religion.

❦ 3/29 – 1563

Les deux nepveux en divers lieux nourris
Navale pugne, terre peres tombez
Viendront si haut esleuez enguerris
Venger l'injure ennemis succombez.

Two nephews, brought up in
   different places
A naval battle, fathers fall
They will rise very high, through
   warfare
Their enemies will die so that the
   insult is avenged.

Said to be concerning the family of the Duke of Montmorency (1493–1567), the

Constable of France who drove the English out of Le Havre in 1563. He died from wounds received at the hands of Huguenot forces, and the insult was most emphatically avenged at the massacre of the Huguenots in Paris five years afterwards.

❦ 8/10 – 1564

Puanteur grande sortira de Lausanne,
Qu'on ne seura l'origine du fait,
Lon mettra hors toute le gente loingtaine
Feu veu au ciel, peuple estranger deffait.

A foul stink will come from Lausanne
No-one will know what caused it
All foreigners will be driven out
Fire will be seen in the sky, the aliens
   defeated.

Nostradamus's bitterest rival was Théodore de Bèze (1519–1605), who originally taught Greek at Lausanne before becoming John Calvin's chief disciple. He evolved into the foremost apostle of Calvinism following Calvin's death in 1564, and made no secret of his disdain for '*Monstre*-damus's' inflated prophecies. In a childish response, Nostradamus called him Bèze the 'beast'. '*Bête Noire*' Bèze would have enjoyed debunking this particular prophecy, because it was never fulfilled.

❦ 4/81 – 1564

Pont on fera promptement de nacelles,
Passer l'armee du grand prince Belgique
Dans profondres et non loing de Brucelles,
Outre passés, detrenchés sept à picque.

A pontoon bridge will quickly be
   built
Over which the Belgian prince's
   army will pass

It will pour forth, not far from
Brussels
Once through, seven will be killed by
pikes.

The word Belgique was archaic when
Nostradamus was writing this quatrain,
and can only refer to the gift of the
Belgae's original tribal territory by
Charles V to his son, Philip II, in 1554.
An invasion of France was attempted in
1564, using a boat-bridge across the
River Scheldt.

❦ 1/33 – 1564

Pres d'un grand pont de plaine spatieuse,
Le grand lion par forces Cesarees
Fera abbattre hors cité rigoureuse,
Par effrai portes lui seront reserées.

Near a large bridge, on an ample
plain
The great lion of the Imperial forces
Will make his kill outside the puritan
city
The gates will then be opened to
him, through fear.

This is wishful thinking on the part of
Nostradamus, in an effort to please one
of his famous clients, the Duke of
Savoy. He is predicting that Geneva will
fall to the Duke, taking with it John
Calvin (1509–1564), spiritual leader of
the Huguenots. Nostradamus, coming
from a family of Jews who converted to
Catholicism, was strongly anti-
Protestant.

❦ 8/6 – 1565

Clarté fulgure à Lyon apparente
Luisant, print Malte subit sera estainte
Sardon, Mauris traitera decepvante
Geneve à Londes à coq trahison fainte.

Bright lightning will appear, shining,
over Lyons
Taken by surprise, Malta will
suddenly be wiped out
St Maurice will deceive Sardinia
From Geneva to London they will
feign treason against France.

It is well-known that the Normans –
Norsemen settled in northern France –
invaded England in 1066. It is not so
well-known that the Normans also
invaded the Mediterranean island of
Malta in 1090, establishing a Christian
culture there that has lasted to this day.
The great siege of Malta by the Turks of
Sultan Suleiman II began in May 1565.
He brought a force of 38,500 men
against 9,000 Maltese defenders. But
contrary to Nostradamus's
expectations, the island was not
overrun. In one of the great battles of
history, Malta repelled all attacks and
became one of the foremost
strongholds of Christianity against
Muslim incursion. Support for Malta
came from all over Europe.

❦ 6/63 – 1566

La Dame seule au regne demeurée
D'unic esteint premier au lict d'honneur,
Sept ans sera de douleur explorée.
Puis longue vie au regne par grand
*   heur.*

The Lady is left alone in the
kingdom
Her only husband dead on the field
of honour
There will be seven years of
mourning
Then she will live long, for the
kingdom's good.

Catherine de Medici, Henri II's widow,
did mourn him for exactly seven years –

until 1 August 1566. She lived another 23 years, and Nostradamus felt certain she would do nothing but good. His loyalty to her was understandable – she spared his life when members of the court accused him of causing the king's death by predicting it – but misplaced.

❦ 7/9 – 1566

Dame à l'absence de son grand capitaine
Sera priee d'amours du Viceroi
Faincte promesse et malheureuse estraine
Entre les mains du grand Prince Barrois.

The lady, in the absence of her great
    Captain
Will be begged for love favours by
    the Viceroy
A fraudulent promise, unhappiness in
    love
She falls into the hands of the Barred
    Prince.

Diane de Poitiers (1499–1566) was the mistress of Henri II of France. Twenty years his senior, she nevertheless outlived him, and after his death in 1559 factions (a Barred prince is one of the royal line) at court sought to maintain her influence. But she sensibly withdrew from public life to her château at Anet.

❦ 8/23 – 1567

Lettres trouvees de la roine les coffres,
Point de subscrit sans aucun nom
    d'hauteur
Par la police seront caché les offres,
Qu'on ne scaura qui sera l'amateur.

Letters are found in the queen's
    cabinet
Without signature, or author's name
The offers are concealed by a ruse
So no-one will know who her lover is.

Nostradamus may well have met the 14-year-old Mary, Queen of Scots (1542–1587), when he was summoned to the French Court in 1556. Eleven years later, the so-called Casket Letters appeared, purporting to reveal the truth about the murder of the Queen's second husband, Lord Darnley. Following Mary's execution for 'sedition', in 1587, the letters, which may well have been fakes, conveniently disappeared.

❦ 10/19 – 1568

Jour que sera par roine saluee
Le jour apres le salut, la priere
Le compte fait raison et valbuee
Par avant humbles oncques ne feut si
    fiere.

One day she will be greeted by the
    queen
The next day she will pray
The rendering is right and good
Among humble women, never was
    there one so proud.

Mary, Queen of Scots (1542–1587), no longer a queen following her abdication in favour of her son James VI in 1567, went to the executioner's block on 8 February 1587. This followed her exile to England in 1568, when she threw herself on the mercy of Elizabeth I. Elizabeth confined her for life, eventually signing her death warrant when news was brought her that Mary was plotting to usurp the English throne for the Catholics. Mary was seen to pray just before the fall of the headsman's axe.

❦ 4/72 – 1560s

Les Artomiques par Agen et l'Estore
A sainct Felix feront leur parlement
Ceux de Basas viendront à la mal'heure
Saisir Concon et Marsan promptement.

The Artomics, through Agen and
  Lectoure
Will hold their discussions at St Felix
Men from Bazas will arrive at a bad
  time
They will promptly seize Condom
  and Marsan.

Artomics are Nostradamian code for
Protestants, so known after *artos*, the
Greek word for leavened bread – which
is taken in the observance of
Communion. Nostradamus is predicting
the growth of the Protestant movement
in southwest France, where all the
towns mentioned are situated.

❦ 6/75 – 1570

Le grand pilot par Roi sera mandé,
Laisser la classe pour plus haut lieu
  attaindre
Sept ans apres sera contrebandé,
Barbare armée viendra Venise craindre.

The great pilot will be ordered by
  the king
To leave the fleet, for a higher rank
Seven years later he will revolt
A Barbarian army will cow Venice.

This successful quatrain refers to
Gaspard de Coligny (1519–1572), who
was admiral-in-chief of Henri II's fleet.
He resigned seven years later, when
the king died, in order to ally himself
with the Calvinist party. He became
instrumental in fomenting the Huguenot/
Catholic wars, which took place at the
same time that Suleiman the

Magnificent and Selim II were harrying
Venice and her possessions in the
Mediterranean.

❦ 2/79 – 1571

La barbe crespe et noir par engin
Subjugera la gent cruelle et fiere
Le grand Chiren ostera du longin,
Tous les captifs par Seline barriere.

The black and curly-bearded one, by
  ingenuity
Subdues a fierce and cruel people
Great Henry will take from far away
All captives of the Turkish banner.

Nostradamus deals with the battle of
Lepanto in numerous quatrains. Under
Charles X of France, 1500 Christian
slaves were freed from enforced
service in the Turkish fleet. Henri III only
took over the throne in 1574, so
Nostradamus would seem to be three
years out in his use of Henry, in line 3.
However the commander of the
crusade against the Turks was a certain
Don John of Austria, who was, indeed,
dark and bearded.

❦ 1/94 – 1571

Au port Selin le tyran mis à mort,
La Liberté non pourtant recouvree
Le nouveau Mars par vindicte et remort
Dame par force de frayeur honoree.

The tyrant will be killed at the port
  of the crescent moon
Liberty, however, will not be
  regained
A new war, caused by vengeance and
  remorse
Will cause Our Lady to be honoured,
  through fear.

The death of Ali Pasha at the battle of Lepanto, on 7 October 1571, did not signal the end of Turkish aggression in the Mediterranean. It persisted for centuries, leading to the eventual loss of Muslim influence over the region, and a return to the Catholic ascendancy through force of arms.

❦ 6/91 – 1571

Du conducteur de la guerre navale,
Rouge effrené, severe horrible grippe,
Captif eschappé de l'aisné dans la basles
Quant il naistra du grand un filz
    Agrippe.

From the commander of the naval war
The unbridled red man, a severe,
    terrible quarrel
A captive, in chains, escapes from the
    elder
The great man will have an Agrippan
    son.

This could be related – at rather a long stretch – to the 1571 Battle of Lepanto (see the surrounding quatrains) in which 15,000 Christian slaves were freed from the Turks.

❦ 3/31 – 1571

Aux champs de Mede, d'Arabe et
    d'Armenie,
Deux grans copies trois fois s'assembleront
Pres du rivage d'Araxes la mesgnie,
Du grand Soliman en terre tomberant.

On the fields of Persia, Arabia and
    Armenia
Two great armies will assemble three
    times
Near the bank of the Araxes the
    household
Of Great Suleiman himself will
    prostrate themselves.

Yet another Battle of Lepanto quatrain. In 1571, sixteen years after the quatrain was first published, Don John of Austria thrashed Selim II, son of Great Suleiman, near a place called Cape Papa, which was then known as Araxum.

❦ 10/95 – 1571

Dans les Espaignes viendra Roi
    trespuissant
Par Mer et terre subjugant or midi
Ce mal fera rabaissant le croissant
Baisser les aesles à ceux du vendredi.

A great king will enter Spain
By sea and land he will subjugate the
    southern gold
This evil will cause the lowering of
    the crescent flag
Clipping the wings of the Muslims.

This very clearly applies to Philip II of Spain (1527–1598) who clipped the wings of the Turks at the Battle of Lepanto, and was responsible for ejecting the Moors from Spain in 1571. His power was in large part due to his inheritance of the extensive Spanish colonies in the New World, on which he came to rely for the replenishment of his treasury.

❦ 10/97 – 1571

Triremes pleines tout aage captif
Temps bon à mal, le doux pour amertume
Proie à Barbares trop tost seront hastifs
Cupid de veoir plaindre au vent la plume.

Triremes full of captives of all ages
Good for nothing times, the sweet
    taken for bitter
In too much haste, they will become
    Barbarian prey
Anxious to see smoke taken by the
    wind.

Both sides in the Crusader Wars forced captured soldiers to row their galleys. It was a cause for great joy when such unwilling crews were liberated, as at the Battle of Lepanto in 1571.

❦ 9/15 − 1572

Pres de Parpan les rouges detenus
Ceux du milieu parpondrez menez loing
Trois mis en pieces, et cinq mal soustenus,
Pour le Seigneur et Prelat de Bourgoing.

The reds are detained near
  Perpignan
Their entrails are drawn, and they
  are quartered
Three are torn apart, and five are
  stretched on the rack
For the Lord and Prelate of
  Burgundy.

This complex quatrain has never been adequately translated until now, most commentators relying on the literal definition of each word rather than on the intended wordplay. The secret lies in line 3, *mis en pieces*. It is quite simply a graphic description of an execution by hanging, drawing and quartering. It could apply to any of the three thousand victims disembowelled and torn limb from limb in front of the baying mob during the massacre of the Huguenots on 24 August 1572.

❦ 4/47 − 1572

Le Noir farouche quand aura essayé
Sa main sanguine par feu, fer, arcs
  tendus,
Trestous le peuple sera tant effrayé
Voir les plus grans par col et pieds pendus.

When the ferocious King will have
  applied
His bloody hand to fire, steel and
  bowstrings

All the people will be so terrified
To see great men hanged by neck
  and feet.

One of the blackest days in the history of France, St Bartholomew's day, 24 August 1572, saw the massacre of the Huguenots in Paris, carried out at the behest of Catherine de Medici with the consent of the son she dominated, King Charles IX. Note that Nostradamus uses the capitalised *Noir* as an anagrammatical code for *Roi*. Aged only 22, Charles not only witnessed the slaughter from a window in the Louvre palace, but joined in by shooting into the crowd. Many Huguenot leaders were hanged in the streets, or had their corpses strung up from gibbets by their feet.

❦ 3/25 − 1572

Qui au Royaume Navarrois parviendra
Quand de Sicile et Naples seront joints
Bigore et Landres par Foix loron tiendra
D'un qui d'Espaigne sera par trop
  conjoint.

He who achieves the kingship of
  Navarre
When Sicily and Naples become
  allies
Will hold Bigorre and Landes
  through Foix and Oloron
From one too strongly allied to
  Spain.

Henri IV, born in 1553 as Nostradamus was producing his *Centuries*, succeeded to the throne of Navarre in 1572. Henri became the first Bourbon king of France in 1589, and restored the nation, through his pragmatic policies, to peace and stability after 40 years of bitter religious wars.

❦ 6/29 – 1572

La veuve saincte estendant les nouvelles,
De ses rameaux mis en perplex et trouble
Qui sera duict appaiser les querelles,
Par son pourchas des razes fera comble.

The widow with a saint's name,
   hearing news
Of her children, is perplexed and
   troubled
Whoever is led to calm the quarrels
Will kill many, in his pursuit of the
   slap-heads.

Nostradamus is referring here to Saint
Catherine of Siena, a famous peace
mediator, and comparing her to her
namesake, Catherine de Medici (1519–
1589), wife of one French king and
mother of three others, and a woman
who most signally failed to live up to
her forebear's saintly reputation. A
mother of nine children, only seven of
whom survived birth, she consistently
played off one child against another,
finally triggering the Massacre of the
Huguenots and the murder of Admiral
de Coligny, in 1572. On the plus side,
she was also responsible for
introducing the haricot bean, broccoli,
frangipani cakes and the macaroon to
France.

❦ 5/83 – 1572

Ceux qui auront entrprins subventir,
Nompareil regne puissant et invincible
Feront par fraude, nuictz trois advertir,
Quant le plus grand à table lira Bible.

Those who will try to undermine
The supreme kingdom, both
   powerful and invincible
Will be acting fraudulently; three
   nights of warning
When the great man reads his Bible
   at table.

This relates to the death of Admiral de
Coligny (1519–1572), who, while
recovering from an earlier assassination
attempt, was set upon by the Catholic
soldiers of Henri de Guise (1550–1588)
while reading his Calvinist bible. He
was disembowelled and thrown, still
alive, from his bedroom window. This
act triggered the Massacre of the
Huguenots lasting for the next three
nights, and during which a further 3000
men, women and children were brutally
killed.

❦ 8/50 – 1573

La pestilence l'entour de Capadille
Un autre faim pres de Sagont s'appreste
Le chevalier bastard de bon senille
Au grand de Thunes fera trancher la
   teste.

The plague surrounds Capellades
Another famine is threatening
   Sagunto
The good old man's bastard knight
Will cause the great man from Tunis
   to lose his head.

The recapture of Tunis by Spain in
1573. The good old man is Charles V
(1500–58), King of Spain and Holy
Roman Emperor and his bastard knight
his illegitimate son Don John of Austria
(1547–78) who commanded the
Spanish forces at Tunis. The mention of
plague is apposite, for Don John died
in the outbreak of 1578.

❦ 9/42 – 1573

De Barcellonne, de Gennes et Venise
De la Secille peste Monet unis
Contre Barbare classe prendront la vise
Barbare, pulse bien loing jusqu'à Thunis.

From Barcelona, Genoa, Venice
And from Sicily, a plague unites
  Monaco
They will take aim against the
  Barbarian fleet
Barbarian, you will be driven back
  beyond Tunis.

The Battle of Lepanto. Don John of
Austria, leader of the fleet that
destroyed the Turkish hopes of a
unified Europe under Turkish rule, went
on to recapture Tunis in 1573. The
Turkish fleet was partly composed of
Barbary pirate ships.

❦ 10/68 – 1573

L'armee de mer devant la cité tiendra
Puis partir sans faire langue alee,
Citoyens grande proie en terre prendra,
Retourner classe, reprendre grand
  emblee.

The naval contingent will stand
  before the city
Then leave, without having to go far
Many citizens will be captured, by
  land
The fleet returns, to seize with great
  robbery.

This could apply to any one of a dozen
notorious buccaneering engagements
during the English Elizabethan era –
but one in particular suggests itself.
Sir Francis Drake (1540–1596) was
responsible for capturing the greatest
treasure in the history of piracy when
he swooped on a hoard of Spanish
silver from the Potosi mines of New
Castile, in 1573, just as the ingots were
being transported by porters across the
Isthmus of Panama prior to their
shipment to Spain.

❦ 9/57 – 1574

Au lieu de Drux un Roi reposira,
Et cherchera loi changeant d'Anatheme,
Pendant le ciel si tres fort tonnera,
Porter neufve Roi tuera soimesme.

A king will take his rest near Dreux
Striving to change the hateful law
During this time the sky will thunder
  so loudly
That the King will kill himself, at the
  new gate.

Charles IX died of a cold in 1574, at the
age of 23. Many felt that he had
succumbed to guilt after allowing
himself to be bullied by his mother,
Catherine de Medici, into sanctioning
the Massacre of the Huguenots. The
hateful law may refer to the 1563 Edict
of Amboise, which allowed limited
freedom of worship to the Protestant
nobility and gentry.

❦ 7/35 – 1574

La grand pesche viendra plaindre, plorer
D'avoir esleu, trompés seront en l'aage
Guiere avec eux ne voudra demourer,
Deçeu sera par ceux de son langaige.

The great fish will come to weep and
  complain
For having chosen, deceit about the
  age
He will not wish to stay with them
He will be deceived by his own
  people.

Pesche in line 1 refers to the way the
Polish nobility traditionally chose their
kings – almost randomly, as if by
fishing. Henri III of France (1551–1589)
was elected King of Poland in just this
way, but threw up the job to return to

France on hearing of the unexpected death of his brother, Charles IX, on 30 May 1574. He was himself deceived and killed by a fellow countryman, Jacques Clément, fifteen years later.

ॐ 6/11 – 1574

Des sept rameaux à trois seront reduicts,
Les plus aisnés seront surprises par mort,
Fratricider les deux seront seduicts,
Les conjures en dormant seront morts.

The seven branches are cut to three
The two elder sons will be surprised
    by death
Both seduced by fratricide
The conspirators will die in their
    sleep.

Of the seven children of Henri II, his second son, Charles IX, died in 1574. He was succeeded by the third, Henri III. The next son in line, François Duc d'Alençon, who espoused the Huguenot cause, tried to overthrow his brother in the fratricidal War of the Malcontents from 1574–76. At the end of it all, the original seven were reduced to three.

ॐ 3/30 – 1575

Celui qu'en luitte et fer au faict bellique,
Aura porté plus grand que lui le prix
De nuict au lict six lui feront la pique,
Nud sans harnois subit sera surprins.

He who, in battle, and warlike action
Shall carry off a prize, greater than
    himself
Will be attacked at night, in bed, by
    six men:
Naked, without armour, he will be
    ambushed.

Another reference to the unfortunate Count Montgomery, unwitting killer of King Henri II in a joust in 1559. Although Henri II had pardoned him before his death, Catherine de Medici, Henri's wife, was not so understanding. She put a price on Montgomery's head. He fled to England. Fifteen years later in 1575, he returned to Normandy at the head of a Protestant rebel army. Forced to surrender at Domfront, he was spared, but was kidnapped from his bedroom by six men, on 27 May, and sent to the Conciergerie, where he later died, probably on Catherine's orders.

ॐ 3/39 – 1576

Les sept en trois mois en concorde,
Pour subjuguer des Alpes Appenines
Mais la tempeste et Ligure couarde,
Les profligent en subites ruines.

For three months the seven agree
To subjugate the Apennine Alps
But storms, and the cowardly
    Ligurians
Destroy them unexpectedly.

A general quatrain, probably referring to the Holy League of Italy, circa 1576.

ॐ 5/72 – 1577

Pour le plaisir d'edict voluptueux,
On meslera le poison dans la foy:
Venus sera en cours si vertueux,
Qu'obfusquera du Soleil tout aloy.

For the pleasure of the licentious
    edict
Poison will mingle into the faith
Venus will be so virtuous at Court
She will obscure the sunlight of
    righteousness.

In 1577 Henri III issued the Edict of Poitiers, permitting France's Protestants to practise their beliefs, and acknowledging the validity of their clergy's marriages. Nostradamus anticipates this liberalism with obvious disapproval, avowing that the acceptance of these voluptuaries at Court will cast a wicked shadow over the celibate priests of the one true, Roman Catholic, faith.

❦ 6/14 – 1578

Loing de sa terre Roy perdra la bataille
Prompt eschappé poursuivi suivant prins
Ignare prins soubs la doree maille
Soubs fainct habit et l'ennemy surprins.

Far from his country, a King will lose the battle
Escaping swiftly, he is followed and captured
The foolish one is taken in his gilded mail
Under false garb; the enemy is surprised.

There is one colourful interpretation of this verse centred on the zealously Catholic Portuguese king Sebastian. Ruler of his country from 1568, when he was just 14, this young evangelist conceived an irresistible urge to lead a crusade against the Moors of North Africa. In 1578 he did so, with an army of Christians, most of them mercenaries and adventurers. The ill-disciplined rabble was utterly crushed by the Moors at the battle of Alcazar-Qivir in Algeria on 4 August. Sebastian himself was reported to have died along with 8,000 others.

The twist in the tale is that Sebastian was soon rumoured not have been killed, but captured – and then to have escaped by exchanging his kingly armour for the clothes of an ordinary soldier. His true fate remains a mystery, but at the time the uncertainty caused acute problems of succession, as Sebastian was without an heir. In 1780 his uncle, King Philip II of Spain, annexed the country, with an army at his back.

❦ 6/83 – 1579

Celui qu'aura tant d'honneur et caresses
A son entrée de la Gaule Belgique
Un temps apres fera tant de rudesses
Et sera contre à la fleur tant bellique.

He who will have so many honours and caresses
When he enters Belgian Gaul
Will shortly afterwards act so grossly
He will be warlike against the flower.

Philip II succeeded his father, Charles V, as king of Spain and the Spanish Netherlands in 1556. Philip spent much of his life in his Flanders palaces but his corruption, extravagance and misguided religious zeal turned the Dutch against him. They revolted on several occasions. In 1576 the Spanish army of the Netherlands mutinied because they had not been paid for years, and in 1579 the seven United Provinces of the Low Countries won effective independence from Spain. Warlike against the flower is likely to refer to Philip's conflicts with the French (symbolised by the *fleur de lys*).

❦ 4/97 – 1580

L'an que Mercure, Mars, Venus retrograde
Du grand Monarque la ligne ne faillit
Esleu du peuple l'usiant pres de Gagdole
Qu'en paix et regne viendra fort envieillir.

In the year when Mercury, Mars and
    Venus retrograde
The Monarch's family line won't fail
Elected by the Portuguese near Cadiz
He'll reign and grow very old in his
    peaceful kingdom.

In 1580, King Philip II of Spain
succeeded to the throne of Portugal by
virtue of his marriage in 1543 to the
Portuguese Infanta Mary (who died
three years later giving birth to their
son, Don Carlos). Philip reigned over
the twin kingdoms until his death in
1598, aged 71.

❦ 6/2 – 1580–1703

En l'an cinq cens octante plus et moins,
On attendra le siecle bien estrange
En l'an sept cens, et trois cieux en
    tesmoings.
Que plusieurs regnes un à cinq feront
    change.

In the year fifteen hundred and
    eighty, give or take
We can expect a very strange century
In the year seventeen hundred and
    three, as the sky will witness
Several kingdoms, one to five, will
    cause changes.

An accurate and date-specific quatrain.
In 1580, France was fighting a virtual
Civil War, known as the 'Seventh War of
Religion'. This effectively began the
seventeenth century, which, in French
terms, lasted until 1703 and Louis XIV's
War of the Spanish Succession. The
five kingdoms mentioned in line 4 are
Spain, the Americas, the Netherlands
and the two Sicilies.

❦ 4/13 – 1581

De plus grand perte nouvelles raportées,
Le raport fait le camp s'estonnera
Bandes unies encontre revoltées,
Double phalange grand abandonnera.

News of the new great loss is
    reported
This will astonish the army
War bands unite against the
    mutineers
A double phalanx will abandon its
    leader.

This relates to the Dutch capture of
Antwerp, in 1581, caused by rumours
of a great defeat and possible mutiny
spreading through the Duke of Parma's
army. The Duke, Alessandro Farnese,
only regained Antwerp on 17 August
1585.

❦ 1/86 – 1587

La grande Royne quand se verra vaincue
Fera excez de masculin courage;
Sur cheval fleuve passera toute nue,
Suitte par fer, a foy fera outrage.

Seeing herself conquered, the great
    Queen
Will excel herself in masculine
    courage
On horseback, naked, she will cross a
    river
Pursued by armed men, she will
    injure her faith.

This is widely interpreted as a
prediction of the fate of Mary, Queen of
Scots, who was married to the Dauphin
of France in 1558, the year Nostradamus's complete *Centuries* were
published. Beautiful and courageous,
but unwise in her choice of political
allies, Queen Mary had a claim on the

English crown as great grand-daughter of King Henry VII. The Dauphin became King Francis II of France in 1559 but died the following year. Childless, Mary returned to Scotland as Queen (she had succeeded to the throne in the year of her birth, 1542). But she found her home country in uproar. Protestant lords were attempting to seize power from the Catholic Stuarts. After marrying the Earl of Bothwell, who had ambitions of his own to control the crown, Mary was forced by an armed confederacy of Scottish lords to abdicate the throne in favour of her son James VI (later also James I of England). Bothwell's forces were defeated in battle and Mary fled to England in 1567 to seek the protection of her cousin, Queen Elizabeth I. She did indeed cross a river, the Solway Firth, in doing so, but was no doubt fully dressed. The reference to nakedness could well allude to Mary's dispossession in Scotland, and her need to throw herself abjectly upon the mercy of the English sovereign. The injury she did to her Catholic faith was to allow Scotland's Protestants to gain control of the country. Mary was executed for treason in 1587, possibly on a false charge of plotting with Catholic insurgents against the life of Elizabeth I.

❦ 3/50 – 1588

La republique de la grande cité
A grand rigueur ne voudra consentir,
Roy sortir hors par trompette cité
L'eschelle au mur, la cité repentir.

The republicans of the great city
Will not wish to accept royal rule
The King, leaving, by a trumpet's
    sound
Swears with ladders to make the city
    repent.

Paris rebelled against Henri III on 12 May 1588 in the celebrated uprising inspired by the Duke of Guise, whom the Catholic League wished to put on the throne in place of the Huguenot-tolerating incumbent. The rising has become famous in history as the *Journée des Barricades*, in which Parisians lifted the very paving stones from the streets to hurl at the King's supporters. Henri was lucky to escape with his life, swearing revenge. He had Guise murdered, and returned to lay siege to Paris, in the following year.

❦ 3/51 – 1588

Paris conjure un grand meurtre
    commettre
Blois fera sortir en plain effet,
Ceux d'Orléans voudront leur chef
    remettre,
Angers, Troye, Langres leur feront un
    meffait.

The committing of murder plotted in
    Paris
Will be carried out openly at Blois
Men of Orléans wish to restore their
    leader
Angers, Troyes and Langres are with
    the king.

Henri III vowed to murder the Duke of Guise following the Paris revolt of May 1588, and carried out his intention at Blois on 25 December of that year. France was divided by this crime: Orléans came out for Guise; Angers, Troyes and Langres for the king.

❦ 10/2 – 1588

Voille gallere voil de nef cachera,
La grande classe viendra sortir la
    moindre.
Dix naves proches le tourneront poulser,
Grande vaincue unis à foi joindre.

The sails of the galleys will hide
  those of smaller ships
The great fleet will call out the
  smaller one
Ten nearby ships will drive it back
The great one vanquished, to join
  those united in faith.

The Catholic Spanish Armada of Philip II was sent against the Protestant Elizabethan English in July 1588. Hopelessly outnumbered, the English sent out fire-ships to harass the Spanish. Driven by contrary winds, the Spanish were then forced to circumnavigate the British Isles, more than half the fleet foundering on the Irish shore. Of 130 galleys sent out, only 67 returned. The defeat almost bankrupted the Spanish Royal treasury.

❦ 1/36 – 1588

Tard la monarque se viendra repentir
De n'avoir mis à mort son adversaire
Mais viendra bien à plus hault consentir,
Que tout son song par mort fera deffaire.

Belatedly, the monarch regrets
That he did not put his adversary to
  death
Soon, however, he will make worse
  mistakes
Which will lead to the end of his line.

This refers to Henri III's perceived mistake in not having the Duke of Mayenne assassinated on the same night that he had arranged for his popular rival, Henri de Guise, and Henri's brother, Cardinal Louis, to be killed. The murders took place at Blois, on 25 December 1588. Henri was later knifed to death by a catholic priest. Mayenne went on to fight against Henri IV of Navarre in the War of Religion. When Henri IV expediently abandoned the Protestant faith, he and Mayenne

made up. The House of Lorraine eventually foundered.

❦ 4/87 – 1588

Un filz du Roi tant de langues aprins,
A son aisné au regne different
Son pere beau au plus grand filz comprins
Fera perir principal adherent.

A king's son, master of many languages
Different from the one who reigned
  before him
His good-looking father will
  understand which son is greater
Causing the main pretender's death.

Henri III (1551–1589), a regular star of the Nostradamus quatrains, spoke several languages fluently, unlike his brother, Charles IX, whom he succeeded. Henri II was his handsome father – the one who died in a joust – and the last line refers to Henri's murder of the Guises, in 1588.

❦ 9/32 – 1588

De fin porphire profond collon trouvee
Dessoubz la laze escriptz capitolin
Os poil retors Romain force prouvee,
Classe agiter ay port de Methelin.

A deep vein of finest porphyry is
  discovered
Beneath the inscriptions at the base
  of the capitol
Bones, hair, the return of an already
  proved Italian army
Mutiny at the port of Mitylene.

Ancient Mitylene was once the capital of Lesbos. In 1588 a large, rose-granite obelisk was discovered in the Basilica of St Peter in Rome. Its finding coincided, fortuitously for Nostradamus, with an invasion of Lesbos.

✌ 5/71 – 1588

Par la fureur d'un qui attendra l'eau
Par la grand raige tout l'exercite esmeu
Chargé des nobles à dix sept bateaulx
Au long du Rosne, tard messagier venu.

The fury of a man waiting for the
   water
His great rage causes the army to
   move
Seventeen ships loaded with nobles
The belated messenger travels the
   length of Rhône.

Poor intelligence (signified by the
belated messenger) made Philip of
Spain's naval Armada against England
in 1588 a doomed venture. Enraged by
continual attacks on his navy, in
harbour as well as on the high seas, by
privateers such as Sir Francis Drake,
Philip ordered his commander, the
Duke of Medina Sidona, to set sail
inadequately prepared for the mission.
In total, after the four-month voyage,
the fleet lost no less than 67 ships
including many (perhaps 17) full of
troops under aristocratic command.

✌ 10/18 – 1588

Le ranc Lorrain fera place à Vendosme
Le hault mis bas et le bas mis en hault
Le filz d'Hamon sera esleu dans Rome
Et les deux grands seront mis en
   deffault.

The House of Lorraine will give way
   to Vendôme
The high will become low, the low
   high
The son of Ham will be elected in
   Rome
And the two great ones will be in the
   wrong.

This is probably a reference to the
murder of the two de Guise brothers by
Henri III on 23 December 1588. Henri
de Guise had usurped the throne of
France that year, with the help of the
Catholic League against the
Protestants. The son of Ham would
imply a black pope; something that has
yet to occur. Perhaps the colour is
meant symbolically.

✌ 10/44 – 1588

Par lors qu'un Roi sera contre les siens,
Natif de Blois subjugera Ligures.
Mammel, Cordube et les Dalmatiens,
Des sept puis l'ombre à Roi estrennes et
   lemurs.

When a king turns against his own
   people
A native of Blois will conquer the
   Genoese
Mammola, Cordoba and the
   Dalmatians
The seven, then the shadow will give
   the king money and ghosts.

Nostradamus's code for Henri III is
'Blois', after his country residence.
Lines 2 and 3 are more difficult to
analyse but line 4 returns to Catherine
de Medici's seven children. The
shadow may refer to the king's murder
of the Duke of Guise and of his brother
on 25 December 1588, which took
place, coincidentally, at Blois.

❦ 10/100 – 1588

Le grand empire sera par Angleterre
Le pempotam des ans plus de trois cens,
Grandes copies passer par mer et terre,
Les Lusitains n'en seront pas contens.

The great empire will be made by
England
All-powerful for more than three
hundred years
Great forces will move by sea and
land
The Portuguese will not be happy.

Nostradamus foresees the British
Empire – the largest in the history of the
world. It seems likely he dates English
ascendancy from the Spanish Armada in
July 1588. This naval disaster, in which
Spain lost 10,000 men and 67 ships,
ended Spain's supremacy and handed
sea power to Britain. The Empire did last
for three hundred years until its
progressive dismantling in the twentieth
century. The Portuguese were firm allies
of Britain for much of that era, but back
in 1588 had been in an unwise alliance
with Spain. It is interesting that
Nostradamus, who was not enamoured
of the English (he thought them a mob of
heretical warmongers), should devote
the very last quatrain of his Centuries to
this remarkable forecast.

❦ 1/85 – 1589

Par la response de dame Roy troublé,
Ambassadeurs mespriseront leur vie,
Le grand ses frères contrefera double,
Par deux mourront, ire, haine et envie.

By agreeing with the disturbed king's
mother
Ambassadors risked their lives
The great man will take his brothers'
places
The two will die by anger, loathing
and fear.

Henry III's mother, Catherine de Medici,
was horrified at her son's complicity in
the assassination of the Duke of Guise in
1588. Her reaction was openly shared
by leading Catholic noblemen, among
them the Duke of Mayenne, who bravely
took the helm of the Catholic League in
place of his two brothers, respectively
the Duke and Cardinal of Guise.

❦ 1/8 – 1589

Combien de fois prinse cité solaire
Seras changeant les loix barbares et vaines
Ton mal s'approche, plus seras tributaire
Le grand Adrie recouvrira tes veines.

How many times, City of the Sun
Will you change your barbarous and
vain laws?
Your nemesis is coming; you must
pay more tributes
The great Hadrian will cover your
veins.

In the first line Nostradamus foresees
not just an important historic event, but
a seminal work of literature. *City of the
Sun* was the title of Tommaso
Campanella's utopian epic, written in
1602 from the prison where he
languished from 1599 to 1626 under
charges of heresy and conspiracy
against Spanish rule in his native Italy.
When Campanella was finally released,
he fled, of course, to Paris. The main
thrust of the quatrain concerns Henri IV,
who succeeded his brother-in-law Henri
III in 1589 and came to Paris to claim it.
The last line refers to the later siege (of
April to September 1860) in which Henri
would conduct himself like that most
cultivated of Roman emperors, Hadrian
(who, like Henri, had Spanish
connections). Nostradamus predicts
correctly that this Hadrian would
mercifully supply food to the besieged
people of Paris – putting flesh on their
veins.

❦ 8/18 – 1589

De Flora issue de sa mort sera cause,
Un temps devant par jeune et vieille
bueira,
Par les trois lys lui feront telle pause,
Par son fruit sauve comme chair crue
mueire.

Flowers will be the cause of her death
Once, soon, by young and old, it will
be drunk
The three lilies will make her pause
for so long
That her children will be saved, just
as the meat is dampened.

Catherine de Medici came from a family
of renowned poisoners, but she actually
died of pneumonia, in 1589. She
married into the lilies of France,
becoming Henri II's queen. Florence,
which is another possible meaning for
'Flora' in line 1, was the capital city of
the Medici Duchy of Tuscany.

❦ 9/19 – 1589

Dans le millieu de la forest Meyenne,
Sol au Lyon la fouldre tombera.
Le grand bastard issu du Grand du
Maine,
Ce jour fougeres pointe en sang entrera.

In the middle of the Mayenne forest
With the Sun in Leo, lightning will
strike
The famous bastard, son of the
Maine man
On that day the sword of Fougères
will enter his blood.

Fougères, 20 miles from the forest of
Mayenne, was once the ancestral home
of a great family which died out in the
thirteenth century. Henri III used the
house while he was Duke of Anjou. He

was to die in August 1589, stabbed by
an assassin in his bedchamber at
Saint-Cloud. Kindly forgive the pun in
line 3. Nostradamus actually calls him
the 'great one of Maine', but then the
Master himself, in his weaker moments,
was not averse to the occasional *jeu de
mots*.

❦ 9/64 – 1589

L'Aemathion passer monts Pyrenees,
En Mars Narbon ne fera resistance,
Par mer et terre fera si grand menee,
Cap. n'ayant terre seure pour
démeurance.

Emathion will cross the Pyrenees
mountains
In March Narbonne will not resist
By sea and land and will make great
progress
Cap. shall not have a safe place to
live.

In Roman mythology, Emathios is the
son of Aurora, goddess of the dawn,
and her earthly lover Tithonus, to whom
Zeus granted immortality on account of
his beauty. It was a paradoxical gift, for
Tithonus grew unbearably old until he
was granted a form of clemency by
Aurora, who turned him into a
grasshopper. Nostradamus may have
chosen Emathios as a code for Henri IV
(1553–1610), the first Bourbon king of
France. Henri, the son of a queen
ranked high above her consort, was
king of Navarre in Spain. He
succeeded to the French throne in
1589 but had to cross the Pyrenees
with an army and march to Paris to
claim it. The cryptic 'Cap.' could refer
to Catholics. Henri was a Protestant.
But Nostradamus's fears were
unfounded. The new king converted to
Catholicism in 1593, and then
guaranteed the safety of Protestants

with the Edict of Nantes in 1598. This
ended the decades of religious wars
that had riven France since the days in
which Nostradamus was writing these
very quatrains.

❦ 1/97 – 1589

Ce que fer, flamme n'a sceu paracheuer,
La douce langue an conseil viendra faire
Par repos, songe, le Roy fera resver,
Plus l'ennemy en feu, sang militaire.

What iron and flame cannot achieve
Sweet words, in council, will contrive
Imagine this; the King, while resting,
　　will not dream
That the enemy at his hearth has
　　military blood.

Henri III of France (1551–89) was
stabbed in the stomach and killed by a
young Dominican monk named
Jacques Clément (the *douce langue* of
Nostradamus's quatrain), on 2 August
1589. Three days before his death,
Henri had dreamed that his royal
emblems would be trodden underfoot
by monks, leading the common people.
in revolt

❦ 4/79 – 1589

Sang Royal fuis, Monhurt, Mas,
　　Equillon
Remplis seront de Bourdelois les landes
Navarre, Bigorre poinctes et eguillons
Profondz de faim vorer de liege glandes.

Flight of the blood royal, Monheurt,
　　Agen, Aguillon
The lands of the Bordelais will be full
Navarre and Bigorre, with point and
　　spur
Starving, they eat the cork oak
　　acorns.

Only Navarre (in Spain) lies outside the
region of southwest France where all
the other named towns are located. An
allusion to Henri of Navarre (1553–
1610) and his struggles for the French
throne, which he claimed on ther
assassination of Henri III in 1589.

❦ 10/45 – 1589–98

L'ombre du Regne de Navarre non vrai,
Fera la vie de fort illegitime
La veu promis incertain de Cambrai
Roi Orléans donra mur legitime.

There is a false shadow over the
　　kingdom of Navarre
It will cast doubts on the life of the
　　strong one
An uncertain vow made at Cambrai
The King of Orléans restores the
　　legitimate border.

There were doubts as to Henri IV of
Navarre's rights of succession after the
murder of Henri III in 1589. He did,
however, bring a measure of stability
back to France after the depredations
of the Wars of Religion. He had many
mistresses, one of whom was the wife
of Balagny, governor of Cambrai. Line 3
may describe his gift to Balagny of
hereditary possession of the town. Line
4 may simply refer to the 1598 Edict of
Nantes, which demarcated the
'legitimate border' between Catholic
and Protestant in France.

❦ 9/45 – 1589

Ne sera soul jamais de demander
Grand Mendosus obtiendra son Empire
Loing de la cour fera contremander
Pimond, Picard, Paris, Tyrron le pire.

There will be no-one left to ask
Great Mendosus will attain his
　　empire

Far from the court, he will
countermand
Piedmont, Picardy, Paris, and
Tuscany the worst.

Mendosus applies to the family of
Vendôme and, in particular, to Henri IV
of Navarre, who finally attained the
kingship of France in 1589, after a long
struggle. He was responsible for the
Edict of Nantes in 1598, giving political
rights to French Protestants and
effectively countermanding the endless
lobbying of the Catholic League.

❦ 8/52 – 1589

Le roi de Blois dans Avignon regner
D'amboise et seme viendra le long de
Lyndre
Ongle à Poitiers sainctes aesles ruiner
Devant Boni.

The King of Blois reigns in Avignon
From Amboise and the Seine he
comes the length of the Indre
His uncle, at Poitiers, destroys the
sacred wings
In front of Boni.

The verse is incomplete. Reference to
the reign of Henri III (1551–89) seems
implied but the last line has clearly
been shortened, perhaps by a
publisher sensitive to the fact that
Catherine de Medici, the Queen
Mother, might be among the readers of
this verse. Henri's uncle had been the
Dauphin Francis, his father Henri II's
elder brother, who died in 1536.
Perhaps the quatrain, complete, had
hinted something about the cause of
that untimely death. Henri himself was
murdered in 1589.

❦ 1/9 – 1590

De l'Orient viendra le coeur punique,
Fascher Adrie, et les hoirs Romullides,
Accompagne de la classe Libique
Trembler Melites et proches Isles vuides.

From the east will come a
treacherous heart
To trouble Hadrian and the heirs of
Romulus
Accompanied by the Libyans
To shake Melites and the nearby
empty islands.

Henri of Navarre (Hadrian) had to quit
the siege of Paris in September 1590 at
the approach of the Duke of Parma.
The 'heirs of Romulus' refers to the
Vatican, which supported Henri against
Parma's sovereign, Philip II of Spain.

❦ 10/38 – 1590

Amour alegre non loing pose le siege
Au Sainct barbare seront les garrisons.
Ursins, Hadrie, pour Gaulois feront
plaige,
Pour peut rendus de l'Armée, aux
Grisons.

The eager lover will not impose a
long siege
The garrisons will be profane clergy
Hadrian will spare street children for
France
So they can serve the army to the
grey-beards.

Another reference to Henri of Navarre's
brief and unsuccessful siege of Paris.
Nostradamus sees Henri (again called
Hadrian – see preceding quatrain) as a
forward-looking man who is careful not
to alienate the urchins of the city,
recognising that they can become
soldiers and live long. Describing Henri

as the eager lover in the first line can only be a reference to the lurid affair the king was having with Gabrielle d'Estrées throughout the siege.

❦ 2/88 – 1590

Le circuit du grand faict ruineux,
Le nom septiesme du cinquiesme sera
D'un tiers plus grand l'estrange belliqueux,
Mouton, Lutece, Aix ne garantira.

The disastrous act is accomplished
The seventh name will now be the fifth
A third greater, this foreign warmonger
Will not manage to keep Paris and Aix in Aries.

The fifth child of Henri II and Catherine de Medici, Henri III became the seventh and last king of the Valois line. Henri IV, Prince of Navarre, who succeeded him, was considered a foreigner, as Navarre was at that time deemed to be unconnected to France. The first line must refer to the Massacre of St Bartholomew's Day, which heralded the end of the Valois line. The last line may indicate Henri de Navarre's siege of Paris in March and April (Aries) of 1590.

❦ 2/63 – 1590

Gaulois, Ausone bien peu subjugera,
Par, Marne et Seine fera Perme l'vrie
Qui le grand mur contre eux dressera,
Du moindre au mur le grand perdra la vie.

The French will fail to subdue southern Italy
Pau, Marne and Seine will cause Parma to sink

Whosoever raises a great wall against them
Will, at that same wall, lose his life.

If Perme, in line 2, is taken as Parma, this quatrain would seem to be referring to the battle of Ivry, in which the Duke of Parma entered France from the Netherlands on behalf of the Catholic League, to fight against Henri of Navarre. An alternative reading would give us the Second World War's French Maginot Line.

❦ 2/55 – 1592

Dans le conflict le grand qui peu valloit
A son dernier fera cas merveilleux,
Pendant qu'Hadrie verra ce qu'il falloit,
Dans le banquet pongnarde l'orgeilleux.

In the argument the great one of little value
Will commit his last marvellous act
While Hadrian watches over his failure
In the banquet he stabs the proud man.

The Duke of Mayenne, successor to his brother the Duke of Guise as leader of the Catholic League, but not a man of great strength or resolve, found himself at odds with the republican government of Paris, known as the *Seize*. Although Mayenne, with an army of the League, had saved Paris from Henri IV's siege, the 16 proud burghers of the city wished to rule independently. Mayenne determined to break them and organised a banquet at which the four leading radicals were stabbed to death. The event divided the city, and began the decline of the Catholic League's influence – as Henri IV (here referred to again by Nostradamus as the wise Hadrian) looked on, no doubt with satisfaction.

❦ 4/76 – 1593

Les Nictobriges par ceux de Perigort
Seront vexez tenant jusques au Rosne
L'associé de Gascons et Begorne
Trahir le temple, le prebstre estant au
    prosne.

The Agenais will be troubled by the
    Perigourdiens
All the way to the Rhône
The man who associates with both
    Gascons and Bigorres
Will betray the church, even as the
    priest delivers his sermon.

The religious wars of southern France
were a constant background in
Nostradamus's own lifetime. Here he
foretells a Protestant linked to Gascony
who betrays the (Catholic) church.
Could he be visualising the future
doctrinal pragmatism of the Protestant
Henri of Navarre, who did so much to
bridge the religious divide by adopting
the Catholic faith before his coronation
with the immortal words *'Paris vaut bien
une messe'* (Paris is well worth a
mass)? Nostradamus, a devout
Catholic, would not have approved.

❦ 9/50 – 1594

Mandosus tost viendra à son hault regne
Mettant arriere un peu de Nolaris
Le rouge blaisme, le masle à l'interregne
Le jeune crainte et frayeur Barbaris.

Mandosus will soon have his great
    reign
Setting aside, somewhat, those of
    Nolaris
The pale red one, he of the
    interregnum
The young man fears the barbaric
    terror.

If Mandosus is Vendôme, and Nolaris is
Lorraine, this quatrain tells of Henri IV's
accession in 1594 and the consequent
decline of the house of Guise. The pale
red one must be the aged Cardinal de
Bourbon, later declared King Charles X,
who only reigned for a year, dying in
1590. Masle would then be the Duke of
Mayenne, and the young man the Duke
of Guise. Barbaris refers to Philip II of
Spain, who laid claim to the French
throne through his daughter, Isabella.

❦ 1/5 – 1596

Chassez seront sans faire long combat,
Par le pais seront plus fort grevés,
Bourg et Cité auront plus grand debat,
Carcas, Narbonne auront coeurs
    éprouvés.

Chased away without a long fight
They will be sorely burdened by the
    peace
Town and city will have a great
    discussion
Carcas and Narbonne will prove
    their hearts.

Carcas is Carcassonne, the fortified
mediaeval city of the Aude in southwest
France. Well-known to Nostradamus,
the city gave itself up to the sovereignty
of Henri IV in 1596 after changing
hands several times during the
century's religious wars. Narbonne,
nearby, had a similar history. In
Nostradamus's day, as now, these
ancient cities were administratively
divided into the original *cité* and the
bourg, or new town.

❦ 8/94 – 1596

Devant le lac ou plus cher fut getté
De sept mois, et son host desconfit
Seront Hispans par Albanois gastez
Par delai perte en donnant le conflict.

In front of the lake where the
    treasure was lost
The army was routed, for seven
    months
The Spanish will be harassed by the
    English
They will delay the battle, and thus
    lose.

Captains Essex, Howard and Raleigh
attacked a Spanish treasure fleet in
Cadiz, in June 1596. The forty galleons
and thirteen warships had just
completed a seven-month voyage from
the newly conquered territories of South
and Central America. All were
destroyed. Nostradamus obviously
foresaw the coming war between
England and Spain, who, at the time of
writing, were allies, due to a marriage
contracted between Mary Tudor,
Queen of England, and Philip II of
Spain.

🐚 3/88 – 1596

De Barcellonne par mer si grand armee,
Tout Marseille de frayeur tremblera
Isles saisies de mer aide fermee,
Ton traditeur en terre nagera.

A great army will come from
    Barcelona, by sea
All Marseilles will tremble in fear
Islands will be seized, help will be cut
    off from the sea
Your betrayer will swim on dry land.

Philip II of Spain blockaded Marseilles
on 17 February 1596, taking over the
islands of Ratonneau and Chateau d'If
(of Monte Cristo fame). Charles de
Casau, a French traitor, was caught
and killed by Pierre Libertat during an
attempt to sell out Marseilles to the
Spanish. Run through by his
opponent's sword, he literally drowned
in his own blood.

🐚 10/37 – 1598

L'assemblee grande pres du lac de Borget
Se ralieront pres de Montmelian
Marchans plus oultre pensifz feront
    proget
Chambry, Moraine combat sainct
    Julian.

A great assembly near the lake of
    Bourget
They will rally near Montmelian
Marching in the van, the thinkers
    draw up a plan
Chambry, Moraine and St Julien
    fight.

The Duke of Savoy, intending to invade
France from Montmélain, was defeated,
near St Julien, by Henri IV, in 1598.
Henri later went on to capture
Chambéry and St Jean-de-Maurienne.

🐚 6/56 – 1598

La crainte armee de l'ennemi Narbon
Effrayera si fort les Hesperiques
Parpignan vuide par l'aveugle darbon
Lors Barcelon par mer donra les piques.

The feared army of the Narbonne
    enemy
Terrifies the Westerners so badly
Perpignan is empty, because of the
    blind one of Arbon
When Barcelona takes up her
    weapons by sea.

The Franco-Spanish war of 1595–98
raged either side of the Pyrenees,
ending in a treaty signed at Vervins
between Philip II of Spain and Henri IV
of France. Philip's Habsburg ambitions
in France effectively came to an end
with his surrender of Picardy, and
France was unified under one crown.

❦ 5/44 – 1500s

Par mer le rouge sera prins de pirates,
La paix sera par son moyen troublee
L'ire et l'avare commettra par fainct
*   acte*
Au grand Pontife sera l'armee doublee.

The red one will be taken at sea by
    pirates
Peace will be troubled because of him
Anger and greed will be reunited by a
    false action
The size of the army will be doubled
    by the Pope.

It's hard to find a source for this. 'Red
one' would normally refer to a cardinal,
and the kidnapping probably took
place in the sixteenth century, when
Popes still had real armies. Beyond
that, interpretation is difficult.

❦ 5/67 – 1500s

Quand chef Perouse n'osera sa tunique
Sens au couvert tout nud s'expolier
Seront prins sept faict Aristocratique,
Le pere et fils mors par poincte au colier.

When the chief of Perugia will no
    longer risk his shirt
And instead walks about stark naked
Seven noblemen will be taken
    prisoner
The father and son dead; struck in
    the throat.

The Pope is indicated in line 1, also his
eventual loss of France ('his shirt'). The
seven are Henri II's children, one of
whom, Henri III, was to die from stab
wounds, just as his father was to die in
a joust.

❦ 9/87 – 1500s

Par la forest du Touphon essartee
Par hermitage sera posé le temple
Le duc d'Estampes par sa ruse inventee
Du mont Lehori prelat donra exemple.

In the cleared forest of Torfou
The hermitage will be placed near
    the temple
The Duke of Estampes, through an
    invented ruse
Will teach a lesson to the priest of
    Montlhéry.

Montlhéry, Torfou and Étampes,
situated 20, 25 and 30 miles south-west
of Paris respectively, are less than ten
miles distant one from the other. All are
situated in the Essonne district of the
Ile-de-France. Three renowned royal
mistresses have held the d'Estampes
title over the years; Anne de Pisseleu,
Diane de Poitiers and Gabrielle
d'Estrées.

❦ 9/67 – 1500s

Du hault des montz à l'entour de Lizer
Port à la roche Valen cent assemblez
De chasteau neuf pierre late en donzere
Contre le crest Romans foi assemblez.

From the high mountains around
    Isère
A hundred people will assemble at
    the gate of the Valencian rock
From Châteauneuf, Pierrelatte and
    Donzère
The steadfast Romans will gather
    against the ridge.

The implication is that these steadfast
Romans are gathering to fight against
the Huguenots. The place-names are
so random that little more can be
deduced.

❦ 9/44 – 1500s

Migres migre de Genesve trestous
Saturne d'or en fer se changera
Le contre Raypoz exterminera tous
Avant l'a ruent de ciel signes fera.

Leave Geneva, all of you, leave
Saturn will change from gold into
    iron
Raypoz will exterminate all who are
    against him
The sky will show signs before the
    attack.

Herodotus writes in his *Histories* of a
certain Zopyrus (of which Raypoz is a
convenient cryptogram) who fearfully
mutilated himself, claiming his master,
King Darius, was responsible. The
Babylonians, whom Darius was
besieging, let him into their city. King
Darius then allowed thousands of his
own Persians to be slaughtered by the
Babylonian forces, under Zopyrus's
command, until he was certain Zopyrus
had the full confidence of the city.
Made Guardian of the Walls, Zopyrus
then opened the Cissian and Belian
gates to Darius, and Babylon fell.
Looked at as an archetype, this story
closely fits the Nostradamian view of
John Calvin (1509–1564), and may now
be seen as an awful warning against
allowing false prophets to enter
Geneva.

❦ 7/12 – 1500s

Le grand puisné fera fin de la guerre,
Aux dieux assemble les excusés
Cahors, Moissac iront long de la serre,
Reffus Lestore, les Agenois razés.

The great late-born one will end the
    war
Those pardoned will face the Gods
Cahors and Moissac will go far from
    prison
A refusal at Lestore, the Agenois cut
    down.

This relates to battles fought during the
Wars of Religion by the de Guise family,
a cadet branch of the ruling House of
Lorraine. All the towns mentioned are in
south-western France, near the de
Guise ancestral lands.

❦ 10/35 – 1500s

Puisnay royal flagrand d'ardent libide
Pour se jouir de cousine germaine
Habit de femme au temple d'Arthemide
Allant murdri par incognu du Marne.

The youngest royal will flaunt his
    wild libido
Desiring to bed his first cousin
Women's clothes in the temple of
    Artemis
A murder by the unknown man from
    the Marne.

This could possibly apply to Marguerite
de Valois (1553–1615), latterly famed
as the lusty and uninhibited Reine
Margot. Her brothers certainly lusted
after her, as did her future husband,
Protestant King Henri of Navarre, who
was a distant cousin. Their childless
marriage was annulled in 1599. The
Massacre of the Huguenots occurred
during the celebrations which
preceded their wedding.

❦ 8/24 – 1500s

Le lieutenant à l'entrée de l'huis,
Assommera la grand de Perpignan,
En se cuidant saulver à Montpertuis.
Sera deceu bastard de Luisgnan.

The lieutenant in the doorway
Will strike down Perpignan's leader
Thinking to save himself at
    Montpertuis
The bastard of Lusignan is deceived.

An involved and only partially
successful quatrain, speculating on
connections between the Count of
Tende, Governor of Provence, and the
Lusignan family of crusader knights,
which ruled Jerusalem and Cyprus until
1489.

❦ 8/25 – 1500s

Coeur de l'amant ouvert d'amour fertive
Dans le ruisseau fera ravir la Dame,
Le demi mal contrefera lassive,
Le pere à deux privera corps de l'ame.

The lover's heart is opened by furtive
    passion
The lady is ravished in the stream
She will pretend to be a little hurt
Her father will deprive them both of
    life.

This bears uncanny echoes to the
legend of Leda and the Swan. Leda
was ravished in a stream by Zeus, in
the guise of a swan. She laid two eggs,
from one of which hatched Helen, who
later became the cause of the Trojan
Wars. Trojan was a common
Nostradamian euphemism for the Royal
House of France, which flattered itself
that it was descended from Priam, King
of Troy. Could Nostradamus be
intimating that a similar ravishing would
affect the course of French history? If
so, he had good reason to use such
obscure language. Plainer words would
have put him at great risk from the
vengeance of Valois kings.

❦ 8/81 – 1500s

Le neuf empire en desolation
Sera changé du pole aquilonaire.
De la Sicile viendra l'esmotion
Troubler l'emprise à Philip tributaire.

The new empire is desolated
Changed by the North Pole
The trouble will come from Sicily
Troubling the enterprise of those
    beholden to Philip.

A straightforward reference to Philip II
of Spain (1527–1598), and to the
possibility of a war with his uncle,
Ferdinand, over the correct division of
Charles V's empire. The uprising, which
was due to start in Sicily, never
occurred.

❦ 8/84 – 1500s

Paterne orra de la Sicile crie,
Tous les aprests du Goulphre de Trieste,
Qui s'entendra jusque à la Trinacrie
Tant de voiles, fui, fuiz, l'horrible peste.

Paterno will hear the cry from Sicily
Preparations will be made in the gulf
    of Trieste
These will be heard as far as Sicily
So many ships, flee, flee the horrible
    plague.

This refers back to the preceding verse,
8/81, and to the wars that never
happened between Philip II of Spain
and his uncle, Ferdinand.

❧ 8/86 – 1500s

Par Arani Tholoser ville franque,
Bande infini par le mont Adrian,
Passe riviere, Hutin par pont la planque
Bayonne entrera tous Bihoro criant.

Through Ernani, Tolosa and
    Villafranca
A great army will pass through
    Mount Adrian
Crossing the river, there will be a
    fight over the plank bridge
Thy will enter Bayonne, shouting
    'Bihoro!'

Geographically, this quatrain holds
together very well, as all the cities
mentioned are encompassed by the old
French province of Navarre. *Bigorre*
was the battle cry of the Navarre
Huguenots, implying that this quatrain
is somehow related to the sixteenth
century Wars of Religion. Beyond that –
peradventure.

❧ 8/89 – 1500s

Pour ne tumber entre mains de son oncle,
Qui ses enfans par regner trucidez.
Orant au peuple mettant pied sur
    Peloncle
Mort et traisné entre chevaulx bardez.

So as not to fall into the hands of his
    uncle
The man who to rule, slaughtered his
    children
Is now pleading with the people, his
    foot on Peloncle
He is killed, and quartered.

Quartering was a common way of killing
in the sixteenth century, with the
condemned man being torn to pieces
between four opposing horses. It was
often preceded by hanging and the

drawing out of the entrails. The word
Peloncle has never been satisfactorily
translated, obscuring the identity of the
unfortunate victim. If the word is seen
as a *jeu de mots*, it could mean peeled
uncle.

❧ 10/84 – 1500s

La naturelle à si hault hault non bas
Le tard retour fera marris contens,
Le Recloing ne sera sans debatz
En empliant et pendant tous son temps.

The bastard girl, so very high, not
    low at all
A late return will make those who
    regret happy
There will be disputes about the
    Reconciled One
In filling, and during all of his time.

The bastard girl is Elizabeth Tudor,
Elizabeth I of England. Pope Pius IV
declared her illegitimate in light of the
perceived illegality of her mother Anne
Boleyn's marriage to Henry VIII. Line 2
shows the Pope (the Reconciled One)
changing his mind, then changing it
back again. The upshot was that Henry
VIII annexed the Abbeys and
Monasteries of England for the benefit
of his Royal Treasury, and Elizabeth,
his daughter, became one of her
country's greatest sovereigns.

❧ 8/78 – 1500s

Un Bragamus avec la langue torte
Viendra des dieux le sanctuaire,
Aux heretiques il ouvrira la porte
En suscitant l'eglise militaire.

A lying mercenary
Will come to the sanctuary of the
    gods
He will open the door to heretics
Giving rise to the church militant.

This is a reference to the mercenary armies who fought for any side that paid them during Europe's Religious Wars of the sixteenth and seventeenth centuries. The actual event is impossible to pin down, but it may contain an oblique reference to the Holy Roman Emperor.

5/50 – 1500s

L'an que les freres du lys seront en aage,
L'un d'eux tiendra la grand Romanie
Trembler les monts, ouvert Latin passage
Pache macher, contre fort d'Armenie

The year in which the brothers of the lily will come of age
Will see one of them holding great Romania
The mountains will tremble, the passage to Italy will open
The Pashas will march against the Armenian fort.

Possibly intended as a provisional quatrain, in case Henri II had taken Nostradamus's advice and not engaged in his fateful joust (see 1/35 on page 11). In that event one of his sons might, just might, have become Holy Roman Emperor.

2/72 – 1500s

Armée Celtique en Italie vexée,
De toutes pars conflict et grande peste
Romains fuis, ô Gaule repoulsé,
Pres du Thesin, Rubicon pugne incerte.

The French army is battered in Italy
On each side conflict, and great loss
The Italians flee, France is repelled
Near Ticino, the battle for the Rubicon is poised, uncertainly.

No-one has satisfactorily interpreted this quatrain. It may refer retrospectively to the Battle of Pavia, in 1525, or to the Habsburg/Valois War of 1547–59. Either way, there are no clinching details.

2/73 – 1500s

Au lac Fucin de Benac le rivage,
Prins du Leman au port de l'Orguion
Nay de trois bras predict bellique image
Par trois couronnes au grand Endymion.

From Lake Fucino, to the banks of Lake Garda
From Geneva to the port of Orguion
Born with three arms, war is predicted
Three crowns competing for great Endymion.

Geographically, this quatrain makes little sense. It possibly refers to Henri II's desire to dominate the Papal states.

9/41 – 1500s

Le grand Chyren soi saisir Avignon
De Romme lettres en miel plein
*   d'amertume*
Lettre ambassade partir de Chanignon
Carpentras pris par duc noir rouge
*   plume.*

The great Chyren will seize Avignon himself
Honeyed letters, full of bitterness, come from Rome
Letters and ambassadors leave from Chanignon
Carpentras is taken by the red-plumed Black Duke.

England's Black Prince lived from 1330–76, so it is unlikely that Nostradamus meant him. Chyren is usually taken to mean Henri II, but Chanignon then presents a problem. De Châtillon was the family name of Gaspard de Coligny, admiral of the French fleet, and the same de Coligny who was killed at the outset of the St Bartholomew's Day massacre of 23 and 24 August 1572.

❧ 10/92 – 1500s

Devant le pere l'enfant sera tué
Le pere apres entre cordes de jonc
Genevois peuple sera esvertué
Gisant le chief au milieu comme un tronc.

The child will be killed in front of its
   father
Later, the father will be confined
   between rush cords
The Genevan people over-exert
   themselves
The leader lying among them like a
   tree trunk.

Nostradamus was obviously rather hoping that Protestantism would be killed in front of its father, John Calvin, and that Calvin (1509–1564) would then be trussed up and treated like a tree trunk, i.e. burned alive.

❧ 7/5 – 1500s

Vin sur la table en sera respandu
Le tiers n'aura celle qu'il pretendoit
Deux fois du noir de Parme descendu
Perouse à Pize fera ce qu'il cuidoit.

The wine will be spilt on the table
The third one will not have what he
   claimed
Twice descended from the black one
   of Parma
Perouse will do just what he thought
   to Pisa.

Parma, Perugia and Pisa were all cities of Italy which changed hands with varying regularity between the Vatican, Italian duchies and foreign powers during and long after Nostradamus's time.

❧ 4/3 – late 1500s

D'Arras et Bourges, de Brodes grans
   enseignes
Un plus grand nombre de Gascons batre
   à pied
Ceux long du Rosne saigneront les
   Espaignes
Proche du mont ou Sagonte s'assied.

From Arras and Bourges, great
   banners from the Brodes
More of the Gascons fight on foot
Those from the Rhône make the
   Spanish bleed
Near the mountain seat of Sagunto.

Nostradamus anticipates continuing wars between Spain's Habsburgs and factions in France.

'Retrospective' Prophecies

There are a number of verses among the *Centuries* describing events which had already taken place. In detailing these earlier occurrences, all in the first half of the sixteenth century, Nostradamus is apparently demonstrating that past and future events can be related with equal facility. How much Nostradamus knew, on a historical basis, of the events detailed in these quatrains is uncertain, but it seems likely that the verses are divined rather than mere reportage. The seer is showing off his powers.

❦ 8/72 – 1512

Champ Perusin d'enorme deffaite
Et le conflict tout au pres de Ravenne,
Passage sacre lors qu'on fera la feste,
Vainqueur vaincu cheval manger la
*   venne.*

What a huge defeat on the Perugian
    battlefield
The conflict is close to Ravenna
After a holy moment, when they
    celebrate the feast-day
The conquered conqueror eats
    horse-meat.

Most commentators take this to be a
retrospective prophecy accurately
describing the victory of Gaston de Foix
at Ravenna in 1512.

❦ 8/74 – 1519

En terre neufue bien avant Roi entré
Pendant subges lui viendront faire
*   acueil,*
Sa perfidie aura tel rencontré
Qu'aux citadins lieu de feste et receuil.

In the new land, well before the king
    entered it
The subjects will come to bid him
    welcome
His treachery will loom so large
That the people will rejoice and
    receive him well.

Another retrospective prophecy,
dealing with the country Nostradamus
already knew as the New World. Before
his Conquest of Mexico in 1519, a white
and bearded God-King resembling
Hernan Cortes (1485–1547) appeared
to Montezuma, Emperor of the Aztecs,
in a dream. Deeply superstitious,
Montezuma at first received Cortes and
his men with honour. Cortes

immediately betrayed Montezuma's
trust by seizing him and forcing him to
swear fealty to the king of Spain.
Montezuma was only released on the
payment of a massive ransom,
consisting of jewels, gold and silver. He
was stoned to death a year later, trying
to quell a riot against Cortes.

❦ 10/41 – 1533–52

En la frontiere de Caussade et Charlus,
Non quieres loing du fonds de la vallee,
De ville franche musicque à son de luths,
Environnez combouls et grand mytee.

At the border between Caussade and
    Caylus
Not very far from the base of the
    valley
The music of lutes will sound from
    Villefranche
Backed by cymbals, and many
    stringed instruments.

A Bacchanalian scene from
Nostradamus's youth? He was living
within a fifty mile radius of all these
towns when he met and fell in love with
his first wife. She and their two children
soon died of the plague.

❦ 1/12 – 1539–62

Dans peu dira faulce brute fragile,
De bas en haut eslue promptement
Puis un instant desloyale et labile,
Qui de Veronne aura gouvernement.

Soon, a treacherous, unstable brute
    will lead
Rising quickly in the ranks
Capable of swift disloyalty
He shall govern Verona.

This may refer to one Jacopo San Sebastiani, who was captain of Verona from 1539 to 1562, and who may have fallen foul of Nostradamus during one of the seer's visits to that city. Nostradamus was not above predicting doom for his enemies.

❦ 4/69 – 1545

La cité grande les exiles tiendront,
Les citadins morts meurtris et chaffés
Ceulx d'Aquilee à Parme promettront,
Monstrer l'entrée par les lieux non
    trassés.

The exiles will hold on to the city
Its citizens murdered and driven out
The Aquileans will promise to show
    Parma
How to enter, by secret trails.

Aqualeia, once an ancient Roman city near Venice, is a euphemism for the great maritime power that Venice was during the sixteenth century. Parma belonged to the papacy from 1511. Once it was made into a duchy, in 1545, Venice agreed to allow Parma restricted access to its port, and the use of its commercial navy.

❦ 9/1 – 1548

Dans la maison du traducteur de Bourc
Seront les lettres trouvees sur la table
Borgne, roux, blanc chanu tiendra de
    cours,
Qui changera au nouveau connestable.

In Bourg, in the translator's house
Letters will be found on the table
One-eyed, with red and white hair,
    he will persist
This will all change with the new
    constable.

This is about Etienne de la Boétie (1530–1563), one of sixteenth century France's best-known scholars. Famed, above all, for his friendship with Montaigne (1533–1592), he fell out with the Constable of France, Anne de Montmorency (1493–1567), over the publication of Boétie's book *Anti-Dictator*, which criticised his violent suppression of a revolt near Bourg.

❦ 10/56 – 1554

Prelat royal son baissant trop tiré
Grand fleux de sang sortira de sa bouche
Le reign Anglique par regne respiré
Long temps mort vif en Tunis comme
    souche.

The royal priest bows far too low
A great gout of blood spurts from his
    mouth
The English queen lives long enough
    to reign
He is half dead, for a long time, like a
    tree stump, in Tunis.

A fascinating and rather grotesque quatrain. It could be ascribed to William Laud (1573–1645), Archbishop of Canterbury to Charles I, and a man who suffered the same fate as his master, on the block. But the last two lines refuse to tally. Thomas Cranmer (1489–1556) seems more likely, although he died during Nostradamus's lifetime, making this a retroactive quatrain. However his torments while being burnt at the stake are graphically described in line 4. *En Tunis* now becomes *entièrement unis*; it was known that Cranmer took back his enforced recantations just before his death, effectively unifying himself once again with his Protestant God. The Queen who lived long enough to reign would then be Lady Jane Grey (1537–1554), who kept the throne for only nine days before her unwarranted execution.

1600–1699

❦ 6/74 – 1603

La deschassee au regne tournera,
Ses ennemis trouvés des conjurés
Plus que jamais son temps triomphera,
Trois et septante à mort trop asseures.

She who is driven from the kingdom,
   will return
Her enemies are found among the
   conspirators
More than ever her era will be
   triumphant
Three and seventy she dies.

Elizabeth I of England (1533–1603) was
imprisoned, exiled and plotted against
in the years preceding her accession to
the throne in 1558. She later
antagonised her Catholic subjects by
reverting to Protestantism, and was
bedevilled by Popish plots during the
entire course of her reign. She presided
over the greatest ever flowering of
English art, culture and music, and died
in 1603, in her seventieth year.

❦ 3/70 – 1607

La grand Bretagne comprinse
   l'Angleterre,
Viendra par eaux si haut à inonder
La ligue neufue d'Ausonne fera guerre,
Que contre eux ils se viendront bander.

Great Britain, including England
Will be covered by deep floods
The new Ausonne league will make
   war against her
So that her various parts will band
   together.

In Nostradamus's time, England,
Scotland and Wales were not united
into the one kingdom of Great Britain.
This process only began under James
I, who formally assumed the title of King
of Great Britain on 24 October 1604.
The floods in this quatrain are probably
those which occurred in January 1607,
when water covered the Somerset
levels for thirty miles in every direction.

❦ 5/75 – 1607

Montera haut sur le bien plus à dextre
Demourra assis sur la pierre quarree
Vers le midi posé à la fenestre
Baston tortu en main, bouche serree.

He will rise high over the one to the
   right of him
He will retain the squared seat
Towards midday, at the window
His mouth pursed, he will hold a
   crooked staff.

Cardinal Richelieu (1585–1642) began
his vertiginous rise to power in France
by being consecrated a bishop (thus
the crooked staff) in 1607, aged only
22. As chief minister to King Louis XIII
from 1629, Richelieu was the *de facto*
ruler of France. Thus did he rise above
the one to the right of him.

❦ 8/71 – 1607

Croistra le nombre si grand des
   astronomes
Chaissez, bannis et livres consurez,
L'an mil six cents sept par sacre glomes
Que nul aux sacres ne seront asseurez.

There will be so many astrologers
That they will be driven out, and
   their books censored
In 1607 the sacred assembly decides
That no-one will be safe from them.

This is a misdating, as no known
assembly decided to censor
Astromancy in the year 1607 – apart
from the fictional Council of Malines,
invented by a desperate Nostradamian
commentator.

❦ 6/54 – 1607

Au poinct du jour au second chant du coq
Ceulx de Tunes, de Fez, et de Bugie
Par les Arabes captif le Roi Maroq
L'an mil six cens et sept, de Liturgie.

At day-break, at the second cock's
   crow
Those of Tunis, of Fez and of Bugie
The King of Morocco is captured by
   the Arabs
In the year 1607, by the liturgy.

The machinations of Moroccan politics
would have been well known to
Nostradamus, if only because
European powers were constantly
interfering in the North African state's
internal affairs. In 1557, the childless
Moroccan king Mahomet IX was
assassinated and his throne passed by
his own will to his nephew, Abdh-Allah
IV, who sought to secure his
succession from his twelve brothers by
attempting to have them all killed. But
two escaped Abdh-Allah's thugs and
fifty years of internecine conflict began.
Finally, in 1607, the throne was secured
by Zidan, who gained victory over rivals
by enlisting British troops from King
Charles I and employing large numbers
of European engineers on his
fortifications and palaces. History
records that the influence of European

expatriates on Muslim society at this
time was not beneficial. Both the sons
of Zidan, for example, became
alcoholics. The liturgy that ends the
quatrain is, some scholars say, a
reference to the Christian ritual of
drinking wine.

❦ 10/91 – 1609

Clergé Romain l'an mil six cens et neuf
Au chef de l'an feras election
D'un gris et noir de la Compagne
Qui onc ne feut si maling.

The Roman Clergy, in 1609
Will have a New Year's election
A grey and black one from Campania
Never was there a wickeder man.

Perhaps due to the rare specific date,
this quatrain can be seen as a failure.
But it certainly could have occurred
had not Pope Paul V, who reigned from
1605 to 1621, recovered from the
serious illness he underwent that year,
amidst the frenetic intrigues of his
entourage to arrange for a possible
successor.

❦ 1/10 – 1610

Serpens transmis dans la caige de fer,
Ou les enfans septaines du Roy sont pris
Les vieux et peres sortiront bas de l'enfer,
Ains mourir voir de fruict mort et cris.

A coffin is placed in the iron vault
Where the seven children of the king
   are held
Their forebears will arise from the
   pit of hell
Lamenting the death of their line.

Following his correct prediction of the death of Henri II (1519–1559) in a joust, Nostradamus foretells the fall of the entire House of Valois. Henri's seven children by Catherine de Medici (1519–1589) all came to unhappy ends, the women in childbirth, the men through premature illness or murder – film buffs will cherish Patrice Chereau's *La Reine Margot*, in which some of their more unfortunate proclivities were aired. The last two lines are tragically self-evident, as Margot, notoriously lewd, was the last of the line.

❦ 7/1 – 1617

L'arc du thresor par Achilles deceu
Aux procrées sceu la quadrangulaire
Au faict Royal le comment sera sceu
Cors veu pendu au veu du populiare.

The treasury chief is deceived by
  Achilles
The crooked man is known to his
  procreators
The Royal act will rectify it
A body will be hung within sight of
  the populace.

Achille de Harlay, President of the Paris Parlement, is said to have played a part in the entrapment of Concino Concini, who rose to great power and wealth in the French court of Marie de Medici. Concini, a favourite minister of the Queen from her native Florence, defrauded the French treasury and made countless enemies at court. When Marie's son King Louis XIII took the reins of power from her on his sixteenth birthday in 1617, he had Concini arrested. Either by accident or design, the troops despatched for the purpose killed Concini in front of a number of passers-by on the bridge to the Louvre palace on 24 April of that year.

❦ 6/7 – 1618

Norvege et Dace, et l'isle Britannique,
Pars les unis frères seront vexées;
Le chef Romain issue du sang Gallique.
Et les copies aux foret repoulsées.

Norway and Dacia, and the British
  Isles
Will be angered by the united
  brothers
The Roman chief, of French blood
And his forces driven back to the
  forest.

The Thirty Years War in Europe broke out in Prague in 1618. 'Norway' signifies the Scandinavian armies who intervened in the war on the Protestant side against the forces of the Holy Roman Emperor Ferdinand II. Dacia is the ancient name for the region of central Europe now mostly occupied by Romania, but then a battlefield between Protestant and Catholic interests. Britain's role in the war was as a frustrated mediator, and a notable supplier of mercenaries to both sides. The Roman chief, Ferdinand, was not of French birth, but Nostradamus would doubtless have wished he had been. Ferdinand, born in Austria, was an ardent Catholic. He started the war – one of the most devastating in history – by insisting that Bohemian (Czech) Protestants convert to Catholicism or be exiled. His objective was to reunite central Europe as a group of Catholic states. But the Protestant influence was increased by the conflict, and the power of the Holy Roman Empire was diminished for ever.

❦ 1/45 – 1618

*Secteur de Sectes, grand paine au
    delateur,
Beste en theatre, dresse le jeu scenique,
Du fait inique ennobli l'inventeur,
Par sectes, monde confus et schismatique.*

The arch sectarian who lives by his
    whispers
The theatrical clown sets up the
    comic scene
This wicked notion will elevate its
    inventor
The world will be confused and
    divided by sects.

Nostradamus here excoriates Martin
Luther (1483–1546) whose Reformation
brought the Protestant and Catholic
sects of Europe into such destructive
conflict in the Thirty Years War of 1618–
48.

❦ 5/13 – 1618

*Par grand fureur le Roi Romain Belgique
Vexer vouldra par phalange barbare
Fureur grinsseant chassera gent Libyque
Despuis Pannons jusques Hercules la hare.*

In a great fury the Roman king will
    come
With a foreign horde, to vex Belgium
Gnashing his teeth, he will chase the
    Libyans
From Hungary to Gibraltar.

The Thirty Years War from 1618–48 was
the most devastating of all European
conflicts up to that time. The Roman
king represents one side of the conflict.
He was the Austrian Archduke
Ferdinand of Bohemia (1578–1637),
soon to become King Ferdinand II of
Hungary and then Holy Roman
Emperor, who provoked the war by
demanding that all his subjects
embrace the Catholic church or face
exile. Ranged on the other side were
the Protestant princes of Germany, the
Low Countries and Scandinivia. All of
Europe from Sweden to Gibraltar was
entangled. Ferdinand did not succeed
in stamping out the Protestant
movement; it was strengthened.

❦ 6/77 – 1618–1648

*Par la victoire du deceu fraudulente,
Deux classes une, la revolte Germaine
Le chef meurtri et son filz dans la tente
Florence, Imole pourchassés dans
    Romaine.*

Because of a fraudulent victory
Two fleets become one, Germany
    revolts
The leader and his son are murdered
    in their tent
Florence and Imola are pursued into
    Romagna.

La revolte Germaine was a euphemism
for any Protestant rebellion, of which
there were many during the Thirty Years
War of 1618–1648. None easily fit the
parameters of this quatrain, however.

❦ 10/71 – 1620

*La terre et l'air gelleront si grand eau
Lorsqu'on viendra pour jeudi venerer
Ce qui sera jamais ne feut si beau
Des quatre pars le viendront honnorer.*

The earth and the air will freeze such
    an expanse of water
When Thursday becomes a day of
    prayer
That which will be was never so
    beautiful
From all four corners they will come
    to venerate him.

Many commentators think that the day of prayer on Thursday refers to Thanksgiving Day in the US, traditionally held on the fourth Thursday in November. The cold snap in line 1 would then be seen to apply to the cold winter of 1620, during which the Pilgrim Fathers lost half of their entire complement of 103 men, women and children. The remainder only survived because of help from the local Indian tribe, with whom they allegedly sat down to dinner, thus instigating the present custom of inviting guests to share in the Thanksgiving turkey.

Nostradamus refers to America as the 'West' in several quatrains. He would have been aware of the existence of the American continents, the object of intense interest in Europe following initial discovery of the Caribbean islands and Mexico by the Genoese explorer Christopher Columbus between 1492 and 1504. By the time Nostradamus was writing the *Centuries*, Spanish explorer Ponce de Leon had made landfall in Florida (1512) – in his quest for the fountain of perpetual youth. Texas was discovered in 1528 by the Spaniard Cabeza de Vaca, who happened to be shipwrecked there. No Texan colony was founded until 1685 – by the French. Louisiana is said to have been discovered in 1519 when the Spaniard Alfonso Alveraz de Piñeda sailed into the mouth of the Mississippi river. Again, Spain made no claim to the territory and it was first colonised by the French in 1682 and named in honour of Louis XIV.

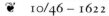 10/46 – 1622

Vie sort mort de L'Or vilaine indigne,
Sera de Saxe non nouveau electeur
De Brunsuic mandra d'amour signe,
Faux le rendant aux peuple seducteur.

Gold causes the life and fated death
    of an unworthy, evil man
He won't be the new Elector of
    Saxony
He will ask for a sign of love from
    Brunswick
The false one returns it to the
    people, seducing them.

A complex and seemingly specific quatrain that may apply to the Thirty Years War of 1618–1648, when the Duchy of Brunswick began to play an important role for the first time in its history. As Duke Christian of Brunswick-Wolfenbüttel chose the Protestant side in the conflict, Nostradamus is not stepping out of Catholic character when he describes him as false.

 6/85 – 1623

La grand cité de Tharse par Gaulois
Sera destruite, captifs tous à Turban
Secours par mer du grand Portugalois
Premier d'esté le jour du sacre Urban.

The great city of Tarsus will be
    destroyed
By the French, all shall be captured
    at Turban
Naval help comes from the great
    Portuguese
Urban is consecrated on the first day
    of summer.

Tarsus and Urban are two good clues here. The great city of Tarsus was no longer great by the time Nostradamus was writing. On what is now the southern coast of Turkey due north of Cyprus's northeasternmost point, Tarsus was a great city of the ancient world, and would have had no more than a few thousand inhabitants by the sixteenth century. One of its claims to fame was that its cosmopolitan populace in ancient times was disapproved of by St Paul. The apostle noted that a motto of the place was 'Eat, drink, play, for nothing else is worth the effort'.

Two popes so far have taken the name Urban since Nostradamus's time. The first, Urban VII, was elected on 15 September 1590 but died only 12 days later, aged 69. Urban VIII, born 1568, lasted longer, from 1623–1644 – the middle years of the Thirty Years War. Urban was a martial pontiff who fortified Rome tremendously and accumulated great personal wealth. To stay on the winning side, Urban was quite happy to ally himself to the Lutherans against the Catholics when necessary. He made an alliance with the French, who entered the war in 1635.

The conclusion is that the cynicism and materialism of Tarsus are used allegorically for Rome in the time of Urban VII. When the Thirty Years War ended in the Treaty of Westphalia, Rome's equivocation disqualified it from participation in the peace talks, and the political influence of the papacy (which Nostradamus would have accounted an invaluable influence) was diminished for ever.

🐦 6/57 – 1624

Celui qu'estoit bien avant dans le regne
Ayant chef rouge proche à la hierarchie
Aspre et cruel, et se fera tant craindre
Succedera à sacré monarchie.

He who was ahead in the reigning stakes
Having a red leader near the seat of power
Harsh and cruel, he will make himself so feared
That he will succeed to the sacred monarchy.

The red leader near the seat of power can only be Cardinal Richelieu (1585–1642), the ruthless statesman who became Minister of State to Louis XIII of France in 1624. Nostradamus seems to anticipate Richelieu's elevation to the Papacy, but the Cardinal took a different direction – later becoming *de facto* ruler of France.

🐦 6/60 – 1625

Le Prins hors de son terroir Celtique
Sera trahi, deceu par l'interprete
Rouan, Rochelle par ceux de l'Armorique
Au port de blaue deceus par moine et
prebstre.

The Prince, outside his French territory
Will be betrayed, deceived by the interpreter
Rouen, La Rochelle, by those of Brittany
Deceived by monks and priests at the port of Blaye.

This seems to be concerned with the suppression of the Huguenots (notably by Cardinal Richelieu at La Rochelle in 1628). The Prince would be Louis XIII under the regency of Marie de Medici, whom Richelieu served as a special adviser. Richelieu made a treaty with the English and arranged the marriage in 1625 of Henrietta Maria, Louis' sister, to Charles I – a union with a Protestant king which many in France would have regarded as a betrayal of the Catholic faith.

5/58 – 1627

De l'acqueduct d'Uticense, Gardoing,
Par la forest et mont inaccessible,
En mi du pont sera tasché au poing,
Le chef nemans et qui tant sera terrible.

Crossing the Gard, by the aqueduct
of Uzés
Through forest and inaccessible
mountain
He will cut a stanchion, halfway
across the bridge
Becoming the chief at Nîmes, and
very terrible.

This a superb quatrain, accurate in
every detail. It refers to the Roman
aqueduct that used to run from Uzès to
Nîmes. In 1627 the Duke of Rohan rode
to the aid of his fellow Calvinists, who
were being besieged at Nîmes. He
moved his artillery by means of the
aqueduct, thus avoiding the heavy
forest and inaccessible mountains of
line 2. Line 3 refers to Rohan's soldiers
cutting some of the stanchions of the
bridge over the Gard to allow the
cannon to be brought forward. When
Rohan and his men finally arrived at
Nîmes, he was immediately put in
command of the garrison.

1/41 – 1628

Siège à cité et de nuit assaillé,
Peu eschapez non loing de Mer conflict
Femme de joys, retour fils, defaillie
Poison et lettres cachées dans le plic.

The city besieged and attacked at
night
A few escape the battle, not far from
the sea
A woman faint with joy at her son's
return
Poison is hidden in the folds of the
letters.

The city is La Rochelle, the Huguenot
stronghold on the Poitou coast
ruthlessly besieged by Cardinal
Richelieu (1585–1642) in 1628. The
identity of the mother and son, with its
flavour of intrigue, is in doubt, but
Queen Marie de Medici, mother of
Louis XIII, whom the Cardinal served as
minister, loathed Richelieu and
certainly attempted to discredit him
with the king and possibly even to
murder him.

3/19 – 1628

En Luques sant et laict viendra plouvoir
Un peu devant changement de preteur
Grand peste et guerre, faim et soif fera
voir
Loing où mourra leur Prince recteur.

Blood and milk will rain down in
Lucca
Just before a change of Governor
War and pestilence and famine and
drought will be seen
Far from where their Governor
Prince will die.

In Nostradamus's time, Lucca in
Tuscany was an important silk town and
the seat of an episcopal see. It was a
leading citizen of the city, Francesco
Burlamacchi, who bravely tried to unite
Italy against all the external powers
who had long kept it divided. He was
executed in 1548 – an event of which
Nostradamus would no doubt have
been aware. A statue to the great man
was finally erected in the city's Piazza
San Michele in 1863. This quatrain
seems to allude to Lucca's successful
assumption of the status of a self-
governing city state in 1628 after a
terrible period of occupations and
liberations by competing invaders from
Bavaria, Genoa, Florence, Pisa and
Verona.

❦ 9/18 – 1632

Le lis Dauffois portera dans Nancy
Jusques en Flandres electeur de l'empire,
Neufve obturee au grand Montmorency,
Hors lieux provez delivre à clere peyne.

The Dauphin's lily will be taken to
    Nancy
The Elector of the Empire will fetch
    up in Flanders
Great Montmorency will have a new
    prison
He will be delivered to Clerepeyne at
    the usual place.

Louis XIII (1601–1643) bore the title of
Dauphin for a brief nine years before
ascending to the lily throne of France in
1610. Twenty-three years later he
entered Nancy, following the capture of
the Elector by Spanish forces, who took
him to Brussels (Flanders). The popular
Constable of France, Henri de
Montmorency, had been executed only
the year before. Following pleas from
his family, he had been transferred to a
new prison, the Hôtel de Ville in Paris,
where he was delivered, in private, to
Monsieur Clerepeyne, his executioner.
Clerepeyne in line 4 is also a play on
words, meaning just punishment.

❦ 6/15 – 1632

Dessoubs la tombe sera trouvé le Prince
Qu'aura le pris par dessus Nuremberg
L'Espaignol Roi en Capricorne mince
Fainct et trahi par le grand Vvitemberg.

The prince will be found beneath the
    tomb
He will have been taken above
    Nuremberg
The Spanish King, thin in Capricorn
Deceived and betrayed by great
    Wittemberg.

In Nostradamus's time, Nuremberg was
one of the wealthiest and most beautiful
cities of Europe. The second city (after
Munich) of what is now Bavaria, it was
the principal centre of manufacturing
and art in northern Europe. But
Nuremberg's great days were to end
with the tragic destruction of the Thirty
Years' War of 1618–48. The city
embraced Protestantism very early in
the Reformation (1525) and allied itself
to the Lutherans. In 1632 as a
stronghold of Gustavus Adolphus, the
Swedish king who took command of the
Protestant forces, Nuremberg found
itself under siege from the Holy Roman
Emperor's General Wallenstein. At least
10,000 citizens died of starvation or
disease and in the devastation of the
region that followed, Nuremberg's
ascendancy came to an end. It is said
that it took Germany 150 years to
recover from the effects of the war –
just in time to face the armies of
Napoleon in the 1790s.

❦ 6/47 – 1632

Entre deux monts les deux grans
*   assemblés*
Delaisseront leur simulté secrette
Brucette et Dolle par Langres acablés,
Pour à Malignes executer leur peste.

The two great men will meet
    between two hills
Abandoning their secret quarrel
Brussels and Dôle will fall to Langres
Their plague will alight on Malines.

This probably refers to the Spanish
Netherlands, during the Thirty Years
War, and to Mechelen, near Maastricht,
which was besieged in 1632. The great
men meeting could refer to any one of a
dozen military alliances which took
place during the period 1618–1648.

❦ 8/5 – 1633

Apparoistra temple luisant orné
La lampe et cierge à Borne et Breteuil
Pour la lucerne le canton destorné
Quand on verra le grand coq au cercueil.

A shining, ornamented temple will
  appear
The lamp and candle at Borne, and
  Breteuil
The canton turns aside because of
  Lucerne
Then we will see the great cock in his
  coffin.

Lucerne is the name both of a canton
and its capital in central Switzerland.
The city is built round the remains of a
mediaeval Benedictine monastery,
already a secular college by
Nostradamus's time and now the great
Hofkirche built from 1633. Is this the
shining temple Nostradamus foresaw?

❦ 10/79 – 1638–1715

Les vieux chemins seront tous embelis
L'on passera à Memphis somentrée
Le grand Mercure d'Hercules fleur de lis
Faisant trembler terre, mer et contree.

The beaten-up roads will be
  improved
They will travel to a place like
  Memphis
The French messenger of Hercules
Will cause land, sea and countryside
  to tremble.

Memphis was the ancient capital of
Egypt during and after the glorious
Ptolemaic Dynasty of 323–30 BC. The
implication here is that Versailles, built
by Louis XIV to encapsulate the
perceived grandeur of France, is the
modern Memphis. Louis XIV (1638–
1715) was renowned not only for the
splendour of his court, but also for the
numerous wars fought during his 72-
year reign.

❦ 8/4 – 1641

Dedans Monech le coq sera receu
Le Cardinal de France apparoistra
Par Logarion Romain sera deceu
Foiblesse à l'aigle, et force au coq naistra.

The French cock will be welcomed in
  Monaco
The Cardinal of France will appear
He will be let down by the Roman
  Legation
The eagle will be weak, the cock will
  be born strong.

The Grimaldi family, originally of
Genoa, who have played a part in the
history of Monaco for a thousand years,
have seen many changes in the
fortunes of the principality they rule
today. Monaguesque princes were
loyal to France until 1524, when
allegiance switched to Charles V, King
of Spain and Holy Roman Emperor. It
was not until 1641 that the French cock
was welcomed back, as a protector of
Monaco, by Grimaldi Honoré II.

❦ 8/68 – 1642

Vieux Cardinal par le jeune deceu,
Hors de sa change se verra desarmé,
Arles ne monstres double soit aperceu,
Et Liqueduct et le Prince embausmé.

The old Cardinal will be deceived by
  the young one
He will lose power, once out of office
Arles, don't let on that you've
  tumbled to the double
Both Liqueduct and the prince are
  embalmed.

An extremely accurate quatrain, detailing the supplanting of the aged Cardinal Richelieu by his young protégé, Cinq-Mars. Richelieu (1585–1642), having lost the favour of his sovereign, Louis XIII, resigns. When visiting Arles, however, he acquires a copy of a treaty, signed by Cinq-Mars and the king's brother. Fatally ill, he returns to Paris on a barge in order to make the king aware of Cinq-Mars's treachery. He dies soon after his return, with the king following him five months later. Both were embalmed. Liqueduct means 'one who has travelled by water'.

❦ 8/69 – 1642

Aupres du jeune le vieux ange baisser
Et le viendra surmonter à la fin
Dix ans esgaux au plus vieux rabaisser,
De trois d'eux l'un huitiesme seraphin.

The old angel falls near the young
  one
He will surpass him in the end
He falls, ten years after equalling the
  oldest
Of the three, one becomes the eighth
  seraphim.

This quatrain follows immediately on from the last, and deals, in a rather oblique manner, with comparisons between Cardinals Richelieu and Mazarin, and their relationships with their two sovereigns, Louis XIII and Louis XIV respectively. Nostradamus would seem to be declaring a dead heat.

❦ 6/53 – 1642

Le grand Prelat Celtique à Roi suspect
De nuict par cours sortira hors du regne
Par duc fertile à son grand Roi,
  Bretaigne
Bisance à Cipres et Tunes insuspect.

The great French prelate is suspected
  by the King
He will flee from the realm by night
Thanks to a duke, loyal to his great
  King, Britain
From Byzantium to Cyprus, Tunis
  unsuspected.

Jules Mazarin (1602–61), who succeeded his patron Cardinal Richelieu as Louis XIII's chief minister in 1642, was a cardinal (a great French prelate) himself. If the king suspected him, he was right to do so, because Mazarin was in love with his Queen, Anne of Austria. It is said that Mazarin and Anne were secretly married after Louis' death in 1643. As to fleeing by night, Mazarin twice fled France during the civil disturbances known as the Frondes – for which he was roundly and rightly blamed – but returned to power on both occasions. His foreign policy was better than his domestic rule: he made a successful alliance in 1648 with Oliver Cromwell to secure his position against Spain. This ended a protracted conflict between France and Spain in which Mediterranean sea battles, eternally aggravated by the incursions of North African and Turkish pirates, had been a considerable drain on France.

❦ 5/37 – 1642–48

Trois cents feront d'un vouloir et accord,
Que pour venir au bout de leur attaincte
Vingt mois apres tous et records,
Leur Roi trahi simulant haine saincte.

Three hundred will be of the same
  mind
Namely that, to reach the end of
  their undertaking
Twenty months to the day after their
  agreement
Their king will be betrayed, feigning
  holy hatred.

Difficult to interpret, as it so generalised. It could possibly relate to Charles I and his betrayal by Parliament, in which case the last line begins to make sense.

❧ 4/62 – 1642–49

Un coronel machine ambition,
Se saisira de la plus grand armée,
Contre son prince fainte invention,
Et descouvert sera soubz sa ramée.

An ambitious colonel will intrigue
Seizing the greater part of the army
He will foment lies about his prince
And will be discovered under his flag.

Sometimes ascribed to Colonel Muhammar Qadaffi (1942–), and even to the unfortunate Admiral de Coligny (1519–1572), this quatrain fits Oliver Cromwell exactly. Cromwell (1599–1658) suborned large parts of King Charles I's army, and later was instrumental in bringing the King first to trial, then to the executioner's block. The final line, which has given many commentators a headache, simply implies that the British flag belonged by right to the monarch, and that Cromwell, through *lèse-majesté*, succeeded in usurping it. An even more ambitious commentator than this one might go so far as to say that the prince in line 3 was the future Charles II, and that Cromwell did indeed end up under his flag when his body was exhumed and hanged, post mortem, at Westminster Hall.

❧ 1/95 – 1643

Devant moustier trouvé enfant besson,
De heroic sang de moine et vestutisque
Son bruit par secte langue et puissance
son,
Qu'on dira fort esleue le vopisque.

A single twin will be found near a
monastery
Fruit of a monk's brave and ancient
lineage
His fame, through force and
erudition
Will more than justify his lucky
survival.

Could this refer to the Man In The Iron Mask, who was reputed to be the son of Queen Anne and Cardinal Mazarin? Alexandre Dumas maintains, in his novel of the same name, that he was the twin brother of Louis XIV, and acceded to the French throne in his brother's stead.

❧ 4/86 – 1643

L'an que Saturne en eau sera conjoinct,
Avecques Sol, le Roi fort et puissant
A Reims et Aix sera reçeu et oingt,
Apres conquestes meurtrira innocens.

In the year that Saturn meets
Aquarius
A strong and powerful king, with the
sun behind him
Will be received and anointed at
Rheims and Aix
After numerous conquests, he will
slaughter the innocents.

Taken by many French monarchists to imply the restoration of the French crown within the next thirty years, this probably refers to King Louis XIV (1638–1715), the 'Sun King', who acceded to the throne of France in 1643, at the age of five, and proceeded to reign for the next 72 years – considerably longer than any other monarch in French history. In 1672 Louis sent an army of 100,000 men across the Rhine in a surprise invasion of the Dutch Republic. A year later, a desperate William III of Orange (1650–1702) opened the sluice gates and flooded his own country in order to save it from the French, thus fulfilling Nostradamus's prediction of a slaughter of the innocents. William later became King of England.

10/89 – 1643–1715

De brique en marbre seront les murs
    reduits
Sept et cinquante annees pacifiques,
Joie aux humains renoué Laqueduict,
Santé, grandz fruict joye et temps
    melifique.

The walls will go from brick to
    marble
Fifty-seven peaceful years
Joy to all, the aqueduct renewed
Health, much fruit, joy and happy
    times.

Following the Battle of the Dunes in 1657, France passed the remaining 57 years of Louis XIV's reign without a war inside its borders. Louis (1638–1715) was responsible for much building, including the aqueduct canals connecting the Atlantic to the Mediterranean. France did indeed enjoy a golden time under her Sun King.

9/93 – 1643–1715

Les ennemis du fort bien eslongnez,
Par chariots conduict le bastion,
Par sur les murs de Bourges esgrongnez,
Quand Hercules battra l'Haemathion.

The enemy is far away from the
    strong one
The bastion is brought by carts
The walls of Bourges are shattered
    from above
When Hercules smites the
    Macedonian.

Some far-fetched interpretations have been found for this one, but it probably refers to Louis XIV (Haemathion), and to the decay of Bourges during his reign.

3/80 – 1646

De regne Anglois l'indigne dechassé,
Le conseiller par ire mis à feu
Ses adherans iront si bas tracer,
Que le bastard sera demi receux.

The worthless one is expelled from
    the English throne
His counsellor will be burnt, in anger
His followers will stoop so low
That the bastard will be half accepted.

Charles I is normally accepted as the worthless one, although some commentators feel that Oliver Cromwell fits the bill more accurately. Nostradamus was a Royalist, and it seems strange that he would slander a king. However Archbishop Laud, one of Charles's counsellors, was burned at the stake, and the King's Scottish supporters did stoop so low as to betray him to Parliament, in 1646. If the bastard is the pretender, Cromwell, this quatrain is remarkably accurate.

9/49 – 1648

Gand et Bruceles marcheront contre
    Anvers,
Senat de Londres mettront à mort leur Roy,
Le sel et vin luy seront à l'envers,
Pour eux avoir le regne en desarroy.

Ghent and Brussels will march
    towards Antwerp
The Senate of London will put their
    King to death
Salt and wine will be turned back to
    front
Having rights to them will put the
    realm in disarray.

Peace came to the Low Countries with the 1648 Treaty of Westphalia with Spain. In the following year, the Senate – Parliament – in London executed King Charles I. The cryptic mention of wine and salt is simpler than it looks: King Charles's insistence on his right to levy taxes without reference to Parliament was a prime source of the conflict – and salt and wine are used by Nostradamus to signify taxable commodities.

4/1 – 1648

Cela du reste de sang non espandu
Venise quiert secours estre donné
Apres avoir bien long temps attendu
Cité livrée au premier cornet sonné.

The remaining blood will not be spilt
Venice looks for help
Having waited for a very long time
The city is surrendered at the first
    trumpet sound.

The siezing of Heraklion on Crete, after a vicious siege, by the Turks in the Ottoman Empire's war with the Venetian Empire.

5/43 – 1648

La grande ruine de sacrez ne s'esloigne,
Provence, Naples, Sicille, Seez et Ponce
En Germanie, au Rhin et la Cologne,
Vexez à mort par ceux de Magonce.

Soon, the clergy will be ruined
Provence, Naples, Sicily, Sées and
    Pons
In Germany, at the Rhine and
    Cologne
They will be driven to their death by
    men from Mainz.

Nostradamus seems to be predicting that Mainz, possibly as a result of the

Thirty Years War of 1618–1648, will turn Protestant, diluting Catholic influence in Southern Europe. If so, he was wrong. Might he therefore have been referring to the 1648 Treaty of Westphalia, which effectively ended the war, diminishing the power of the Holy Roman Empire and the Habsburgs, in favour of France?

10/7 – 1648–60

Le grand combat qu'on appreste à Nancy,
L'aemathieu dira tout je soubmetz,
L'isle Britanne par vin, sel, en solci,
Hem. mi deux Phi. long temps ne
    tiendra Metz.

The great battle being prepared at
    Nancy
Aemathien will say 'I shall subjugate
    all'
Great Britain frets over wine and salt
Hem. and Philip two won't hold
    Metz for long.

This may reflect European events in the years 1648–60. First, the Treaty of Westphalia ceded Metz to France in 1648. Then, in 1649, Charles I of England lost his head. Later, in 1660, Nancy was finally taken by the French. An unsatisfactory quatrain.

8/37 – 1649

La forteresse aupres de la Tamise
Cherra par lors le Roi dedans serré
Aupres du pont sera veu en chemise
Un devant mort, puis dans le fort barré.

The fortress near the Thames will
    fall
When the King is locked inside it
He will be seen in his shirt, near the
    bridge
One facing death, then locked inside
    the fort.

A chilling prediction of the execution of King Charles I of England on 30 January 1649. The fallen fortress near the Thames is not the Tower of London, but Windsor Castle, seized by Parliament, where Charles was held until his trial. He went to the block, in shirtsleeves, at Whitehall Palace, within sight of London Bridge.

❦ 8/76 – 1649

Plus Macelin que roi en Angleterre
Lieu obscure nay par force aura l'empire
Lasche sans foi, sans loi saignera terre,
Son temps approche si presque je soupire.

More of a butcher than a king of
    England
Born in obscurity, he will seize the
    kingdom
A coward with no faith, the lawless
    land will bleed
I sigh, because his time is so near.

This certainly applies to Oliver Cromwell (1599–1658), whom Nostradamus would have regarded as a Protestant heretic. Born in obscurity, he was known as 'the butcher of Drogheda' after he stormed the Irish town of the same name in 1649 and massacred all its inhabitants. The reference to coward in line 3 may refer to Cromwell's habit of wearing a chain-link shirt out of fear of assassination.

❦ 3/57 – 1649–1939

Sept fois changer verrez gent Britannique
Taintz en sang en deux cents nonante an:
Franche non point par appuy
    Germanique,
Aries doubte son pole Bastarnien.

The British nation will see seven
    changes
Over 290 bloodstained years
German support will not bring
    freedom
Aries brings fear for Poland.

Starting with the decapitation of King Charles I and the creation of a republic (called the Commonwealth) in 1649, 290 years takes Britain's bloodstained history, unnervingly, to the declaration of war on Germany in 1939, following Hitler's invasion of Poland (Bastarnien). Aries is taken by astrologers to refer to the Zodiacal sign of the ram. But Nostradamus will also have known *aries* as the Latin for battering ram – in the language of the Nazis, the *Blitzkrieg*.

From 1558, the British monarchy was distrusted in much of France after Catholic Mary Tudor was succeeded by her Protestant younger half-sister Elizabeth. To Nostradamus, a Catholic sympathiser, the execution of the English sovereign and declaration of a republic would certainly count as a pivotal change.

Accepting that the quatrain relates entirely to Britain's future, culminating in the events of 1939 which left the UK with the salvation of the world almost entirely in its hands, what could the intervening five events be? These are among the most popular interpretations:

1660 Monarchy restored with accession
    of King Charles II.
1688 Exile of King James II in the
    'Glorious Revolution'.
1707 United Kingdom created by union
    of England and Scotland.
1714 Hanoverian succession, of King
    George I, to British throne.
1832 Great Reform Act enfranchises
    wider population.

❧ 6/30 – 1650

Par l'apparence de faincte saincteté
Sera trahi aux ennemis le siege
Nuict qu'on cuidoit dormit en seureté
Pres de Braban marcheront ceux du
  Liege.

Due to the appearance of a false
  sanctity
The siege will be betrayed to the
  enemy
At night, when they expected to sleep
  safely
The Liègeois will march near
  Brabant.

For much of the Middle Ages, the great
fortified town of Liége was in an almost
perpetual state of revolt against the
prince-bishops who ruled there.
Successive Dukes of Brabant were
called upon by the church to put down
rebellions. Nostradamus sees these
troubles continuing into the future –
which they did until the city came under
the control of Bishop Maximilian Henry
of Bavaria (1650–1688) who stripped
the citizens' guilds of all their powers
and disabled them from raising
objections, let alone armies. Liége was
assigned to the new state of the
Netherlands under the Congress of
Vienna in 1815, but the citizens joined
the Belgian revolt of 1830 and the city
has been a provincial capital in the
Kingdom of Belgium since that date.

❧ 8/56 – 1650

La bande faible la terre occupera,
Ceux qui haut lieu ferant horribles cris,
Le gros trouppeau d'estra coin troublera,
Tombe près Dinebro descouvers les
  escrits.

The weaker army will hold the field
Men of the highlands will make
  horrible cries
The larger force will be cornered
Falling near Edinburgh, the plans
  discovered.

Oliver Cromwell's bid to subjugate the
Scots very nearly ended in disaster
when his army was cornered by a large
force of baying Highlanders at Dunbar
in September 1650. Brilliant
generalship earned Cromwell a
surprise victory, gaining him control of
Edinburgh.

❧ 1/28 – 1650

La Tour de Bouk craindra fuste barbare
Un temps, long temps après barque
  Hesperique
Bestial, gens, meubles, tous deux feront
  grand tare
Taurus et Libra quelle mortelle pique.

The tower in the Bouches dreads a
  foul odour
Once and for long after the Spanish
  ship
Livestock, people and goods all pay a
  high price
Taurus and Libra, what mortal
  offence.

A reference to the arrival of plague,
brought on board a Spanish ship to the
coastline of the Bouches du Rhône in
southern France. Plague was rife in the
1650s.

❦ 8/40 – 1651

Le sang du Juste par Taurer la daurade,
Pour se venger contre les Saturnines
Au Nouveau lac plongeront la Maynade,
Puis mercheront contre les Albanins.

The blood of the just shed for the
    church
For vengeance against the Saturnines
Will plunge into a new lake of blood
Then march against the English.

This cryptic quatrain has been held
since the eighteenth century to
describe the raising of an army in
Scotland by supporters of King Charles
II of England following his father's
execution. But the new army was
defeated in bloody battle by Oliver
Cromwell at Worcester on 3 September
1651.

❦ 10/4 – 1651

Sus la minuict conducteur de l'armee
Se saulvera, subit evanoui,
Sept ans apres la fame non blasmee
A son retour ne dira oncq oui.

At the stroke of midnight the army
    commander
Will save himself, vanishing suddenly
Seven years later, his fame still
    unblemished
They will be all for his return.

Following the Battle of Worcester, in
1651, Charles II of England was forced
to flee to France. His opponent, Oliver
Cromwell, reigned in his stead for
seven years. Charles returned, to
popular acclaim, in 1660, to reclaim his
usurped throne.

❦ 8/58 – 1651

Regne en querelle aux frères divisé,
Prendre les armes et le nom
    Britannique,
Titre Anglican sera tard avisé
Surprins de nuict mener à l'air
    Gallique.

The kingdom divided in war between
    brothers
Takes up arms and the name Britain
The English king will be counselled
    too late
Surprised and forced by night to seek
    French air.

A remarkably clear vision of King
Charles II's flight to France after the
defeat of his army at Worcester in the
English Civil Wars. He landed safely in
France on 20 October 1651, to begin
15 years of exile.

❦ 8/43 – 1653

Esleu sera Renard, ne sonnant mot,
Faisant le saint public, vivant pain
    d'orge,
Tyrannizer après tant à un cop,
Mettant à pied des plus grands sur la
    gorge.

Renard, who keeps silent, will be
    elected
Playing the saint, eating coarse bread
Ruling as tyrant after a coup
Placing his foot on the throats of the
    greatest.

Oliver Cromwell dissolved the Long
Parliament in 1653, bringing debate to
an end, and appointing himself head of
a ruling Puritan Convention.

❦ 7/23 – 1653

Le Royal sceptre sera contrainct de prendre
Ce que ses predecesseurs avoient engaigé
Puis que l'aneau on fera mal entendre
Lors qu'on viendra le palais saccager.

The Royal sceptre will be forced to take
That which its predecessors had pledged
Because they don't fully understand the ring
When they do come, they sack the palace.

Nostradamus, always sensitive to the fate of royal families, anticipates the interruption of Stuart rule in England on the execution of King Charles I in 1649. Oliver Cromwell, Charles's nemesis, was himself offered the throne by Parliament, but refused it. He disdained the worldly trappings of office, famously saying of the royal sceptre when it was offered him, 'take away that fool's bauble.' The occasion was at the dismissal of the Rump Parliament, 20 April 1653.

❦ 3/87 – 1655

Classe Gauloise n'approches de Corsegne,
Moins de Sardaigne tu t'en repentiras
Trestout mourrez frustrez de l'aide grogne,
Sang nagera, captif ne me croiras.

Do not approach Corsica, French seamen
Much less Sardinia; you will regret it
Despite help from the cape, you will all die
Blood will flow, and Captif won't believe me.

This is a very specific quatrain, with numerous double meanings. In 1655, part of the French fleet was destroyed near Sardinia and Corsica. Many seamen were lost because they could not reach the Cap de Porceau. Grogne, in line 3, can mean either cape or pig, as in *porceau*. Their pilot, Jean de Rian, known as *le captif* due to his earlier enslavement by Barbary corsairs, refused to listen to advice.

❦ 9/11 – 1655

Le juste à tort à mort l'on viendra mettre
Publiquement et du millieu estaint
Si grand peste en ce lieu viendra naistre,
Que les jugeans fouir seront constraint.

They will put the worthy man to a wrongful death
He will be killed publicly, and visibly
So great a plague will arise in this place
That his judges will be forced to flee.

Charles I of England (born 1600) was beheaded in 1649 on the pretext that he had committed treason against the state. The Great Plague of London followed six years later, in 1655–6, wreaking a terrible revenge on his persecutors and their families.

❦ 9/25 – 1659

Passant les ponts venir pres des rosiers
Tard arrivé plustot qu'il cuidera
Viendront les noves espaingnolz à Beziers
Qui icelle chasse emprinse cassera.

Crossing the bridges, approaching Les Rosiers
Arriving late, it was still earlier than he intended
The new Spanish will come to Béziers
This hurry will destroy the enterprise.

There are a number of towns called Les
Rosiers in France, but none near
enough the Spanish border to count.
Béziers, however, is on the invasion
route, and only became a formal part of
France in 1659.

🐦 10/58 – 1660

Au temps du deuil que le felin monarque
Guerroiera le jeune Aemathien
Gaule bansler perecliter la barque
Tenter Phossens au Ponant entretien.

At a time of mourning, the cat-like
    monarch
Will fight the young Aemathien
France shudders, the ship is in
    danger
Marseilles will try to negotiate with
    the West Wind.

There have been many very different
interpretations of this verse. The most
likely has Louis XIV as the young
Aemathion, or Sun King. The feline
monarch would then be Philip IV of
Spain. Louis XIV entered Marseilles in
1660.

🐦 2/23 – 1662

Palais, oiseaux, par oiseau deschassé,
Bien tost apres le prince parvenu
Combien que hors fleuve ennemi repoulsé,
Dehors sousi trait d'oiseau soustenu.

The palace, and its birds, by a bird
    sent hence
Soon afterwards the prince reaches
    his goal
Despite the enemy being repulsed
    beyond the river
The bird, upheld, is seized from
    outside, through trickery.

Until now, commentators have been
mystified by this quatrain. Here, for the
first time, is the true meaning. Charles I
of England (1600–1649) and his royalist
courtiers (who wore bird feathers in
their hats), fought and lost a bitter civil
war with the puritan Parliamentarian
forces, under their leader, Oliver
Cromwell (1599–1658). The Cromwells,
whose name was originally Williams,
had risen from obscurity thanks to the
favour of Henry VIII's minister, Thomas
Cromwell, whose family name they took
in gratitude, thus making virtual
courtiers (birds) of them. The man who
most influenced young Oliver Cromwell
was his teacher, Thomas Beard, an
outspoken puritan, whose name further
highlights the bird connection. Later,
when Cromwell dissolved Parliament on
19 April 1653, he was told that the
'birds have flown.' King Charles's son,
Prince Charles, soon to be Charles II
(1630–1685), later reached his goal,
despite being exiled across the
channel, by becoming king a mere two
years after Cromwell's death, in 1660.
The bird, Cromwell, was later upheld to
public view by being disinterred from
Westminster Abbey and hanged,
despite being two years dead, as a
traitor. His head was put on a pole
above Westminster Hall, and his body
was buried at the foot of the gallows.
This new interpretation makes this one
of the most prescient and specific of all
Nostradamus's quatrains.

2/53 – 1665

La grand peste de cité maritime
Ne cessera que mort ne soit vengée,
Du juste sang par pris damné sans crime,
De la grand dame par feincte n'outragée.

The great plague of the maritime city
Will not cease until death is avenged
For the righteous blood of the
    condemned innocent
Of the cathedral outraged by false
    saints.

Nostradamus vows that London will pay
the price of plague for the execution of
King Charles I in 1649 and for the
desecration of churches. The Great
Plague struck in the summer of 1665
and killed about 100,000. It subsided
only when London was visited with
another disaster – the Great Fire of the
following year.

2/51 – 1666

Le sang du juste a Londres sera faute
Bruslez par foudres de vingt trois les six,
La dame antique cherra de place haute,
De mesme secte plusieurs seront occis.

The blood of the just will be lacking
    in London
Burned up in the fire of '66
The ancient lady will topple from her
    high place
Many of the same sect will be killed.

A prediction of extraordinary accuracy
in time. The Great Fire of London
destroyed three-quarters of the city in
1666. Eighty-four of the city's 109
churches (including St Paul's cathedral)
were burned, bringing many votive
effigies of the Virgin Mary crashing
down. But the casualties of the inferno,
Christians or otherwise, were fewer than
Nostradamus foretold. Only six people
died in the fires.

4/96 – 1677

La Soeur aisnée de l'Isle Britannique,
Quinze ans devant le frère aura
    naissance,
Par son promis, moyennant verrifique,
Succedera au Regne de Balance.

The elder Sister of the British Isle
Aged fifteen, and before her
    brother's birth
By her promise, being confirmed
Will succeed to the King in a
    partnership.

Princess Mary, sister of King James II
of England, married her cousin, William
of Orange, on 4 November 1677 when
she was 15. William and Mary became
joint sovereigns of England – a unique
partnership – in 1688, when the
autocratic and irrational James II was
obliged by Parliament to flee to France.

8/36 – 1678

Sera commis conte oingdre aduché
De Saulne et sainct Aulbin et
    Bell'oeuvre
Paver de marbre de tours loing espluché
Non Bleteram resister et chef d'oeuvre.

An act will be committed against the
    anointed one
Brought from Saulnier, St Aubin and
    Bell'oeuvre
Paved in marble plucked from distant
    towers
Irresistible Bleterans and his
    masterpiece.

Bleterans in Franche-Comté may be the
key. The region was part of the
Habsburg Empire (and thus seen as
irresistible) until obtained by France in
1678.

❦ 4/91 – 1678

Au duc Gauloise contrainct battre au duelle
La nef Mollele monech n'approchera
Tort accusé, prison perpetulle
Son fils regner avant mort taschera.

The Mollele ship will not approach Monaco
Because of the French duke's duel
Wrongly accused and jailed for life
His son will attempt to reign before he dies.

It is hard to resist one interpretation of this quatrain, namely that it refers to the alleged conspirator against King Louis XIV of France arrested in 1678. The accused, a nameless aristocrat, was falsely convicted and incarcerated, his identity hidden by an iron mask.

❦ 10/61 – 1683

Betta, Vienne, Emorre, Sacarbance,
Voudront livrer au Barbares Pannone
Par picque et feu, enorme violance,
Les conjurez descouvers par matrone.

Betta, Vienna, Emorte and Sopron
Will wish to deliver Hungary to the barbarians
Great violence, by pike and fire
The conspirators discovered by a go-between.

This may describe the Relief of Vienna by the Holy League in 1683. The barbarian Turks were then driven from Sopron and the rest of Hungary by the Christian pike men, culminating in the 1699 Treaty of Karlowitz.

❦ 9/38 – 1685

L'entrée de Blaye par Rochelle et l'Anglois,
Passera outre le grand Aemathein
Non loing d'Agen attendra le Gaulois,
Secours Narbonne deceu par entretien.

The English will enter Blaye, via La Rochelle
They will go further, even, than Alexander the Great
The French will wait near Agen
Help from Narbonne fails through discussion.

A tricky quatrain, which seems to apply to help given by the English to the Huguenots of La Rochelle, at the time of the Revocation of the Edict of Nantes in 1685.

❦ 9/72 – 1685

Encor seront les saincts temples pollus
Et expillez par Senat Tholossain
Saturne deux trois cicles revollus
Dans Avril, Mai, gens de nouveau levain.

Once again the holy churches will be polluted
And plundered by the Toulouse Senate
Saturn having completed two or three cycles
In April and May, people of the new bread will come.

The new bread refers to the Calvinists, who were disputing the Eucharist with the Toulouse Senate during Nostradamus's lifetime. Saturn takes 29.5 earth years to complete a cycle, and it might be assumed that Nostradamus was dating the cycles from the sack of Toulouse and the killing of 4000 Huguenots in 1562.

Three cycles would arrive at about 1650, and the reign of Louis XIV (1638–1715) who finally revoked the Edict of Nantes – which guaranteed a certain measure of religious tolerance to the Huguenots – in 1685. Alternatively, dating the cycles from the actual signing of the Edict of Nantes, in April 1598, three Saturn cycles would arrive at the precise year of its revocation.

❦ 3/16 – 1685

Un prince Anglais Mars a son coeur de ciel
Voudra poursuivre sa fortune prospere
Des deux duelles l'un percera le fiel
Hai de lui, bien aimé de sa mere.

An English prince, with Mars in his
    heavenly heart
Will wish to continue on his
    prosperous way
Of two duels fought, one pierces the
    faithful
Hated by him, but loved by his
    mother.

James Scott, Duke of Monmouth (1649–85) was the son of Charles II of England and his mistress Lucy Walter. On his father's death, Monmouth was persuaded that he, rather than his uncle James II, was the rightful heir to the throne. A brave soldier made very prosperous by his marriage to one of the nation's richest heiresses, Anne, Countess of Buccleuch, he led an uprising against King James in the West Country, but was captured and executed.

❦ 2/64 – 1685

Seicher de faim, de soif, gent Genevoise,
Espoir prochain viendra au defaillir
Sur point tremblant sera loi Gebenoise.
Classe au grand port ne se peut acuillir.

Desiccated by hunger and thirst, the
    people of Geneva
Will see their urgent hopes come to
    nothing
The law of the Cevennes will tremble
    on the precipice
The fleet cannot find shelter at the
    great port.

This is yet another reference to Nostradamus's favourite *bête noire*, John Calvin. Calvin lived in the Cevennes, and had enormous influence there. When Louis XIV revoked the Edict of Nantes in 1685, the Cevennois revolted. It is certainly conceivable that their Calvinist allies in Geneva might have sent ships to their aid, although this is hard to prove.

❦ 10/63 – 1687

Cydron, Raguse, la cité au sainct Hieron.
Reverdira le medicant succours,
Mort fils de Roi par mort de deux heron,
L'Arabe Ongrie feront un mesme cours.

Canea, Dubrovnik and Bosnia
Will be healed again
The king's son will die because of the
    death of two heroes
Arabia and Hungary will move in the
    same direction.

Part three of the history of the Austro-Turkish War, started in quatrains 10/61 and 10/62 (see pages 64 and 67). Line 3 may apply to Sultan Mohammed IV, who was deposed by his Janissaries on 8 November 1687, and sent to prison, where he died in 1692. He was succeeded by his brother, Suleiman II.

🐛 2/67 – 1688

Le blond au nez forchu viendra
commettre,
Par le duelle et chassera dehors
Les exilés, dedans fera remettre,
Aux lieux marins commettant les plus
fors.

The blond man will fight the hook-
nosed one
In a duel, driving him out
The exiles will return, restoring the
status quo
The strongest will be chosen for sea
duties.

The blond man is William of Orange,
who drove England's James II out of
office in 1688. The exiled Stuarts rallied
behind their leader, who was sheltering
in Ireland, aided by the French fleet.
They almost won, but their hopes of a
restoration were dashed when William
III won the Battle of the Boyne. James
fled to France, never to return. The
British fleet finally triumphed over the
French at Cap La Hague, in 1692.

🐛 2/69 – 1688

Le Roy Gaulois par le Celtique dextre,
Voyant discorde de la grande Monarchie
Sus les trois pars fera florir son sceptre
Contre la Cappe de la grande
Hierarchie.

The French king, from the Celtic
right hand
Seeing the disarray of the great
Monarchy
Will flourish his sceptre on the other
three sides
Against the great Hierarchy of the
Capets.

Following on from 2/68 (see page 67),
this quatrain seems to show the French
monarchy – the Capets – mistrusting
William of Orange's intentions in
England. They allied themselves with
his enemy, James II, supplying him with
soldiers and ships. James was
eventually defeated, escaping to
France, where he died in 1701.

🐛 4/89 – 1688–9

Trente de Londres secret conjureront,
Contre leur Roi sur le pont entreprinse,
Lui, satalites la mort degousteront.
Un Roi esleu blonde, natif de Frize.

Thirty Londoners, in secret, will
conspire
Against their king; the plan will come
by sea
He and his courtiers are disgusted by
death
The elected king will be fair; a native
of Friesland.

An extraordinary quatrain, showing, in
detail, the events leading up to the
accession to the English throne of
William III of Orange (1650–1702),
during what has become known as the
Glorious Revolution of 1688–9. Married
to Mary, daughter of James II, current
holder of the kingship, William insisted
that the English nobles who supported
his cause sign their names to a piece of
paper before he would set sail with his
fleet. James II, not wishing to die, fled
to France, upon hearing that the
commander of his army, the Duke of
Marlborough, had deserted his cause.

6/41 – 1689

Le second chef de regne d'Annemarc,
Par Ceux de Frise et l'isle Britannique,
Fera despendre plus de cent mille marc,
Vain exploicter voyage en Italique.

The second chief of the kingdom of
  Mark Anthony
Because of the Friesians and the
  British
Will be forced to spend more than
  100,000 marks
In a vain attempt to reach Italy.

William of Orange (1650–1702) came
from Friesland, and took the throne of
England as William III, in 1689,
following the Glorious Revolution. The
reference to Mark Anthony is a purely
metaphorical one, implying the taking
over of a foreign kingdom, just as
Anthony did, in 33 BC Egypt. The figure
of 100,000 may refer to the number of
French soldiers Louis XIV sent across
the border against the Dutch in 1672,
which led directly to William's election
as captain-general, and to his ultimate
accession to the English throne.

2/68 – 1690

De l'aquilon les efforts seront grands.
Sus l'Occean sera la porte ouverte
Le regne en l'isle sera reintegrand,
Tremblera Londres par voille
  descouverte.

From the North, great efforts will be
  made
The doors will open over the ocean
On the island, dominion will be
  restored
London, fearful of the fleet, will
  tremble

William of Orange (1650–1702), King of
England. The British fleet was sorely
harried by the French in naval actions
off Beachy Head and at Bantry Bay.
William's main strength, however, lay in
his land army, which allowed him to
confirm his dominion at the Battle of the
Boyne, in 1690. The last line may refer
back to William's leading of a Dutch
fleet up the Thames in 1667, on a raid.

10/62 – 1697

Pres de Sorbin pour affaillir Ongrie,
L'herault de Bude les viendra advertir
Chef Bizantin, Sallon de Sclavonie,
A loi d'Arabes les viendra convertir.

Near Saxony, to assail Hungary
The herald of Budapest will come to
  warn them
The Byzantine leader will come to
  Salona of Slavonia
In an effort to convert them to Islam.

This follows on from 10/61 (see page
64), and covers much of the same
ground. The Byzantine leader at the
time was Sultan Suleiman II, who did
not live to see Turkey finally humbled at
the Battle of Senta in 1697.

2/8 – 1600s

Temples sacrez prime facon Romaine
Rejecteront les goffres fondements
Prenant leurs loix premieres et humaines
Chassant, non tout des saincts les
  cultements.

Temples consecrated in the original
  Roman way
Will reject the deep foundations
Taking over their first and human
  laws
And chasing out nearly all the cults of
  the saints.

Nostradamus correctly foresees that the influence of the Protestant movement will increase with the Reformation.

❦ 5/86 – 1600s

Par les deux testes, et trois bras separés,
La cité grande par eaux sera vexee
Des grands d'entre eux par exile esgarés,
Par teste Perse Bisance fort pressee.

Divided by two heads and three arms
The fine city will be harried by water
The great among them will be lost,
    in exile
Byzantium will be hard pressed by
    the Persian leadership.

This probably describes the Paris floods of the early seventeenth century, at a time when the Turks were being harassed by Persia.

❦ 5/87 – 1600s

L'an que Saturne hors de servage,
Au franc terroir sera d'eau inundé
De sang Troyen sera son mariage,
Et sera ceur d'Espaignols circundé.

The year in which Saturn goes free
The Frankish terrritory will be
    flooded
He will marry one of Trojan blood
And be surrounded by the Spanish

Possibly following on from the last quatrain, Trojans usually means a member of the French Royal line, who were reputed to be descended from the kings of ancient Troy. However the quatrain is too general in tone to allow for a more accurate interpretation.

❦ 6/3 – 1600s

Fleuve qu'esprouve le nouveau nay
    Celtique,
Sera en grande de l'empire discord
Le jeune prince par gent ecclesiastique,
Ostera le sceptre coronel de concorde.

The newly born French heir will
    attempt to cross a river
There will be great discord in the
    empire
The young prince will, because of the
    clergy
Remove the crowned sceptre of
    peace.

Crossing the river was an ancient rite of passage required of early French Kings. Newly-born, they were placed on a straw target and floated up the Rhine. If they fell off and drowned they were not legitimate – if they survived, they were the genuine article. The young prince in this instance is probably Louis XIV (1638–1715), who was never required to perform the test. He was dominated by the clergy, in the form of Cardinal Mazarin (1602–1661), during his early years, and engaged in many battles along the edge of the Rhine, indirectly testing himself for legitimacy.

1700–1799

☙ 1/26 – 1700

Le grande du fondre tomb d'heure diurne,
Mal et predit par porteur populaire,
Suivant presage tombe d'heure nocturne,
Conflit Rheims, Londres, Etrusque,
Pestifère.

At daybreak the founder's eldest falls
An ill-fortune popularly believed
The next prophecy follows at
    nightfall
Conflict between London and Reims;
    plague in Italy.

The War of Spanish Succession in Europe involving the English and French kings (the latter were crowned in Reims in Nostradamus's time). Charles II, the last Habsburg king of Spain, died childless in 1700 and King Louis XIV of France was anxious to unite the two crowns. The war raged from 1701 to 1713, when it was concluded by the Treaty of Utrecht. The plague in Italy (the Etruscan empire of the ancient world) might represent the nation's division between Savoy and Austria as a term of the treaty.

☙ 4/5 – 1700

Croix, paix, soubz un accompli divin
*   verbe*
L'Espaigne et Gaule seront unis
*   ensemble*
Grand clade proche, et combat tresacerbe
Coeur si hardi ne sera qui ne tremble.

Peace and the cross are achieved
    through the divine word
Spain and France are unified
A great disaster looms, the fighting
    will be ferocious
Even brave hearts will tremble.

The union of France and Spain, a principal ambition of Louis XIV of France, would have taken place in 1700 on the death of Spain's King Charles II, but for the intervention of European states concerned at the consequences for the balance of power. The War of Spanish Succession ensued.

☙ 4/46 – 1701

Bien defendu le faict par excellence
Garde toy Tours de ta proche ruine
Londres et Nantes par Reims fera defense
Ne passe outre au temps de la bruine.

For its excellence, the product is
    forbidden
Beware, Tours, your ruin approaches
London and Nantes will defend
    through Reims
Don't go further, in the season of
    mists.

Tours lies about 100 miles due east of Nantes in the Loire river valley of central France. Reims is about 200 north-north-east of Tours. What links these three cities? One theory is that it is wine: the famed rosé of Touraine, the Muscadet of Nantes and the champagne of Reims. These wines have long been popular in England, but have regularly been embargoed during Anglo-French conflicts. The season of mists is autumn, harvest-time. Nostradamus was a keen gourmet, and would have known the importance of the British market for his country's proudest product. The worst period of import bans for French wines was during the war of Spanish Succession (1701–1713) when Britain turned to Portugal as an alternative supplier, and the nation acquired a lasting thirst for port.

☙ 4/2 – 1701

Par mort la France prendra voyage à faire,
Classe par mer, marcher monts Pyrenées,
Espaigne en trouble, marcher gent militaire,
Des plus grands Dames en France emmenées.

Death will lead France to make a voyage
Ships will sail, the Pyrenees will be crossed
Spain will experience a military invasion
The greatest ladies will be brought into France.

The War of the Spanish Succession arose from King Louis XIV of France's belief that his marriage to the daughter of a Spanish king entitled him to that country's throne – as confirmed in the will of Spain's Charles II, who died in 1700. The rest of Europe was not convinced that the union of two nations as powerful as France and Spain would be entirely beneficial to the balance of power, and war broke out in the following year.

☙ 9/64 – 1701–14

L'Aemathion passer montz Pyrenees
En Mars Narbon ne fera resistance
Par mer et terre fera si grand menee
Cap. n'ayant terre seure pour demeurance.

The Aemathian will cross the Pyrenees in March
Narbonne will not resist
He will carry his intrigues by land and sea
The Capets will have nowhere left to hide.

Aemathion may refer either to Louis XIV (the Sun King) or to a man with a Macedonian name (possibly his grandson, Philip V). During the 1701–14 War of the Spanish Succession Philip fought against the Grand Alliance of England, the Netherlands, Denmark, Austria and Portugal, for his right to the Spanish throne. The matter was finally settled, to nobody's satisfaction, in the Treaty of Utrecht.

☙ 1/51 – 1702–1802

Chef d'Aries, Jupiter et Saturne,
Dieu eternel quelles mutations?
Puis par long siecle son maling temps retourne
Gaule, et Italie quelles emotions?

The head of Aries, Jupiter and Saturn
God Eternal, what changes can be expected?
Following a long century, evil will return
France and Italy, what emotions will you undergo?

Louis XIV's War of the Spanish Succession was underway in 1702, the year of a conjunction between Jupiter and Saturn in Aries. Nostradamus foretells the long century of upheaval that ensued, culminating in France invading Italy in 1802, following which Napoleon saw himself declared President of the Italian Republic.

7/19 – 1705 & 1891

Le fort Nicene ne sera combatu,
Vaincu sera par rutilant metal
Son faict sera un long temps debatu,
Aux citadins estrange espouvantal.

The fort at Nice will not be attacked
It will fall through shining metal
The truth will be long debated
The people will find it strange and
    terrifying.

The image of shining metal in line 2 has
seduced many commentators into
unwise speculation about flying
saucers and other extra-terrestrial
objects. But why Nice? The 'metal'
probably just refers to the shells used
during bombardments of the city by
French armies in 1705 and 1891
respectively.

6/53 – 1709

Le grand Prélat Celtique à Roy suspect,
De nuict par cours sortira hors de regne,
Par Duc fertile à son Grand Bretaine,
Bisance a Cypres et Tunes insuspect.

The great French Prelate suspected
    by the King
Will leave the kingdom in haste by
    night
Enabled by the conquering Duke to
    Great Britain
Undetected through Bisance, Cyprus
    and Tunis.

Since the eighteenth century, this has
been believed to refer to the escape of
the Cardinal de Bouillon from his
master, King Louis XIV of France. The
Cardinal was aided by the Duke of
Marlborough, who spirited him to Britain
via a (very) circuitous route.

5/85 – 1712

Par les Sueves et lieux circonvoisins,
Seront en guerre pour cause des nuees
Gamp marins locustes et cousins,
Du Leman fautes seront bien desnuees.

Through Switzerland and its
    surrounding area
A war will be fought, on account of
    the clouds
From the sea will come locusts and
    gnats
Geneva's faults will be open to
    scrutiny.

There have been very few wars fought
over Swiss soil, however Swiss
Protestants and Catholics did clash on
a number of occasions, culminating in
the Bernese triumph at Villmergen, on
25 July 1712, which established the
dominance of the Protestant cantons.
Clouds may therefore be taken as a
euphemism for spiritual matters. It
should be remembered that John
Calvin (1509–1564), the 'gnat' sucking
the blood of Catholicism, had lived in
Geneva for two years, from 1536 to
1538.

4/16 – 1713

La cité franche de liberté fait serve,
Des profligés et resveurs faict asile
Le Roy changé à eux non si proterve
De cent seront devenus plus de mille.

The free and democratic city will be
    enslaved
Becoming an asylum for the corrupt
    and feckless
A change of king makes things easier
    for them
From a hundred, they become a
    thousand.

There were many free cities in Europe during the sixteenth century, but Nostradamus is referring here to Orange, which was only ceded to the French in 1713. Before then it was a haven for French Protestants, whom Nostradamus would certainly have defined as corrupt and feckless.

☙ 3/67 – 1713

Une nouvelle secte de Philosophes
Mesprisant mort, or, honneurs et
richesses
Des monts Germains ne seront
limitrophes
A les ensuivre auront appuy et presses.

A new sect of philosophers
Scorning death, gold, honours and
　riches
They will refuse to confine
　themselves to the German
　mountains
They will have the support of many
　people.

A marvellous prediction of the Philosophes, France's great men of letters – led by Denis Diderot (1713–84) and followed up by the likes of Jean-Jacques Rousseau and Voltaire – whose writings on political philosophy in the eighteenth century inspired the new age of materialism, religious scepticism and interest in popular democracy. France under the Bourbons was inimical to many of these men's ideas, and they regularly sought refuge and sponsorship abroad. Diderot was supported by Catherine the Great of Russia and Voltaire by Frederick the Great of Prussia.

☙ 6/13 – 1714

Un dubieux ne viendra loing du regne
La plus grand part le voudra soustenir
Un Capitole ne voudra point qu'il regne
Sa grande charge ne pourra maintenir.

A doubtful man will approach the
　kingdom
The greater part will wish to support
　him
The Pope will not want him to reign
He will not be able to support his
　great burden.

The accession of George I, Elector of Hanover, to the newly (1707) united kingdom of Great Britain and Ireland in 1714. King George I was the great grandson of King James I of England, but spoke not a word of English. His succession to Queen Anne was not universally popular, but as a Protestant he was preferred to the other claimants, the Roman Catholic Stuarts – whom the Pope of course wished to see on the throne. George's popularity was considerably increased in 1715 when James Stuart (son of the late, exiled James II) landed with an army in Dorset in an attempt to overthrow the government, and failed. George I did not bear the burden of his reign well, but chose to leave the administration of the country to the Whigs, notably under the leadership of Britain's first 'prime' minister, Robert Walpole. The king never learned English and spent as much time as possible at home in Hanover.

❧ 2/87 – 1714

Apres viendra des extremes contrées
Prince Germain, dessus le throsne doré
La servitude et eaux rencontrées,
La dame serve, son temps plus n'adore.

Later, from a distant country, there
  will come
A Germanic Prince, upon a golden
  throne
Servitude and waters meet
Our Lady is subordinated, no longer
  worshipped.

This relates to the accession of George
I of Hanover (1660–1727) to the throne
of England, in 1714. England was a
great prize, and thus golden. The
German prince had been invited to
succeed to the throne, hence the
concept of servitude. Catholicism
continued its long decline under the
ensuing Protestant Hanoverian
ascendancy.

❧ 5/38 – 1715

Ce grand monarque qu'au mort
  succedera,
Donnera vie illicite et lubrique,
Par nonchalance à tous concedera,
Qu'à la parfin faudra la loi Salique.

He who succeeds, following the
  death of the great monarch
Will lead an illicit and lubricious life
Not caring, he will make many
  concessions
Leading to the failure of Salic law.

Louis XV (1710–1774) was recognised,
after his death, as the most wayward
and decadent of all French Kings.
Succeeding his great-grandfather,
Louis XIV, in 1715, at the age of five, he
later undid the great King's legacy and

laid the foundations for what would
eventually become the French
Revolution. The failure of Salic Law
refers to his arrogation of power to
Madame de Pompadour and Madame
du Barry, who metaphorically became
kings in his stead, something illegal
under the law.

❧ 3/15 – 1715

Coeur, vigueur, gloire, le regne
  changera,
De tous points contre ayant son
  adversaire:
Lors France enfance par mort
  subjuguera,
Un grand Regent sera lors plus
  contraire.

Heart, vigour, glory, the rule will
  change
In all ways against having his
  adversary
Then a child will come to power by
  death
A powerful Regent will then be more
  contrary.

Nostradamus looks forward with
misgivings to the appointment of a
Regent, Philippe, Duke of Orléans, to
rule on behalf of Louis XV – who
succeeded to the French throne aged
only five on the death of his great-
grandfather, the brave, vigorous and
glorious Louis XIV. Orléans was a
cultured man, but led a scandalous
private life; he was suspected of
complicity in the deaths of both
previous heirs to the throne, Louis XV's
father and grandfather.

❦ 1/78 – 1715

D'un chef vieillard naistra sens hébeté,
Degenerant par scavoir et par armes,
Le chef de France par sa soeur redouté,
Champs divisez, concedez aux gens
l'armes.

To an old chief will be born a dullard
Degenerating in knowledge and arms
The chief of France, feared by his
   sister
Divides in the battlefield, conceding
   to men of arms.

The old chief is Louis XIV, who reigned
from 1638 until his death in 1715 aged
77. He outlived his direct heirs and was
succeeded by his great-grandson, five-
year-old Louis XV, whose own long
reign of 39 years was marked by good
intentions and disastrous policies at
home and abroad. France suffered
humiliating military defeats through
much of the reign, and the prestige of
the monarchy reached a new nadir
under his tenure. The flip remark of
Louis' favourite mistress, Madame de
Pompadour, '*Après nous le déluge*',
perfectly encapsulates the witless
descent of the French monarchy,
shrewdly foreseen by Nostradamus in
so many acutely observed respects.

❦ 9/27 – 1722

De bois la garde, vent clos rond pont sera,
Haut le reçu frappera le Dauphin,
Le vieux teccon bois uni passera,
Passant plus outre du Duc le droit confin.

Dubois the guard, closed shutters in
   the apse
Empowered, will strike the Dauphin
The old wooden ball will roll about
Going beyond the Duke's
   instructions.

The traditional interpretation depends
on Nostradamus intending 'De bois' as
an ill-disguised code for the priest
Guillaume Dubois (1656–1723) who
rose to be first minister of France under
the Regency of the Duke of Orléans in
1722. Dubois had charge of the young
King Louis XV's spiritual welfare, and
Nostradamus forecasts that he will fail
in this duty, submitting the young king
to more discipline than the Duke would
ordain. The reference to the old
wooden ball may well be a pun on
Dubois' ability to ride the ebb and flow
of the political tides.

❦ 3/77 – 1727

Le tiers climat sous Aries comprins,
L'an mil sept cens vingt et sept en Octobre
Le Roy de Perse par ceux d'Egypte prins,
Conflit, mort, perte: à la croix grand
approbre.

The third climate will be under Aries
In October, of the year 1727
The Persian king will be taken by the
   Egyptians
Battle, death and losses: the cross will
   be excoriated.

This is extraordinarily specific, with
Nostradamus giving the actual year
and month of an event that took place
161 years after his death. In October
1727, a peace was indeed arranged
between the Turks and the Persians. As
a result, Ottoman influence was
consolidated throughout the region, to
the detriment of the Christian powers.

❦ 4/78 – 1734

La grande armee de la pugne civile
Pour de nuict Parme à l'estrange trouvée
Septante neuf meurtris dedans la ville
Les estrangiers passez tous à l'espee.

The great army of the civil war
Finds Parma, taken at night by
    foreign forces
Seventy-nine are murdered in the
    town
All the strangers are put to the
    sword.

Parma in the Emilia-Romagna region of
Italy was a papal possession for most
of Nostradamus's life, but was given by
Pope Paul III to his son as a duchy in
1545, beginning a succession of heirs
which endured until 1731. The last duke
died childless and Parma passed to the
crown prince of Spain, Charles of
Bourbon. Now Parma's troubles began.
Charles succeeded as King of Naples
in 1734 and handed Parma to Austria,
but in 1745 Spanish troops reclaimed
the city, only to lose it back to Austria in
the next year. In 1748, Spain regained
possession. By this time, much of the
population had perished in sieges, and
Parma's fabulous art treasures had
been almost entirely lost.

🐚 8/49 – 1736

Saturn: au beuf joue en l'eau, Mars en
    fleiche
Six de Fevrier mortalité donra
Ceux de Tardaigne à Briges si grand
    breche
Qu'à Ponteroso chef Barbarin mourra,

Saturn: Taurus plays in Aquarius,
    Mars in Sagittarius
The sixth day of February brings
    death
The Sardinians will make such a big
    breach at Bruges
That the barbarian chief will die at
    Ponteroso.

Astrologers have not arrived at a
satisfactory future date based on this
seemingly specific celestial pattern, but
one claim is that this heavenly
configuration pertained in 1736. On 6
February of that year, the most notable
event was the landing of John Wesley,
the founder of Methodism, in America –
where he received a distinctly hostile
reception from the Georgia colonists,
but did not lose his life.

🐚 8/3 – 1736

Au fort chasteau de Viglanne et Resviers
Sera serré le puisnay de Nancy
Dedans Turin seront ards les premiers
Lors que de dueil Lyon sera transi.

At the fortress of Viglanne and
    Resviers
They will imprison the youngest
    born of Nancy
The leading citizens of Turin will be
    burned
When Lyons is transported with
    grief.

There are several clues in this verse.
The most interesting is Nancy, the
former capital of the province of
Lorraine. Here Stanislas Leczinski, last
Duke of Lorraine, who abdicated the
Polish throne in 1736 and was given
Lorraine by his son-in-law Louis XV of
France, established one of the most
beautiful cities in Europe. The reference
to burning in line 3 (though referring,
inexplicably, to Turin) is also interesting,
because Stanislas died from burns
received in an accident in 1766, at the
age of 89.

❦ 5/3 – 1737

Le successeur de la Duché viendra
Beaucoup plus outre que la mer de
   Tosquane
Gauloise branche la Florence tiendra
Dans son giron d'accord nautique Rane.

The heir to the Duchy will come
From far beyond the sea of Tuscany
A French branch will hold Florence
In his lap will be a naval agreement
   with the frog.

This is a remarkably sharp insight into
the future of Florence, which passed
from Medici possession into that of
Francis, Duke of Lorraine, in 1737.

❦ 9/61 – 1743

La pille faite à la coste marine
La cita nova et parents amenez
Plusieurs de Malte par le fait de Messine
Estroit serrez seront mal guardonnez.

Pillage occurs on the sea coast
Family relations are favoured in the
   new city
Some Maltese, because of Messina's
   acts
Will be locked up, and poorly
   rewarded.

The island of Malta is situated in the
Mediterranean, south of Sicily. Messina
separates the north-western corner of
Sicily from mainland Italy. In 1743
Messina was decimated by a plague.
Any merchants passing through the
straits of Messina from Malta would
have been forcibly quarantined to
prevent the spread of the pestilence,
thus ensuring that they were poorly
rewarded for their pains.

❦ 5/93 – 1745

Soubs le terroir du rond globe lunaire,
Lors que sera dominateur Mercure,
L'isle d'Escosse fera un luminaire,
Qui les Anglais mettra à déconfiture.

On this world beneath the moon
While Mercury is in the ascendant
The isle of Scotland will produce a
   leader
Who will cause the English
   discomfort.

Prince Charles, the 'Young Pretender'
intent on regaining the crowns of
Scotland and England for the Stuart
dynasty dispossessed of it in 1588,
landed in Inverness, Scotland in 1745.
He collected together an army of
highlanders and succeeded in seizing
Edinburgh, proclaiming himself king.
But what really discomforted the
English was Bonnie Prince Charlie's
march south. Even though the young
prince never received the
reinforcements he was promised by the
perfidious French, he got as far as
Derby before the series of reverses that
was to culminate in the carnage at
Culloden, and the end of this luminary's
pretensions, on 16 April 1746.

2/33 – 1755

Par le torrent qui descent de Veronne
Par lors qu'au Pau guidera son entrée
Un grand naufrage, et non moins en
*   Garonne*
Quand ceux de Gennes marcheront leur
*   contree.*

Near the river which flows down
   from Verona
Near the place where the Pau guides
   its entrance
There will be a great wreck, in the
   Garonne too
When the Genoese march their
   country.

Geographically, a remarkably diverse
quatrain, extending from Bordeaux to
Italy. It seems likely to refer to the
uprising against the Genoese in
Corsica in 1755. The island was bought
by France from Genoa in 1768.

9/54 – 1755

Arrivera au port de Corsibonne,
Pres de Ravenne qui pillera la dame,
En mer profonde legat de la Ullisbonne
Souz roc cachez raviront septante ames.

At Porto Corsini a man will arrive
Who will plunder Our Lady, near
   Ravenna
On the high seas, the legate from
   Lisbon
Hidden beneath a rock, will snatch
   seventy souls.

A presage of the earthquake that
devastated Lisbon in November 1755.
Three-quarters of the city, including
churches dedicated to the Virgin, was
destroyed by tremors and fires and
10,000 died. News of the disaster was
spread by onlookers in ships far

enough out to sea to survive the
gigantic seismic wave which crashed
on to Lisbon following the quake.

4/51 – 1764

Un Duc cupide son enemi ensuivre,
Dans entrera empeschant la phalange
Hastez à pied si pres viendront
*   poursuivre,*
Que la journee conflite pres de Gange.

A Duke, eager to harry his enemy
Will succeed in breaking through
   their phalanx
Hastily, on foot, they will follow so
   closely
That the day of the battle will occur
   near the Ganges.

The Ganges could indicate either the
river in India, or the small town in
France, near Montpellier, which was
where Nostradamus earned his medical
degree. There is also a Ganges in
North Columbia, not to speak of those
in Michigan and Ohio. But the most
obvious source for the battle mentioned
in line 4 would be in India. In 1764,
when the British were trying to re-
establish their domination of Bengal, Sir
Hector Munro routed the vastly superior
forces of Mir Kasim, Nawab of Bengal,
near Buxar, on the river.

1/60 – 1769

Un Empereur naistra pres d'Italie
Qui a l'Empire sera vendu bien cher
Diront avec quels gens il se ralie,
Qu'on trouvera moins prince que boucher.

An Emperor will be born near Italy
Who will cost the Empire dearly
Judged by the people who surround
   him
He will be considered less Prince,
   than butcher.

Napoleon was born 'near Italy', in 1769, on the island of Corsica. It can be argued that he cost the French Empire dearly, both in terms of life and prestige. In English popular newspapers of the time, Napoleon was known as the 'French Butcher', a reference both to his humble birth and military tactics.

❦ 1/76 – 1769

D'un nom farouche tel proferé sera,
Que les trois soeurs aurant fato le nom
Puis grand peuple par langue et faict
* dira*
Plus que nul autre bruit et renom.

He will be known by a savage name
The name is the destiny of three
  sisters.
He will address a great people in
  words and actions
His fame and renown greater than
  any other.

A new Messiah? Possibly, but a more earthly paragon is likelier: France's incomparable exemplar, Napoleon Bonaparte (1769–1821). The name Napoleon is a savage one, deriving from the Greek word for destroyer – and Bonaparte's campaigns destroyed more lives, including one and a half million French ones, than any previous conflict in history. He was a great orator and legislator as well as soldier. He had three sisters, Elisa, Pauline and Caroline, who each benefited from their brother's eager desire to make the Bonapartes the first family of Europe.

❦ 4/54 – 1769–1821

Du nom qui onques ne fut au Roy
* Gaulois,*
Jamais ne fut un fouldre si craintif
Tremblant l'Italie, l'Espaigne et les
* Anglois,*
De femme estrangiers grandement
* attentif.*

From a name never held by French
  kings
Comes a fear-inducing thunderbolt
Italy, Spain and the English tremble
He will be drawn to foreign women.

The king who was not a king has to be Napoleon Bonaparte, whose name had never before ranked among the rulers of France. Lines 2 and 3 are self-evident, and Napoleon's proclivity for foreign-born women is also well documented: Josephine, his first wife, was a Creole, born in Haiti; his mistress, Guiseppina Grassini, was Italian; another mistress, Maria Walewska, who bore him an illegitimate child, was Polish.

❦ 1/70 – 1774

Pluys, faim, guerre, en Perse non cesée,
La foy trop grande trahira le Monarque,
Par la finie en Gaule commencée,
Secret augure pour a un estre parque.

Rain, hunger, unceasing war in the
  east
His excess of faith will betray the
  monarch
It's the beginning of the end for
  France
A secret augury for one who lives
  apart.

King Louis XVI of France succeeded his grandfather, Louis XV, in 1774 aged

20. The kingdom was bankrupt through prolonged war and endemic official corruption. Louis' reign was marked by a series of poor harvests, mass starvation and unjust burdens of taxation imposed on all classes except the aristocracy. The king, remote from his people and ill-served by his advisors, must indeed have had premonitions of his country's and his own fate in the looming Revolution. His execution on 20 January 1793 brought 1,025 continuous years of French monarchy to an end.

❦ 5/57 – 1783

Istra du Mont Gaulfier et Aventin,
Qui par trou avertira l'armée
Entre deux rocs sera prins le butin,
De S E X T. mansol faillir le renommee.

From Montgaulfier and Aventin will
   go forth
One who, through a hole, will warn
   the army
The booty will be taken from
   between two rocks
The renown of Sextus the celibate
   will diminish.

This quatrain has tormented commentators for many years. It would appear to foretell, even down to their names, the invention of the hot air balloon by the Montgolfier brothers, in 1783. The balloon was immediately used to scout enemy positions at the Battle of Fleurus in 1794. This victory then led, by a circuitous route, to Napoleon's sack of Rome, indicated by the booty being taken between two rocks. Pius VI ('sextus') was captured by Napoleon, and his influence and renown were indeed diminished by the Treaty of Tolentino, in 1797.

❦ 1/66 – 1789

Celui qui lors portera les nouvelles,
Apres un peu il viendra respirer
Viviers, Tournon, Montferrand et
   Pradelles,
Gresle et tempestes les fera soupirer.

The one who will subsequently carry
   the news
Will stop for a short while to catch
   his breath
Viviers, Tournon, Montferrand and
   Pradelles
Will be stricken by hail, and
   tempests.

This quatrain resists easy interpretation, but probably refers to the spread of the French Revolution. The towns mentioned would, at first glance, seem to have nothing in common. If Montferrand is changed to Montferrat, however, and if Pradelles is changed to Pradelle, it emerges that they are all situated in the Rhônes-Alpes and the revolutionary connection is hinted at.

❦ 1/14 – 1789

De gent esclave chansons, chants et
   requestes,
Captifs par Princes et Seigneur aux
   prisons
A l'avenir par idiots sans testes,
Seront reçus par divines oraisons.

Songs, chants and demands will come
   from the enslaved
Held captive by the nobility in their
   prisons
At a later date, brainless idiots
Will take these as divine utterances.

The French Revolution was caused by social unrest, stemming from the power of the aristocracy and their abuse of it.

The Paris mob, thinking themselves liberated, howled and chanted outside the walls of Louis XVI's prison. Men like Danton (1759–1794) and Robespierre (1758–1794) took these cries quite literally to heart, a mistake which cost them their own heads on the guillotine.

❦ 7/14 – 1789

Faux esposer viendra topographie,
Seront les cruches des monuments ouvertes
Pulluler secte saincte philosophie,
Pour blanches, noirs, et pour antiques verts.

He will come to expose the false topography
The monumental urns will be opened
Sects, and sacred texts will thrive
Black instead of white, new for old.

Following the National Assembly of 22 December 1789, everything changed in France. The funeral urns of the French Kings were destroyed and their ashes scattered. Even the Church was abolished, to be replaced by the cult of Reason.

❦ 2/10 – 1789

Avant long temps le tout sera rangé
Nous esperons un siecle bien senestre
L'estat des masques et des seuls bien changé
Peu trouverant qu'à son rang vueille estre.

Before long everything will be settled
We can expect a very bad century
The condition of the masked and alone, much changed
Few will wish to retain their rank.

A clear allusion to the French Revolution at the end of the eighteenth century.

❦ 9/58 – 1789

Au costé gauche à l'endroit de Vitry
Seront guettez les trois rouges de France
Tous assomez rouge, noir non murdri
Par les Bretons remis en asseurance.

In Vitry, on the left side
The three reds of France will be ambushed
Only the reds are killed, not the blacks
Confidence is restored by the Bretons.

At a stretch, this could be referring to the Breton, later the Jacobin, Club, which at first harboured only the more moderate revolutionary faithful. Vitry-le-François was the site of the first victory by French Republican forces during the Revolutionary Wars.

❦ 1/44 – 1789

En bref seront de retour sacrifices,
Contrevenans seront mis a martyre,
Plus ne seront moins, abbez ne novices
Le miel sera beaucoup plus cher que cire.

Briefly sacrifices will be made again
Protesters will be martyred
No more monks, abbots or novices
Honey will be costlier than candles.

The murderous destruction of the English monasteries in 1536, ordered by Henry VIII in his unilateral Reformation, will have been in Nostradamus's mind as he predicted a similar fate for France's abbeys. The Church in France hung on to its influence and its vast wealth right up to the Revolution – longer, perhaps than the seer expected. Priests were murdered (judicially or otherwise) in vast numbers. Most of the land and property was seized by the moneyed 'notables' of the Revolution – and remains in the hands of their heirs today.

9/17 – 1789–93

Le tiers premier pis que ne fait Neron,
Vuidez vaillant que sang humain
*   respandre*
R'edifier sera le forneron,
Siecle d'or, mort, nouveau roi grand
*   esclandre.*

The first of the third behaves worse
   than Nero
Go, brave one, that human blood
   may flow
The oven will be rebuilt
Golden century, dead, a new king
   and a great scandal.

The first of the third is the Tiers Etat, precursor of the French Revolution in 1789. The blood-letting it engendered would be far worse even than Nero's. The guillotine was placed in the Place de la Revolution, where before there had only been kilns (ovens) for baking tiles. The golden century refers to the reign of the three Louis, XIV, XV and XVI. The scandal is the beheading of Louis XVI.

4/17 – 1789–99

Changer à Beaune, Nuy, Chalons et
*   Dijon,*
Le duc voulant amander la Barrée
Marchant pres fleuve, poisson, bec de
*   plongeon,*
Vers la queue; porte sera serrée.

Changes to Beaune, Nuits, Chalon
   and Dijon
The king wishes to improve the lot of
   the Carmelites
Merchants near the rivers; fish; the
   beaks of diving birds
Towards the end the gates will be
   shut.

Barée in line 1 refers to the Carmelites, an order of nuns whose silent and contemplative lives consisted of prayer, penance, and hard work, and who were forcibly deprived of their nunneries during the French Revolution of 1789–99.

6/23 – 1789–99

D'esprit de regne munismes descriées,
Et seront peuples esmuez contre leur Roi
Paix, faict nouveau, sainctes loix
*   empirées,*
Rapis onc fut en si tres dur arroi.

The spirit of the kingdom
   undermines its defences
People will rise against the king
A new peace is made, holy laws
   deteriorate
Paris has never before found herself
   in such dire straits.

This certainly applies to the French Revolution of 1789–99, in which the people rose against King Louis XVI (1754–1793) and his wife, Marie Antoinette (1755–1793), causing them both to be beheaded. During this terrible period the Catholic Church was almost completely undermined, many churches being either sacked or destroyed. Paris continued in dire straits until Napoleon Bonaparte's election as commander of the Army of the Interior in 1794, in gratitude for his saving of the Tuileries Palace.

❦ 9/63 – 1789–99

Plainctes et pleurs cris et grands
urlemens
Pres de Narbon à Bayonne et en Foix
O quel horrible calamitz changemens
Avant que Mars revolu quelques fois.

Laments and howls and terrible cries
Near Narbonne, at Bayonne and in
    Foix
Oh what horrible calamities and
    changes occur
Before Mars has made several
    revolutions.

Mars revolves around the earth once
every 687 days. The horrors of the
French Revolution lasted for the space
of five Martian circuits, and culminated
in the election of Napoleon, on 19
November 1799, as First Consul of
France.

❦ 4/24 – 1789–99

Oui soub terre saincte dame voix fainte,
Humaine flamme pour divine voix luire
Fera les seuls de leur sang terre tainte,
Et les saincts temples par les impurs
    destruire.

The faint voice of Our Lady is heard
    underground
The earthly flame will burn for the
    divine voice
The blood of priests will stain the
    earth
And the churches will be destroyed
    by unbelievers.

This is usually taken to refer to the
French Revolution of 1789–99, in which
countless churches were sacked, and
many priests and nuns killed. The
Catholic Church was forced
underground until Napoleon restored its

rights in 1804, in the same year that he
was crowned Emperor by Pope Pius
VII. However a fascinating and never-
before-suggested alternative reading
would have it referring to the Cristeros
Rebellion of 1926–29, in Mexico, which
Graham Greene described so
powerfully in his novel The Power And
The Glory.

❦ 2/76 – 1790

Foudre en Bourgongne fera cas
    portenteux,
Que par engin oncques ne pourrait faire,
De leur senat sacriste fait boiteux
Fera scavoir aux ennemis l'affaire.

Lightning in Burgundy will portend
    more
Than could ever have been suggested
    by trickery
From their hidden councils, a lame
    priest
Will make known the truth to their
    enemies.

Charles de Talleyrand-Périgord (1754–
1838) was the consummate diplomat.
Crippled as a child by the fall of a chest
of drawers, he gave up his position as
Bishop of Antin in 1790 to join the
Revolutionaries. He became a
supporter of Napoleon, but was later
instrumental in having the Bourbons
returned to office, exhibiting, during his
long and fascinating life, the *volte-face*
capacities of a latter-day Janus.

❦ 2/12 – 1790

Yeux clos ouverts d'antique fantasie
L'habit des seules seront mis a néant;
Le grand monarque chastira leur
* frenaisie,*
Ravir des temples le thrésor par devant.

Eyes closed to truth but open to
  ancient paganism
The priesthood will be reduced to
  nothing
The great monarch will punish their
  frenzy
Stripping the temples of their
  treasure.

Nostradamus looks fearfully ahead to
the ravishing of the French church in
the Revolution. The great monarch is
Louis XVI, who was forced on 22 July
1790 to issue the Civil Constitution of
the Clergy, under which church
property was nationalised and priests
became employees of the state.
  The new constitution altered the
French church radically. While once
there were 139 dioceses, there were
now just 83, each designated in line
with the administrative departments of
the country. It also heralded the end of
Vatican influence in France. While the
new French Catholic church
acknowledged the supremacy of Rome,
its clergy were no longer answerable to
the Pope. The immense possessions of
the church throughout France,
including the famed vineyards of
Burgundy, now passed into the hands
of the state, and thence into the
ownership of private families – many of
whom remain in possession to this day.

❦ 3/93 – 1791

Dans Avignon tout le Chef de l'empire
Fera arest pour Paris desolé
Tricast tiendra l'Annibalique ire,
Lyon par change sera mel consolé.

The empire's supreme chief will stop
  at Avignon
Because Paris is deserted
The three towers will contain African
  anger
The lion, on the other hand, will be
  consoled by honey.

Avignon ceased to belong to the
Vatican in 1791, a time when Paris no
longer even paid lip-service to the
Catholic Church. Large parts of Africa,
however, were later evangelised,
containing her potential power and
Europeanising her. The Protestant
British lion, master of most of what
remained of the continent, was
secularly consoled by possession of
the honey of world trade.

❦ 9/20 – 1791

De nuict viendra par la forest de Reines,
Deux pars, vaultorte, Herne la pierre
* blanche,*
Le moyne noir en gris dedans Varennes:
Esleu Cap. cause tempeste, feu, sang,
* tranche.*

By night through the forest of Reines
  will come
The couple, via a circuitous route,
  Herne the white stone
The black monk in grey towards
  Varennes:
The elected Capet, causing storm,
  fire, blood, cut.

A chillingly perceptive vision of the flight of the royal couple, King Louis XVI and Marie-Antoinette, from Paris, through the forest at night, only to be intercepted and arrested at Varennes on 21 June 1791. Interpreters of this famous quatrain agree that Herne is an anagram for Reine and *la pierre blanche* refers to the recorded fact that on the occasion the Queen was dressed in white. The black monk is the King – a man of chaste habits who was disguised in grey on the day. The elected Capet also refers to the King, for under France's Revolutionary Constituent Assembly, Louis had lately been 'elected' the first constitutional head of state (Cap. or Capet) in French history. The last words describe the fate that awaited the royal family: uprisings and invasions by foreign powers trying to save them, then death by guillotine.

❦   7/44 – 1791

Alors qu'un bour, sera fort bon,
Portant en soy les marques de justice,
De son sang lors portant son nom.
Par fuite injuste recevra son supplice.

When a bourbon will be truly bon
Having the marks of justice in his
    personage
Of his blood then bearing his name
By his flight he will be unjustly
    condemned.

The first line contains a Nostradamian pun, putting the *bon* (good) into the Bourbon, France's royal line. The quatrain is another describing King Louis XVI's attempt to flee the Revolution, and what Nostradamus considers to be his unwarranted punishment for it.

❦   9/34 – 1792

Le part solus mari sera mitré,
Retour conflict passera sur le thuille
Par cinq cens un trahir sera tiltré,
Narbon et Saulce par conteuax avons
*   d'huile.*

The lonely, separated husband will
    be forcibly hatted
On his return, there will be conflict
    at the Tuileries
Of the five hundred, one traitor will
    be ennobled
Narbon and Saluces will have oil for
    their blades.

Nostradamus is always good on Louis XVI, and here he surpasses himself. When Louis and Marie Antoinette fled from their detention in Paris, they were stopped at Varennes (actually named in another quatrain). That night they stayed in a Monsieur Saluces' house. On his return to Paris on 20 June 1792, Louis was separated from his family and humiliated, in the Tuileries, by being forcibly hatted with a revolutionary cap by a mob of five hundred in August 1792. A moderate called Narbon later tried to persuade the Council to pardon Louis, but to no avail.

❦   9/22 – 1792

Roy et son cour au lieu de langue halbe,
Dedans le temple vis à vis du palais,
Dans le jardin Duc de Mantor et d'Albe,
Albe et Mantor, poignard, langue et
*   palais.*

The King and his court in the
    debating chamber
Within the temple facing the palace
In the garden the Duke of Mantor
    and Albe
Albe and Mantor, dagger, talk and
    palace.

On 14 August 1792, King Louis XVI and his family were moved to the Legislative Assembly opposite the Temple, the old Knights Templar palace in Paris. The Duke of Mantor and Albe is believed to be a coded anagrammatic reference to the Duke of Normandy, the Dauphin, who would have played in the garden.

🦎 9/23 – 1792

Puisnay jouant au fresch dessoubs la
  tonne,
Le haut du toict du milieu sur la teste,
La père Roy au temple sainct Salonne,
Sacrifiant sacrera fum de feste.

The youngest playing in the fresh air
  below the tower
The highest point directly above him
The King his father in the temple of
  St Salonne
Will be crowned amidst the smoke of
  festive sacrifice.

Nostradamus returns to the melancholy theme of the imprisonment of the French royal family in the temple in August 1792, with King Louis looking out at his son playing below. The last line is opaque, but ominous.

🦎 8/98 – 1792

Des gens d'eglise sang fera espandu,
Comme de l'eau eu si grand abondance
Et d'un long temps ne sera restranche
Ve, ve au clerc ruine et doleance.

Blood will flow from the church
  people
Abundantly, like water
It won't be stanched for a long time
Woe and alas, the clergy will grieve,
  and be ruined.

Following the same line as numerous other quatrains, this bemoans the

Persecution of the Clergy in France in 1792, during the Revolution.

🦎 5/12 – 1792

Aupres du lac Leman sera conduite
Par garse estrange cité voulant trahir
Avant son meurtre à Auspourg la
  grande suitte
Et ceux du Rhin la viendront invahir.

He will be led to near Lake Geneva
By a foreign minx who wants to
  betray the city
Before her murder a great throng will
  enter Augsburg
The Rhinelanders will come to
  invade it.

Marie Antoinette, about whom Nostradamus often speaks in unflattering terms, was the daughter of the Empress Maria Theresa of Austria. Aware of her imminent fate in 1792, Austria and her allies threatened dire retribution against France. But she was executed just the same, in October 1793, and Austrian invaders, among others, were repelled from France by revolutionary armies.

🦎 6/69 – 1792

La pitié grande sera sans loing tarder
Ceux qui donoient seront contrains de
  prendre
Nudz affamez de froit, soif, soi bander
Les monts passer commettant grand
  esclandre.

The terrible event won't be long in
  coming
Those who gave will now be forced
  to take
Naked, starving, cold and thirsty,
  they will band together
To cross the mountains, causing
  great outrage.

Widely held to be a foretelling of the dissolution of the French established church during the Revolution. Thousands of churches were desecrated and hundreds of priests murdered, with or without trial. Many members of the clergy, utterly dispossessed, fled to Italy in the hope of protection from the church of Rome. Europe was scandalised by this ill-treatment of priests.

❧ 5/5 – 1792

Souz ombre faincte d'oster de servitude
Peuple et cité l'usurpera lui mesmes
Pire era par fraux de jeune pute
Livré au champ lisant le faux proesme.

Under the weak pretence of a
    removal from servitude
The people and the city will usurp it
    themselves
He will do worse because of the wiles
    of a young whore
Delivered to the fields, making false
    promises.

Nostradamus uses strong words to warn of the malign influence on King Louis XVI of his consort Queen Marie Antoinette, who became his bride in 1770 aged only 15. She is said to have hampered Louis' attempts to come to terms with popular demands for political reform and prevailed on him to deceive their Revolutionary guards that the royal family would not attempt to escape house arrest in Paris in 1792 when they had every intention of doing so. They were intercepted at Varennes, and were both thus condemned. Marie Antoinette went to the guillotine on 16 October 1793, eight months after her husband met a similar fate.

❧ 10/17 – 1792

La Royne Ergaste voyant sa fille blesme
Par un regret dans l'estomach enclos,
Cris lamentables seront lors d'Angolesme,
Et au germain mariage forclos.

The imprisoned Queen seeing her
    wan daughter
By a regret in the closed stomach
There will be lamenting cries at
    Angoulême
And a marriage to a first cousin.

The captive Queen is Marie Antoinette, imprisoned in the Temple with her husband Louis XVI and their two children. Her daughter, Marie Thérèse Charlotte, pale and wan because of her family's unhappy predicament, is aged 14, but has been betrothed since she was nine to her first cousin, the Duke of Angoulême. Marie Thérèse, known to history as 'the orphan of the Temple', survived and the wedding took place in 1799. The closed stomach must allude to the sad fact that the marriage was childless, perhaps due to the ill-treatment the girl had received at the hands of the revolutionaries. But Marie Thérèse lived a long life. She died on 19 October 1851, aged 73.

❧ 4/85 – 1793

Le charbon blanc du noir sera chassé,
Prisonnier faicte mené au tomberreau
More Chameau sus piedz entrelassez,
Lors le puismé sillera l'aubereau.

The white coal is driven out by the
    black
He is made a prisoner, taken to the
    tumbril
The rogue's feet are tied, as is the
    custom
The youngest will let slip the falcon.

The first line consists of wordplay identifying the Bourbon king, Louis XVI (1754–1793). Imprisoned in the Temple and later condemned to death by the Convention, who voted 683 to 38 in favour of Madame Guillotine, Louis was forced into a tumbril by the revolutionary guards, where his feet were tied. He was executed later that day, 21 January, in the Place de la Revolution.

9/77 – 1793

Le regne prins le Roi conviera,
La dame prinse a mort jurez a sort,
La vie a Royne fils on desniera,
Et la pillex au fort de la consort.

The King will acknowledge his realm
   is taken
The Queen is taken to a death
   ordained by a jury
Which will deny her son his life
And the prostitute goes the same way
   as the consort.

It looks an accurate depiction of the fate of Louis XVI at the hands of the Commune in October 1793, along with Marie-Antoinette. The Dauphin was spared the Guillotine, but indeed denied his life. The prostitute could very well be the renowned mistress of Louis XV, Madame du Barry, who went to the block in the same year.

3/59 – 1793

Barbare empire par le tiers usurpé,
La plus grand part de son sang mettra à
*   mort,*
Par mort senile, par luy le quart frappé,
Pour peur que sang par le sang ne soit
*   mort.*

The barbarous state, usurped by the
   third party
Will put to death many people of its
   own blood
An old man's death will hurt the
   fourth party
For fear that blood will not wish to
   die by blood.

Robespierre's French Revolutionary Reign of Terror, in which at least 25,000 citizens went to the guillotine, inspires this curious quatrain. The third party refers to Robespierre himself. The identities of the old man and the fourth party remain uncertain.

9/68 – 1793

Du mont Aymar sera noble obscurcie,
Le mal viendra au joinct de Saone et
*   Rhône*
Dans bois caché soldats jour de Lucia,
Que ne fut un si horrible thrône.

From Mount Aymar an unknown
   nobleman
Will come to harm at the confluence
   of the Saone and Rhône
Soldiers hidden in the woods on St
   Lucia's Day
Nothing could make such a horrible
   throne.

The confluence of the Saone and Rhône is the city of Lyons where, in 1793, the city's Royalists and Girondists rose against the Convention of the Revolution. But an army of the republic laid siege for seven weeks, entering the city on 10 October. Appalling atrocities were committed against the townsfolk.

☙ 1/57 – 1793

Par grand discord la trombe tremblera
Accord rompu dressant la teste au ciel
Bouche sanglante dans le sang nagera,
Au sol la face ointe de laict et miel.

The horn sounds discordantly
Following a broken vow, he raises his
    head to the sky
His blood-stained mouth awash with
    blood
His fallen face is anointed with milk
    and honey.

This is one of Nostradamus's most
successful quatrains, describing in
considerable detail, the execution of
Louis XVI on the 21 January 1793.
Following his broken vow not to attempt
escape from Paris, the trumpets
sounded ironically as he ascended the
steps of the guillotine. Reciting the third
verse of the third psalm, exaltus capum
meum (Lord, I lift my face to heaven),
Sanson, his executioner, triggered
Madame Guillotine, then raised the
king's head, quite literally, on high. It
has been well-documented that
severed heads bleed from the mouth.
The fallen king's face, had, of course,
been anointed with milk and honey
nineteen years before, during his
coronation.

☙ 1/58 – 1793

Tranche le ventre, naistra avec deux
    testes,
Et quatre bras: quelque ans entiers vivra
Jour qui Alquiloie celebrera ses festes,
Fossen, Turin, chef Ferrare suivra.

A creature with two heads and four
    arms will burst
From the stomach; he will survive
    some years

The day on which the eagle holds his
    festival
Fossano, Turin, and the chief of
    Ferrara will follow.

The creature with two heads bursting
from a cut in the belly is Louis XVI,
reluctant star of the preceding quatrain,
1/57. He was the antecedent of two
heads of state, Louis XVIII and Charles
X. His four arms were the Dukes of
Angoulême, Bordeaux, Berry and
Normandy respectively. The eagle is
Napoleon, who brought Louis' family
down. Napoleon also imprisoned Pope
Pius VIII, humbling Italy.

☙ 5/33 – 1793

Des principaux de cité rebellee
Qui tiendront fort pour liberté ravoir
Detrencher masles, infelice meslee,
Cris hurlemens à Nantes piteux voir.

The leading citizens of the rebellious
    city
Will struggle hard to regain their
    liberty
The men will be torn apart, a sad
    mess
The cries and howls at Nantes will be
    piteous to see.

Another very specific quatrain, detailing
the horrors of the Noyades at Nantes
which took place in 1793, a time of
terrible excesses in the French
Revolution. A thousand eminent Nantais
citizens were guillotined for resisting
the National Convention, and hundreds
more, men and women, priests and
nuns, were tied naked together on
barges in the middle of the Loire river,
which were then sunk.

🐦 4/20 – 1793

Paix uberté long temps lieu louera;
Par tout son regne desert la fleur de lis
Corps morts d'eau, terre là lou apportera,
Sperants vain heur d'estre là ensevelis.

Peace and plenty will last long in that
  place
Throughout its kingdom, the fleur de
  lys will be abandoned
Drowned bodies will be brought
  from the land
They will wait in vain to be buried.

The preceding verse, 5/33 tells of the
massacre of women and priests on
sinking barges in the river Loire during
the bloodiest period of the French
Revolution. This quatrain seems to refer
to the same event, counterpointing it
against the peace and prosperity which
existed in the region before the *fleur de
lys*, symbol of French kings, was
temporarily abandoned.

🐦 6/92 – 1793

Prince de beauté tant venuste,
Au chef menee, le second faict trahi
La cité au glaive de poudre face aduste,
Par le trop grand meutre le chef du Roi
hai.

The beautiful prince, so handsome
Taken to the leader, he betrays the
  second deed
The city is put to the sword, its
  facade burnt by gunpowder
The king's head is spited, for too
  much murdering.

Louis XVI (1774–1792) was considered
beautiful in his youth. Forced to agree
that the monarchy should become
purely constitutional, he betrayed his
oath by fleeing to Varennes as part of a
misguided counter-revolution.

Guillotined in 1793, his head was spited
(ridiculed) in front of the crowd, then
thrown into a quick-lime pit.

🐦 2/83 – 1793

Le gros traffic d'un grand Lyon changé
La plus part tourne en pristine ruine.
Proie aux soldats par pille vendengé
Par Jura mont et Sueve bruine.

Great Lyons sees a change in her vast
  trade
The greater part transformed into
  pristine ruin
Vulnerable to the harvesting and
  looting of soldiers
A fog comes across the Jura
  mountains from Switzerland.

During the course of the French
Revolution, in October 1793, the great
city of Lyons was sacked for alleged
counter-revolutionary activity.
Nostradamus uses the term *bruine*,
which equates remarkably closely to
the renamed Revolutionary month of
Brumaire, which lasted from mid-
October to mid-November. The
concept of '*pristine ruin*' is a delicate
one, implying that the people were
killed while the buildings of the town
were allowed to remain standing. This
proved, in fact, to be the case.

🐦 8/22 – 1793

Gorsan, Narbonne, par le sel advertir
Tucham, la grace Parpignam trahie,
La ville rouge n'y vouldra consentir
Par haulte vol drap gris vie faillie.

Gorsan and Narbonne, warning him
  by salt
Tucham, betraying the Paris pledge
The red city refuses its consent
Life is ended by grey drape's flight.

A superb and detailed quatrain. Anoine Joseph Gorsas (1725–1793) was a journalist, founder of the *Courier de Paris à Versailles*. Together with Count Louis de Narbonne, he tried to send a message, hidden inside a salt shaker, to Louis XVI, who was imprisoned at the Temple. The Revolutionary committee had previously wrung a promise from the king that he would not leave Paris, but the king nevertheless decided to flee to Varennes, disguised in the grey drapes of a Carmelite monk. This was just the pretext needed by the revolutionary regime to order his death. Louis XVI was executed, by guillotine, on 21 January 1793.

8/87 – 1793

Mort conspiree viendra en plein effect,
Charge donnee et voiage de mort,
Esleu, crée, receu par siens deffait.
Sang d'innocence devant foi par remort.

The plotted death will occur
A charge will be made, the death voyage undertaken
Elected, made, first accepted, then betrayed by his own
An innocent man, remorse through faith.

This encapsulates the sad fate of Louis XVI (1754–1793), who paid with his life for his father's shortcomings as a monarch. 'Elected' as constitutional monarch, he made a death voyage to Varennes, which provided the National Convention with just the excuse they needed to sentence him to the guillotine. He was executed on 21 January 1793. Nostradamus rather quaintly sees the French people blaming themselves for his unnecessary death after the event.

9/98 – 1793

Les affligez par faute d'un seul taint,
Contremenant à partie opposite,
Au Lygonnois mandera que contraint
Seront de rendre le grand chef de Molite.

One man is responsible for afflictions of the many
The transgressor comes from the opposing party
He will say to the Lyonnais that they must
Give up the great leader of Molite.

This could be seen to relate to the sack of Lyons by Republican forces under the notorious anti-royalist mayor, Nivière Chol, in October 1793.

10/88 – 1793

Piedz et cheval à la seconde veille
Feront entrée vastient tour par la mer,
Dedans la poil entrera de Marseille,
Pleurs, cris, et sang onc nul temps si amer.

Foot and horse, during the second watch
Will make their entrance, devastating all from the sea
He will enter the port of Marseilles
Tears, cries and blood, never was there so bitter a time.

The mention of horses would appear to rule out a modern conflict. Marseilles is the oldest city in France, founded by the Greeks in 600 BC. It has been invaded countless times. The most recent near-miss was the siege of Toulon by the English in 1793.

🍂 10/43 – 1793

Le trop bon temps trop de bonté royalle
Fais et deffois prompt subit negligence,
Legier croira faux despouse loyalle,
Lui mis á mort par sa benevolence.

Too many good times, too much
    Royal generosity
To make and to unmake can often
    cause negligence
He will believe too easily that his
    loyal spouse is faithless
His benevolence causes his death.

A kindly man, Louis XVI (1754–1793) was indirectly the cause of his own downfall. Like Othello, he chose to believe the worst of his wife, Marie Antoinette (1755–1793) in the 1785–6 affair of the Diamond Necklace. His error of judgement led to a notorious court case which seriously dented the reputation of both the queen and the monarchy. He and Marie would both be guillotined in 1793.

🍂 7/13 – 1793

De la cité marine et tributaire,
La teste raze prendra la satrapie
Chasser sordide qui puis sera contraire
Par quatorze ans tiendra la tyrannie.

From the marine and tributary city
The crop-head will take up the
    government
He will chase his evil opponent
The tyranny will last for fourteen
    years.

Napoleon retook Toulon from the English in 1793. He later shaved off his revolutionary locks and adopted a hairstyle that resembled his idol, Julius Caesar. The evil opponent in line 3 may refer to General Moreau, Napoleon's chief rival, who later offered his services to the allied coalitions fighting for the Bourbon restoration. Napoleon enjoyed absolute power for fourteen years, from 9 November 1793 to 13 April 1814.

🍂 9/68 – 1793

Du mont Aymar sera noble obscurcie
Le mal viendra au joinct de sonne et
    rosne
Dans bois caichez soldatz jour de Lucie
Qui ne fut onc un si horrible throsne.

A great darkening will come from
    Mount Aymar
The evil will appear at the confluence
    of the Saone and the Rhône
Soldiers conceal themselves in the
    woods on St Lucy's day
Never was there such a horrible
    reign.

St Lucy's day falls on the 13 December, and Lyons is the city situated at the confluence of the Saone and the Rhône. Following the terrible sack of Lyons by the Republicans (Jean Baptiste Amar was the speaker of the Public Committee who suggested the deed), the pro-Royalist forces were finally defeated at the battle of Le Mans, on 13 December 1793. The reign, of course, is the Reign of Terror, which followed hard on the final defeat of the Royalists.

🍂 2/35 – 1793

Dans deux logis de nuict le feu prendra
Plusieurs dedans estouffes et rostis
Pres de deux fleuves pour seul il
    adviendra
Sol, l'Arq et Caper tous seront amortis.

Fire will engulf two houses at night
Several within are suffocated and
    burnt
It will certainly happen near two
    rivers
When the Sun, Sagittarius and
    Capricorn are transited.

Girondists allied with Royalists seized
power in Lyons in 1793 but were
burned out by an army of the
revolutionary Convention. Lyons is a
very important city to Nostradamus, as
it was here, at the confluence of the
Rhône and Saône rivers, that Pope
Clement V was crowned in 1305.

❦ 3/10 – 1793

De sang et faim plus grand calamité
Sept fois s'appreste à la marine plage
Monech de aim, lieu pris, captivité
Le grand mené croc en ferree caige.

An even greater calamity, of blood
    and famine
Seven times it approaches the sea
    shore
Monaco is taken, captured, through
    hunger
The great one is hooked into an iron
    cage.

Monaco, the tiny but ancient coastal
state entirely surrounded by the French
department of Alpes-Maritimes has
been a sovereign principality for eight
centuries, but was annexed in 1793 by
France's revolutionary National
Convention. It was restored to the ruling
Goyon Grimaldi family in 1814.

❦ 9/46 – 1793–4

Vuidez, fuyez de Tholose les rouges
Du sacrifice faire expiation
Le chef du mal dessouz l'ombre des
    courges
Mort estranger carne omination.

Be gone you red ones, fly from
    Toulouse
Expiation for the sacrifice must be
    made
The lord of evil hides among the
    empty-headed ones
Death is a stranger to omens of the
    flesh.

Although this could have many
meanings, the most obvious application
is to Revolutionary France, and in
particular to the massacres of the
1793–4 Reign of Terror. Nostradamus,
who would have been profoundly
shocked by the *lèse-majesté* of any
revolution against the monarchy, is
calling on the revolutionaries to leave
Toulouse and to make amends for the
horrors they have brought on their own
people.

❦ 2/42 – 1794

Coq, chiens et chats de sang seront repeus
Et de la playe du tyran trouvé mort.
Au lict d'un autre jambes et bras
    rompus,
Qui n'avait peur de mourir de cruelle
    mort.

Dogs, cats and cockerels will feed on
    blood
The tyrant will die of his wounds
In the bed of another, his arms and
    legs broken
Unafraid of death, he yet dies cruelly.

This tells of the death of Robespierre (1758–1794), responsible, with others, for much of the horror of the Reign of Terror, 12–28 July 1794, in which 1285 people lost their lives to Madame Guillotine's blade. Sickened by what he had perpetrated, he tried to bring the whole thing to a premature end on 26 July. He was arrested, but freed by troops of the Commune, who took him to a 'strange bed' in the Hôtel de Ville. He was immediately recaptured by the National Guard, during which he was injured by a bullet in the jaw. With his arms and legs bound, he was executed on 29 July at the Place de la Revolution, later renamed the Place de la Concorde.

8/19 – 1794

A soubstenir la grand cappe troublee,
Pour l'esclaircir les rouges marcheront,
De mort famille sera presque accablee.
Les rouges rouges le rouge assomeront.

To support the great, troubled cappe
The reds will march to clarify it
A family nearly overcome by death
The bloody reds will strike the red
   one down.

Cappe signifies Capulet, a family name of the French Royal line at the time of the French Revolution. Despite the support of the more moderate Girondins, all the surviving family, bar one, died under the guillotine. A year later, Maximilien Robespierre (1758–1794), the red one, who had led the paradoxically-named Committee of Public Safety during the terrible months between April 1793 and July 1794, was himself executed.

8/45 – 1794–95

La main escharpe et la jambe bandée,
Louis puisne de palais partira,
Au mot du guet la mort sera tardée,
Puis dans le temple a Pasque saignera.

His hand in a sling and his leg
   bandaged
Young Louis will quit the palace
The watchman's word will delay his
   death
Then in the temple he will bleed at
   Easter.

This famous quatrain, with its oblique allusions to Christ's Passion, may solve one of the vilest crimes in French history, the murder of the young son of King Louis XVI and Queen Marie Antoinette. Aged 11, the prince was taken away from his parents at the time of their execution in October 1793. The last record of Louis XVII was made by a Dr Harmand who examined him a year later when in the custody of a citizen known as Simon the Shoemaker, billeted in a seized palace. The child had been cruelly abused. The physician noted injuries to his left arm and to both knees, which had been dressed and bandaged for months. Perhaps the doctor's protests delayed the boy's fate. A report the following spring from the Temple prison in Paris referred to a body under a bloodstained sheet. Royalists claimed it was the child king, and that he had been beaten to death.

5/1 – 1795

Avant venu de ruine Celtique
Dedans le temple deux parlementeront
Poignard coeur, d'un monté au coursier
   et pique
Sans faire bruit le grand enterreront.

Before the ruin of France
Two will parley inside the temple
Stabbed in the heart by a mounted
     knight
They will bury the great one in
     secret.

The temple is taken to be the Temple in Paris where King Louis XVI and his family were confined in 1792 during the French Revolution. The Dauphin, heir to Louis and thus Louis XVII on his father's execution in 1793, died some time soon after of unknown causes. News of his death was made official in 1795 and his body was never discovered.

🍂 6/52 – 1795

En lieu du grand qui sera condemné
De prison hors son ami en sa place
L'espoir Troien en six mois joinct,
     mortnay
Le Sol à l'urne seront prins fleuves en
     glace.

In place of the condemned worthy
They will put his friend; he'll be
     outside the prison
The Trojan hope lasts for six
     months, then still-born
The Sun is in Aquarius, the rivers
     will be frozen.

Trojan is Nostradamian code for French royalty – based on the unsubstantiated assertion that the earliest French kings somehow descended from Francus, son of Troy's King Priam. One attractive theory is that this quatrain pertains to the son of Louis XVI reported to have died or been murdered in the Temple after his parents' executions – in 1794 or 1795. In the tradition of Dickens's *Tale of Two Cities*, the prince has been spirited away and replaced with a brave substitute. The sun in Aquarius indicates the last weeks of February

and the first of March, but the official acknowledgement of Louis XVII's death was made in June (1795).

🍂 8/14 – 1795

Le grand credit d'or, d'argent l'abondance
Fera aveugler par libide honneur
Sera cogneu d'adultere l'offense,
Qui parviendra à son grand deshonneur.

So much gold and silver
Will blind honour, through lust
The adulteress's offence will become
     known
Causing her great dishonour.

The geographical boundaries of the present day United States were created on the back of an unstoppable land and gold-lust, at the expense of some 300 native tribes. Beginning with the Treaty of Greenville in 1795, the offences perpetrated in the name of the adulteress (the Statue of Liberty) have only recently been acknowledged, somewhat tarnishing US claims to be the 'land of the free'.

🍂 1/93 – 1795

Terre Italique pres des monts tremblera,
Lyon et coq non trop confederez
En lieu de peur l'un l'autre s'aidera,
Seul Catulon et Celtes moderez.

Alpine Italy will tremble
Cock and lion will be disunited
In a place of fear, one will help the
     other
Only liberty will moderate the
     French.

Napoleon began his Italian campaign in 1795, for ever changing the face of Italy. The French cock and the English lion were consequently thrown into open conflict. At Waterloo, the

Prussians helped the English, liberating France from Napoleon's stranglehold, and Europe from tyranny.

❦ 9/24 – 1795

Sur le palais au rochier des fenestres
Seront ravis les deux petits royaux
Passer aurelle Luthece Denis cloistres
Nonain, mallods avaller verts noiaulx.

The two small Royal children will be
  carried off
Through the windows of the rocky
  palace
They will pass Orléans, Paris and the
  cloisters of St Denis
A nun, bad odours, the unripe nuts
  will be swallowed up.

Marie-Thérèse and the Dauphin, the two young children of Louis XVI, were held in the Temple following the beheading of their parents. Both unripe nuts died through neglect, although rumours circulated for many years that Marie escaped execution and later married the Duke of Angoulême, her cousin.

❦ 6/79 – 1796

Pres du Tesin les habitans de Loire,
Garonne et Saonne, Seine, Tain, et
  Gironde
Outre les monts dresseront promontoire,
Conflict donné Pau granci, submergé
onde.

Near Ticino the inhabitants of the
  Loire
The Garonne, Saone, Seine, Tain
  and the Gironde
Will build a promontory beyond the
  mountains
War is waged, Pau is seized, he will
  be submerged under the waves.

During the Battle of Lodi, on 10 May 1796, Napoleon I, the *pau* of line 4, in hot pursuit of the Austrians, was knocked from a bridge into the Adda river by his over-exuberant men. History reveals that he was snatched out just in time to save his life, but lost his Wellingtons.

❦ 6/67 – 1796

Au grand Empire par viendra tout un
  autre,
Bonté distant plus de felicité;
Régi par un issu non loing du peautre
Corruer Regnes grand infelicté.

To the great Empire will come a very
  different man
Far from kindness and ever farther
  from happiness
Ruled by one from whose bed he has
  just risen
To bring the Kingdom great
  unhappiness.

Widely believed to refer to the influence exerted on Napoleon Bonaparte by Joséphine de Beauharnais (1763–1814), whom he married in 1796. Napoleon had their marriage dissolved in 1809 for lack of any surviving children.

❦ 8/12 – 1796

Apparoistra aupres de Buffalore
L'hault et procere entré dedans Milan
L'abbé de Foix avec ceux de saint Morre
Feront la forbe abillez en vilan.

Appearing near Buffalora
The high-born one entered Milan
The abbé of Foix, with those of St
  Maur
Will foment mischief, dressed as
  commoners.

A difficult quatrain, linking, as it does, the Benedictine and the Augustinian monastical orders to the small town of Buffalora, near Milan. The only possible connection can be Napoleon, who entered Milan with an army in 1796.

❦ 6/38 – 1796

Au profligez de paix les ennemis
Apres avoir l'Italie superee
Noir sanguinaire, rouge sera commis
Feu, sang verser, eaue de sang couloree.

The enemies of those weakened by peace
Having already overcome Italy
Red deeds will be done by the bloody black being
Fire, spilled blood, blood-stained water.

It is important to bear in mind the affection Nostradamus felt for Italy, where he travelled widely as an itinerant physician. He often speaks in fearful tones about the country's future, and quite blithely refers to it as Italie, even though its unification under that name was more than 300 years off in the future. Here, he is using 'red' in the late eighteenth century context of revolution, and looking ahead to 1796, when Napoleon Bonaparte was appointed to lead France's revolutionary army in Italy.

❦ 3/37 – 1796

Avant l'assaut l'oraison prononcee,
Milan prins d'aigle par embusches decevez
Muraille antique par canons enfoncee,
Par feu et sang à mercy peu receus.

A speech is delivered before the assault
Milan is ambushed and captured by the eagle
Ancient walls are breached by cannon
In the ensuing fire and bloodshed, few receive quarter.

Napoleon took Milan twice, on 15 May 1796, then again on 2 June 1800, each time allowing his soldiers to sack the city. He made a famous speech before the first assault, in which he promised his men glory and booty in profusion if they followed him. History records that they did, and obtained both.

❦ 8/11 – 1797

Peuple infini paroistra à Vicence
Sans force feu brusler la Basilique
Pres de Lunage deffait grand de Valence,
Lors que Venise par more prendra pique.

The French will appear at Vicenza
A weak fire will burn the Basilica
Near Lunage the chief of Valencia will be defeated
Then Venice will take up the quarrel, by default.

Vicenza was the capital of the Venetian Republic. Napoleon passed through it, in 1797, on his march from Verona to capture Venice. Lunage probably describes the valley of Lunigiana, which Napoleon knew well, using it on more than one occasion as a short-cut during his Italian campaign.

❦ 5/30 – 1797

Tout à l'entour de la grand Cité,
Seront soldats logez par champs et villes
Donner assaut Paris, Rome incité,
Sur le pont lors sera faicte grande pille.

All around the great city
Soldiers will be garrisoned in the
    fields and towns
Paris will make the assault, Rome
    incited
The Pope will be subjected to many
    depredations.

The sad history of Rome, between 1797
and 1809, incorporates two
ransackings by France and the
relinquishment of part of the Papal
States by Pope Pius VI. It was followed,
twelve years later, by a total
capitulation under his successor, Pius
VII, the States being incorporated into
Napoleon's nascent French Empire.

❦ 2/94 – 1798

Grand Po grand mal pour Gaulois
*   recevra,*
Vaine terreur au maritim Lyon,
Peuple infiny par la mer passera
Sans eschapper le quart d'un million.

The great river Po will be hurt by the
    Frenchman
Unjustified terror to the maritime
    Lion
Uncountable people will pass by the
    sea
A quarter of a miilion will not escape.

The Gaulois is Napoleon, who had
conquered Austria in the Italian wars (in
which the River Po figured
strategically), and now determined to
set out by sea for Egypt with a great
invasion force. This makes the maritime

Lion – code for Britain, which
dominated the seas – unwarrantably
nervous, as Napoleon had no plans to
attack the British. Casualties in the
ensuing land and sea battles were
high.

❦ 5/14 – 1798

Saturne et Mars en Leo Espagne captive,
Par chef Libique au Conflit attrape;
Proche de Malte, Herodde prinse vive,
Et Romain sceptre sera par Coq frappé.

With Saturn and Mars in Leo, Spain
    is captive
By a Libyan chief taken in battle
At Malta Rhodes heroes are quickly
    taken
And the Roman sceptre is struck by
    the Cock.

Napoleon occupied the island of Malta
in 1798, seizing it with little resistance
from the Knights of Rhodes.

❦ 3/23 – 1798

Si France passes outre mer Lygustique,
Tu le verras en isles et mers enclos,
Mahomet contraire, plus mer
*   Hadriatique,*
Chevaux et d'asnes tu rangeras les os.

France, if you go beyond the
    Lygustian sea
You will see yourself trapped in
    islands and seas
Mohammed will oppose you, more in
    the Adriatic
You will be grawing the bones of
    horses and mules.

A warning to Napoleon Bonaparte lest
he extend himself too far (beyond the
Lygustian sea – the Gulf of Genoa) to
invade Egypt. On islands including

Malta, as well as at Alexandria, French forces were starved under siege by Mohammed in the shape of the Turks, while in the Adriatic they faced the terrors of the British fleet, later that year to wreck the French fleet in Aboukir Bay.

❦ 8/1 – 1798

Pau, Nay, Loron, plus feu qu'à sang sera
Laude nager, fuir grand au surrez
Les agassas entrée refusera
Pampon, Durance les tiendra enferrez.

Pau, Nay, Loron, more fire than blood
Swimming in praise, the great man hurries to the confluence
He will refuse entry to the magpies
Pampon and Durrance will confine them.

The three town names (all in southwest France) are a Nostradamian anagram for Napoleon. This quatrain is concerned with the two magpies, the respective Popes Pius VI and VII, captured and imprisoned by Napoleon Bonaparte in 1798 and 1809.

❦ 3/24 – 1798

De l'entreprise grande confusion,
Porte de gens thresor innumerable,
Tu n'y dois faire encore extension,
France à mon dire fais que sois recordable.

From this enterprise, great confusion
Loss of countless lives and treasures
You must not try to extend there again
France must heed my words.

Nostradamus continues to urge France not to extend herself as far as Egypt again.

❦ 8/88 – 1798–1802

Dans la Sardaigne un noble Roi viendra
Que ne tiendra que trois ans la royaume,
Plusieurs couleurs avec soi conjoindra,
Lui mesmes apres soin someil marrit scome.

A noble king will come to Sardinia
Who will only reign for three years
Many colours will join him
After sleeping, he will be taunted.

A fine quatrain. There were no kings of Sardinia until the eighteenth century, when King Charles Emmanuel IV retired there. He reigned for three years, from 1798–1802. On his abdication in favour of his brother, Victor Emmanuel I, he retired, humiliated, to Rome, where, no doubt in desperation, he became a Jesuit. He died there in 1819.

❦ 1/98 – 1799

Le chef qu'aura conduit peuple infiny
Loing de son ciel, de meurs et langue estrange
Cinq mil en Crete et Thessalie fini
Le chef fuyant, sauvé en marine grange.

The chief who will have lead an infinity of people
Far from their homeland, where customs and language are strange
Five thousand will die in Crete and Thessaly
Their leader fleeing in a cargo ship.

Many commentators have insisted that this quatrain foretells a nebulous Captain Kirk leading what remains of the human race into the far reaches of space on board an inter-galactic Noah's Ark. It more likely refers to Napoleon's expedition to Egypt, and his escape from the British in a wooden ship. The Turks, who ruled Thessaly and Crete at the time, massacred his remaining army of 5,000 men.

❦ 8/1 – 1799

Pau, Nay, Loron plus feu qu'a sang sera,
Laude nager, fuir grand aux surrez,
Les aggasas entre refusera,
Pampon, Durance, les tiendra enserrez.

Pau, Nay, Loron shall be more fire
    than blood
To swim in praise, to flee in
    carriages, the great man
Will refuse the magpies entry
Heretics of France will keep them
    imprisoned.

It is not stretching credulity too far to surmise that the first three words (each a common place name) of this obscure verse, form an anagrammatic rendering of the name Napoleon, who proclaimed himself First Consul of Revolutionary France in 1799. Nostradamus anticipates a great man, not high-born, but coming to fame as a soldier (more fire than blood). The reference to fleeing in carriages and refused magpies have been connected to Napoleon's heretical (Pampon is a wrongdoer) act of ordering the kidnap and imprisonment of Pope Pius VI and his successor Pius VII.

❦ 2/97 – 1799

Romain Pontife garde de t'approcher
De la cité que deux fleuves arrouse.
Ton sang viendra auprès de là cracher,
Toy et les tiens quand fleurira la rose.

Roman Pontiff, take care of
    approaching
The city irrigated by two rivers
Your blood will come close to the
    spitting
You and yours when the rose comes
    into bloom.

Pope Pius VI (1717–99) is warned to avoid the city at the confluence of the rivers Rhône and Saône, namely Lyons. It was good advice, which the Pontiff did not take. He died at Valence, close by, in August 1799, of a violent coughing fit. He had been taken there, as a captive, by the French forces who had seized Rome in the previous year on the pretext that Pius had ordered the murder of a member of the French embassy there.

❦ 4/26 – 1799

Lou grand eyssame se levera d'abelhos,
Que non sauran don te siegen venguddos
De nuech l'embousque, lou gach dessous
    las treilhos
Cuitad trahido per cinq lengos non
    nudos.

A great swarm of bees will arise
From where, no-one will know
A night ambush, a sentinel beneath
    the vine
A city betrayed by five who cannot
    hold their tongues.

This quatrain, written in Provençal rather than French, describes Napoleon Bonaparte engaged in a coup d'état on 9 November 1799 – 18 Brumaire, in the revolutionary calendar. Five members of the Directory were bribed to allow the swarm of bees (Napoleon's coat of arms) to take over the building. The Provençal word *treilhos* can be taken to apply to the Tuileries, where the coup was arranged.

❦ 7/22 – 1799

Les citoyens de Mesopotamie
Yrés encontre amis de Tarraconne
Jeux, ritz, banquetz, toute gent endormie
Vicaire au Rosne, prins cité, ceux
    d'Ausone.

The citizens of Mesopotamia
Are angry with their friends from
   Tarragona
Games, rites, banquets, everyone
   asleep
The Pope near the Rhône; the city,
   and the Italians, taken.

Mesopotamia is Nostradamian code for a land between two rivers (the Tigris and Euphrates of biblical Mesopotamia). In this case it may well mean that part of southern France encompassed by the Rhône and Saône rivers. The allusion here is to Pope Pius VI's detainment during the French advance into Italy of 1799.

❦ 6/25 – 1799

Par Mars contraire sera la monarchie,
Du grand pecheur en trouble ruineux
Jeune noir rouge prendra la hierarchie,
Les prodateurs iront jour bruineux.

Mars will adversely influence the
   monarchy
The Pope will be in terrible trouble
The young red king will take over
The traitors will choose a misty day
   to act.

Revolutionary Mars, the God of War, overthrows the Bourbon monarchy and threatens the stability of the Catholic Church. In 1799, Napoleon, the young red king, chooses the month of mists, Brumaire, to engage in his coup d'état. As a result, Pope Pius VI is imprisoned, and later dies, in Valence. An altogether remarkable quatrain.

❦ 6/46 – 1700s

Un juste sera en exile renvoyé,
Par pestilence aux confins de Nonseggle,
Response au rouge le fera desvoyé,
Roi retirant à la Rane et à l'aigle.

A good man will be returned to exile
Through plague, to the confines of
   Nonseggle
His reply to the red one will lead him
   astray
The king will retire to the Frog and
   the Eagle.

This reads like something out of Alice in Wonderland. 'Nonseggle' has never been solved, but if taken literally, implies bread that is not made of rye. In geographical terms it may be taken as Monségur, in the Pyrenées, scene of a notorious massacre of Cathars (a mediaeval heretical sect) that Nostradamus would certainly have known about. The Frog and the Eagle, in this context, refer to the 'Royalists' and the 'Bonapartists', whose symbols they were. The Bonaparte connection is further strengthened by the use of 'red one', in line 3.

❦ 8/82 – 1700s

Ronge long, sec faisant du bon valet,
A la parfin n'aura que son congie
Poignant poison et lettres au collet
Sera saisi eschappé en dangie.

Thin, tall and desiccated, playing the
   good valet
In the end he will have nought but
   his dismissal
What a sad poison, he takes letters
   with him
He will be seized, then escape in
   more danger.

A difficult quatrain. There are suggestions that it refers to Jean Jacques Rousseau (1712–1778), who began his life as a valet, and whose writings, the 'letters' of line 3, provided the philosophical underpinning for the French Revolution of 1789–99.

1800–1899

10/36 – 1800

Apres le Roi du saucq guerres parlant
L'isle Harmotique le tiendra à mespris
Quelque ans bous rongeant un et pillant
Par tyrranie à l'isle changeant pris.

After the king of markets speaks of
  war
The united island despises him
Several good years of plundering and
  pillaging
The island changes because of tyranny.

Saucq (Souk) is the Arabic word for
market, and is a far more likely
translation in this context than stump,
which has been generally accepted,
until now, as the meaning. The united
island would appear to be Great Britain,
although the final coming together only
took place following the Act Of Union
with Ireland in 1800. Wales had already
joined England in 1536, and Scotland in
1707. Fortunately, few instances of real
tyranny can be found in Britain during
the nineteenth and twentieth centuries,
due to the purely constitutional role of
the Sovereign. Britain was, of course,
pre-eminently a trading nation,
therefore the King could justifiably be
seen as the King of Markets. Could
Nostradamus be referring to the War of
Independence in the United States,
which predated the Act of Union by 24
years?

4/37 – 1800

Gaulois par saults, monts viendra
  penetrer
Occupera le grand lieu de l'Insubre
Au plus profond son est fera entrer
Gennes, Monech pousseront classe rubre.

The leaping Gauls will penetrate the
  mountains
Occupying the main seat of
  Lombardy
The army will penetrate to the very
  depths
Genoa and Monaco will repulse the
  red fleet.

Leaping Gauls is a well-imagined
description of the army Napoleon
brought at astonishing speed across
the Alps to invade Italy in 1800,
capturing Milan, the Lombardy capital.
Genoa and Monaco were both under
naval attack (from Austrian and British
fleets) at the same time.

4/35 – 1800

Le feu estaint, les vierges trahiront
La plus grand part de la bande nouvelle
Fouldre à fer, lance les seulz Roi
  garderont
Etrusque et Corse, de nuict gorge
  allumelle.

When the fire is extinguished, raw
  recruits will betray
The greater part of the new army
Steel lightning, only lances will guard
  the king
Tuscany and Corsica; throats slit by
  night.

Inexperienced Italian soldiers will offer
scant resistance to France's forces
during the Napoleonic wars.

❦ 8/79 – early 1800s

Qui par fer pere perdra nay de Nonnaire,
De Gorgon sur la sera sang perfetant
En terre estrange fera si tant de taire,
Qui bruslera lui mesme et son enfant.

Born of a prostitute, he will lose his
    father to the sword
The Gorgon's blood will live again
He will try to remain silent in a
    strange land
And burn both himself, and his child.

Nonnaire can be read to mean either
nunnery or prostitute, depending on
which version of low Latin you use.
Nostradamus was canny enough to
have implied both in his first line, but
that still brings us little closer to a
reading. The implication in line 2 is that
this man turns whatever he sees to
stone, like the Gorgon of Greek myth.
However we also know that winged
Pegasus sprang from the Gorgon's
blood. This returns us to the
Bellerophon connection in 8/13 (see
page 114), which links the 'man lamed
through vanity' with Napoleon.

❦ 7/15 – 1800

Devant cité de l'Insubre contree,
Sept ans sera le siege devant mis
Le tres grand Roi y fera son entrée,
Cité puis libre hors de ses ennemis.

Before the city of the Insubrian plain
The siege will last for seven years
The supreme king will make his
    entrance there
The city will be free, and rid of its
    enemies.

Milan was never besieged for seven
years, but it did suffer under a seven
year war with Napoleon Bonaparte,
which began in 1793. This culminated
in Napoleon's triumphal entrance into
the city on 2 June 1800.

❦ 7/39 – 1800

Le conducteur de l'armée Françoise,
Cuidant perdre le principal phalange
Par sus pave de l'avaigne et d'ardoise,
Soi parfondra par Gennes gent estrange.

The commander of the French army
Fearing the loss of his main force
On the pavement of oats and slate
A foreign race will be undermined
    through Genoa.

Napoleon sacrificed Massena's
starving garrison of 15,000 men at
Genoa, on 4 June 1800, to gain a brief
respite for his main army before the
Battle of Marengo, 14 June, in which he
unequivocally defeated the Austrians
under Baron von Melas.

❦ 8/53 – 1802

Dedans Boulogne voudra laver ses fautes;
Il ne pourra au temple du soleil.
Il volera faisant choses si hautes,
Qu'en hierarchie n'en fut onc un pareil.

In Boulogne he will wish to expiate
    his failings
He will not be allowed in the temple
    of the sun
His achievements will be so great
That none of any hierarchy can be
    his equal.

Napoleon determined to invade
England from Boulogne, but
Nostradamus considers that for all the
great man's achievements, he'll never
make it.

❦ 8/57 – 1804

De soldat simple parviendra en empire,
De robbe courte parviendra à la longue:
Vaillant aux armes, en Eglise, ou plus
  pyre,
Vexer les prestres comme l'eau fait
  l'espagne.

From simple soldier he progressed to
  Empire
From the short robe he progressed to
  the long
Valiant in arms, more of a scourge to
  the Church
Wringing out the priests like water
  from a sponge.

Napoleon Bonaparte crowned himself
Emperor on 2 December 1804,
exchanging the modest attire of First
Consul for the orotund Imperial regalia.
Pope Pius VII was in attendance, but the
honour of placing the crowns on the
heads of Napoleon and the Empress
Josephine was accorded not to His
Holiness, but to the Emperor himself. This
was symptomatic of the esteem in which
Bonaparte held the Church. Five years
later, the French annexed the Papal
estates, and Pope Pius was arrested.

❦ 10/30 – 1804

Nepveu et sang du sainct nouveau venu
Par le surnom soustient arcs et couvert
Seront chassez mis à mort chassez nu
En ruge et noir convertiront leur vert.

Blood nephew of the newly-created
  saint
His surname will uphold the arches
  and the roof
Naked, they will be chased and put to
  death
Their green will be converted to red
  and black.

After much pressure on Pope Pius VII,
Saint Napoleon, an early Christian
allegedly martyred by the emperor
Diocletian, was duly honoured every
year on the 15 August birthday of his
illustrious namesake, Napoleon
Bonaparte. To the Napoleonic French
Army, he became the patron saint of
warriors. His blood nephew, Bonaparte,
even had his own image superimposed
over that of the saint on religious icons.
Red and black are the symbolic colours
of death and blood, while green
generally symbolises life.

❦ 8/61 – 1804

Jamais par le descouvrement du jour
Ne parviendra au signe sceptrifere
Que tous ses sieges ne soient en sejour,
Portant du coq don du TAG amifere.

Never by sunrise
Will he reach the sign of the sceptre
Even if all sieges end
And he brings more armies to the
  Cock.

This is a royalist's reference to
Napoleon's assumption of the title
Emperor, in 1804. Nostradamus implies
that Napoleon will never have the same
right to rule as those with Royal blood,
not even if he were to end all sieges
and add to France's armies.

🐝 6/55 – 1805

Au chalme Duc, en arrachant l'esponce
Voile Arabeque voir, subit descouverte
Tripolis Chio, et ceux de Trapesonce
Duc prins, Marnegro et la cité deserte.

The easy-going Duke, drawing up
   the contract
Sees an Arabian sail, a sudden
   discovery
Tripoli, Chios and those of
   Trebizond
The Duke wins; Black Sea and City
   are deserted.

Pirates. In the modern era of Colonel
Gadaffi and his terrorist war against the
interests of the United States, it is
forgotten that two hundred years ago,
Libya was the centre of Mediterranean
piracy, and that American ships –
trading in important centres such as
Chios (where the original chewing gum
comes from) and Trebizond on the
Black Sea – were principal among the
targets. On 17 July 1801, an American
battle fleet blockaded the Libyan port-
capital Tripoli after the pasha, Yusuf
Karamanli, declared war on the United
States. The dispute was financial. The
pasha demanded 'protection' money to
dissuade Libyan corsairs from
attacking American shipping, and the
US refused to pay up. The blockade
lasted until 4 June 1805, when Yusuf
Karamanli signed a peace treaty with
the Americans (the 'easy-going Duke'
describing a strong adversary but one
taking an unconventional approach to
international affairs) and pirates were
suppressed. An early example of
successful US sanctions against Libya.

🐝 9/97 – 1805

De mer copies en trois parts divisees,
A la seconde les vivres failliront,
Desesperez cherchant champs Helisees,
Premier en breche entrez victoire auront.

The naval forces will be divided into
   three parts
The second force will lack supplies
In despair, they will seek Elysian
   fields
The first ones through the breach
   will snatch the victory.

Admiral Lord Horatio Nelson (1758–
1805) fought and won the battle of
Trafalgar on 21 October 1805, losing
his life in the process. Three parts
refers to the three combatants, France,
Spain and England. The Spanish
vessels were known to have lacked
supplies. Nelson drove a breach
through both navies, snatching victory
(Victory was also the name of Nelson's
flagship) by a margin of 20 French and
Spanish ships sunk, to the loss of no
English vessels.

🐝 1/77 – 1805

Entre deux mers dressera promontoire,
Qui puis mourra par le mors du cheval,
Le sien Neptune pliera voile noire,
Par Calpre et classe auprès de Rocheval

A promontory will lie between two
   seas
Someone will die by a horse's bit
Neptune's own will unfold a black
   sail
Via Gibraltar and a fleet close to
   Cape Roche.

The promontory must be Cape
Trafalgar, which gave its name to the
sea battle of 21 October 1805, fought

between Gibraltar (Calpre) and Cape Roche. Nelson, the victor – Neptune's own – was killed, and was borne back to England in a ship rigged with a black sail. Admiral Villeneuve, commander of the vanquished French fleet, was captured. When released, he was ordered to Paris, but rather than face Napoleon, he hanged himself in a livery stable, possibly with his horse's bridle.

❧ 3/1 – 1805

Apres combat et bataille navale,
Le grand Neptune à son plus haut befroi
Rouge adversaire de peur deviendra pasle
Mettant le grand Ocean en effroi.

After battle and naval conflict
Great Neptune, in his highest belfry
Will cause his red adversary to
   blanch with fear
Putting the mighty ocean into
   turmoil.

Often taken as yet another Battle of Lepanto quatrain, this actually refers to the Battle of Trafalgar, fought on 21 October 1805, in which Admiral Horatio Nelson, 'Great Neptune', lost his life after securing a stunning victory over the French and Spanish 'reds'. The clinching detail is that a 100 ft column was erected in London's Trafalgar Square in 1849 commemorating Nelson's victories. The column is dominated by a colossal statue of the victorious Admiral by E. H. Baily, uncannily fulfilling the prophecy of the first two lines.

❧ 5/61 – 1806

L'enfant du grand n'estant à sa naissance,
Subjugera les hauts monts Apennis
Fera trembler tous ceux de la balance,
Et de monts feux jusques à mont Senis.

The child of the great man, who will
   not be at his birth
Will conquer the high mountains of
   the Apennines
He will make the Librans tremble
And the mountains will burn, all the
   way to Mt Cenis.

This may relate to Eugène de Beauharnais (1781–1824), son of the Empress Joséphine and stepson of Napoleon Bonaparte, who was therefore 'not at his birth'. Beauharnais became a famous general, harrying the Habsburgs ('Librans') on many occasions. He became Viceroy of Italy in 1806.

❧ 6/40 – 1806

Grand de Magence pour grand soif
*   estaindre,*
Sera privé de sa grand dignité
Ceux de Cologne si fort le viendront
*   plaindre,*
Que le grand groppe au Rin sera getté.

To quench his great thirst, the leader
   of Mainz
Will be deprived of his grand dignity
The people of Cologne will complain
   so much about him
That the great rump will be thrown
   into the Rhine.

The office of the Elector of Mainz was abolished on 6 August 1806, when the Holy Roman Empire came to an abrupt end – thanks to Napoleon's diligent efforts.

✹ 5/35 – 1807

Par cité franche de la grand mer Seline,
Qui porte encores à l'estomac la pierre
Angloise classe viendra soubs la bruine
Un rameau prendre, du grand ouverte
guerre.

From the fair city of the great
crescent sea
Which still carries the stone in its
stomach
An English fleet will come through
the fog
To seize one branch; war is declared
by the great one.

Genoa is normally taken to be the 'city
of the crescent sea', but the name
could also be applied to Constantinople, known, since 1930, as Istanbul. In
which case the 'English fleet' may refer
to Admiral Sir John Thomas Duckworth's squadron, which appeared
before Constantinople in 1807 and
attempted to force the Dardanelles. The
Turks succeeded in driving him out,
with the loss of two of his ships.

✹ 5/99 – 1807

Milan, Ferrare, Turin et Aquillaye
Capne Brundis vexés par gent Celtique
Par le Lion et phalange aquilee
Quant Rome aura le chef vieux
Britannique.

Milan, Ferrara, Turin, Aquileia
Capua and also Brindisi will be
troubled by the Celts
By the lion and the eagle's phalanx
When Rome has the old British
chief.

Napoleon Bonaparte's conquest of
Italy. One plausible naming of the old
Briton is Henry Stewart, Cardinal of
York, last of the Scottish royal dynasty,
who died in Rome in 1807.

✹ 1/52 – 1807

Les deux malins de Scorpion conjoinct,
Le grand seigneur meutri dedans sa salle
Peste à l'Eglise par le nouveau roy joinct
L'Europe basse et Septentrionale.

The two evil ones will join in Scorpio
The great Lord will be murdered in
his hall
The new king will plague both the
church
And Europe, north and south.

Mars and Saturn, the two evil ones,
conjoined in Scorpio in 1807, when
'Seigneur' Selim III of Turkey was
deposed from his throne. He was
murdered a year later. At the same
time, in France, Napoleon was holding
Pope Pius VII prisoner, following his
defeat of Austria, Prussia and Russia.

✹ 4/70 – 1808

Bien contigue des grands monts Pyrenees
Un contre l'aigle grand copie addresser
Ouvertes veines, forces exterminées
Comme jusque à Pau le chef viendra
chasser.

Near the great Pyrenees mountains
One man will raise a great army
against the Eagle
Veins will be opened, soldiers
exterminated
The chief will chase them as far as
Pau.

Arthur Wellesley (1769–1852), later
Duke of Wellington, was despatched to
Portugal in 1808 to lead the war against
the occupying French (as in Napoleon's
Eagle) in the Iberian peninsular. After
five years' fighting, British troops
crossed into France in pursuit of the
retreating occupying force.

THE PROPHECIES OF NOSTRADAMUS

❦ 3/62 – 1808

Proche del duero par mer Cyrrene close
Viendra percer les grands monts Pyrenées
La main plus courte et sa percee gloze
A Carcassonne conduira ses menées.

From near the Douro, by the Bay of
  Biscay
He will cross the great Pyrenees
He will choose the shortest route
Leading his men to Carcassonne.

The Duke of Wellington triumphed over
the French in Portugal during the
Peninsular War between 1808 and 1810
and earned the title Baron Douro (after
the river that flows into the sea at
Oporto) from the Portuguese King in
gratitude. Wellington went on to defeat
the French in Spain, crossing over the
Pyrenees to invade France in late 1813.
He did choose a short route through the
mountains, but met stiff resistance from
an army under his arch-rival Marshal
Soult. Casualties were very high on
both sides, and Wellington did not enter
French territory until the following year,
reaching Carcassonne in the spring. It
was on his return to England from this
campaign that Wellesley was elevated
to his dukedom.

❦ 2/99 – 1809

Terroir Romain qu'interpretoit Augure,
Par gent Gauloise par trop sera vexée.
Mais nation Celtique craindra l'heure,
Boreas classe trop loing l'avoir poussée.

Roman territory, comprising that of
  the Augur
Will be much troubled by the French
But the Celtic nation will not endure
  it this time
Their winter fleet will have pushed
  too far.

In May 1809 Napoleon Bonaparte
annexed the Papal States (the Pope is
seen as the successor to the Augur of
ancient Rome). With his armies and
fleets extended all over Europe and the
Russian campaign looming, the Emperor
will live to regret coming this far.

❦ 2/93 – 1809

Bien pres du Timbre presse la Lybitine
Un peu devant grand inondation
Le chef du nef prins, mis à la sentine
Chasteau, palais en conflagration.

The Death Goddess threatens very
  near to the Tiber
A short while before the great flood
The captain of the ship is put in the
  scuppers
Both the palace and castle are burnt
  down.

The river of Rome goes into flood and a
palace and castle – surely the Vatican –
are burnt. The captain of the ship must
be the Pope, in this case Pope Pius VII,
arrested by Napoleon. The destruction
of the Vatican is figurative – unless this
quatrain refers to some disaster yet to
be visited upon the Holy See..

❦ 6/9 – 1809

Au sacrez temples seront faicts escandales,
Comptez seront par honneurs et louanges.
D'un que on grave d'argent, d'or les
  medalles,
La fin sera en torments bien estranges

There will be scandals in the
  churches
Some will be thought honest and
  praiseworthy
One, whose image is engraved on
  coins and medals
Will die, strangely tormented.

We are back to Napoleon and his persecution of the Italian clergy in 1809. Napoleon's image certainly appeared on the coins of the French realm, and he did die, on the isle of St Helena, tormented by stomach cancer.

❦ 1/88 – 1809

Le divin mal surprendra le grand Prince,
Un peu devant aura femme espousée,
Son Appuy et credit à un coup viendra
  mince,
Conseil mourra la teste rasée.

God's vengeance will fall on the great
  Prince
Just before he will have taken a wife
Acclaim for him at this action will
  grow thin
Support will dry up for the shaven-
  headed one.

Nostradamus refers almost vindictively to Napoleon I in the last line, alluding to the undoubted fact that the great man went prematurely bald. The theme of the quatrain is clearly Napoleon's December 1809 divorce from the Empress Josephine, and the disapproval with which it was met. Napoleon immediately afterwards married the Arch-duchess Marie Louise of Austria.

❦ 5/15 – 1809

En naviguant captif prins grand Pontif,
Grand après faillier les clercs tumultuez:
Second esleu absent son bien debiffe,
Son favory bastard à mort tué.

While navigating, the great Pontif
  will be taken prisoner
In the aftermath the clergy will be in
  tumult
This second absent elected one will
  lose all
The false one he favoured will kill him.

Pope Pius VII traduced by Napoleon Bonaparte. The Pope attended Napoleon's imperial coronation in 1804, thus favouring this false monarch. He was humiliated at the ceremony, and opposed Napoleon thereafter. He was arrested by the French in 1809, a fate shared by his predecessor Pius VI, which made him the second elected pope to be absent from Rome. Napoleon did not have him killed; he was released in 1814 and returned to Rome, where he died in 1823, aged 81.

❦ 8/92 – 1812

Loin hors du regne mis en hazard voyage
Grand host duira pour soi l'occupera,
Le roi tiendra les siens captif ostrage
A son retour tout pays pillera.

Far from the realm, on a hazardous
  journey
He will lead his own great army
The king will hold his own people to
  ransom
On his return, he will lay waste the
  country.

This is probably yet another reference to Napoleon, although commentators have mooted both Mao Tse Tung and Charles XII of Sweden, both of whom fit equally well. Nostradamus tended to confine his quatrains to France and the surrounding territories of Europe, with only the occasional foray further afield, so Napoleon is likelier. The hazardous journey is therefore the invasion of Russia, in 1812, followed by his devastating rearmament before the German campaign of 1813.

✇ 4/82 – 1812

Amas s'approche venant d'Esclavonie,
L'Olestant vieux cité ruinera
Fort desolee verra sa Romanie.
Puis la grand flamme estaindre ne sçaura.

A mass of men will approach from
   Slavonia
The Destroyer will ruin an old city
He will see his dreams of empire
   shattered
He will not know how to extinguish
   the flames.

Napoleon Bonaparte arrived in Moscow
on the night of the 14 September 1812.
While his soldiers camped in the
deserted streets, citizens of the ancient
wooden city raced around, setting fire
to its buildings. The fires raged for five
days, during which four fifths of the city
was destroyed. Napoleon began his
retreat from Moscow on 19 October,
but the retreat turned into a rout after
Marshal Kutuzov led the Russian army
to victory at Smolensk, in November,
against Marshals Ney and Davout.

✇ 9/99 – 1812

Vent Aquilon fera partir le siege,
Par murs gerer cendres, chauls, et
   pousiere,
Par pluie apres qui leur fera bien piege,
Dernier secours encontre leur frontiere.

The siege will be raised by the North
   Wind
Cinders, lime and dust will be thrown
   over the walls
Later, rain will make matters worse
Their last chance of hope lies at the
   frontier.

Another reference to the burning of
Moscow following the Battle of
Borodino, in 1812, and to Napoleon's

desperate retreat to the safety of the
'frontier' in October of that year.

✇ 3/68 – 1812–13

Peuple sans chef d'Espaigne et d'Italie
Morts, profligez dedans le Cherronesse
Leur dict trahi par legiere folie
Le sang nager par tout à la traverse.

Leaderless people from Italy and
   Spain
Dead, they are overcome within the
   peninsular
Their dictator is betrayed by
   senseless folly
Blood will flow through everything.

The closing stages of the Napoleonic
Wars. Napoleon's appointees as kings
of Naples and Spain, his brother-in-law
Joachim Murat and his brother Joseph
respectively, both failed him.

✇ 3/53 – 1813

Quand le plus grand emportera le pris
De Nuremberg, d'Auspourg et ceux de
   Basle
Par Agrippine chef Frankfort repris
Traverseront par Flamant jusqu'au
   Gale.

When the great man carries off the
   prize
Of Nuremberg, Augsburg, and Basle
Frankfurt will be retaken by the
   leader of Cologne
They will cross Flanders into France.

King Frederick William III of Prussia
called his people to arms against the
French on 3 February 1813, beginning
the process by which Germany
contributed to the defeat of Napoleon,
and subsequently became the
dominant continental power in Europe.

❦ 3/52 – 1813

En la campaigne sera si longue pluie
Et en la Pouille si grand siccité
Coq verra l'Aigle, l'aesle mal accompli
Par Lyon mise sera en extremité.

Heavy rains will dog the campaign
In Puglia there will be a drought
The Cock will see the Eagle, its wing
   unfinished
The Lion will drive it to the brink.

Napoleonic wars. Nostradamus often
construes Napoleon as an eagle, and
the cock would be expected to
symbolise France. The lion is usually
associated with Britain. The last
campaigns of 1813 in the run-up to the
crushing defeat of the French at Leipzig
were conducted in an exceedingly wet
autumn. As for drought in Puglia, this
might symbolise Napoleon's loss of
power in Italy as his king of Naples,
Joachim Murat, went over to the
Austrians in hope of saving his throne.

❦ 4/94 – 1813

Deux grans freres seront chassez
   d'Espaigne
L'aisné vaincu sous les monts Pyrenees
Rougir mer, rosne, sang lemam
   d'Alemaigne
Narbon, Blyterre, d'Agath contaminees.

Two great brothers will be driven
   from Spain
The elder will be beaten under the
   Pyrenees
The sea and the Rhône will redden
   with Genevan blood from
   Germany
Narbonne and Beziers will be
   contaminated by Agde.

Europe-wide conflict. The brothers
driven from Spain could be Napoleon
Bonaparte and his brother Joseph,
whom the Emperor appointed to the
country's throne during the French
occupation until his defeat at Vittoria in
1813 – Joseph was, indeed, the elder
brother.

❦ 1/89 – 1813

Tous ceux de Iler seront dans la Moselle,
Mettant à mort tous ceux de Loyre et
   Seine,
Le cours marin viendra d'haute velle,
Quand l'Espagnol ouvrira toute veine.

Men of the Iller will be in the Mosel
Putting to death those of the Loire
   and Seine
The marine power will come near the
   high valley
When the Spanish will open every
   vein.

Napoleon is losing the war in 1813,
caught in the pincer movement of
attacks from Austria, Prussia and Spain.
Nostradamus makes poetic use of river
names to delineate the northern front:
the Iller is a tributary of the Danube, so
it is Germans who are killing those of
the Loire and Seine – the French. The
marine power, England, has conquered
Spain and advances to the Pyrenees.
Vengeful Spaniards in the allied force
will kill everyone they find as they cross
into France on 8 October.

❦ 2/44 – 1813/4

L'aigle pousée entour de pavillions,
Par autres oiseaux d'entour sera chassée
Quand bruit des cymbees, tubes et
   sonaillons,
Rendront le sens de la dame insensée.

The eagle will be driven back to the tents
And chased by other, nearby birds
At the sound of the cymbals, the trumpets and the bells
Sense will be restored to the angry woman.

Napoleon, the Eagle, was driven back from Moscow during the winter of 1813–14, chased by the Imperial eagles of Russia, Austria and Prussia. The angry woman may refer either to France, in the shape of Marianne, the republican symbol, or to Joséphine, Napoleon's discarded wife. He had their marriage annulled on the grounds of her supposed infertility.

8/85 – 1814

Entre Bayonne et à Saint Jean de Lux
Sera posé de Mars la promottoire
Aux-Hanix d'Aquilon Nanar hostera lux,
Puis suffocqué au lict sans adjutoire.

Between Bayonne and St Jean de Luz
Mars's promontory will be placed
Nanar will take the light from the unconquerable Northerners
He will be suffocated in bed, with no one to help him.

This accurately deals with the closing days of Napoleon's Empire in November 1814, when the Duke of Wellington crossed the Pyrenees with his Anglo-Spanish army and camped at St Jean de Luz. He later moved to besiege Marshal Soult's forces at Bayonne. 'Nanar', at a stretch, could be seen as an abbreviation for Napoleon Bonaparte. The Emperor died on the island of St Helena, on 5 May 1821, from stomach cancer. Could Nostradamus be implying that he was helped on his way? The news of his death took seven weeks to travel to England.

5/100 – 1814

Le boutefeu par son feu attrapé
De feu du ciel à Carcas et Cominge
Foix, Aux, Mazere, haut veillart eschappé
Par ceux de Hasse, des Saxons et Turinge

The incendiary will be trapped by its own fire
Fire in the sky at Carcassonne and Comminges
Foix, Auch and Mazeres, the important old man escapes
Helped by the Hessians, the Thuringians and the Saxons.

The Duke of Wellington closes in on France in the south as German forces invade from the north. The last stages of the Napoleonic Wars.

10/23 – 1814

Au peuple ingrat faictes les remonstrances,
Par lors l'armee se saisira d'Antibe,
Dans l'arc Monech feront les doleances
Et à Frejus l'un l'autre prendra ribe.

Protests are made to the ungrateful people
Despite this, the army will seize Antibes
They will mourn in the Monegasque arch
And at Fréjus, one will seize the other's shore.

Antibes was the only town in France that remained loyal to Napoleon Bonaparte after Louis XVIII issued a proclamation urging fidelity to the crown. The ex-Emperor had used Antibes as his embarkation point on his journey to exile in Elba.

❦ 10/34 – 1814

Gaulois qu'empire par guerre occupera,
Par son beau frère mineur traby;
Par cheval rude voltigeant trainera,
Du fait le frère long temps sera bay.

The Frenchman who gains an empire
  by war
Will be traduced by his youngest
  brother-in-law
On his rugged, leaping horse he
  leaves all behind him
But this brother will long be hated.

A startlingly astute summary of Joachim
Murat (1767–1815). He was the most
brilliant, dashing and courageous
cavalry officer of his time. He enlisted in
the cavalry in 1789 and Napoleon
Bonaparte promoted him to general
rank during the Egyptian campaign of
1799. In the next year, Murat married
Napoleon's youngest sister, Caroline.
This qualified him for further elevation,
and in 1806 he was given the throne of
Naples. Murat's cavalry exploits were
legendary, and he made a colourful
Italian sovereign. But in 1814, as the
tide of war turned against his imperial
brother-in-law, Murat made a fatal error
of betrayal. In what he may have
imagined were the best interests of the
kingdom he'd learned to call his own,
Murat signed treaties with Austria and
Britain in January 1814, agreeing to an
Italian alliance with them in exchange
for a promise that the allies would
guarantee his throne at the conclusion
of hostilities. Napoleon never forgave
Murat, and refused his offer to take
command of the cavalry during the
Hundred Days before Waterloo.
Napoleon later bitterly reflected that
had he swallowed his pride and
reconciled himself to Murat, this great
cavalryman's presence on the field
might well have turned defeat into

victory. In 1815, Murat attempted to
recover his Neapolitan throne
(Metternich, inevitably, went back on
the deal with him) by landing with a
small force in Calabria. He failed to
summon up local support and was
arrested. He died, courageously, in
front of an Austrian firing squad on 13
October 1815.

❦ 5/34 – 1814

Du plus profond de l'occident Anglois,
Où est le chef de l'isle Britannique
Entrera classe dans Gironde par Blois,
Par vin et sel, feux cachez aux barriques.

From the deepest part of Western
  England
Where the leader of the British lives
A fleet will enter the Gironde, from
  Blois
Wine and salt will be offered; fires
  are hidden in the casks.

Arthur Wellesley (1769–1852), the 'Iron
Duke' of Wellington, took his title from
the small town of Wellington, in
Somerset, situated in the 'deepest part
of Western England'. In 1814 he
entered the Gironde with his army,
taking Bordeaux on 12 March. He beat
the French twice again, at Arcis-sur-
Aube, and at La Fère-Champenoise,
before storming Montmartre on 30
March, and entering Paris the following
day. The 'wine and salt' offered in the
quatrain could be an oblique reference
to Prime Minister Wellington's passing
of the Catholic Emancipation Bill, in
1829, giving British Catholics the right
to vote and sit in Parliament, on
condition that they recognise the
Protestant succession and deny papal
power to intervene in British domestic
affairs. 'Fires hidden in the casks' may
refer back to Guy Fawkes (1570–1606),
who was the cause of much religious

discord when he tried to blow up the Protestant King James I by placing casks of gunpowder beneath the cellars of the Houses of Parliament, in 1605.

❦ 3/45 – 1814

Les cinq estranges entrez dedans le temple,
Leur sang viendra la terre prophaner,
Aux Tholosains sera bien dur example
D'un qui viendra ses loys exterminer.

The five outsiders will enter within the temple
Their blood will profane the ground
Toulouse's people will be a hard example
From one who comes to extinguish their rights.

The five outsiders are the allies – Britain, Austria, Prussia, Russia and Spain – who will invade France. Toulouse did indeed suffer. The Duke of Wellington defeated a French army (under the command of his old adversary Marshal Soult) north-east of the city in one of the bloodiest battles of the occupation. The hardness of the example was the worse for the fact that the battle was completely unnecessary. Napoleon had already abdicated, but his commanders at Toulouse did not receive the news in time to effect a surrender.

❦ 9/76 – 1814

Avec le noir Rapax et sanguinaire,
Yssu du peaultre de l'inhumain Neron
Emmy deux fleuves main gauche militaire,
Sera murtry par Joyne chaulveron.

The rapacious and bloody monarch
Sprung from the rudder of the inhuman Nero
Between two rivers the army's left hand
Will be murdered by a young cavalier.

Napoleon Bonaparte is driven back towards Paris (between the two rivers Seine and Marne) and surrender. The name Nero is a Nostradamian code for the Revolution. The reference to murder is likely to be allegorical in the context of military defeat.

❦ 10/24 – 1815

Le captif prince aux Italles vaincu
Passera Gennes par mer jusqu'à Marseille,
Par grand effort des forens survaincu
Sauf coup de feu barril liqueur d'abeille.

The beaten, captive prince, at Elba
Will cross by sea from Genoa to Marseilles
He is overcome, after much effort, by foreigners
Safe from assassination, a barrel of bee's liquor.

Following on from 4/26 (see page 99), this once again mentions Napoleon's 'bee' emblem. With commendable detail, it tells of Napoleon's final hundred days, in 1815, his escape by sea, from Elba, the 'effort' entailed in his march up through France, and his final nemesis at Waterloo.

❦ 9/26 – 1815

Nice sortie sur nom des lettres aspres
La grande cappe sera present son sien
Proche de Vultry aux murs de vertes
   capres
Apres plombin le vent à bon essien.

Leaving Nice in the name of the
   bitterly-worded letters
The great caped one will stay with
   his own people
Near Voltri, at the walls of the green
   corsairs
The wind will get up beyond
   Piombino.

Capres in line 3 has nearly always been
mistranslated as capers, which makes
no sense at all. It actually means
corsair in old French, or one who
travels in a corsair. It can now be seen
to apply to Napoleon, who set sail in a
corsair from near Piombino during his
flight from exile in Elba, in February
1815. He began his seventeen day
march to Paris from behind Nice, on
what is now the Route Napoleon,
entering the capital on 19 March.

❦ 1/38 – 1815

Le sol et l'aigle an victeur paroistront
Response vaine au vaincu l'on asseure
Par cor ne cris harnois n'arresteront,
Vindicte paix par mors si acheve à
   l'heure.

The sun and the eagle will appear to
   the victor
An empty message reassures the loser
Neither bugle nor shouts will stop
   the soldiers
Peace is justified if achieved, in time,
   through death.

Twinned with 1/23 (see page 116) in
the original manuscript, this quatrain

describes the final hours of the battle of
Waterloo, on 18 June 1815. Napoleon's
Imperial Eagle shines in the thin
evening sun, appearing to the soon-to-
be victorious Wellington through the
mist-enshrouded battlefield. Seeing
men massing to the left, Napoleon
sends a message to his army that
Grouchy's relief troops have at last
arrived. Reassured, they attack with
fury. The smoke of battle disperses,
only to reveal von Blücher's Prussians.
The main French force breaks and
runs, leaving the Imperial Guard to take
the brunt of the final assault. Forty-
seven thousand men were to die that
day, so that peace might be achieved
throughout Europe.

❦ 8/13 – 1815

Le croisé frere par amour effrenee
Fera par Praytus Bellesophon mourir,
Classe à mil ans la femme forcenee,
Beu le breuvage, tous deux apres perir.

The crusading brother, loving
   fervently
Will cause Bellerophon, through
   Proteus, to die
The imprisoned woman, and the
   thousand year army
The potion will be drunk, both will
   later die.

The myth of Bellerophon and Proteus
deals with the dangers of vanity. The
goddess Athena gave Bellerophon the
horse Pegasus with which to kill the
Chimera. Later, wishing to boast of his
prowess, Bellerophon was lamed when
Zeus sent a gadfly to sting his mount.
Napoleon was exiled to St Helena on
board the Bellerophon, in 1815. Slowly
dying of stomach cancer, Napoleon
chose to think that he was being
poisoned by the British. He too, had
been brought down by a surfeit of vanity.

❦ 5/88 – 1815

Sur le sablon par un hideux deluge,
Des autres mers trouvé monstre marin
Proche du lieu sera faict un refuge,
Tenant Savone esclave de Turin.

Across the sands, a hideous flood
Will reveal a sea monster, from other
    parts
A keep will be built near the place
In which Savona, slave of Turin, will
    be held.

Savona, a part of Genoa, was given, in
1815, to the House of Savoy, which also
boasted the city of Turin among its
holdings. The 'sea monster' presents
difficulties, unless it is an oblique
reference to Genoa, which had, until
that time, virtually ruled the waves for
upwards of five hundred years.

❦ 2/66 – 1815

Par grans dangiers le captif eschapé,
Peu de temps grand a fortune changée
Dans le palais le peuple est attrapé,
Par bon augure la cité assiegée.

The prisoner escaped, braving great
    danger
Soon the great one sees his fortune
    changed
The people are trapped inside the
    palace
By good luck, the city is besieged.

Napoleon escaped from Elba on 1
March 1815. Faced with the bayonets
of the Fifth Infantry regiment barring his
route to Grenoble, Napoleon risked his
life by confronting the soldiers. Despite
their commander giving the order to
fire, Napoleon succeeded in convincing
the regiment to mutiny against their
leader, Louis XVIII. Arriving in Paris,
Napoleon was carried to the Royal
Apartments on the shoulders of the
crowd, which was so large that people
were trapped inside the palace for
hours. Louis XVIII was restored to the
throne on 8 July 1815, following
Napoleon's defeat at Waterloo.
Nostradamus, a devout monarchist,
would have considered this a good
omen.

❦ 1/32 – 1815

Le grand empire sera tost translaté,
En lieu petit, qui bien tost viendra
    croistre
Lieu bien infime d'exigue comté,
Ou au milieu viendra poser son sceptre.

The great empire will soon be moved
To a smaller environment. This, too,
    will begin to grow
A good place, though too small for an
    earldom
Here he will place his sceptre.

After his exile on Elba, Napoleon
Bonaparte (1769–1821) escaped,
moving his dreams of empire back to
mainland France. Those dreams were
destroyed by the Duke of Wellington
(1769–1852) and his Prussian ally, von
Blücher (1742–1819), on 18 June 1815,
at Waterloo. Napoleon was exiled to the
island of St Helena, in the South
Atlantic, where he died in 1821.

❦ 2/82 – 1815

Par faim la proye fera loup prisonnier,
L'assaillant lors en extreme detresse,
Le nay ayant au devant le dernier,
Le grand n'eschappe au milieu de la
presse.

Wild with hunger, the quarry will
    imprison the wolf
Causing its attacker great distress
With the young preceding the old
The great man cannot escape, hidden
    by the crowd.

Le Nay in line three, may well apply to
Marshall Ney (1769–1815), whose
gallant but ultimately futile efforts on the
battlefield of Waterloo may have gone
some way towards costing Napoleon
his expected victory. Napoleon, the
'great man', did not escape in the midst
of his troops, but was swiftly made a
prisoner by the English and sent on his
way to final exile in St Helena.

❦ 1/23 – 1815

Au mois troisième se levant le Soleil
Sanglier, Leopard, aux champs Mars
    pour combatre
Leopard lasse au Ciel estena son oeil,
Un Aigle autour du Soleil voit sesbatre.

At the sun's rise in the third month
The wild boar and leopard are in the
    battlefield
The leopard left alone, raises his eyes
    to heaven
An eagle is seen to fight against the
    sun.

Waterloo, 15 June 1815, a hundred
days (three months) after Napoleon
Bonaparte landed back on French soil.
The leopard, Britain, has determined to
make a stand here to face the French.

Wellington anxiously awaits his ally the
boar – Blücher, at the head of the
Prussian forces. The imperial eagles of
Napoleon's army came first, out of the
sun, and battle was joined.

❦ 10/86 – 1815

Comme un griphon viendra le roi
    d'Europe
Accompaigné de ceux d'Aquilon,
De rouges et blancz conduira grand
    trappe
Et iront contre le roi de Babilon.

The king of Europe will come like a
    griffin
Accompanied by the northerners
He will lead a great force of red and
    whites
They will go against the king of
    Babylon.

A griffin is part eagle, part lion, so
Nostradamus is predicting a composite
King of Europe who is part English, part
Austrian. This is reinforced in line 3
when he speaks of the red uniforms of
the English, and the white of the
Austrians. This could then apply to the
joint Anglo-Austrian army that went
against Napoleon, 'the king of Egypt',
during the battle of Waterloo, in 1815.

❦ 4/75 – 1815

Prest à combattre fera defection.
Chef adversaire obtiendra la victoire,
L'arrière garde fera defension,
Les defaillans mort au blanc territoire.

The one ready to fight will not come
The opposing chief will obtain the
    victory
The vanguard will make the defence
The losers dead against the white
    territory

Napoleon's defeat at Waterloo. The one ready to fight, the Marquis de Grouchy, who had supported Napoleon brilliantly after his return from Elba and routed Blücher at Ligny, failed to arrive in time to play a useful part in the battle. Wellington, the opposing chief, won the day. Napoleon's élite Imperial Guard provided a stout, but futile defence. The white territory against which the losers died represents the restored Bourbons in their uniformly white regalia.

☙ 7/24 – 1815

L'ensevely sortira du tombeau,
Fera de chaines lier de fort du pont:
Empoysoné avec oeuf de barbeau,
Grand de lorraine par le Marquis du
    Pont.

The buried one leaves his grave
He will forge the links of a strong
    bridge
Poisoned with fish roe
Is the big man of Lorraine by the
    Marquis du Pont.

The significant line is said to be the first, predicting the restoration of the Bourbon monarchy after Napoleon's defeat at Waterloo. The buried one is Louis XVIII, who had been restored in the previous year, but looked politically dead when Napoleon escaped from Elba and returned to France.

☙ 9/86 – 1815

Du bourg Lareyne ne parviendront droit
    à Chartres
Et feront pres du pont Anthoni panse
Sept pour la paix cantelleux comme
    martres
Feront entrée d'armee à Paris clause.

They won't come straight to
    Chartres from Bourg-la-Reine
They will pause near Pont d'Antony
Seven, as crafty as martens, are for
    peace
Armed, they will enter tightly-sealed
    Paris.

The seven allied nations of England, Prussia, Portugal, Austria, Sweden, Spain and Russia entered Paris on 3 July 1815, following Napoleon's final defeat at the Battle of Waterloo on 18 June. As per its agreement, the main French Army had already pulled back through Bourg-la-Reine, on its way to Chartres. To further leaven the success of this quatrain, the army is even said to have camped beneath the Pont d'Antony.

☙ 10/16 – 1815

Heureux au regne de France, heureux de
    vie,
Ignorant sang, mort, fureur et rapine,
Par nom flatteur sera mis en envie:
Roy desrobé, trop de foye en cuisine.

Happy on the throne of France,
    happy in life
Ignorant of blood, death, fury and
    plunder
Flattered by a name the speaks of
    desire
A king without majesty, too
    interested in food.

King Louis XVIII of France (1755–1824) to a tee. Brother of the executed Louis XVI, he escaped the Revolution and found comfortable sanctuary in England, far from the tribulations of war. Restored after Napoleon's defeat, he was happy indeed, and had the popular nickname Le Désiré, signifying the strength of feeling with which so many in France had awaited the restoration. A notorious glutton, Louis was a good deal more interested in matters of the table than he was in matters of state.

❦ 3/96 – 1820

Chef de Fosan aura gorge coupee,
Par le ducteur du limier et laurier
La faict patre par ceux de mont Tarpee,
Saturne en Leo 13 de Fevrier.

A leader from Fossano will have his
    throat slit
By one who trains hounds
The deed is done by a criminal
When Saturn is in Leo, on the 13
    February.

Another remarkable dating, this time to the assassination of the Duke de Berry, on 13 February 1820 (see 3/91 below). Berry's maternal grandfather was the King of Fossano, in Sardinia. Louvel, Berry's assassin, was a Republican, and worked in the Royal stables, thus the reference to the Tarpean Rock, from which Republican Rome was wont to throw her criminals. Louvel stabbed the Duke on his exit from the Opéra.

❦ 3/91 – 1820

L'arbre qu'estoit par long temps mort
    seché,
Dans une nuict viendra à reverdir
Cron Roy malade, Prince pied estaché,
Criant d'ennemis fera voile bondir.

A tree, which had for a long time
    been thought dead of drought
Will flourish again, in the course of
    one night
The old sick king and the prince with
    one leg
Will set sail, fearing enemies.

The Duchess of Berry gave birth to a son on 29 September 1820, seven months after her husband was assassinated, thus ensuring the continuation of the Bourbon line. The boy later injured his leg falling from a horse, causing him a permanent limp. He and his grandfather, Charles X, were forced into exile in 1830, and he never succeeded to the throne of France.

❦ 4/73 – 1820

Le nepveu grand par forces prouvera
Le pache faict du coeur pusillanime
Ferrare et Ast le Duc esprouvera
Par lors qu'au soir sera le pantomime.

The great nephew will prove by force
The cowardly-hearted crime
The Duke will try Ferrara and Asti
Of an evening, when the comedy
    takes place.

The assassination of the Duke de Berry on 13 February 1820 when leaving the Opéra in Paris. The nephew in question is Charles Louis Napoleon Bonaparte (1808–73), later Napoleon III.

❦ 4/93 – 1820

Un serpent veu proche du lict royal,
Sera par dame nuict chiens n'abayeront:
Lors naistre en France un Prince tant
    royal,
Du ciel venu tous les Prines verront.

A snake comes close to the royal bed
Seen by the lady on the night the
    dogs did not bark
When there is born in France a
    Prince so royal
That others Princes will see him as
    come from heaven.

The birth of Henri Charles, Comte de Chambord. He was the son of the Duchess of Berry, who had been widowed by her husband's assassination months earlier, and was thereby a Bourbon heir to the throne of France. As such he was seen by another pretender, the Duke of Orléans, who attended the Duchess's confinement in disbelief that she could be giving birth. Nostradamus clearly considered Henri was a prince among princes and the rightful heir, and that Orléans was a villain. As events turned out, Henri never gained the throne. He died in 1883.

❦ 10/90 – 1821

Cent fois mourra le tyran inhumain;
Mis à son lieu scavant et debonnaire,
Tout le Senat sera dessous sa main,
Fasché sera par malin temeraire.

A hundred deaths the inhuman tyrant
  will die
Replaced by a scholarly and debonair
  man
The government will be in his thrall
He will be troubled by wicked
  temerity.

Napoleon Bonaparte died the last of his hundred deaths after a miserable six years' confinement on St Helena in 1821. Louis XVIII, who was scholarly and debonair by any standards, had a good start to his reign, but later years were marred by the assassination of his nephew, an heir to the throne.

❦ 9/75 – 1821–32

De l'Ambraxie et du pays de Thrace
Peuple par mer mal et secours Gaulois
Perpetuelle en Provence la trace
Avec vestiges de leur coustume et loix.

From Arta and the country of Thrace
People are made ill by the sea, there
  is help from France
Their traces will remain forever in
  Provence
With vestiges of their costumes and
  laws.

This refers back to the ancient Greeks, and to their colony of Provence, which still bears traces of their culture. In modern times, France came to the aid of Greece during her 1821–32 War of Independence against the Ottoman Turks.

❦ 3/73 – 1824

Quand dans la regne parviendra la
  boiteux,
Competiteur aura proche bastard
Lui et le regne viendront si fort roigneux,
Qu'ains qu'il guerisse son faict sera bien
  tard.

When the lame man achieves the
  kingdom
His close competitor will be a bastard
Both he and the kingdom will
  become mean
So that, when he recovers, his actions
  will come too late.

Franklin D. Roosevelt has been nominated for the lame man, as has the Duke of Bordeaux, heir of Charles X of France. The trouble is, neither of them recovered. The most famous poet in Europe, Lord Byron (1788–1824), was also lame, and certainly achieved the kingdom, if only by notoriety; a number of his close competitors were most certainly bastards, a few of which he fathered himself. He sailed to Greece at the end of his life with the intention of helping the Greeks shake off Turkish rule, and died at Missolonghi on 19 April 1824.

❦ 2/17 – 1826

Le camp du temple de la vierge vestale
Non esloingé d'Ethne et monte Pyrenées
Le grand conduict est caché dans la male
North getez fleuves et vignes mastinées.

The field of the Vestal Virgin's
  Temple
Not far from Ethne and the Pyrenees
The great one led and hidden in a
  tree trunk
In the North the rivers overflow and
  vines are bruised.

A reference to Tibur, now Tivoli, north-east of Rome, the site of the spectacular Villa d'Este, started in 1549 (no doubt to Nostradamus's knowledge) by the architect Pirro Ligorio for Cardinal Ippolito d'Este. Tivoli narrowly escaped complete destruction in November 1826 when the river Arno flooded disastrously, washing away large expanses of vineyards and olive groves. The references to Vestal Virgins and the Pyrenees are thinly veiled disguises for the name Este and the Sabine mountains, through which the river Arno flows.

❦ 6/76 – 1828–1861

La cité antique d'antenoree forge.
Plus ne pouvant le tyran supporter
Le manchet fainct au temple couper gorge,
Les siens le peuple à mort viendra
  boucher.

The ancient city of Antananarivo,
  forged
No longer able to support the tyrant
The false amputee cuts throats in the
  temple
The people will drive his followers to
  their deaths.

No commentator has yet made the connection between *d'antenoree* and Antananarivo. In 1828, Madagascar's benevolent king Radama I died, leaving his wicked queen, Ranavalona I, as head of state. She reigned for the next thirty-three years, closing the island to both the French and the British, who had the usual colonial ambitions. She was renowned for her cruelty, and particularly relished having Christians thrown off cliffs – in the event that they chose not to commit suicide by 'slitting their throats'. She drove out the European missionaries and laid waste their schools and churches, and encouraged slavery, debauch and barbarity. Nostradamus does her full justice.

❦ 1/39 – 1830

De nuict dans lict le supresme estrangle,
Par trop avoir sejourné, blond esleu
Par trois l'empire subrogé exanche,
A mort mettra carte, et pacquet ne leu.

The last one is strangled in his bed,
  at night
For having spent too much time with
  the blonde pretender
The empire is enslaved by three
  substitutes
His death occurs with the Will still
  unread.

The last in the line of Bourbon-Condés was found hanging in his bedroom. His assassins had strangled him in his bed, then hung him with a rope to conceal the marks of their deed. The substitutes in question are Louis Philippe, Napoleon III and the Third Republic of Thiers and MacMahon. Condé had written a will, but it was destroyed by his assassins and replaced with a new one, favouring the Duke of Aumale, son of Louis Philippe.

🐝 6/84 – 1830

Celuy qu'en Sparte Claude ne peut
regner,
Il fera tant par voye seductive,
Que de court, long le fera araigner,
Que contre Roy fera sa perspective.

He who cannot reign as Claude in
Sparta
Will do much by way of seduction
In a short time, after long conspiring
The King will prevail over views
against him.

Possibly a view of the events of July
1830 in Paris. The reigning king,
Charles X, was forced to abdicate in
the *Révolution de Juillet* because he
could not reconcile his notions of divine
right with those of the democratic
ambitions of his nation. His place was
taken by the 'Citizen King' Louis-
Philippe. The reference to Sparta is a
witty allegory of a state once ruled by
two kings at once.

🐝 2/7 – 1830

Entre plusieurs aux isles deportés
L'un estre nay à deux dents en la gorge
Mourrant de faim les arbres esbrotés
Pour eux neuf Roy, nouvel edict leur
forge.

Among the many who are deported
to the islands
A man will be born with two teeth in
his neck
Dying of hunger, the trees uprooted
They will have a new king who will
pass new laws.

In 1830, the British public was outraged
by news of 'abo hunting' in the penal
colony of Australia. Native Australians
were driven from their land and into the
guns of bloodthirsty settlers. Aboriginal

ritual dress included teeth threaded on
to necklaces. It was, unhappily, some
time before legislators put an end to the
savagery.

🐝 10/82 – 1830

Cris, pleurs, larmes viendront avec
coteaux
Semblant fouir donront dernier assault.
Lentour parques planter profons plateaux,
Vifs repoulsez et meurdris de prinsault.

Cries, weeping, tears, come with the
knives
Pretending to flee, they will make
one last assault
They will set up high platforms
around the parks
The living are repulsed, and
straightway murdered.

This harks back to the Fall of Troy, and
the Greeks use of the Trojan Horse.
'Trojan' was often used by
Nostradamus as a euphemism for the
French Royal house. Is he foretelling
the slow downfall of the French
monarchy? If so, the image is accurate.
The monarchy raised itself a number of
times, before finally bowing its head
before the unstoppable Republican
onslaught in 1830.

🐝 3/27 – 1830

Prince libinique puissant en Occident
François d'Arabe viendra tant enflammer
Scavans aux lettres sera condescendant
La langue Arabe en François translater.

This Libyan Prince will be powerful
in the West
The French will become enamoured
of Arabia
A learned man, he will condescend
To translate the Arab tongue into
French.

The French colonisation of north Africa came about by accident. On 14 June 1830, after a series of military skirmishes and diplomatic tiffs between Paris and Algiers, French troops were landed in Algeria with a vew to persuading the ruler to desist from supporting corsairs in their attacks on French shipping in the Mediterranean. In the ensuing war, the French found themselves in possession of a valuable overseas territory. The translator may be Si-Hamza of the Walid-sidi-Sheikh family, who remained a loyal ally of France until his death in 1861.

❦ 8/42 – 1830

Par avarice, par force et violence
Viendra vexer les siens chef d'Orléans
Près Saincte Memire assant et resistance
Mort dans sa tente, diront qu'il dort leans.

By his greed and violent abuse of
   power
Orléans will come to upset his own
   supporters
Near St Memire there will be assault
   and resistance
He will skulk in his tent, saying he is
   asleep in it.

Orléans is Louis-Philippe, king of France between the revolutions of 1830 and 1848. He was the son of the Duke of Orléans, but renounced his titles and joined the National Guard in the 1789 Revolution.

❦ 5/69 – 1830

Plus ne sera le grand en faux sommeil,
L'inquietude viendra prendre repoz
Dresser phalange d'or, azur, et vermeil,
Subjuger Affrique la ronger jusques oz.

No longer will the great man pretend
   to sleep
Unease will take the place of rest
A phalanx of gold, blue and
   vermillion will be raised
To subdue Africa and gnaw it to the
   very bone.

In 1830 Louis Philippe usurped the French crown, becoming the first Bourbon to accept the 'tricolour' flag. In an effort to popularise himself with the French people he invaded and conquered Algeria, storing up much trouble for the century to come.

❦ 9/89 – 1830

Sept ans sera Philipp. fortune prospere:
Rabaissera des Arabes l'effort;
Puis son midi perplex, rebors affaire,
Jeune Oignon abismera son fort.

For seven years Philipp's fortunes
   will prosper
He will humble Arab ambitions
His middle years will face a
   perplexing affair
Young Onion will reduce his
   strength.

King Louis-Philippe had an excellent start to his reign as the 'Citizen King' of France from 1830–38 but there were then political troubles in the Middle East. The curious reference to the Young Onion is extremely intriguing. Ogmiom was the classical hero depicted on the five-centime coins minted by the young Republic of 1848, which brought Louis-Philippe's reign to an end.

🍎 9/5 – 1831

Tiers doit du pied au premier semblera.
A un nouveau monarque de bas hault
Qui Pise et Lucques Tyran occupera
Du precedant corriger le deffaut.

The third toe will resemble the first
And belong to a low-born king
He will occupy Pisa and Lucca by
    force
Correcting the faults of his
    predecessor.

This could refers to the Third Estate, established, for the second time, in 1848. The link is strengthened when one knows that Louis Napoleon (1808–1873) had attempted to besiege Civila Castellana, in 1831, which is situated not far from Lucca and Pisa, in Tuscany. A nephew of Napoleon I, he would be considered 'low-born' by a royalist such as Nostradamus.

🍎 1/73 – 1835

France à cinq parts par neglect assaillie
Tunys, Argiels esmeuz par Persiens,
Leon, Seville, Barcelone faillie
N'aura la classe par les Venitiens.

France, neglectful, is assailed on five
    sides
Tunis and Algeria are stirred up by
    Persians
Leon, Seville and Barcelona go
    wrong
There won't be recruitment by the
    Venitians.

A vision of an embattled France. In 1835 the French army in Algeria suffered a shock defeat by Muslim (Persian) rebels, starting a lengthy and bitter war between the French colonists and their reluctant subjects. Spain, like America, was demanding reparations for the ravages of the Napoleonic wars – even though France was mired in poverty. And on 28 July an Italian, Giuseppe Maria Fieschi, attempted to assassinate King Louis Philippe. The attempt failed even though 18 passers-by were killed in the assassin's hail of bullets. Recruitment to Fieschi's Republican cause certainly suffered as a result.

🍎 2/37 – 1836

De ce grand nombre que l'on envoyera
Pour secourir dans le fort assiegez
Peste et famine tous les devorera
Hors mis septante qui seront profligez.

Of the great number sent
To relieve the captured fort
Disease and hunger will devour them
    all
Save seventy, who will die in other
    ways.

In the war for possession of Texas in 1836, the capture by 5,000 troops under the command of Mexican tyrant Santa Anna of a fort at the Alamo, now occupies a special place in American history. The garrison at the Alamo on 6 March 1836 consisted of 183 men, including Colonel William Bowie and the frontiersman Davy Crockett. It is said that Santa Anna lost a thousand men in taking the fort. All the garrison were slaughtered. But only a few days later, Santa Anna's army was resoundingly defeated by a Texan force under the command of Sam Houston. The Mexicans not killed or captured melted away to die of disease or lack of food.

🐝 10/42 – 1837–1901

Le regne humain d'Anglique geniture,
Fera son regne paix union tenir,
Captive guerre demi de sa closture,
Long temps la paix leur fera maintenir,

The human throng, governed from
  England
Its reign will hold in peace and union
Half its extent will have been
  captured by war
For a long time, peace will be
  maintained for them.

Victorian England (1837–1901) can be
accounted the heyday of the British
Empire, during which peace reigned or
was maintained for many long years. At
its height Britain controlled nearly a
quarter of the world's land area and
population. Despite occasional lapses,
the Empire was largely benevolent, and
depended on trading and diplomacy
rather than on military threats for its
survival.

🐝 7/38 – 1842

L'aisné Royal sur coursier voltigeant,
Picquer viendra si rudement courir
Gueulle, lipee, pied dans l'estrein
  pleignant
Trainé, tiré, horriblement mourir.

The Royal eldest, on a leaping horse
Will spur it so badly that it bolts
Mouth, lips, foot will be injured in
  the stirrup
Dragged, pulled horribly to his
  death.

A grim prognosis for a royal heir – and
indeed the fate on 13 July 1842 of
Ferdinand Philippe, eldest son of King
Louis-Philippe of France, who was
killed when he fell from his carriage,
catching his foot in the door, as the
horses bolted.

🐝 5/7 – 1845

Du Trumvir seront trouvez les os,
Cherchant profond tresor aenigmatique,
Ceux d'alentour ne seront en repos
Ce concaver marbre et plomb metallique.

The bones of the Triumvir will be
  found
In the deep search for an enigmatic
  treasure
Those in attendance will have no rest
In hollowing out marble and metal of
  lead.

Napoleon Bonaparte's remains are
brought from St Helena to the Invalides
in Paris. He was a 'triumvir' in the sense
that he was one of three members of
the Directory left in power by the *coup
d'état* of 1801.

🐝 5/39 – 1846

Du vrai rameau de fleur de lys issue
Mis et logé heretier de Hetrurie
Son sang antique de long main tissu
Fera Florence florir en l'armoirie.

Born of the true branch of the fleur
  de lys
Put in place as the heir of Etruria
His noble and ancient blood
Will cause Florence's coat of arms to
  flourish.

Presumptive heir to King Charles X
(1757–1836), but with his legitimacy
questioned, the Count of Chambord
was exiled to Venice with his mother,
the Duchess of Berry. In 1846 he
married the daughter of Duke Francis
IV of Florence, thereby joining the *fleur
de lys* of the French coat of arms to the
fleur de lys of Florence, both of which
flourished, effectively completing
Nostradamus's pun.

❧ 4/65 – 1846

Au deserteur de la grand fortresse,
Apres qu'aura son lieu abandonné
Son adversaire fera si gran prouesse,
L'Empereur tost mort sera condamné.

The one who left the great fortress
Some time after he abandons his post
Will see his adversary display such
    great skill
That the emperor, soon to die, will
    be condemned.

On 25 May 1846, Louis Napoleon
(1808–73), later Napoleon III, escaped
to England from the fortress of Ham.
Louis Philippe (1773–1850) abandoned
his kingship of France during the 1848
revolution, after which Louis Napoleon
was voted Prince President. He was
later held responsible for the Franco-
Prussian war and its disastrous effects
on France, in which his adversaries, the
Prussians, undoubtedly displayed great
skill.

❧ 4/9 – 1847

Le chef du camp au milieu de la presse
D'un coup de fleche sera blessé aux cuisses
Lors que Geneve eu larmes et detresse
Sera trahi par Lozan et Souisses.

The leader of the army, standing in a
    crowd
Will be injured in the thigh by an
    arrow
At the same time distressed and
    troubled Geneva
Will be betrayed by Lausanne and
    the Swiss.

Switzerland, troubled by strife between
Calvinist protestants and militant
Catholics almost continuously since the
Reformation, was plunged into a civil

war in November 1847 as a league of
Catholic cantons rebelled against the
rule of the federal government. But the
cantons were violently put down and
surrendered within weeks. The
wounding of their leader was not with
the arrow of Nostradamus's vision, but
with a Swiss-made firearm.

❧ 3/14 – 1848

Par le rameau du vaillant personnage
De France infime, par le pere infelice
Honneurs, richesses, travail en son vieil
    aage
Pour avoir creu le conseil d'homme nice.

The offspring of the brave person
Becomes infamous in France, his
    father unhappy
Honours, riches, much work in old
    age
All because he believed an
    inexperienced man.

Son of the Duke of Orléans, Louis
Philippe was elected King of France in
1830, but failed in his role of 'citizen
monarch' by accepting bad advice that
he should retain his hold on the crown
through censorship and the abolition of
trial by jury. He was unseated, at the
age of 75, in the revolution of 1848.

❧ 5/92 – 1848

Après le siege tenu dix-sept ans,
Cinq changeront en tel revolu terme:
Puis sera l'un esleu de mesme temps,
Qui des Romains ne sera trop conforme.

After keeping his seat for 17 years
Five will change in a similar period
Then one will be elected at the same
    time
Who will not conform closely to the
    Romans.

King Louis-Philippe's reign in France ended in its seventeenth year with the Revolution of 1848, disinheriting five princes. The elected one is Louis Napoleon, nephew of Napoleon Bonaparte, who became President of the Republic that year and Emperor in 1852. He conducted military campaigns in Italy.

❦ 5/6 – 1848

Au Roy l'augure sur le chef la main mettre,
Viendra prier pour la paix Italique,
A la main gauche viendra changer le sceptre,
De Roy viendra Emperor pacifique.

The Augur will put his hand on the King
He comes to pray for peace in Italy
The sceptre will be handed over furtively
After the King will come a peaceful Emperor.

The displacement of King Charles X of France by Louis Napoleon in the role of President of the Republic, in 1848. Louis Napoleon later became Emperor as Napoleon III.

❦ 8/41 – 1848

Par le decide de deux choses bastards,
Nepveu du sang occupera le regne,
Dedans lectoure seront les coups de dards.
Nepveu par pleira l'enseigne.

By the demise of two illegitimate things
The nephew of the blood will have the realm
History will speak of him in forked tongues
The nephew will bend to the signs.

Following two illegitimate governments in France (those of King Louis-Philippe and the Second Republic) the nephew takes over – Louis Napoleon, son of Napoleon Bonaparte's brother Louis. Later Emperor, his reign was ended by his unwise declaration of war against Prussia in July 1870.

❦ 3/95 – 1848–1989

La loy Moricque on verra deffaillir,
Apres un autre beaucoup plus seductive
Boristhenes premier viendra faillir,
Par dons et langue une plus attractive.

Moorish law will be seen to fail
As a result of another, more seductive version
The Russians will be the first to succumb
Gifts and language will make the other more appealing.

This predicts both the rise and fall of Communism, but fails to supply a date. With hindsight, we can now date the rise as coinciding with the publication of the 'Communist Manifesto' by Marx and Engels in 1848, and the fall to the tearing down of the Berlin Wall in 1989.

❦ 1/6 – 1849

L'oeil de Ravenne sera destitué
Quand à ses pieds les aisles sailliront;
Les deux de Bresse auront constitué
Turin, Verceil, que Gaulois fouleront.

The eye of Ravenna will weep
When at her feet the wings flutter aloft
The two of Bresse will have established
Turin, Venice, when Frenchman once trod.

Nostradamus knew Ravenna, the ancient and beautiful capital of Emiglia in Italy, well. The eye referred to is probably a favourite window in one of the city's great churches. It was in Ravenna in 1849 that Giuseppe Garibaldi (1807–82), father of the Italian Risorgimento, stopped to rest with his wife Anita on their long retreat from Rome. Tragically, Anita died from exhaustion there. Nostradamus foresees that the church where the great patriot took his wife's body to mourn her, shed tears for her departing soul. The 'two of Bresse' refers to Garibaldi, who was born in France, and his wife. Turin, Venice and Ravenna were all occupied on more than one occasion by France up to the unification of Italy in the 1860s. Turin was the Italian capital from 1860–65; Venice was liberated from Austrian suzerainty into the Italian union in 1866 and Ravenna was one of the first cities to declare for unity, in 1859 – the tenth anniversary of the sad event of 1849.

❦ 10/8 – 1856

Index et poulse parfondra le front
De Senegali le Conte à son filz propre
Les Myrnarmee par plusieurs de prin
*   front*
Trois dans sept jours blesses mors.

The Count of Senigallia
Will baptise his own son
The Mimnermians will get through
    several, quickly
Three, in seven days, wounded and
    killed.

Pope Pius IX, godfather to the Prince Imperial, son of Napoleon III, baptised his 'son' on the 15 June 1856. The Pope's own father was Count Mastoi Ferretti of Senigallia.
    Mimnermia was a surname of Venus,

implying either the Empress Eugenie or the Venetians. The latter is more probable, in this context. The last line is unexplained.

❦ 7/20 – 1856

Ambassadeur de la Toscane langue
Avril et May Alpes et mer passer,
Celuy de veau exposera harangue,
Vie Gauloise ne venant effacer.

The Tuscan-speaking Ambassador
Crosses the Alps and sea in April and
    May
He of the calf will expose in a
    harangue
That France is incompatible.

A reference to attempts made by Italy to obtain independence of French and Austrian influence and to find its own unity. The Ambassador was Camillo Benso, Count of Cavour, representing Victor Emmanuel, the future Italian King, whose centre of power was Turin – the city of the bull.

❦ 6/51 – 1858

Peuple assemblé, voir nouveau epectacle
Princes et Rois par plusieurs assistans
Pilliers faillir, murs, mais comme
*   miracle*
Le Roi sauvé et trente des instants.

People are assembled to see the
    spectacle
Princes and Kings with several aides
Walls and pillars fall, but
    miraculously
The King is saved, and thirty
    bystanders.

Italian republican Felice Orsini's attempt on the life of Napoleon III on 14 January 1858. Orsini's bomb killed eight bystanders and wounded more than a hundred in the crowd gathered outside the Paris Opera. The building was badly damaged, but the Emperor and his consort Empress Eugenie, along with others, escaped injury.

❦ 5/9 – 1858

Jusques au fond le grand arq demolué,
Par chef captif l'ami anticipé
Naistra de dame front face chevelue,
Lors par astuce Duc à mort attrappé.

At the foot of the great demolished
   arch
A friend's quick action saved the
   chief
Brought about by the hairy-faced
   lady
Then caught in a deadly trap by the
   shrewd Duke.

The failed assassination attempt by disguised bombers on Emperor Napoleon III as he left the Opera on 14 January 1858.

❦ 5/10 – 1858

Un chef Celtique dans le conflict blessé,
Auprès de cave voyant siens mort abattre,
De sang et playes et d'ennemis pressé,
Et secours par incogneus de quatre.

A French chief wounded in the
   conflict
Seeing his subjects struck down at
   the theatre
Blood and wounds and enemies
   pressing close
And help by unknown local people.

A double vision from Nostradamus – one of the rare occasions in *Centuries* when he refers to the same incident in succeeding quatrains. He must have

had a very clear picture indeed of this assassination attempt. The Emperor was indeed wounded, and several members of his party were killed.

❦ 5/20 – 1859

Dela les Alpes grande armée passera,
Un peu devant naistra monstre vapin;
Prodigieux et subit tournera
Le grand Toscan à son lieu plus propin.

A great army will pass beyond the
   Alps
Shortly before, a consuming monster
   will arise
Suddenly and prodigiously it will
   turn out
That the great Tuscan will return
   home.

Napoleon III of France invaded Italy in 1859, driving the Grand Duke of Tuscany, Leopold II, a Habsburg, back to Austria where he came from. The consuming monster is the Italian *Risorgimento*.

❦ 5/26 – 1860

La gent esclave par un heur martial
Viendra en haut degré tant esleuee
Changeront prince, naistre un provincial
Passer la mer copie aux monts levee.

The slave people, through good
   fortune in war
Will become so highly elevated
That they will change their prince,
   born in the provinces
An army raised in the mountains will
   cross the sea.

Abraham Lincoln (1809–65), a former provincial shopkeeper, was elected President of the United States in 1860 on an anti-slavery ticket. But the

Confederacy of seven southern states would not submit to national policy on the matter of abolition and withdrew from the Union in the following year, pitching America into a bitter civil war. Lincoln was assassinated but the Union triumphed, and on 6 April 1866 all people in the United States were guaranteed liberty under the Civil Rights Act. Many armies were raised and 600,000 killed, but the last line of the quatrain evokes Lincoln's famous recurring dream, which came to him on the nights before battles and on the night, too, before his death. He dreamt, he said, that he was moving across water to a dark and distant shore.

❦ 8/97 – 1860

A fin du Var changer le pompotans,
Pres du rivage les trois beaux enfants
* naistre.*
Ruine ay peuple par aage competans.
Regne ay pays changer plus voir croistre.

At the end of the Var, the all-
    powerful will change
Three beautiful children will be born
    near the bank
When they come of age, the people
    will be destroyed
Kingdom and country change, and
    are seen to prosper.

The river Var delineated the eastern boundary of France's border with Savoy. This quatrain tells of the eventual integration of Savoy into France, in 1860.

❦ 2/36 – 1860

Du grand Prophete les lettres seront
* prinses.*
Entre les mains du tyran deviendront,
Frauder son Roy seront ses entreprinses,
Mais ses rapines bien tost le troubleront.

The great Prophet's writings will be
    seized
They will come into the hands of the
    tyrant
His purposes will be to cheat his
    King
But soon his plunderings will trouble
    him.

In 1860, a leading Nostradamus interpreter, the Abbé Torné, published a volume entitled *L'Histoire prédité et jugée* in which he clearly predicted that Napoleon III of France would be deposed. The Emperor ordered the book confiscated on the grounds that it was seditious.

❦ 5/42 – 1860

Mars esleue en son plus haut befroi,
Fera retraire les Allobrox de France
La gent Lombarde fera si grand effroi,
A ceux de l'aigle comprins souz la
* Balance.*

A mighty warrior, raised high
Will restore the Savoyards to France
The Lombardians will cause much
    terror
To the Eagle's followers, including
    the Librans.

Savoy belonged to France at the time Nostradamus was writing, so here he is predicting not only its loss, which occurred in 1559, but also its eventual restoration, which took place 301 years later, on 22 March 1860, when King Victor-Emmanuel II presented Savoy to Napoleon III in gratitude for French help against the Austrians (the Librans).

❦ 9/3 – 1861

La magna vaqua à Ravenne grand
trouble,
Conduictz par quinze enserrez à Fornase
A Rome naistre deux monstres à teste
double
Sang, feu, deluges, les plus grands à
l'espase.

The great cow of Ravenna will cause
much trouble
Led by the fifteen imprisoned at
Fornese
Two monsters with twin heads will
be born in Rome
Blood, fire, floods, the most
important will hang.

Nostradamus saw two monsters during
a prophetic dream, and took them to
symbolise disunity. Here he applies the
image to Italy. Magnavacca was a port,
near Ravenna, renamed Porto de
Garibaldi after the reunification of Italy
in 1861 by Giuseppe Garibaldi (1807–
1882). The remainder of the quatrain is
rather obscure.

❦ 1/24 – 1862

A Cité Nevue pensif pour condamner,
Loisel de Proie au ciel se vient offrir,
Après Victoire a captifs pardonner
Cremone and Mantoue grands maux
auront offert.

For condemning the unseen city of
prayer
The hawk will come to offer himself
After victory, the prisoners are
forgiven
Cremona and Mantua will risk great
harm.

In 1862 and 1867, Garibaldi marched

on Rome, but failed to get within sight
of the city on either occasion. The
victory referred to may be that of
Victor Emmanuel II's entry into Rome
of 1870.

❦ 5/28 – 1865

Le bras pendu et la jambe liée
Visage pasle au seing poignard caché
Trois qui seront jurez de la meslee
Au grand de Gennes sera le fer lasché.

One arm hanging, and with his leg
bandaged
His face is pale, he has a dagger
hidden at his breast
Three who were there tell of the
scuffle
The blade strikes the great man of
Genoa.

An assassination. There were three
others in Abraham Lincoln's box at
Ford's Theatre in Washington on the
night of 15 April, 1865, when the
President was fatally shot by John
Wilkes Booth – who was tracked down
after he sought medical help for a leg
injury sustained in making his escape.
Interestingly, Lincoln's secretary of
state, William Seward, was seriously
hurt by a knife wound on the same
night. Could he be the encoded great
man of Genoa? Seward survived the
injury and later successfully negotiated
the purchase of Alaska from Russia for
7.2 million dollars.

❦ 5/79 – 1865

La sacree pompe viendra baisser les aisles
Par la venue du grand legislateur
Humble haulsera vexera les rebelles
Naistra sur terre aucun aemulateur.

The sacred pomp will lower its wings
At the coming of the great law-giver
He will raise the meek and trouble
    the rebellious
His like will not be seen again.

More than one modern interpreter has
read Abraham Lincoln into this
quatrain.

❦ 1/25 – 1865

Perdu, trouvé caché de si long siècle
Sera Pasteur demi-Dieu honoré,
Ainsi que la Lune achève son grand
    siècle,
Par autre vents fera dishonoré.

Lost but found hidden for long
    centuries
Pasteur will be honoured as a demi-
    god
Just as the moon reaches her high
    point
Other opinions will revile him.

Nostradamus looks three centuries
ahead to the work of a figure he may
well have seen as his own natural
successor, Louis Pasteur (1822–95).
The great French chemist was the
father of bacteriology. From 1865
onwards, he revealed how diseases
such as plague were spread by micro-
organisms. He was indeed elevated to
the highest status by the scientific
community – although he had his
detractors elsewhere.

❦ 3/43 – 1867

Gens d'alentour de Tarn Loth, et
    Garonne
Gardez les monts Apennines passer
Vostre tombeau pres de Rome et
    d'Anconne
Le noir poil crespe fera trophee dresser.

You people from the Tarn, the Lot
    and the Garonne
Don't cross the Appenine mountains
Your tomb will be near Rome and
    Ancona
The man with the dark curly hair will
    triumph.

France is warned not to invade Italy,
but it was a French force that prevented
Giuseppe Garibaldi (1807–82) seizing
Rome in 1867. Garibaldi's
Risorgimento, the rise of united Italy,
triumphed in the end, and the
revolutionary made his peace with
France, being elected a deputy to the
Bordeaux Assembly in later life.

❦ 4/100 – 1870

De feu celeste au Royal edifice
Quant la lumiere de Mars defaillira
Sept mois grand guerre, mort gent de
    malefice
Rouen, Eureux au Roi ne faillira.

Fire will fall from the sky on to the
    Royal building
Just as the war is weakening
Seven months the great war lasted,
    many evil killings
Rouen and Evreux will not fail the
    king.

The Franco-Prussian War of 1870–71, in
which the Palace of the Tuileries in
Paris was submitted to artillery fire. The
war, declared by France on Prussia on
16 July 1870, ended seven months later
by a provisional treaty signed on 26
February 1871 at Versailles. While
much of France capitulated to the
Prussian invasion immediately,
Normandy towns such as Rouen
supported the king, Napoleon III. An
astonishingly astute prophecy in every
respect.

❦ 10/51 – 1870

Des lieux plus bas du pays de Lorraine
Seront les basses Allemaignes unis,
Par ceux du siege Picards, Normans, du
*   Maine,*
Et aux cantons se seront reunis.

Regions south of Lorraine
Will be united to southern Germany
By the besieged of Picardy,
    Normandy and Maine
And they will be reunited to the
    cantons.

The Franco-Prussian war. The
Prussians' first thrusts were into
precisely the regions mentioned.

❦ 2/25 – 1870

La garde estrange trahira forteresse
Espoir et umbre de plus hault mariage
Garde deçeue, fort prince dans la presse,
Loire, Son, Rosne. Gar à mort oultrage.

The foreign guard will betray the
    fortress
There will be hope, the shadow of an
    all-powerful conjunction
With the guards deceived, the fort
    will be stormed, then taken
The Loire, the Saone, the Rhône and
    the Garonne, all mortally
    outraged.

The capitulation of Metz took place in
1870. General Bazaine retreated there,
rather than taking advantage of his
defeat of the Prussians at St Privat and
Gravelotte. His decision allowed the
Prussian troops access to the interior of
France. During his court-martial, in
1872, accusations were made that he
had received bribes from the Prussians.

❦ 1/92 – 1870–1

Sous un la paix par tout sera clamee
Mais non long temps pillé et rebellion
Par refus ville, terre, et mer entamee,
Mors et captifs le tiers d'un million.

Thanks to one man, peace will be
    declared
Though soon afterwards there will be
    riot and looting
Because of pride, both city, land and
    sea will be broached
And a third of a million killed, or
    taken captive.

This refers to Napoleon III (1808–1873)
of France's statement 'L'Empire c'est la
paix,' indicating that he considered his
Second Empire the empire of peace.
However, following Kaiser Wilhelm I
(1797–1888) of Prussia's refusal to
accede to France's humiliating
demands relating to Hohenzollern
rights to the Spanish throne, the
Prussians declared war on an
unprepared France. Between 300,000
and 350,000 people were killed in the
ensuing fighting.

❦ 5/82 – 1870–1

Au conclud pache hors de la forteresse,
Ne sortira celui en desespoir mis
Quand ceux d'Arbois, de Langres, contre
*   Bresse,*
Auront monts Dole, bouscade d'ennemis.

The despairing one will not venture
Outside the fortress once the truce is
    over
When the people of Arbois and
    Langres, fighting Bresse
Will be ambushed in the mountains
    of Dôle.

Geographically, this would seem to apply to the eastern area of France defended by General Charles Bourbaki's army before its defeat in the Franco-Prussian War of 1870–71. Out of 185,000 men, Bourbaki (1816–1897) escaped into Swiss territory with only 85,000. In despair, he later tried to commit suicide.

❦ 7/11 – 1879

L'enfant Royal contemnera la mère,
Oeil, pieds blessez, rude, inobeisant.
Nouvelle à dame estrange et bien amere,
Seront tuez des siens plus que cinq cens.

The Royal child disdains his mother
Defiant, footloose, hard, disobedient
News to the foreign lady is very
    bitter
He and 500 of his men will be killed.

The death of the Prince Imperial, son of Napoleon III of France, at the hands of Zulus in South Africa, in 1879. Exiled to Chislehurst in Kent, the Emperor had died in 1873 and the Empress was very reluctant to let her son join the British expedition against the Zulus (the prince had been educated at Woolwich), but he defied her and was killed in battle – with 530 of his comrades. With him died all hopes of a restoration of the Napoleonic dynasty to the throne of France.

❦ 8/33 – 1883

Le grand naistra de Veronne et Vicence,
Qui portera un surnam bien indigne,
Qui a Venise voudra faire vengeance,
Luy mesme prins homme de guet et fine.

The great one will be born of Verona
    and Vicenza
Who will bear a very undignified
    surname
Who at Venice will wish to gain
    vengeance
But will himself be taken by a sharp
    and wary man.

Benito Mussolini was born in the Romagna in 1883, the son of a blacksmith, whose name means maker of muslin. When he later became dictator of Italy, Mussolini met Adolf Hitler in Venice to discuss an alliance that would help Italy avenge past defeats by European enemies. But Hitler was not a man with whom a wise statesman made agreements for any purpose.

❦ 1/11 – 1867

Le mouvement de sens, coeur, pieds et
    mains,
Seront d'accord Naples, Lyon, Sicille
Glaves, feux, eaux puis aux nobles
    Romains,
Plongez tuez mors par cerveau debile.

The motion of the senses, heart, feet
    and hands
Naples, Lyons and Sicily will agree
Swords, fire, water, then the noble
    Romans
Immersed, stone dead, due to a weak
    mind.

Probably relates to the Spanish Habsburg Empire, but could equally refer to Garibaldi's attack on Rome, via Naples, in 1867. Either seems tendentious, as both rely on different readings of the word *Lyon*. The Habsburg camp would replace it with Leon, the Garibaldi one with Lion.

❦ 6/4 – 1870

Le Celtiq fleuve changera de rivaige,
Plus ne tiendra la cité d'Agripine
Tout transmue ormis le vieil langaige,
Saturne, Leo, Mars, Cancer en rapine.

The French river will alter its course
Cologne will no longer hold
All, save the old language, will
     change
Saturn, Leo and Mars will ravage
     Cancer.

A reference to the fate of Alsace-
Lorraine, and to France's many efforts
to secure that part of the Rhineland for
itself. These efforts came to nothing as
a result of the Franco-Prussian war,
which began in the month of Cancer,
July 1870. Thanks to their victory, the
Prussians reclaimed the region, which
did, however, retain its use of the
French language. France eventually
claimed back Alsace in 1919, under the
Treaty of Versailles.

❦ 5/32 – 1870

Où tout bon est tout bien Soleil et Lune,
Est abondant sa ruine s'approche
Du ciel s'advance vaner ta fortune,
En mesme estat que la septiesme roche.

Where all is good, the sun as well as
     the moon
Is abundant; but ruin approaches
Coming from the heaven while you
     boast of your fortune
It will resemble the seventh rock.

The sun and moon are euphemisms for
money, and the second person singular
was reserved by Nostradamus for
references to France. France was at the
height of her powers in 1867, at the
time of the Exposition Universelle, but
only three years later, on 19 July 1870,

the Prussians declared war on her, and
won. The seventh rock is a reference to
the seventh rock of the apocalypse,
and refers back to the desolation
caused by the Prussian attack.

❦ 1/62 – 1889–2243

Le grand parte las que feront les lettres,
Avant le cycle de Latona parfaict
Feu grand deluge plus par ignares
*   sceptres,*
Que de long siecle ne se verra refaict.

There will be a great loss of learning
Before the moon's full cycle is
     completed
Fire and floods will be fomented by
     ignorant rulers
Much time will go by before it is
     rectified.

The current lunar cycle began in 1889,
and will end in 2243. During this period,
if the situation today is anything to go
by, learning will be degraded, and our
rulers will become increasingly under-
educated and ignorant. The destruction
of all great civilisations has been
preceded by the abuse and side-lining
of the learned. Today, political
correctness threatens to subsume
scholarship. The philosopher
Montaigne, sensing a similar tendency
in his own era, retreated to his 'white
tower' in horror. 'Let us not be ashamed
to speak what we are not ashamed to
think,' he said.

❦   2/31 – 1800s

En Campanie le Cassilin fera tant
Qu'on ne verra que d'aux des champs
*   couvers*
Devant apres le pluie de long temps
Hors mis les arbres rien l'on verra de
*   vert.*

In Campania the Capuan river will
    rise
Water will cover all the fields
Both before and after the great rains
The only green thing visible will be
    the trees.

A fascinating extrapolation of Appius
Claudius's building project from Rome
to Capua of 312 BC. The Appian Way, a
magnificent paved road running for 132
miles, is foreseen by Nostradamus to
'cover all the fields' – with the buildings
which now submerge the Campania,
leaving trees as the only green life
visible.

1900–1999

❦ 8/75 – 1908

Le pere et fils seront meurdris ensemble
Le prefecteur dedans son pavillon
La mere à Tours du filz ventre aura enfle
Caiche verdure de feuilles papillon.

The father and son will be murdered
    at the same time
The prefect will be found in his
    pavilion
The mother, at Tours, will be with
    child
A green chest, with torn paper inside
    it.

The only notable father and son
assassination within living memory
occurred outside France, in 1908, when
Carlos I and Louis Philippe of Portugal
were murdered in Lisbon. The two last
lines remain unexplained.

❦ 2/15 – 1910

Un peu devant monarque trucidé
Castor, Pollux en nef, estre crinite
L'erain public par terre et mer vuidé
Pise, Ast, Ferrare, Turin, terre
    interdicte.

A little before a king is killed
Castor and Pollux on board ship, a
    comet is seen
The public wealth is emptied, by land
    and sea
Pisa, Asti, Terrara and Turin are
    forbidden territory.

A presage of the First World War
(1914–18), triggered by the
assassination of Archduke Ferdinand in
Sarajevo. Halley's comet was seen in
the sky in 1910.

❦ 3/40 – 1910

Le grand theatre se viendra se redresser
Les des jettez et les rets ja tendus
Trop le premier en glaz viendra lasser
Par ares prostrais de long temps ja
    fendus.

The great theatre will rise again
The dice are thrown, the nets
    stretched
The first one to toll the knell will tire
    too much
Destruction by beams split long ago.

Is Nostradamus groping far into the
future to visualise the age of that
limitless theatre, the broadcast? The
stretching of the nets and the tolling of
the knell suggest performances seen
and heard over distances. Wireless
telegraphy dates from around 1910.

❦ 10/80 – 1912

Au regne grand du grand regne regnant
Par force d'armes les grands portes
    d'airain
Fera ouvrir le roi et duc joignant,
Port demoli nef à fons jour serain.

In the kingdom of the great one,
    reigning well
The king and the duke, allied
    together
Will force the brass gates open, by
    strength of arms
The port is demolished, the ship
    sunk, the day is serene.

Foretelling the loss of the *Titanic*, this is
one of the most remarkable of all

Nostradamus's quatrains. It has never before been correctly interpreted. The great one is Cronus, king of the twelve Titans. Together they ruled the universe for aeons until Cronus was dethroned by his son, Zeus. Cronus is the king, Zeus the duke. The *Titanic*, the apparently unsinkable flagship of the British White Star Line, was named in honour of the Titans. The ship struck an iceberg off the Grand Banks of Newfoundland with its port side just before midnight on 14 April 1912. The 'port was demolished' as plates buckled along the ship's hull at the water line. Allied together, Zeus and Oceanus, another of the Titans, forced the brass gated bulkheads open and sunk the ship in a little less than three hours. Of the 2224 people on board, 1513 died. It is the most famous disaster in maritime history. The weather on the night, as Nostradamus says in line 4, was serene.

🐝 8/59 – 1914

Par deux fois hault, par deux fois mis à bas
L'orient aussi l'occident faiblira
Son adversaire apres plusieurs combats
Par mer chassé au besoin faillira.

Twice raised high, twice put down
The West will weaken, and the East, too
Its adversary, after many battles
And a chase on the sea, will fail when needed.

The two world wars of the twentieth century, in which Germany on both occasions has been put down by alliances of western and eastern powers on land and sea.

🐝 1/54 – 1914

Deux revoltes faicte du maling falcigere,
De regne et siecles faict permutation
Le mobil signe à son endroit si ingere,
Aux deux egaux et d'inclination.

Two revolutions will be fomented by the evil scythe-bearer
Kingdoms will alter at the turn of the century
Libra moves into its house
And both sides are well balanced.

Saturn is the scythe bearer, and the two revolutions are those of France in 1789 and Russia in 1917. Libra is the house that governs Austria, whose Empire foundered following the death of Archduke Ferdinand in 1914. His assassination led directly to the First World War, in which the two sides were, for most of the war at least, equally balanced.

🐝 10/50 – 1914

La Meuse au jour terre de Luxembourg
Descouvrira Saturn et trois en lurne
Montaigne et plein, ville, cité et Bourg
Lorrain deluge trahison par grand hurne.

The Meuse, by day, enters Luxembourg
Saturn and three will be found in Aquarius
Mountain and plain, town, city and borough
A flood in Lorraine, and Aquarian treason.

The astrological clues imply that this event took place in September 1914, during the British and French withdrawal from the Meuse region, prior to the first Battle of the Marne.

❦ 1/65 – 1914

Enfant sans mains jamais veu si grand
*   faudre,*
L'enfant royal au feu d'oesteuf blessé
Au pui brises fulgures allant mouldre,
Trois souz les chaines par le milieu
*   troussés.*

A child without hands will cause the
    fiercest storm ever
The royal child will be wounded in
    the heat of revenge
Lightning will strike the broken well
Leaving three men in bondage
    beneath the oak trees.

No commentator has yet made the
connection between the child without
hands and Kaiser Wilhelm II of
Germany (1859–1941). During his
difficult birth, on 27 January 1859,
Wilhelm was delivered by forceps,
permanently deforming his arm. So
embittered was he by this perceived
defect that one could argue that his
judgement was permanently impaired
by it, indirectly leading to the First
World War – the fiercest storm ever.
Wilhelm's youngest son, Prince
Joachim, shot himself at a hunting
lodge near Potsdam, in 1920,
disillusioned with Germany's revenge
on the Kaiser, his exiled and
disinherited father. Joachim's brothers,
Crown Princes Wilhelm, August Wilhelm
and Adalbert were later arrested by the
allies and interned after the Second
World War, beneath the oak trees of
their native Germany.

❦ 1/56 – 1914

Vous verrez tost et tard taire grand
*   change,*
Horreurs extremes, et vindications
Que si la lune conduicte par son ange,
Le ciel s'approche des inclinations.

Sooner or later great changes will
    occur
Vengeances, and extreme horrors
The moon, led by its angel
Will see the heavens approaching
    Libra.

The assassination of Archduke
Ferdinand, at Sarajevo. It foretells the
horrors of the First World War trenches.

❦ 5/70 – 1914–18

Des region subjectes à la Balance
Feront troubler les monts par grand
*   guerre*
Captifz tout sexe deu et tout Bisance
Qu'on criera à l'aube terre à terre.

From the Libran regions will come
    men
To disturb the mountains with a
    great war
Both sexes will be captured, and all
    Byzantium
So that cries will be heard at dawn,
    from land to land.

Libra sometimes signifies Britain in
Nostradamian code. If true here, the
likely theatre is the Middle East during
the First World War of 1914–18, when
the Turks (Byzantium) were expelled by
Arab forces with the inspirational
assistance of TE Lawrence (1888–
1935) as well as that of the British army
commanded by General Allenby which
relieved Damscus in October 1918.

❦ 6/72 – 1916

Par fureur faincte d'esmotion divine,
Sera la femme du grand fort violee
Juges voulans damner telle doctrine,
Victime au peuple ignorant imolee.

Through the feigned fury of divine
    emotion
The wife of the great one will be
    badly wronged
Judges, wishing to condemn such a
    doctrine
The victim will be sacrificed to the
    ignorant people.

This tells the story of Grigori Rasputin
(1872–1916), the 'mad monk' whose
magnetic personality and ability to
alleviate the Tsarevich's haemophilia
endeared him to Empress Alexandra,
Tsar Nicholas II's wife. His power
became so great that in 1916 he was
assassinated by a group of noblemen.
He was first poisoned, then beaten,
then shot, and finally, when all that
failed to kill him, drowned.

❦ 1/3 – 1917

Quand la littière du tourbillon versée
Et seront faces de leurs manteaux
    couverts,
La République par gens nouveaux vexée,
Lors blancs et rouges jugeront à l'envers.

When litter is blown on the wind
And faces hide under cloaks
The Republic will be angered by new
    people
Whites and reds will be deemed
    opposites.

A prediction, perhaps, of the samizdat
pamphleteers of the Russian
Revolution, pursued by the secret
police amidst the conflict between the
Bolsheviks and landed Whites.

❦ 4/41 – 1917

Gymnique sexe captive par hostage
Viendra de nuit custodes decevoir
Le chef du camp deceu par son langage
Lairra à la gente, sera piteux à voir.

A female prisoner will arrive by night
To deceive the guards
The camp leader, deceived by her
    tongue
Hands her to his people; it is pitiful
    to see.

Can Nostradamus have foreseen the
short, eventful life and pitiable death of
Mata Hari, the Dutch dancer arrested
on ludicrous spying charges in Paris in
1917 and shot by firing squad?

❦ 4/32 – 1917

Es lieux et temps chair un poisson donra
    lieu
La loi commune sera faicte au contraire
Vieux tiendra fort plus osté du millieu
Le Pánta chiona philòn mis fort arriere.

When meat gives way to fish
Common law will dictate the
    opposite
The old order will hold, then be
    ousted
The Common Order will fall behind.

Meat giving way to fish equates to the
contemporary phrase about frying pans
and fires. The people of Russia lost
their despotic tsar in 1917, only to have
his regime replaced with an equally
tyrannical communist rule. And as
Nostradamus predicts, this new
Common Order will fail in its time, as it
did in 1990.

🐦 1/68 – 1918

O quel horrible et malheureux tourment,
Trois innocens qu'on viendra à livrer
Poison suspecte, mal garde tradiment,
Mis en horreur par bourreaux enivrez.

Three innocent people will find
  themselves subjected
To a most terrible and wretched
  torture
Poison will be suspected, and
  treason; through lack of care
They will be delivered up, in horror,
  to their drunken executioners.

Russian Tsar Nicholas II (1868–1918),
his wife Aleksandra, his son Alexis, and
his four daughters, Olga, Tatiana, Marie
and Anastasia, were put to death on 16
July 1918 at Yekaterinburg, Siberia. The
three innocent people mentioned in the
quatrain were, arguably, their
physician, Prince Dolgorolkoff, Alexis's
nurse, and the Tsarina's lady-in-waiting,
who were executed at the same time as
their masters – presumably to stop
them from talking. Their executioners
were indeed drunk, on vodka. The
family knew nothing of their impending
murder, for the jailers kept silent,
passing on only the paradoxically true
information that another removal was
imminent.

🐦 4/45 – 1918

Par conflict Roi, regne abandonnera
Le plus grand chef faillira au besoing
Mors profligés peu en rechapera
Tous destranchés un en sera tesmoing.

The king abandons his kingdom
  because of a battle
The greatest leader will fail when
  needed
Death, ruination, few will escape
All killed, save one witness.

The fate of Kaiser Wilhelm II, forced to
abdicate after Germany's defeat in the
First World War. Contrary to the allied
propaganda of the time, the Kaiser was
not a ferocious warmonger, but the
impotent puppet of his generals.

🐦 1/7 – 1918

Tard arrivé, l'execution faite
Le vent contrare, lettres au chemin
  prinses,
Les conjurez quatorze d'une secte,
Par le Rousseau seront les entreprinses.

Arriving late, the execution carried
  out
The wind against them and letters
  lost on the way
The beseeching group of fourteen
The Red ones will be their
  undertakers.

The murder of Tsar Nicholas II of
Russia with his family and household by
Red Guards on the day they arrived at
Yekaterinberg in the Urals on 16 July,
1918. Bolshevik officials in Moscow,
wishing to distance themselves from
the crime, claimed bad weather and
communications had prevented their
intervention in a decision taken without
consultation by local secret police.

❦ 3/17 – 1918

Mont Aventine brusler nuict sera veu
Le ciel obscur tout à un coup en Flandres
Quand le monarque chassera son neveu
Leurs gens à Eglise commettront les
esclandres.

They will see Mount Aventine
burning by night
The sudden obscuring of the heavens
in Flanders
When the monarch chases out his
nephew
Their church people will cause
scandals.

The end of the First World War. Kaiser
Wilhelm II's forces were driven out of
France and the Low Countries by
forces under the titular control of his
blood relation, George V of Great
Britain.

❦ 9/35 – 1918

Et Ferdinand blonde sera descorte,
Quitter la fleur suivre le Macedon.
Au grand besoin faillira sa routte,
Et marchera contre le Myrmidon.

Fair Ferdinand will lose everything
Leaving the flower to follow
Macedonia
In great necessity his course will fail
him
He will march against the
Myrmidons

King Ferdinand of Bulgaria abandoned
his beloved France and sided with
Germany during World War I, in the
mistaken belief that the Kaiser would
help him regain Macedonia. The Kaiser
abandoned him in 1918, leaving him to
face the French and the Serbs
(Myrmidons) alone. Stripped bare by

the treaty of Versailles, he fled Bulgaria
at the end of the war, to be succeeded
by his son, Boris III.

❦ 8/80 – 1919

Des innocens le sang de vessue et vierge.
Tant de maulx faitz par moyen se grand
Roge
Saintz simulacres tremper en ardent
cierge
De frayeur crainte ne verra nul ne boge.

The blood of innocents, widows and
virgins
The great Red One commits many
evils
Holy images burn in ardent flame
Terrified and fearful, no-one will
dare to move.

This describes the Russian Revolution
of 1919, in which the great Red One
was responsible for the destruction of
countless Orthodox churches, and the
murder of many innocents, which, to
Nostradamus's royalist eyes, would
include the Tsar and his family.

❦ 10/99 – 1919

La fin le loup, le lyon, boeuf, et l'asne
Timide dama seront avec mastins
Plus ne cherra à eux la douce manne
Plus vigilance et custode aux mastins.

The end, the wolf, the lion, bull and
donkey
The timid deer will sit among the
mastiffs
No longer will sweet manna fall on
them
The mastiffs will be more cautious
and vigilant.

The wolf is Italy; the lion is England; the
bull is Spain; the donkey is Palestine;

the deer is Germany; the mastiff is another euphemism for England, and, in this context again, Italy. Timid Germany is caught between Italy and England. When did this happen? Possibly in the First World War, when both Italy and England belonged to the allied Central Powers. However Germany, under the Kaiser, seemed far from timid during the conflict. Perhaps this is a reference to the 1919 Treaty of Versailles, concluded after the abdication of the Kaiser, and in which Germany was stripped of nearly all her possessions and power – the same Versailles Treaty which first mooted the League of Nations, drawing in Palestine and Spain.

❦ 8/60 – 1919

Premier en Gaule, premier en Romanie
Par mer et terre aux Anglois et Paris
Merveilleux faitz par celle grand mesnie
Violent terax perdra le Norlaris.

First in France, first in Romania
By land and sea to the English and
    Paris
Marvellous deeds by that great
    alliance
The violent brute will lose Lorraine.

Kaiser Wilhelm II (1859–41) invaded France in 1914, crushing Rumania two years later. His intention was to take Paris and isolate England. The German advance was halted, however, following the loss of millions of French and English lives. Germany lost the province of Lorraine following the Treaty of Versailles in 1919.

❦ 8/28 – 1919–29

Les simulacres d'or et argent enflez,
Qu'apres le rapt au lac furent gettez
Au desouvert estaincts tous et troublez.
Au marbre script prescript intergetez.

The inflated copies in gold and silver
Which, after the rapine, are thrown
    into the burning lake
On their discovery, exhaustion, and
    debt
All scrips and bonds are null and
    void.

This could apply to Germany, at the end of the First World War, when the German mark began its downward spiral, culminating in its reduction to a billionth of its pre-war value against the gold standard, and the issue of worthless million mark notes.

❦ 8/31 – 1922

Premier grand fruit le prince de Perquiere
Mais puis viendra bien et cruel malin
Dedans Venise perdra sa gloire fiere
Et mis à mal par plus joune Celin.

First, the great fruit of the prince of
    Peschiera
Afterwards will come a cruel and
    wicked man
In Venice he will lose his proud glory
He is led into evil by the youngest
    Selin.

The prince of Peschiera is King Victor Emmanuel III of Italy (1869–1947), who brought his country into the First World War against Germany and bravely commanded his army. In 1922, to save Italy from civil war, he offered the premiership to Benito Mussolini and thereby effectively lost control of his realm.

❦ 9/7 – 1923

Qui ouvrira le monument trouvé
Et ne viendra le serrer promptement.
Mal lui viendra et ne pourra prouvé,
Si mieux doit estre roi Breton ou
* Normand.*

The man who opens the tomb, after
  its discovery
And does not shut it straight away
Evil will strike him, no-one can prove
  it
He should rather have been a Breton
  or Norman king.

Howard Carter (1873–1939), a British
archaeologist, and his patron, George
Herbert, 5th Earl of Carnarvon (1866–
1923), discovered the opulent tomb of
Tutankhamen, an eighteenth dynasty
Egyptian Pharaoh, in 1922. Despite
rumours of a curse, they opened the
tomb in 1923. It was untouched, and
contained the magnificent mummy of
the boy-king, together with his
immensely valuable funeral relics.
Carnarvon died two months later, in
Cairo, as the result of an infected
mosquito bite he inadvertently cut,
while shaving. At exactly the same
moment, back in England, his beloved
dog also died.

❦ 9/2 – 1924

Du hault du mont Aventin voix ouie,
Vuidez, vuidez de tous les deux costez,
Du sang des rouges sera l'ire assomie,
D'Arimin Prate, Columna debotez.

A voice is heard from the Aventine
  heights
Leave, leave, all of you, on both sides
Anger will only be appeased with the
  blood of the reds
Colonna is expelled from Rimini and
  Prato.

Roman senators used to retreat to the
Aventine heights when no further
dialogue was possible. In 1924, the
Italian socialist opposition left the
Chamber in protest at the murder, by
fascists, of Deputy Matteoti. Mussolini,
who was born near Rimini and Prato,
and who, like Colonna, had the Vatican
on his side, used their absence to force
through new vote-rigging tactics.

❦ 3/63 – 1925

Romain pouvoir sera du tout abas
Son grand voisin imiter les vestiges
Occultes haines civiles et debats
Retarderont aux bouffons leurs folies.

Roman power will be humbled
In imitation of its great neighbour
Too much talk, too many oblique
  feuds
Will slow the folly of these buffoons.

Surely a reference to Benito Mussolini,
bombastic Italian dictator from 1925–
43, whose alliance with Nazi Germany
cost his country so dearly.

❦ 5/29 – 1925

La Liberté ne sera recouvrée,
L'occupera noir, fier, vilain, inique,
Quand la matière du pont sera ouvrée,
D'Hister, Venise faschée la république.

Liberty will not be recovered
Power will be held by a proud,
  villainous, iniquitous man
When the matter of the bridge is
  opened
By Hister at Venice, angering the
  republic.

Benito Mussolini, dictator of Italy from
1925 to 1943, first met Adolf Hitler in
Venice, and began the dialogue that

was to cost him his country and his life. The matter of the bridge is very likely the agreement between the Pope (pont equates to bridge which equates to pontiff) and Mussolini of 1928. The name Hister is unnervingly close to that of the Führer.

🐝 9/80 – 1925

Le Duc voudra les siens exterminer,
Envoyera les plus forts lieux estranges,
Par tyrannie Bize et Luc ruyner,
Puis les Barbares sans vin feront
   vendanges.

The Duc will want to eliminate his
   own people
He will send the strongest into exile
By tyranny he will ruin Italy
Then the Barbarians will have
   harvests but no wine.

Mussolini comes to power, and immediately gets rid of the comrades (especially the socialist ones) who put him there. Wine is an occasional Nostradamian code for blood.

🐝 9/96 – 1935

Dans cité entrer excercit desniee,
Duc entrera par persuasion,
Aux foibles portes clam armee amenee,
Mettront feu, mort de sang effusion.

The army is denied access to the city
The Duc enters by persuasion
The army is led, in secret, to
   vulnerable gates
They will put the place to fire and
   sword; blood will flow.

Following on from the previous quatrain, 'Duc' may once again be taken for 'Duce', the title Benito Mussolini assumed as fascist head of

the Italian State after 1924. The vulnerable gates would then be those of Makale, the provincial capital of Ethiopia, which fell to the Duce on 8 November 1935.

🐝 4/4 – 1935

L'impotent Prince faché, plaincts et
   querelles
De rapts et pille, par coqz et par Libiques
Grand est par terre par mer infinies
   voilles
Seule Italie sera chassont Celtiques.

The powerless Prince is angry, he
   complains and quarrels
There is rape and pillage, both by the
   cock and the Libyans
The great one stays on land, at sea,
   many sails
Only Italy chases out the Celts.

France continues to be troubled by its rebellious territories in north Africa, and now the independence of the last free state on the continent is challenged as Italian fascists invade Abyssinia (Ethiopia), starting their campaign on 3 October by shelling a hospital clearly displaying the Red Cross flag.

🐝 9/33 – 1935

Hercules Roi de Rome et d'Annemarc
De Gaule trois Guion surnommé
Trembler l'Italie et l'unde de sainct Marc
Premier sur tous monarque renommé.

Hercules becomes king of Rome and
   of Annemarc
A man named De Gaulle is a three
   time leader
Italy, and the waters of Venice will
   tremble
The president will be renowned
   above all monarchs.

Just as annemarc signifies Mark Anthony in another quatrain (4/27), Hercules here applies to Benito Mussolini (1883–1945), who became leader of Rome and Abyssinia (Mark Anthony's land) during the 1920s and 1930s respectively. Remarkably, General Charles de Gaulle (1890–1970), one of his chief opponents, is mentioned here by name. He was, and remains, 'renowned above all monarchs' by a certain body of opinion in France.

❦ 6/45 – 1936

Le gouverneur du regne bien scavant,
Ne consentir voulant au faict Royal
Mellile classe par le contraire vent,
Le remettra à son plus desloyal.

The learned governor of the realm
Not wishing to consent to the royal
    deed
The fleet of Melilla, through a lee
    wind
Will return him to his most disloyal
    subject.

General Francisco Franco (1892–1975) launched his revolt against the elected Spanish Government from Melilla, a Spanish colony near Morocco, on 18 July 1936, just five years after King Alfonso XIII (1886–1941) had abdicated and left the country. Franco was instrumental in restoring the Bourbon monarchy to Spain, when he named Prince Juan Carlos, Alfonso's grandson, as his successor, in 1969.

❦ 3/35 – 1936

Du plus profond de l'Occident d'Europe
De pauvres gens un jeune enfant naistra
Qui par sa langue seduira grande troupe,
Son bruit au regne d'Orient plus croistra.

From the deepest part of Western
    Europe
A baby will be born, to a poor family
He will seduce many by his speeches
His reputation will rise in the
    Eastern kingdom.

Thanks to the last line, this quatrain applies to Adolf Hitler (1889–1945), and not to Napoleon. Born in Austria, in the small village of Braunau am Inn, Hitler was the son of an impoverished customs official. Renowned for the power of his oratory, which held even his opponents spellbound with horror, Hitler signed a pact with Japan (the Eastern Kingdom) in 1936. Japan later allied itself with Hitler against the Allies during the Second World War.

❦ 10/22 – 1936

Pour ne vouloir consentir à divorce,
Qui puis apres sera cogneu indigne,
Le Roi des Isles sera chassé par force
Mis à son lieu que de roi n'aura signe.

For not wishing to approve the
    divorce
And who, incidentally, shall later be
    considered unworthy
The King of the Islands will be
    forced out
A man will replace him who never
    expected to be king.

A very successful quatrain, linked to 10/40 (see page 147), which correctly describes the abdication of Edward VIII of England, on 10 December 1936. In love with divorcée Wallis Simpson, Edward was forced into voluntary exile after their marriage, and was later considered unworthy for his tactless dealings with the Nazis. His diffident brother George succeeded him as George VI (1895–1952), becoming one of England's most popular monarchs and the father of the present Queen.

🐝 10/40 – 1936

Le jeune nay au regne Britannique,
Qu'aura le pere mourant recommandé,
Icelui mort Lonole donra topique,
Et à son fils le regne demandé.

The young man, born to rule
  England
Which his dying father had
  commended to him
Once his father is dead, London will
  cavil
The kingdom is taken back from his
  son.

Following on from 10/22, this is clearly also about Edward, Prince of Wales, later to become Edward VIII of England. The kingdom was taken back from him in 1936, when he abdicated in favour of his brother, the Duke of York, following the scandal surrounding his affair with a divorced woman, Wallis Simpson.

🐝 9/16 – 1936

De castel Franco sortira l'assemblee
L'ambassadeur non plaisant fera scisme
Ceux de Ribiere seront en la meslee
Et au grand goulphre desnier ont l'entrée.

Franco will bring the army from
  Castille
The ambassador will complain,
  causing a schism
Rivera's men will be part of the force
The great man will be denied entry
  to the gulf.

One of the most famous of all Nostradamus's quatrains, mentioning the names of both Francisco Franco (1892–1975) and Primo de Rivera (1870–1930), his fascist precursor. On Rivera's death, his son, José Antonio, created a Falange movement in his father's honour; its members later fought on Franco's side in the Spanish Civil War of 1936–39. In 1936 the Republican government of Spain had exiled Franco to the Canary Islands, denying him entry to the Mediterranean gulf.

🐝 10/47 – 1936

De Bourze ville à la dame Guirlande,
L'on mettra sus par la trahison faicte,
Le grand prelat de leon par Formande,
Faux pellerins et ravisseurs defaicte.

From Burgos to the garlanded lady
People will be downtrodden by
  treason
Through Formande, the grand
  prelate of Leon
Is undone by ravishers and false
  pilgrims.

Francisco Franco established his military junta at Burgos in 1936, and from there began his push towards Madrid (the garlanded lady). Meanwhile Formentara (formande) and Ibiza had been taken by the Republicans, although why Nostradamus takes the trouble to mention Formentara by name is a mystery, as it is nothing but a tiny and windswept island, with few inhabitants.

🐝 5/21 – 1936

Par le trespas du monarque latin
Ceux qu'il aura par regne secouruz
Le feu luira, divisé le butin
La mort publique aux hardis incoruz.

Because of the Latin king's passing
Those whom he assisted during his
  reign
The fire glows, the booty is divided
A public death for the hardy
  usurpers.

Victor Emmanuel II (1869–1947), last effective king of Italy, ceased to wield even constitutional power in the 36th year of his reign, in 1936, when Benito Mussolini stripped him of power, conferring on him the ludicrous title of Emperor of Abyssinia. But the king supported Mussolini loyally, even as Italy was devastated in war, until his usurper's execution.

❦ 3/54 – 1936

L'un des grands fuira aux Espagnes,
Qu'en longue playe après viendra
saigner,
Passant copies par les hautes montaignes,
Devastant tout, et puis en paix regner.

One of the great will rise in Spain
Which will bleed from a long wound
 after
Comrades passing by the high
 mountains
Devastating all, and then to reign in
 peace.

The rise of Francisco Franco (1892–1975). He became Generalissimo of the Spanish army, and head of the Nationalist state, in September 1936.

❦ 3/8 – 1936–39

Les Cimbres joints avecques leurs voisins,
Depopuler viendront presque l'Espaigne
Gens amassez, Guienne et Limosins,
Seront en ligue, et leur feront
compaigne.

The Cimbrians, together with their
 neighbours
Will decimate nearly the whole of
 Spain
The people will gather, Guiennese
 and Limousins
Allying themselves to their company.

The Cimbrians, an ancient North German tribe, here refer to the German and Italian forces who supported Franco's fascist army during the Spanish Civil War. Six hundred thousand Spaniards and their supporters were killed during the conflict, which lasted from 1936–39, many of them congregating in South West France (Guyenne and Limousin) before crossing the border to fight on the side of the Republicans.

❦ 2/82 – 1938

Quand les colomnes de bois grande
tremblée,
D'auster conduicte couverte de rubriche,
Tant vuidera dehors une grande
assemblée,
Trembler Vienne et le pays d'Austriche.

When the great wooden columns
 tremble
Correct behaviour as covered by the
 rubric
Will do so much to drive a great
 assembly outside
Shaking Vienna and the country of
 Austria.

A vision of Anschluss Day in Austria, 14 March 1938. Huge crowds greeted Hitler in the streets of Vienna. Peace treaties – the rubrics – forbad union between Germany and Austria but Hitler, and many supporters in Austria, swept these sanctions aside.

❦ 9/94 – 1938

Foibles galleres seront unies ensemble,
Ennemis faux le plus fort en rampart
Faible assaillies Vratislaue tremble,
Lubecq et Mysne tiendront barbare part.

Weak ships are joined together
False enemies, the strongest holds
    the rampart
The weak are attacked, Bratislava
    trembles
Lubeck and Meissen will take the
    side of the barbarian.

The barbarian is Hitler, drawing
together the weak ships of France and
Great Britain in the Munich Pact of
1938, in which Czechoslovakia is
carved up in appeasement, giving
Germany control of the Sudetenland
and an excuse to annexe the rest of
Czechoslovakia.

❦ 7/20 – 1938

Ambassadeurs de la Toscane langue
Avril et Mai Alpes et mer passer
Celui de veau exposera l'harangue
Vie Gauloise ne venant effacer.

Tuscan-speaking ambassadors
Will cross the sea and the Alps in
    April and May
The man from Vaud will expose their
    harangue
They will not wipe out the French
    way of life.

Benito Mussolini's declaration of 7 May
1938 that the Fascist union of Italy and
Germany would sweep all of Europe
before it. Nostradamus asserts
optimistically that France will resist.

❦ 6/17 – 1938

Apres les limes brusler les asiniers
Contraints seront changer habits divers
Les Saturnins bruslez par les meusniers
Hors la plupart qui ne sera convers.

After the penance, the refuges are
    burned
They will be forced to change into
    other clothing
Those of Saturn burned by the
    millers
Excepting the greater part, who will
    not be converted.

Believed to be a reference to the
persecution of German Jews by Nazis,
culminating in the terrible night of
thuggery, arson and looting of 9
November 1938, known as *Kristallnacht*
after the seas of broken glass to be
found in the streets from buildings
attacked in Jewish quarters of cities
throughout the country.

❦ 6/90 – 1938

L'honissement puant abhominable
Apres le faict sera felicité,
Grand excusé, pour n'estre favourable,
Qu'à paix Neptune ne sera incité.

The abominable, stinking disgrace
Will be lauded after the fact
The great man will be excused for
    not being favourable
Let us hope that Neptune cannot be
    persuaded towards peace.

Neville Chamberlain (1869–1940) was
British Prime Minister at the time of the
Munich Pact of 1938. His instincts were
to appease rather than to confront
Hitler, and he colluded in allowing Hitler
to annexe the Sudetenland region of
Czechoslovakia on the understanding

that Germany would immediately thereafter cease its expansion into Europe. He was welcomed back to Britain as a hero. In retrospect he is seen as a kindly, though misguided man. Nostradamus, in line 4, foresees the dangers of appeasement and sends Great Britain – Neptune – a coded message across nearly four centuries that only Winston Churchill (1874–1965) seemed capable of understanding.

❦   10/48 – 1939

Du plus profond de l'Espaigne enseigne,
Sortant du bout et des fins de l'Europe,
Troubles passant aupres du pont de
*   Laigne,*
Sera deffaicte par bands sa grand troppe.

Banners, from the deepest corners of
    Spain
From both ends of Europe, also
Troubles occur near the Laignes
    bridge
Its great army will be routed by
    guerillas.

Lines 1 and 2 detail the involvement of the Italians and the Germans in the Spanish Civil War of 1936–39. Leganés is a part of Madrid that saw much fighting during the battle to take the capital city, which was a Loyalist stronghold until its fall in 1939.

❦   6/49 – 1939

De la partie de Mammer grand Pontife,
Subjugera les confins du Danube
Chassera les croix par fer raffe ne riffe,
Captifz, or, bagues plus de cent mille
rubes.

The Pope, speaking for Mother
    Church
Will subdue the borders of the
    Danube
By a hooked cross he will cause the
    true cross to be harried
Captives, gold, rings, more than
    100,000 rubies.

An indictment of Pope Pius XII (1876–1958), who refused to condemn or to excommunicate either Hitler or Mussolini, following his election to the Pontificate in 1939. The hooked cross in line 3 is the swastika, under whose symbol the Nazis invaded Poland that same year, harrying the Catholic majority. The last line refers to the millions of Jews who were to lose their lives and worldly possessions partially due to the Pope's intransigence. If he had spoken out earlier, Catholic Italy might have rejected Mussolini at an earlier date.

❦   2/40 – 1939

Un pres apres non point longue
*   intervalle*
Par mer et terre sera faict grand
*   tumulte*
Beaucoup plus grande sera pugne
*   navalle,*
Feux, animaux, qui feront plus d'insulte.

A short while after an even shorter
    interval
A great storm will rise, by land and
    sea
Even fiercer sea battles will be fought
With fire, monstrous armaments, and
    an even greater tumult.

This refers to the Second World War, which followed a scant twenty-one years after the First. Adolf Hitler unleashed his *Blitzkrieg* on land and sea, and the naval battles of the First World War were dwarfed by those of the Second, thanks to a massive increase in fire-power and to the sophistication of modern armaments.

2/38 – 1939

Des condamnez sera fait un grand nombre
Quand les monarques seront conciliez
Mais l'un deux viendra si malencombre
Que guere ensemble ne seront reliez.

A great number will be condemned
When the monarchs are reconciled
But one of them will be so unfortunate
That they won't stay allies for long.

Of the scores of broken treaties in the last 450 years, the non-aggression pact of 24 August 1939, when Adolf Hitler vowed never to attack Russia, has to have been the most unfortunate of all. The pact lasted less than two years, and its breach cost Germany the war, and eastern Europe its liberty for half a century.

7/18 – 1939

Les assiegés couloureront leur paches,
Sept jours apres feront cruelle issue
Dans repoulsé feu, sang. Sept mis à l'hache
Dame captive qu'avoit la paix tissue.

Those besieged will exaggerate their pacts
Seven days later they will attack, cruelly
Driven back with fire, and blood; seven are executed
She who negotiated the peace is captured.

A very tricky quatrain which can, however, be unpicked, line by line. Line 1 refers to the Soviet-German Non-aggression Pact of 1939; line 2 to the fact that Germany invaded Poland seven days later leading to the outbreak of the Second World War. Line 3 indicates the seven countries overrun by Germany during the course of 1939–41, and line 4 refers in particular to France, one of the chief negotiators of the Peace Treaty of Versailles in 1919, the unfairness of which Hitler used as one of his main pretexts for the outbreak of hostilities in 1939.

9/90 – 1939

Un capitaine de la grand Germanie
Se viendra rendre par simulé secours
Un roi des rois aide de Pannonie,
Que sa revolte fera de sang grand cours.

A captain of greater Germany
Will arrive to offer false help
King of kings, support will come from Hungary
His war will cause a great shedding of blood.

Grossen Deutschland, or greater Germany, was Adolf Hitler's name for the Third Reich empire he hoped to create. In 1939 he invaded Poland, claiming that he was offering help to the German speaking minority. King of kings describes Hitler's paradoxical position as ruler of the Kaiser, who had been forced to abdicate in 1919. The 300,000 men from Hungary were sent to support Hitler's invasion of Russia. By the end of the war (which Hitler had triggered, making it 'his' war) a total of fifty million lives had been lost.

❦ 10/11 – 1939

Debouz louchere du dangereux passage
Fera passer le posthume sa bande
Les monts Pyrens passer hors son bagaige
De Perpignam courira duc à tende.

Standing up and squinting in the
  dangerous passage
The soon-to-be-dead man enfilades
  his group
They will cross the Pyrenees without
  baggage
The Duke will hasten from
  Perpignan to Tende.

A difficult quatrain to pin down, but it
could certainly be applied to the final
days of the Spanish Civil War (1936–39)
following Franco's victory at the Battle
of the Ebro, when Juan Negrín and the
remnants of his Nationalist government
fled across the Pyrenees to found a
government in exile in south-western
France.

❦ 5/51 – 1939

La gent de Dace, d'Angleterre et Polonne
Et de Boesme feront nouvelle ligue
Pour passer outre d'Hercules la colonne
Barcins, Tyrrens dresser cruelle brique.

The Dacians, the English, the Poles
And the Czechoslovakians will form a
  new alliance
Hoping to pass beyond the pillars of
  Hercules
The Spanish and the Italians will
  hatch a cruel plot.

This refers to Britain's alliance with the
Balkan states at the outset of World War
Two. The Polish connection provided
the impetus for Britain's entry into the
conflict in September 1939. The Italians
allied themselves with Nazi Germany
while the Spanish remained technically

neutral, although Franco's sympathies
were always with the Axis forces.

❦ 7/32 – 1939–45

Du mont Royal naistra d'une casane,
Qui cave, et compte viendra tyranniser
Dresser copie de la marche Millane,
Favene, Florence d'or et gens espuiser.

Born in poverty, he will take supreme
  power
He will bankrupt the country
Raising an army in the Milanese
  marches
He will drain Faenza and Florence of
  gold and people.

This could be taken to apply to Benito
Mussolini (1883–1945), born to a poor
family, and the man who eventually
bankrupted Italy with his dreams of
Empire. He was directly responsible for
the deaths of hundreds of thousands of
her people.

❦ 3/32 – 1939–45

Le grand sepulchre du peuple
*   Aquitanique,*
S'approchera aupres de la Toscane
Quand Mars sera pres du coing
*   Germanique,*
Et au teroir de la gent Mantuane.

The gaping tomb of the French
  people
Will approach from Tuscany
Once war touches the German
  corner
And the land of the Mantuan people.

This foretells the Second World War.
Nostradamus was adamant that a major
war would one day occur, pitting the
French against the Germans and the
Italians. Tuscany and Mantua stand for
the Italians.

☙ 3/99 – 1939–45

*Aux champs herbeux d'Alein et du
Vaineigne,
Du mont Lebrou proche de la Durance,
Camps de deux parts conflict sera si aigre
Mesopotamie defaillira en la France.*

In the verdant fields of Alleins and
Vernègues
From the Lubéron mountains, near
the Durance river
The fighting in both camps will be so
extreme
That Mesopotamia will fail in
France.

The two villages in line 1 are situated
close to Nostradamus's birthplace, and
all three are not far from the Lubéron
hills. Mesopatamia has often been
taken as referring to France. This
implies that the quatrain could be yet
another reference to the Second World
War.

☙ 10/5 – 1939–45

*Albi et Castres feront nouvelles lique,
Neuf Arriens Lisbons et Portugues,
Carcas, Tholosse consumeront leur brigue
Quand chef neuf monstre de Lauragues.*

Albi and Castres will unite once more
Nine Aryans, Lisbon and the
Portuguese
Carcassone and Toulouse will join
their plot
When a new leader appears from
Lauragues.

The French towns mentioned are all in
south-western France, and the link up
of Aryans, Lisbon and the Portuguese
leads many commentators to assume
that the quatrain refers to the cross-
border activities of the French

Resistance during World War II. Lisbon,
being neutral, was the transit point for
many escaped prisoners of war.

☙ 4/15 – 1939–45

*D'où pensera faire venir famine,
De là viendra le rassasiement
L'oeil de la mer par avare canine
Pour de l'un l'autre donra huile, froment.*

From the place where he thinks to
bring famine
Will come relief
The eye of the sea, like a greedy
dog's
One will give oil, the other, wheat.

This is the second quatrain referring to
Great Britain's isolation and blockade
by Nazi Germany's submarines during
the early stages of the Second World
War. The eye of the sea is the
submarine's periscope, and greedy
dogs refers to the wolf-packs, a name
used more than once about the U boats
which cruised so effectively beneath
the North Atlantic destroying Allied
shipping.

☙ 10/60 – 1939–45

*Je pleure Nisse, Mannego, Pize, Gennes,
Savone, Sienne, Capue, Modene, Malte
Le dessus sang et glaive par estrennes,
Feu, tremblera terre, eau, malheureuse
nolte.*

I weep for Nice, Monaco, Pisa and
Genoa
Savona, Siena, Capua, Modena and
Malta
Above them, blood; a sword for a
new year's gift
Fire, earthquake, flood, miserable
unwillingness.

All of these cities were affected, in one way or another, by the Second World War, with most being occupied by the German army. Beyond that, it's hard to see any connection. The unwillingness of line 4 can be taken for granted.

☙ 3/13 – 1939–45

Par fouldre en l'arche or et argent fondu
De deux captifs l'un l'autre mangera
De la cité le plus grand estendu
Quand submergée la classe nagera.

Gold and silver are melted by
 lightning in the box
One captive eats the other
The leader of the city is racked
When the fleet travels under water.

Submarines are an acknowledged theme in several of the quatrains, placing them no earlier than the twentieth century. The theme of this appears to be the Second World War, when German U-boats did so much to starve Great Britain of desperately needed supplies from across the Atlantic.

☙ 3/33 – 1939–45

En la cité où le loup entrera,
Bien pres de là les ennemis seront
Copie estrange grand pays gastera,
Aux murs et Alpes les amis passeront.

In the city that the wolf enters
Enemies will be close by
An alien force will sack a great
 country
Allies will cross the mountains and
 the borders.

The German wolf enters Paris, going on to occupy and sack a large proportion of mainland France. The Nazis are only

driven out when the Allies join together to push them back across the mountains and borders in order to harry them in their own back yard.

☙ 4/21 – 1940

Le changement sera fort difficile,
Cité, province au change gain fera
Coeur haut, prudent mis, chassé lui
 habile,
Mer, terre, peuple son estat changera.

The change will be a difficult one
Both city and province will gain by it
A great-hearted and prudent man will
 be forced to flee
By a cunning one; sea, land and
 peoples will change.

Vichy's Marshal Pétain was the cunning one who forced great-hearted Charles de Gaulle, of the Free French, to flee to London in 1940, during the early stages of the Second World War.

☙ 7/33 – 1940

Par Fraude regne, forces expolier,
La classe obsesse, passages à l'espie
Deux fainctz amis se viendront rallier,
Esveiller haine de long temps assoupie.

The kingdom will be stripped of its
 power through fraud
The fleet blockaded, spies can still
 get through
Two false friends will rally together
Hatred, for a long time dormant, will
 reawaken.

This refers to the destruction of the French Fleet by the British, on 3 July 1940, at Mers-el-Kebir, near Oran, Algeria. Fearful that the fleet, commanded by Vichy-led Admiral Gensoul, would be commandeered by the Germans for the invasion of Britain, the British blockaded the port and issued an invitation to the French to ally themselves with Britain. When this was refused they opened fire, destroying all but one of the battleships. Britain's action, though technically justified, caused the death of 1,297 French sailors, and reopened old wounds between the French and the British.

🐚 10/83 – 1940

De batailler ne sera donné signe,
Du parc seront contraint de sortir hors,
De Gand lentour sera cogneu l'ensigne,
Qui fera mettre de tous les siens à mors.

No sign of battle will be given
They will be obliged to leave the
  park
Around Ghent, the banner will be
  recognised
Of one who put all his own men to
  death.

A reference to the fall of Belgium in 1940, under the Flag of the Nazi invaders. The Swastika is for ever associated with Adolf Hitler, who was responsible for the death of millions of his fellow countrymen.

🐚 8/64 – 1940

Dedans les isles les enfans transportez,
Les deux de sept seront en desespoir,
Ceux du terrouer en seront supportez
Nom pelle prins des ligues fui l'espoir.

The children are transported in the
  islands
Two out of seven will despair
Farmers will live off the land
The name 'pelle', hope of the allies,
  is adopted.

This is usually taken to apply to the mass evacuation of British children from the main UK target areas in the opening months of World War II. Two out of every seven children had to leave their homes 'in despair'. The Nazi blockade meant that Britain relied on its farms and allotments for food. *Pelle* means spade, a reference to the digging that would be required if the country was to be able to feed itself.

🐚 8/65 – 1940

Le vieux frustré du principal espoir,
Il parviendra au chef de son empire
Vingt mois tiendra le regne à grand
* pouvoir,*
Tiran, cruel en delaissant un pire.

The old man's main hope is
  frustrated
He will lead the Empire, however
For twenty months he will reign
He is a cruel tyrant, making way for a
  worse one.

The old man is Marshal Pétain (1883–1945), 83-year-old leader of the Vichy Government of unoccupied France. Invested with plenary powers on 10 July 1940, he gave up most of his authority to Pierre Laval (1883–1945) in April 1942. Laval went on to collaborate with the Nazi regime. He was executed for treason in 1945.

❦ 4/48 – 1940

Plannure, Ausonne fertille, spacieuse,
Produira tabons si tant de sauterelles:
Clarté solaire deviendra nubileuse,
Ronger tout, grand peste venir d'elles.

The wide, fertile plain of St Emilion
Will produce so many hornets and
   grasshoppers
The sunlight will be clouded
They will devour all, bringing great
   pestilence.

A vision, perhaps, of the massed
aircraft first seen over Europe in the
Second World War. Grasshoppers take
to the air as locusts. Ausonius, in the
first line, was the Roman tribune at St
Emilion in Bordeaux, where a great
wine château is named after him.

❦ 1/20 – 1940

Tours, Orléans, Blois, Angers, Renes and
*   Nantes,*
Cités vexées par soudain changement,
Par langues étranges seront tendues
*   tentes.*
Fleuves, Darts, Rennes, Terre & Mer
*   tremblement.*

Tours, Orléans, Blois, Angers, Renes
   and Nantes
Cities harassed by sudden change
Banners in foreign languages will be
   stretched
Rivers, Darts, Rennes, Land and Sea
   will tremble.

Nostradamus forsees the Nazi insignia
and German-language proclamations
going up as the cities of France submit
to occupation in the Second World War.
The last line seems impenetrable.

❦ 1/61 – 1940

La republique miserable infelice
Sera vastee de nouveau magistrat
Leur grand amus de l'exile malefice,
Fera Sueve ravir leur grand contracts.

The wretched, unhappy republic
Will be devastated by a new
   government
Ill will, accumulated in exile
Will cause the Swiss to break their
   vows.

Unoccupied France was devastated by
the Vichy government of Marshal Pétain
(1856–1951), who took office in 1940
following the German invasion. In the
same year, Charles de Gaulle (1890–
1970) escaped into exile in London,
where he set up an alternative French
National Committee. Switzerland
enacted a Banking Secrecy Law in 1934
to protect the accounts of Jews living
under Nazi rule. This law was arguably
broken, when monies held on behalf of
Jewish families murdered during the
Holocaust were not restored to the
descendants of their rightful owners.
This situation is only now being rectified
by the Swiss government, following
considerable international pressure.

❦ 6/43 – 1940

Long temps sera sans estre habitée,
Ou Signe et Marne autour vient
*   arrouser*
De la Tamise et martiaux tentée,
Decevez les gardes en cuidant repouser.

For a long time no-one will inhabit
The place watered by the Seine and
   the Marne
Attempts by London, and its soldiers
Will deceive the guards into thinking
   them rebuffed.

This could refer to the Fall of Paris on 14 June 1940, when four-fifths of the population fled, abandoning the city to the invading German troops. The final two lines would then refer to the evacuation of Dunkirk, ten days earlier, when Hitler not unreasonably assumed that he had England on the run. On that day 200,000 British and 140,000 French troops abandoned French shores, leaving over 30,000 of their companions dead or captured.

10/98 – 1940

La splendeur claire à pucelle joyeuse
Ne luyra plus, long temps sera sans sel,
Avec marchans, ruffiens, loups oudieuse,
Tous pesle mesle montre universel.

The shining splendor of the joyful
  virgin
Will bring no light this time; for long
  there will be no salt
With marketeers, ruffians, ravening
  wolves
All pell-mell everywhere.

No Joan of Arc to save France from the terrors of occupation this time, as Hitler invades.

5/94 – 1940

Translatera en la grand Germanie,
Brabant et Flandres, Gand, Bruges et
* Bolongue,*
Le treue sainte le grand duc d'Armenie,
Assaillira Vienne et la Cologne.

He will take into the greater
  Germany
Brabant and Flanders, Ghent, Bruges
  and Boulogne
The sacred tryst with the Armenian
  duke
Will lead to the destruction of
  Vienna and Cologne.

Hitler will roll up most of northern Europe into his Reich, but treaties he makes will ultimately lead to the destruction of his own homelands.

1/72 – 1940

Du tout Marseille des habitants changée
Course & pour fritte jusques près de
* Lyon,*
Naron, Tholoze par Bordeaux outragée,
Tuez, captifs, presque d'un million.

All the people of Marseilles are
  unsettled
They are pursued almost to Lyons
Bordeaux insults Narbonne and
  Toulouse
Almost a million are killed or
  captured.

The figure of a million strongly suggests the Second World War. By the time the Germans marched into Paris on 14 June 1940, the French government had removed to Bordeaux (via Tours). Marshal Pétain's Vichy regime, centered in the south, took over from the legitimate government on 16 June and signed the armistice on the 22nd.

1/34 – 1940

L'oiseau de proie volant à la semestre,
Avant conflict faict aux François pareure
L'un bon prendra l'un ambigue sinistre,
La partie foible tiendra par bon augure.

The bird of prey, flying widdershins
  (left-handed)
Appears to the French before the
  battle is met
Some will take it as a good omen,
  others an evil one
The weaker side will view it
  favourably.

Taken by most scholars to apply to the Second World War. The bird of prey is Adolf Hitler (1889–1945), or alternatively his Dornier spy planes, circling over Paris before its fall in 1940. Collaborationist, anti-semitic and fascist elements among the French would have viewed the birds as good omens, heralding the arrival of the German army and the restoration of order. Others, the stronger ones, would have taken a different view.

❦   2/50 – 1940

Quand ceux d'Hainault, de Gand et de Bruxelles,
Verront à Langres le siege devant mis:
Derrier leur flancs seront guerres cruelles
La playe antique fera pis qu'ennemys.

When men of Hainault, Ghent and Brussels
See the siege set before Langres
Behind their flanks will be cruel wars
The old wound made worse than enemies.

Nazi forces continue their rapid progress between Europe's capitulating cities.

❦   10/85 – 1940–3

Le vieil tribun au point de la trehemide.
Sera pressee captif ne deslivrer,
Le veuil non veuil ne mal parlant timide
Par legitime à ses amis livrer.

The old tribune, on the point of weakening
Will be urged not to release the captive
The old, not old, fearful of speaking evil
In order lawfully to free his friends.

Marshal Pétain, leader of Vichy France, conducted lengthy and futile negotiations with the German high command from 1940 to 1943, concerning the release of over a million French prisoners who were being used by the Nazis as slave labour.

❦   7/34 – 1940–44

En grand regret sera la gent Gauloise
Coeur vain, legier croirera temerité
Pain, sel, ne vin, eaue: venin ne cervoise
Plus grand captif, faim, froit, necessité.

The French nation will grieve greatly
Vain-hearted and shallow, they will trust to boldness
Bread, salt, no wine, water; neither ale nor poison
Their leader captured, hunger, cold and want ensues.

This could only apply to the Occupation of France, 1940–44, which was caused by the woeful vanity of the French military leadership. Despite numerous indications to the contrary, France's commanders persisted in their belief that the Maginot Line fortifications would ensure their country's safety from the German Panzers. Following the Allied D-Day landings of 6 June 1944, Marshal Pétain (1856–1951), the French Vichy leader, was taken to Germany, at a time when occupied Paris was suffering considerable privations.

❦   2/85 – 1940–44

Le vieux plain barbe soubs le statut severe,
A Lyon faict dessus l'Aigle Celtique
Le petit grand trop autre persevere,
Bruit d'arme au ciel: mer rouge Ligustique.

Under the stern authority of the old
and bearded one
Lyons is raised above the French
eagle
The great man, small of stature,
persists too long, however
In the sky there is the noise of
weapons: the Ligurian sea turns
red.

Nostradamus is fond of punning, and if
Lyons is taken to mean the English lion,
then the old and bearded one may well
be Marshal Pétain (1856–1951),
president of the collaborationist Vichy
Government of 1940–44. The English
lions are the warplanes, based in
England, that flew over France in order
to liberate her. The great man, small of
stature, is Hitler, who persisted too long
in his megalomaniac ambitions, most
notably by invading Russia. The
Ligurian sea did indeed turn red under
the Allied bombardments of Genoa and
the southern littoral of France.

🐝 1/59 – 1940–5

Les exilez deportez dans les isles,
Au changement d'un plus cruel
monarque
Seront meurtris: et mis deux les scintiles,
Qui de parler ne seront estez parques.

The exiles deported to the islands
By the advent of an even crueller
monarch
Will be murdered; two at a time they
will be burnt
Especially those not sparing in their
speech.

Commentators hesitate before
accepting that this quatrain foretells the
holocaust, most notably on account of a
mistranslation of *et mis deux les
scintiles*. The present translation

rectifies this, throwing a new, more
sinister light on the quatrain. The
concentration camps were certainly
islands, cut off from the comforts and
laws of ordinary humanity. The ovens at
Auschwitz and Dachau are beyond
description. The philosopher Ludwig
Wittgenstein (1889–1951) said, 'Of that
which cannot be spoken, thereof
remain silent.'

🐝 4/68 – 1940

En lieu bien proche non esloigné de
Venus,
Les deux plus grans de l'Asie et
d'Affrique
Du Rhin et Hister qu'on dira sont venus,
Crys, pleurs à Malte et costé ligustique.

In a nearby place, not far from
Venice
The leaders of Africa and Asia
Who are said to have come from
Hister, and the Rhine
Will cause weeping and tears in
Malta, and the Italian coast.

On 27 September 1940, a ten-year
military and economic tripartite pact
was made between Germany, Italy and
Japan, which thereafter became known
as the Axis. Adolf Hitler and Benito
Mussolini met a week later, in the
Brenner Pass, to discuss their future
war plans, which included the blanket
bombing of the island of Malta. The
pact ultimately led to the US Fifth Army
landing at Salerno, on 9 September
1943, which triggered the full scale
invasion of Italy by the allied forces, in
1944.

❦ 4/80 – 1940

Pres du grand fleuve, grand fosse, terre
egeste,
En quinze pars sera l'eau divisee
La cité prinse, feu, sang, cris conflict
mettre
Et la plus part concerne au collisee.

Near the great river there is a vast,
excavated trench
The water will be divided into fifteen
channels
The embattled city will fall, amidst
fire, cries and blood
The coliseum will be much involved.

The Maginot line, which faces the great
river of the Rhine, indirectly led to the
downfall of France, in 1940. Broken in
fifteen places by rivers, the massive
fortifications were said to have been
suggested to the Abbé Torné-
Chavigny, their progenitor, by a
misreading of Nostradamus (easily
done). French war minister André-
Louis-René Maginot (1877–1932)
oversaw their immensely costly
construction. Hitler's armies simply
bypassed them, and came back later.

❦ 5/45 – 1940

Le grand Empire sera tost desolé
Et translaté pres d'arduenne silve
Les deux bastardz par l'aisné decollé,
Et regnera Aenodarb, nez de milve.

The mighty empire will soon be
desolated
And moved near the forest of
Ardennes
Two bastards will be beheaded by
their older brother
Aenobarbus, the hawk-nosed one,
will rule.

As late as 1940 the French high
command refused to believe that the
Nazis could pierce the Forest of
Ardennes with their armour. France was
lost as a direct result of this failure of
judgement. Further battles would be
fought around the Ardennes in 1944/5,
culminating in the Battle of the Bulge.
The two bastards in line 3 refers to the
French generals captured by the
Germans in 1940, following upon which
General de Gaulle (the hawk-nosed
one) and his 4th Armoured Division put
up the only remaining defence against
the crack Nazi Panzer units.

❦ 5/81 – 1940

L'oiseau royal sur la cité solaire,
Sept mois devant fera nocturne augure
Mur d'Orient cherra tonnerre esclaire,
Sept jours aux portes les ennemis à
l'heure.

The royal bird will fly over Paris
Nightly prophecies will occur for
seven months
The Eastern borders will fall, in
thunder and lightning
In seven days the enemy will be at
the gates.

The German eagle (royal bird) flew
regularly over Paris during the phony
war of December 1939 to April 1940,
dropping propaganda leaflets among
which were to be found quatrains by
Nostradamus apparently prophesying
French defeat. Eastern borders refers
to the Maginot line, which effectively fell
in the seven days of the *Blitzkrieg*, 5–11
June 1940, laying open the gates of
Paris to the German invader.

❦ 3/71 – 1940–1

Ceux dans les isles de longtemps assiegez,
Prendront vigeur force contre ennemis
Ceux par dehors mors de faim profligez,
En plus grand faim que jamais seront
mis.

Those besieged for a long time in the
islands
Will fight their enemies with vigour
Those outside will be overcome by
hunger
It will be a worse famine than ever
before.

Britain was effectively blockaded by
Nazi Germany from June 1940 to July
1941, never having more than a six
week reserve of food available to feed
the population at any one time. The
German people, and in particular the
Berliners, suffered an even worse fate
in 1945, in the closing stages of the
war, when they had no food at all. Many
thousands starved, until the victorious
Allies came to their aid.

❦ 5/16 – 1940

A son hault pris la lerme sabee
D'humaine chair par mort en cendres
mettre
A l'isle Pharos par croisars perturbee
Alors qu'à Rodes paroistra dur espectre.

Sabine tears will no longer seem to
count
Dead human flesh is burnt into ashes
Pharos is troubled by crusaders
A terrible apparition appears at
Rhodes.

The Sabine women are the heroines of
a touching Roman story. The Sabine
people of central Italy were among the
last to submit to the power of Rome in
the third century BC. Roman troops
ravished a group of women from the

tribe then found themselves confronted
by a mob of bitterly vengeful men. To
prevent a bloodbath, the women threw
themselves, clutching their babies to
their breasts, between the two snarling
hordes. Peace was made.

Thus Nostradamus uses the analogy
of Sabine tears for pleas for peace or
clemency. But in this quatrain such
pleas are ignored and corpses are
being burned. To many modern
interpreters, this represents the
Holocaust of the 1940s, an episode of
such scale and horror that it seems
impossible Nostradamous should not
have foreseen it.

There is classical allusion, too, in the
last two lines. Pharos and Rhodes are
both sites of wonders of the ancient
world, the lighthouse and the Colossus.
Both the islands were the scenes of
invasions and battles during the
Second World War.

❦ 5/4 – 1940

Le gros mastin de cité deschassé
Sera fasché de l'etrange alliance
Apres aux champs avoir le cerf chassé
Le lous et l'Ours se donront defiance.

The great mastiff is driven from the
city
He will be angry about the foreign
alliance
After having chased the stag from the
field
The wolf and the bear will defy each
other.

The mastiff is Nostradamian code for
England, whose expeditionary force
was expelled from France by the Nazis
in 1940. The stag, the mastiff's prey, is
Germany and the wolf and bear are
respectively Italy and the USSR.
German alliances with the Italians and
Russians did indeed anger Great
Britain.

❦ 2/59 – 1940

Classe Gauloise par appuy de grande
garde
Du grand Neptune, et ses tridens souldars
Rongée Provence pour soustenir grand
bande
Plus Mars Narbon, par javelots et dards.

The French fleet, with the full
support
Of great Neptune and his trident
warriors
Provence is raped to support such an
army
More war in Narbonne, with javelins
and arrows.

Neptune may well refer to Britain,
whose rising sea power Nostradamus
predicted on many occasions. This
seems very likely to predict the
destruction by the Royal Navy of most
of the French fleet in the Mediterranean
on 3 July 1940, to prevent it falling into
the hands of Germany – with whom
France had signed an armistice a
fortnight earlier.

❦ 5/8 – 1940

Sera laissé feu vif, mort caché,
Dedans les globes horrible espouvantable,
De nuict à classe cité en poudre lasché
La cité à feu, l'ennemy favorable.

Living fire will be unleashed, hidden
death
Inside horrible, terrifying globes
By night the city will be ground into
powder
The fire in the city will be favourable
to the enemy.

Nazi Germany began the Blitz over
London in September 1940.
Nostradamus has a good idea of the

appearance and function of bombs,
and foresees night raids, in which the
burning city was itself a navigational
beacon for the waves of bombers.

❦ 3/7 – 1940

Les fugitifs, feu du ciel sus les piques.
Conflict prochain des corbeaux s'esbatans,
De terre on crie aide secours celiques,
Quand pres des murs seront les
combatans.

Fire from heaven above will sting the
fugitives
The next conflict will be that of
bickering ravens
On earth they beg heaven for
assistance
When the fighters near the walls.

This describes the fall of France in
1940, when hundreds of thousands of
refugees took to the roads only to be
harried back to Paris by the advancing
German forces. Stuka dive-bombers
strafed the innocent civilians, causing
untold casualties. A few days later, on
14 June, the Nazis entered the city in
triumph.

❦ 9/51 – 1940–44

Contre les rouges sectes se banderont,
Feu, eau, fer, corde par paix se minera,
Au point mourir, ceux qui machineront,
Fors un que monde surtout ruinera.

Sects unite against the reds
Fire, water, steel, the peace treaty
will weaken
The plotters are near death
Save one, who will ruin the world.

Each line must be taken separately
here, as Nostradamus is sketching in a
detailed political picture of the Second

World War and of Germany's part in it. Line 1 refers to the Nazi invasion of Russia on 22 June 1940, and line 2 to the breakdown of the non-aggression treaty between the two countries. Line 3 refers to the Von Stauffenberg bomb plot against Hitler's life on 20 July 1944, and line 4 to Hitler's near-miraculous survival and his subsequent descent into paranoia which, if German scientists had managed to complete the atomic bomb in time, might very well have led to the ruin of the world.

❦ 1/37 – 1941

Un peu devant que le soleil s'excuse,
Conflict donné grand peuple dubiteux
Profliges, port marin ne faict response,
Pont et sepulchre en deux estranges lieux.

Shortly before sunset
Battle is engaged; a great people
    doubt the outcome
Brought low, the sea port no longer
    answers
Bridge and tomb are in two different
    places.

A little before sunset, Greenwich mean time, on 7 December 1941 – or early morning, local Pacific time – Pearl Harbour was bombed by the Japanese. Submarines and carrier aircraft pounded the sea port, destroying 200 US planes and damaging or sinking eight battleships. Three thousand men were either killed or injured. The United States immediately declared war on Japan. For four more years, until the Hiroshima atom bomb of 6 August 1945, the American people doubted the outcome of the war. The final sentence, in which bridge and tomb are in two different places, can now only mean one thing – the destroyed ship's bridges jut out above the water, while the men who sailed the ships lie beneath them.

❦ 2/54 – 1941

Par gent estrange, et Romains lointaine
Leur grand cité apres eaue fort troublée
Fille sans trop different domaine
Prins chef, ferreure n'avoir este riblée.

Because of a foreign people, and far
    off Romans
Their great city will be damaged by
    water
A girl from nearby
Is taken by the leader, her bonds still
    in place.

This has been interpreted by several scholars as a presage of Japan's attack on the American naval base at Pearl Harbour on 7 December 1941. The far-off Romans is Nostradamian for a distant imperial power. The captive girl is less easily delineated.

❦ 5/11 – 1941

Mer par solaires seure ne passera
Ceux de Venus tiendront toute l'Affrique
Leur regne plus Saturne n'occupera
Et changera la part Asiatique.

The sun people will not cross the
    seas in safety
The Venusians will occupy the whole
    of Africa
Saturn will no longer hold their
    kingdom
The Asiatic portion will change.

An extraterrestrial assault on the dark continent? Not so. Venus is a Nostradamian rendering of Venice, signifying Italy, and the occupation of Africa is that of the Second World War, which ended in 1943 as the Allies drove the Italian-German axis out. The Asian element of the sun people is, of course, Japan, whose assault on the US Navy did not leave them safe enough to cross the seas (the strategically vital aircraft carriers were at sea when Pearl Harbour was struck on 7 December 1941). Japan, for centuries the dominant military power in the Far East, ceased to be so after the Second World War.

❦ 4/52 – 1942

En cité obsesse aux murs hommes et
femmes,
Ennemis hors le chef prest à soi rendre
Vent sera fort encontre les gendarmes,
Chassez seront par chaux, poussiere, et
cendre.

Both men and women man the walls
of the besieged city
The enemy, though not their leader,
are prepared to surrender
A strong wind will delay the
constables
They will be driven off by lime, dust
and cinders.

This relates to the 160 day siege of Stalingrad, begun on 20 August 1942, in which both Russian men and women manned the desperate defensive lines against Adolf Hitler's army. The Germans only raised the siege after losing 300,000 of their men. The combined Russian losses totalled nearly a million.

❦ 3/100 – 1942

Entre Gaulois le dernier honnoré,
D'homme ennemi sera victorieux
Force et terroir en mouvement exploré
D'un coup de traict quand mourra
l'envieux.

Among the French the last to be
honoured
Will be victorious over his enemy
Lands and strength will be actively
explored
The envious one will die from a shot.

This applies to General de Gaulle, the last to be honoured, and to his Vichy opponent, Admiral Darlan, who was assassinated on 24 December 1942. Darlan was, however, instrumental in persuading the French North and Western African territories to go over to the Allies, after 1942.

❦ 10/32 – 1942–45

Le grand empire chacun an devoir estre
Un sur les autres le viendra obtenir
Mais peu de temps sera son regne et estre
Deux ans aux naves se pourra soustenir.

The great empire will continue, year
by year
One man will take it from the others
His life and reign will both be short
He will last for two years in the
boats.

Adolf Hitler was riding high in 1942, but a year later his would-be empire was in tatters. It was only due to his U-boats that he was able to eke out the final two terrible years of the Second World War.

❦ 6/31 – 1943

Roy trouvera ce qu'il désiroit tant,
Quand le Prelat sera repris à tort,
Response au Duc le rendra mal content,
Qui dans Milan mettra plusieurs à mort.

The King will find what he has
    desired so much
When the Prelate is wrongfully
    seized
The Duke's response will make him
    unhappy
Who in Milan will put several to
    death.

The Duke is Il Duce, Mussolini. When
he was arrested by his German ally in
1943, Italy's king, Victor Emmanuel III,
had what he wanted – an end to the
fascist regime and the opportunity to
change sides in the war.

❦ 3/86 – 1943

Un chef d'Ausonne aux Espaignes ira,
Par mer fera arrest dedans Marseille
Avant sa mort un long temps languira
Apres sa mort on verra grand merveille.

An Italian leader will visit the
    Spanish
By sea; he will stop at Marseilles
He will languish a long time before
    dying
After his death great marvels will be
    seen.

Could this be about Benito Mussolini
(1883–1945), who sent troops, by sea,
to support the fascists, under General
Franco, during the Spanish Civil War?
Mussolini was effectively side-lined in
1943, when he was sacked by Victor
Emmanuel III, after which he
languished in Northern Italy, leading a
puppet fascist government until his
death in 1945. The great marvels in line

4 could refer either to the defeat of the
Axis powers or to the eventual
unification of Europe.

❦ 6/68 – 1943

Lorsque soldats furent seditieuse,
Contre leur chef feront de nuict fer luire,
Ennemy d'Albe soit par main furieuse,
Lors vexer Rome, et principaux seduire.

As soldiers become mutinous
Against their chief they shine in the
    night
Albion's enemy will struggle
    furiously
Then Rome will stir, seduced from
    its principles.

Possibly concerning Pietro Badoglio,
Italy's Commander-in-Chief in the
Second World War, who signed the
treaty with the Allies (Albion) in 1943
after Mussolini's arrest by Hitler. There
was much changing of sides.

❦ 2/16 – 1943

Naples, Palerme, Sicille, Syracuses
Nouveau tyrans, fulgures feux celestes
Force de Londres, Gand, Bruxelles, et
    Suses
Grand hecatombe, triomphe faire festes.

Naples, Palermo, Sicily and Syracuse
New tyrants, exploding fire in the sky
An army from London, Ghent,
    Brussels and Susa
A great slaughter, triumph is fêted.

The Allied landings on Sicily and the
Italian mainland, August 1943. Italy had
a new tyrant in the shape of Germany
after the fall of Mussolini a month
earlier. British and allied troops were
wildly fêted as they entered cities such
as Palermo and Naples.

❦ 7/6 – 1943

Naples, Palerme, et toute la Secille
Par main barbare sera inhabitee
Corsicque, Salerne et de Sardeigne l'isle
Faim, peste, guerre fin de maux
*   intemptee.*

Naples, Palermo and all Sicily
Will be forcibly depopulated by
    foreigners
Corsica, Salerno and the isle of
    Sardinia
Hunger, plague, hardly the end of
    lengthy evils.

The Allied invasion of Italy in 1943. Italy surrendered on 8 September, but found itself now opposed by rather than allied with, the forces of Nazi Germany.

❦ 10/1 – 1943

A l'ennemy l'ennemy foi promise
Ne se tiendre les captifs retenus
Prins preme mort et le rest en chemise,
Damné le reste pour estre soustenus.

The enemy make a promise to their
    enemy
It isn't kept, the captives aren't
    released
One is captured, near death, the rest
    in their shirts
The rest are damned for sustaining
    them.

The Vichy Regime in France beautifully fits the image of an enemy making a promise to an enemy. The promise, of course, wasn't kept, and Vichy leader Marshal Pétain (1856–1951) found himself facing trial for treason after the war. Near death refers to the sentence of death passed on him by the court, which was then commuted to life imprisonment. The captives may refer to the thousands of Jews who were rounded up by the notorious Vichy Milice and delivered willingly to the Germans. The Milice were fascists, or black shirts, and many people were later damned for collaborating with them.

❦ 2/77 – 1944

Par arcs feux poix et par feux repoussés,
Cris hurlements sur la minuit ouis
Dedans sont mis par les remparts cassez
Par cunicules les traditeurs fuis.

By bow-shot and fiery pitch they'll be
    repulsed
Screams and cries at witching hour
They break through the smashed
    ramparts
Only to see the traitors escape
    through secret passages.

This is so generalised a quatrain that it could apply to more than thirty engagements in the Second World War alone, among them Montecassino and Les Arcs. The monastery of Montecassino, bombed flat on 15 February 1944, would appear to be the most obvious contender. General Frido von Senger und Etterlin's troops held out heroically until May, when Polish forces finally overwhelmed the honeycomb of tunnels and secret passages the German troops had been using for protection. Some were known to have escaped.

9/53 – 1944

Le Neron jeune dans les trois cheminées
Fera de paiges vifs pour ardoir getter,
Heureux qui loing sera de telz menees,
Trois de son sang le feront mort guetter.

The new Nero, in the three chimneys
Will burn, in his ardour, only living
pages
Happy the one far from such goings-
on
Three of the same blood will try to
kill him, by trickery.

The three chimneys have been seen as
a sinister reference to the chimneys of
Auschwitz, in which the new Nero,
Adolf Hitler, sought to destroy the
Jewish race in Nazi-occupied Europe.
Three of Hitler's own people plotted to
kill him by placing a bomb, in a
briefcase, near his chair. The plot
narrowly failed, and its perpetrators
were tortured and executed.

4/23 – 1944

La legion dans la marine classe,
Calcine, Magnes soulphre, et paix
bruslera
Le long repos de l'asseuree place,
Port Selyn, Hercle feu les consumera.

An army will sail with the fleet
Burning with lime, magnesium,
sulphur and pitch
A long rest in a safe place
Genoa and Monaco will be consumed
by fire.

This is a description of Greek Fire, used
by the Greeks and Byzantines in times
past to cripple and destroy enemy
fleets. The port of Genoa was severely
bombed in mid-July 1944, and
Nostradamus could be using the image

of Greek Fire to suggest the
incendiaries that rained down on the
harbour facilities. The reference to
Monaco is harder to pin down.

3/9 – 1944

Bordeaux, Rouan, et la Rochelle joints,
Tiendront autour la grand mer Occeane,
Anglois, Bretons, et les Flamans
conjoints,
Les chafferont jusque au pres de Rouane.

Bordeaux, Rouen and La Rochelle
will join
Holding everything near the Oceanic
sea
The English, Bretons and Flemish
will unite
Driving them as far as Roanne.

This probably refers to the Allied
landings in 1944, and to the eventual
driving out of the German Axis forces
from French territory.

1/29 – 1944

Quand le poisson, terrestre and aquatic,
Par forte vague au gravier sera mis,
Sa forme étrange suave et horrifique
Par mer aux murs bier tort enemies.

When the amphibious fish
Is put on shore by the strong wave
In its strange, beguiling, horrid form
Enemies twist by the sea walls.

The D-Day landings of 6 June, 1944.

❦ 3/6 – 1944

Dans le temple clos le foudre y entrera,
Les citadins dedans leur fort grevez
Chevaux, boeufs hommes, l'onde mur
*   touchera,*
Par faim, soif, soubs les plus faibles
*   armez.*

Lightning will enter the closed
    temple
Harming the citizens in their
    stronghold
Horses, livestock, men, the force will
    strike the walls
Even the weakest will arm themselves
    through hunger and thirst.

On 10 June 1944, only four days after
the successful Allied invasion of
Normandy, the inhabitants of Oradour
sur Glane, a small village near Limoges
in South Western France, were rounded
up by a company of SS soldiers and
murdered. The 192 men were
separated from their wives and
children, tortured for information, then
shot. The remaining 450 women and
children were herded into the church,
which was then set on fire. Anyone who
tried to escape was machine-gunned.
Grenades were tossed through the
church windows. Four men escaped
the massacre in the barns, and one
woman escaped from the church.
Altogether 642 people died. Oradour
has been left exactly as it was found on
the day the massacre was discovered.

❦ 2/61 – 1944

Euge, Tamins, Gironde et la Rochele,
O sang Troyen Mort ay port de la flesche
Derrier le fleuve au fort mise l'eschele,
Pointes feu grand meurtre sur la bresche.

Well done men of the Thames, of
    the Gironde and La Rochelle
O French blood of Troy, killed at the
    harbour by an arrow
Behind the river a ladder is placed
    against the fort
Gunfire, and terrible slaughter in the
    breach.

The Spring 1944 Allied 'D' Day victory
in Normandy brought the Second World
War significantly closer to its inevitable
end. The arrow may refer to Hitler's V-1
and V-2 rockets, which fell in profusion
on Cherbourg and other French ports
following the landings.

❦ 2/56 – 1944

Que peste et glaive n'a sceu definer
Mort dans le puis sommet du ciel frappé
L'abbé mourra quand verra ruiner
Ceux du naufrage l'esceuil voulant
*   grapper.*

Having survived both plague and
    sword
He dies in the mountains, struck
    from the sky
The priest will die when he sees the
    ruin
Of the lost ones, as they try to climb
    the ladders.

Nostradamus knew Italy well, and will
certainly have visited Monte Cassino,
midway between Naples and Rome,
where a monastery was first
established by St Benedict in the sixth
century. The beautiful buildings
Nostradamus knew were those of the
third monastery on the site, erected
around 950 after the earlier one was
destroyed by Saracens in 885. In 1866,
the place narrowly escaped dissolution,
but was saved by a vigorous campaign
organised by British expatriates in Italy.

Monte Cassino became a national monument, and a boys' school was established there. But no intervention could save this beautiful place from the ravages of the Second World War. The monastery was relentlessly shelled and bombed by the Allies in their advance on Rome. It was believed that the monastery had been turned into a stronghold by retreating Germans, but the garrison's strength in no way merited the destruction wrought upon it. Monte Cassino was occupied by British and Polish troops on 18 May 1944.

☙ 8/47 – 1944

Lac Trasmenien portera tesmoignage
Des conjurez serez dedans Perouse
Un despolle contrefera le sage
Truant Tedesque de sterne et minuse.

Lake Trasimene will bear witness
That the conspirators are locked
    inside Perugia
A fool will imitate the sage
Killing, overthrowing and cutting to
    pieces the Teuton.

Collaborators are imprisoned as the Nazis are driven from Italy.

☙ 3/79 – 1944

L'ordre fatal sempiternal par chaisne,
Viendra tourner par ordre consequent
Du port Phocen sera rompu la chaisne,
La cite prinse, l'ennemi quant et quant.

The fated and chained eternal order
Will veer, by consequence of an
    ensuing order
The chains guarding Marseilles will
    be broken
And the city will be taken, as will the
    enemy.

The port of Marseilles was held by the Germans until August 1944, when General De Lattre's Free French division fought an eight day running battle through the streets to liberate it. The enemy was indeed 'taken', when Major General Shaefer finally surrendered, together with the 7000 exhausted survivors of his garrison.

☙ 2/1 – 1944

Vers Acquitaine par insuls Britanniques
De pars eux mesmes grands incursions
Pluies gelées feront terroirs uniques
Port Selin fortes fera invasions.

The British assault Aquitaine
Making great inroads
Rain and frost torture the ground
They will even invade the mighty
    crescent port.

The Hundred Years War, in which France battled for nearly a century to expel English occupiers from Aquitaine, ended on 17 July 1453, exactly a century before Nostradamus wrote these words, predicting the next occasion on which British and Allied troops would enter Bordeaux, liberating the region from four wintry years of Nazi occupation in August 1944.

❦ 6/99 – 1944

L'ennemi docte se tournera confus,
Grand camp malade, et de faict par
*   embusches,*
Monts Pyrenees et Poenus lui seront
*   faicts refus*
Proche du fleuve decouvrant antiques
*   cruches.*

The erudite enemy will turn in
   confusion
The great army sickens, defeated by
   ambush
The hills of the Pyrenees and the
   Pennines will be refused to him
Ancient urns will be discovered near
   the river.

A convoluted word-game with many
possible meanings. Adolf Hitler would
probably not be considered erudite by
most people, but General Field Marshal
Gerd Von Rundstedt (1875–1953),
Hitler's Supreme commander, certainly
was. He was relieved of his command
after his perceived failure in allowing
the Allies to land on D-Day, thus
depriving him of eventual victory in
England (the Pennines), and
unoccupied France (the Pyrenees).

❦ 4/61 – 1944

Le vieux mocqué et privé de sa place,
Par l'estrangier qui le subornera
Mains de son filz mangées devant sa face,
Le frere à Chartres, Orl. Rouan trahyra.

The old man, mocked, and deprived
   of his place
By the foreigner who bribes him
Will see the power of his son
   humbled before him
He will betray his brother at
   Chartres, at Orléans, and at
   Rouen.

Marshal Henri Philippe Pétain (1856–
1951), Chief of the Vichy Government of
unoccupied France, was known as *le
vieux*. This quatrain details his
humbling and gradual loss of power,
culminating in his deportation to
Sigmariggen on the very day that
Chartres, Orléans and Rouen were
liberated, on 19 August 1944.

❦ 1/22 – 1944

Ce qui vivra and n'aura aucen sens,
Viendra le fer à mort son artifice,
Autun, Chalons, Langres, les deux Sens,
La guerre et la glasse fera grand malefice.

He who lives on will lack direction
His invention will be the weapon of
   death
Autun, Chalons, Langres will go both
   ways
War and the death knell will do great
   harm.

Adolf Hitler survived an assassination
attempt in 1944 at the time he was
unleashing the first flying bombs
against Britain in a desperate,
directionless bid to reverse the fortunes
of the war. These terrible weapons were
the precursors of the intercontinental
ballistic missiles of the modern era.

❦ 9/69 – 1944

Sur le mont de Bailly et la Bresle
Seront caichez de Grenoble les fiers
Oultre Lyon, Vien. eulx si grande gresle
Langoult en terre n'en restera un tiers.

On the mountains of Bayons and La
   Bréole
The brave men of Grenoble will hide
There will be a terrible hailstorm
   beyond Lyons and Vienne
The locust will leave only a third of
   the land.

The two villages mentioned in line 1 are in the Provençal Alps, a scant fifty-five miles from Grenoble. They have never been correctly identified before. Fierce battles were fought in the triangular piece of country delineated by the three locations during the summer of 1944. The hailstorm in line 3 probably refers to the bombarding of the German columns by the US near the notorious Montélimar Gap, down river from Lyons and Vienne.

9/70 – 1944

Harnois trenchant dans les flambeaux cachez
Dedans Lyon le jour du Sacremont
Ceux de Vienne seront trestous hachez
Par les cantons Latins Mascon ne ment.

Sharp armour is hidden in the torches
In Lyons, on the day of the sacrament
Those from Vienne will be cut to pieces
By the Latin cantons; Macon does not lie.

This could be a continuation of 9/69, describing the German retreat through Vienne and Lyons in 1944. The image in line 1 is particularly striking, and would appear to describe the flame-throwing tanks of the Allied and Nazi armoured divisions. A possible misprint in line 4 would give us cannons instead of cantons.

10/69 – 1944

Le fait luisant de neuf vieux eslué
Seront si grand par midi aquilon,
De sa seur propre grande alles levé.
Guyant meurdri au buisson d'ambellon.

The shining deed of the newly-elected elder
They will be exalted in both South and North
Great crowds are raised by his own sister
Fleeing, he is murdered in the bushes of Ambellon.

The first two lines refer to Marshal Pétain, who was initially lauded for his role in the post-invasion Vichy Government of 1940. Disillusion soon set in, leading to considerable resistance activity on behalf of Marianne, symbol of Republican France. Ambel is a small village close to the Vercors Plateau, near Grenoble, which was the scene, in 1944, of a bloody guerila battle between 20,000 crack SS troops and 950 *maquisards*. Seven hundred and fifty of the maquisards were killed during the battle, which lasted from 9 June to 24 July. Fifty badly wounded men, left hiding in the bushes, were systematically beaten to death by the SS.

1/100 – 1945

Longtemps au ciel sera veu gris oiseau,
Aupres de Dole et de Touscane terre
Tenant au bec un verdoyant rameau,
Mourra tost grand et finera la guerre.

For some time a grey bird will be seen
In the skies above Dôle and Tuscany
In its beak will be a flowering branch
But the chief will soon die and the war will end.

The grey bird is a traditionally grey-painted Nazi warplane, seen constantly over Italy following the fall of Mussolini. Dorniers, in particular, had cannons in their nose sections, vividly illustrated by

Nostradamus's image of a grey bird with a flowering branch in its beak. Hitler, of course, committed suicide in 1945, directly leading to the cessation of hostilities by the Germans.

❦ 4/40 – 1945

Les fortresses des assiegés serrés
Par poudre à feu profondés en abisme
Les prodireurs seront tous vifs serrés
Onc aux sacristes n'advint si piteux
scisme.

The besieged fortresses will be closed off
They will plumb the depths because of gunpowder
The traitors will be buried alive
Never has such a piteous division beset the Saxons.

This is widely interpreted to predict the fate of Adolf Hitler on 30 April 1945 in his bunker under Berlin.

❦ 7/21 – 1945

Par pestilente inimitié Volsicque
Dissimulee chassera le tyran
Au pont de Sorgues se fera la traffique
De mettre à mort lui et son adherent.

By the plague-ridden enmity of Languedoc
The pretender will chase out the tyran
The bargain will be struck by the bridge of Sorgues
He and his accomplice will be put to death.

Pierre Laval, traitorous prime minister of Vichy France from 1942–44, openly collaborated with the Nazis. He was executed, with a number of other collaborators, in 1945.

❦ 3/72 – 1945

Le bon vieillard tout vif enseveli,
Pres du grand fleuve par fausse souspeçon
Le nouveau vieux de richesse ennobli,
Prins a chemin tout l'or de la rançon.

The good old man will be buried alive
Falsely suspected, near the great river
The new old man will rise, through riches
Having taken all the ransom gold.

An intriguing interpretation is the defeat of Winston Churchill (1874–1965) in the landslide victory by the Labour Party in Britain's General Election of 1945. Thus was this very good old man (he was then 72) buried alive. But he and his Conservative Party came back in the following election. It is said that the British people naively believed that even if they did not elect the Conservatives after the war, Churchill would still remain Prime Minister. When re-elected, he set about restoring Britain's shattered economy and did so with remarkable success.

❦ 9/95 – 1945

Le nouveau faict conduira l'exercite,
Proche apamé jusques au pres de rivage,
Tendant secour de Milannoile eslite,
Duc yeux privé à Milan fer de cage.

A new general will command the army
Soon to be cut off near the river bank
Help will be offered by the Milanese élite
The Duc will be sightless in Milan; an iron cage.

The first two lines detail the final days of the Third Reich, when Hitler was replacing his generals with astonishing regularity. The Milanese turned violently against Mussolini in 1945, culminating in his murder by communist partisans. The sightless dead bodies of the Duce, Mussolini, and his mistress, Clara Petacci, were later strung upside down on the iron cage of a burnt-out petrol station, and abused by the crowd.

In 1945, the Italians were driven back across the Po and the Ticino rivers by the Allies during their attack on the Fascist Republic at Salò. Benito Mussolini, their leader, and his mistress, Clara Petacci, later had their bodies paraded and abused before an angry crowd in Milan.

8/91 – 1945

Frymy les champs des Rodans entrée
Ou les croisez seront presque unis,
Les deux brassieres en Pisces rencontrees
Et un grand nombre par deluge punis.

Entering the Rhodians fields
Where the people of the cross are
  nearly united
The two cords are joined in Pisces
A great number are punished in the
  flood.

This refers to the island of Rhodes, which belonged to the Turks between 1523 and 1912. It became Greek in 1945, falling, once again within the Orthodox fold, having been a Christian colony pre–1523. The flood may refer to the woeful influx of tourists which this beautiful island has since suffered.

2/26 – 1945

Pour la faveur que la cité fera,
Au grand qui tost prendra camp de
  bataille,
Puis le rang Pau Thesin versera
De sang, feux mors noyés de coup de taille.

Because of the favour shown by the
  city
To the great man, soon to fail on the
  battlefield
The rank and file will flee,
  overflowing the Po and the Tessin
Much blood and fire, the fallen
  drowned and cut by sabres.

4/56 – 1945

Apres victoire de babieuse langue
L'esprit tempte en tranquil et repos
Victeur sanguin par conflict faict
  harangue,
Roustir la langue et la chair et les os.

Following the raving tongue's victory
The spirit moderates itself, resting in
  tranquillity
Throughout the battle the bloody
  victor harangues his enemy
The tongue, the flesh and the bones
  are roasted.

This must apply to Adolf Hitler, whom Nostradamus mentions on many occasions, calling him the great speechmaker, and the 'seducer of the many by his speeches'. After Hitler's suicide, age 56, in the Berlin bunker, on 30 April 1945, his body was burnt, to prevent desecration by the Russians.

10/64 – 1945

Pleure Milan, pleure Luques, Florance,
Que ton grand Duc sur le char montera,
Changer le siege pres de Venise s'advance,
Lors que Colomne à Rome changera.

Weep, Milan, Lucca and Florence
As your great Duc climbs aboard his
  vehicle
The seat of government moves near
  Venice
The Colonnas will change in Rome.

Milan, Lucca and Florence were all fought over during World War II, directly as a result of Benito Mussolini's actions. When the Duce climbed aboard the truck that he thought would carry him to liberty over the Swiss border in April 1945, he little knew that he and his mistress, Clara Petacci, would be dead within a few hours. The fall of his government had been announced, seven months before, at the Piazza Colonna in Rome.

❦ 3/81 – 1945

Le grand crier sans honte audacieux,
Sera esleu gouverneur de l'armee
La hardiesse de son contentieux,
Le pont rompu cité de peur pasmee.

The great speechmaker, bold, and
   without shame
Will be elected chief of the army
The strength of his contentions
Will cause the bridge to break, and
   the city to quake with fear.

In 3/35 (see page 146), Nostradamus described Adolf Hitler (1889–1945) as seducing many by his speeches. Here he is talking about Hitler again, this time as the great speechmaker. Hitler was elected chief of the army (Chancellor) in 1933, by popular vote. Once in office, he set about consolidating his totalitarian power and convincing the German people that they were the master race and entitled to whatever they could get (the strength of his contentions). The bridge in line 4 refers to the bridge over the Elbe, upon which Russian, US and British soldiers met on 25 April 1945, to celebrate their combined victory over Nazi forces. Realising that all was now lost, Hitler committed suicide in his bunker only 5 days later.

❦ 3/82 – 1945

Friens, Antibor, villes autour de Nice,
Seront vastees fort par mer et par terre
Les saturelles terre et mer vent propice,
Prins, morts, troussez, pillés, sans loi de
   guerre.

Fréjus, Antibes, and the towns
   around Nice
Will be badly damaged, by land and
   sea
The winds of land and sea being
   propitious, the locusts
Plunder, kill, rape and take captives,
   outside the laws of war.

This possibly refers to the landing of the US Seventh Army near Fréjus, in August 1944. The image of locusts accurately portrays the sight of parachutists floating down onto land and sea. However the final line is problematical, as these American locusts had not come to abuse France, but to liberate it. The verse may simply describe the end of the war.

❦ 2/24 – 1945

Bestes farouches de faim fleuves tranner,
Plus part du champ encontre Hister sera.
En caige de fer le grand fera treisner,
Quand rien enfant de Germain
   observera.

Beasts, insane with hunger, will cross
   the river
Most of the field will be against
   Hister
The great leader will be paraded in a
   cage of iron
While the German child sees
   nothing.

This is one of the most famous of all Nostradamus's quatrains, linking, as it does, the words Hister (Hitler), and German. A further twist is that the Latin name for the Danube, near which Hitler grew up in Linz, Austria, is Ister. Goebbels (1897–1945), Hitler's propaganda minister, had the Nostradamus quatrains brought to his attention by his wife, and made full use of them. He little knew that Hitler's ally, Benito Mussolini (1883–1945) would have his body paraded in an iron cage – the charred frame of a fire-bombed petrol station – and that the world would pass judgement on German children for the very fact that they did, indeed, see nothing. Beasts, in line one, refers to the Russian army, who crossed the Elbe, raping up to 50,000 German women in revenge for the siege of Stalingrad in which only 1515 people were left alive out of the original population of 500,000; the rest were either starved or killed, many having recourse to cannibalism.

❧ 1/31 – 1945

Tant d'ans les guerres en Gaule dureront
Outre la course du Castalon monarque
Victoire incerte trois grands couronneront,
Aigle, coq, lune, lion, soleil en marque.

The wars in France will last so many years
Beyond the reign of the Castulon kings
A shaky victory will lead to the crowning of three great ones
The eagle, the cock, the moon, the lion, and the sun at its zenith.

The Castulon kings are the Spanish. They ceased to reign when the Spanish Republic was formed in 1923. The Second World War lasted, as far as the French were concerned, for seven long years. The war was crowned with victory, in particular for the American eagle, the French cock and the British lion. The image of the sun at its zenith could indicate that Japan (the land of the rising sun) had briefly touched its peak, or, alternatively, refer to the capitulation of the Japanese on 12 August 1945, during the sign of Leo.

❧ 1/47 – 1945

Du Lac Lemans les sermons fasceront,
Des jours seront reduit par des sepmains,
Puis mois, puis an, puis tous dafaliront,
Les Magistrats damneront leurs loix vaines.

Lake Leman's sermons will cause anger
Days will turn into weeks
Then into months and years, then fail
The lawmakers will damn their empty laws.

A clear vision of the tragic failure of the League of Nations, which was set up in 1920 at Geneva (archaically called Lake Leman) in hope of preventing any further outbreaks of world war. The League was superseded by the United Nations after the Second World War.

❧ 3/84 – 1945

La grand cité sera bien desolee,
Des habitans un seul n'y demoura
Mur, sexe, temple et vierge violee,
Par fer, feu, peste, canon peuple mourra.

The fine city will be desolated
Not a single inhabitant will remain
Walls, sexes, temples and virgins violated
The people will die from cannon, plague, sword and fire.

Berlin was sacked by Russian troops in April 1945, during which mass rapes are known to have taken place. In the course of the battle nearly a million people lost their lives. Berlin was virtually obliterated from the map, having already been pounded for many months by non-stop Allied bombardments in an effort to demoralise the population.

❦ 2/70 – 1945

Le dard du ciel fera son estendre,
Mors en parlant: grande execution
La pierre en l'arbre la fiere gent rendue,
Bruit humain monstre purge expiation.

The heavenly dart will stretch its
   course
Death in the speaking: a great
   achievement
The proud nation brought low by the
   stone in the tree
Rumours of a monstrous human
   bring purge, then expiation.

6 August 1945. Hiroshima. The atomic bomb released by the Americans killed 129,558 people and destroyed 68% of Hiroshima's buildings. A further 24% were damaged. The stone in the tree describes the shape of the mushroom cloud that engulfed the city, which is an effective rendering of the paradoxical image – at least to contemporaries of Nostradamus – of something inherently land-bound (a bomb) falling unexpectedly from above.

❦ 10/13 – 1945

Soulz la pasture d'animaux ruminant
Par eux conduicts au ventre herbipolique
Soldatz caichez les armes bruit menant
Non loing temptez de cité Antipolique.

Underneath the hay
Led there from the fields
The soldiers hide their noisy weapons
In preparation for an attempt on
   Antibes.

Very generalised, although possibly applying to an episode during the Second World War when German troops were driven from their final footholds on the Riviera by the soon-to-be victorious Allied forces.

❦ 4/95 – 1945

La regne à deux laissé bien peu tiendront
Trois ans sept mois passés feront la guerre
Les deux vestales contre eux rebelleront
Victor puis nay en Armorique terre.

With two of them ruling, it won't last
In three years and seven months they
   will go to war
The two vestals will rebel against them
The victor is then born on American
   soil.

A chilling presage of the superpower confrontations of the late twentieth century. The brinkmanship between the United States and Soviet Union that began the Cold War from 1945 came close on many occasions (more than are ever likely to be acknowledged by either side) to intercontinental war, and resulted in terrible conflicts such as Korea, Vietnam, and bitter civil wars in Latin America and Africa. As to the rebellious vestals, these must be the vassal states of either empire – the unreliable allies of the US in Nato (France wouldn't join) and anti-communist rabbles of the developing world on one side, and the corrupt regimes of the Warsaw Pact client states of the Soviet Union of the other. And is the victor Ronald Reagan (born 1911), the US President who finally faced the Soviet Union down?

10/20 – 1945 onwards

Tous les amis qu'auront tenu parti,
Par rude en lettres mis mort et saccagé,
Biens publiez par sixe (fixe) grand neanti,
Onc Romain peuple ne feut tant outragé.

All the friends who took part
Are robbed and killed by those of
little learning
The great one set at naught, his
goods auctioned illegally
Never were the Roman people so
wronged.

This is now acknowledged, with
convenient hindsight, to apply to post-
Fascist Italy.

1/63 – 1945 onwards

Les fleurs passés diminue le monde,
Long temps la paix terres inhabitées
Seur marchera par ciel, serre, mer et
onde:
Puis de nouveau les guerres suscitées.

With the plague scars gone, the earth
becomes smaller
Peace will reign for a long time
People will travel by land, sea and air
Before war once again takes over.

A perfect description of post-Second
World War western society. The world
seems smaller, thanks to an explosion
in communications, and peace, to all
intents and purposes, has reigned for
an unprecedentedly long time. Air
travel has become a commonplace, as
well as travel by sea and land. In
Nostradamus's time, travel was only for
the rich and learned. His final line is
intended to puncture our equanimity.
Never, in the history of mankind, has
war been absent from our
consciousness for so long. We have
been warned.

2/71 – 1946

Les exilés en Sicile viendront,
Pour delivrer de faim la gent estrange
Au point du jour les Celtes lui faudront
La vie demeure à raison: Roi se range.

The exiles will enter Sicily
To deliver the alien nation from want
At sunrise, they will need the French
Life remains: the king enters the fray.

Many interpretations have been found
for this one, most notably that of the
Mafia returning to Sicily after the
Second World War and trying to reach
an agreement with their French
counterparts. How can this be squared
with the Mafiosi delivering an alien
nation from want, in line 2? Only on the
basis that Lucky Luciano was an agent
of the US government, and that they
deported him to Italy in 1946
specifically to counter a perceived
threat from the Italian Communists.

3/49 – 1946

Regne Gaulois tu seras bien changé
En lieu estrange est translaté l'empire
En autres moeurs et lois seras rangé
Roan, et Chartres te feront bien du pire.

You will change, Kingdom of France
Your Empire will expand to foreign
places
Other laws and customs will appear
Rouen and Chartres will do their
worst.

Here Nostradamus predicts not the
military expansion of France – as a
colonial power, the Republic's record
has been dire – but its extraordinary
success in retaining world influence by
dominating the European Community.
This achievement is largely due to the

efforts of Charles de Gaulle (1890–1970), President of France, who formed the Coal and Steel Union with West Germany after the Second World War, successfully turning this unlikely economic alliance into the Common Market, from which de Gaulle deliberately exluded Great Britain, and thence into the modern European Union, in which France remains the most manipulative and self-serving member, earning benefits and influence far beyond the degree merited.

❧ 3/97 – 1948

Nouvelle loi terre neufve occuper,
Vers la Syrie, Judee et Palestine
Le grand empire barbare corruer,
Avant que Phoebus son siecle determine.

A new land will be occupied by a new law
Towards Syria, Judea and Palestine
The great barbarian empire will decay
Before the sun ends its century.

This relates to the foundation of the new State of Israel, on 14 May 1948. The implication is that the Arab empire will decay before the end of the twentieth century (the century of the sun). According to the Jewish lunar calendar, 1997 was the true end of the millennium.

❧ 9/66 – 1952

Paix, union sera et changement
Estatz, offices bas hault, et hault bien bas
Dresser voyage le fruict premier torment
Guerre cesser, civil proces debatz.

There will be peace, union and change
Estates and offices that were once high, fall, and vice versa

The eldest child is tormented by the preparations for a voyage
The war ceases amidst legal process and debate.

This is a remarkably astute prediction for the future of Great Britain after the Second World War, and the steady break-up of the British Empire. Queen Elizabeth II is the eldest child, and the voyage is the funeral of her beloved father, George V, following his death in 1952. During the early course of her reign over forty colonies were to become independent, and many ancient offices overturned.

❧ 2/29 – 1954

L'Oriental sortira de son siege,
Passer les monts Apennins voir la Gaule
Transpercera le ciel les eaux et neige,
Et un chacun frappera de sa gaule.

The oriental man will leave his seat
And pass across the Apennines, to France
He will pierce the skies, the sea and the snow
He will strike all with his rod.

This quatrain may refer to General Vo Nguyen Giap who vanquished the French at Dien Bien Phu on 7 May 1954 after a 56 day siege, driving them out of Vietnam for ever. The report of his exploits crossed the Apennines via the Geneva Conference to France, piercing the very skies, just as his 105 Howitzers did, taking the French camp completely by surprise. On 20 July 1954 Vietnam was partitioned along the seventeenth parallel, a fact which led to US intervention in 1960, culminating in a disastrous second Vietnamese War.

❦ 1/21 – 1950–1960

Profonde argile blanche nourrit rocher,
Qui d'un abysme istra l'acticineuse
En vain troublez ne le seront toucher,
Ignorant être au fond terre argileuse.

A white clay from the deep nourishes
    the rock
Which will bring actinium from an
    abyss
No one will want to touch it
Being ignorant of the clay in the
    earth's heart.

Actinium is a radioactive metal (atomic
number 89). A clear prediction of
mining for radioactive materials and the
development of atomic power – with the
fears of contamination that attend it.

❦ 3/54 – 1955

L'un des plus grands fuira aux Espaignes
Qu'en longue playe apres viendra
*   saigner*
Passant copies par les hautes montaignes
Devastant tout et puis en paix regner.

One of the greatest will flee to Spain
Which will thereafter bleed from a
    terrible wound
Armies will cross the high mountains
Devastating everything – later he will
    reign in peace.

It is likely that this predicts the roller-
coaster career of Juan Domingo Perón
(1895–1974), the Argentine leader who
modelled himself on Benito Mussolini.
At the time of Perón's birth, Argentina
was a major economy, with a gross
national product similar in size to that of
the United States. But the nation went
into decline from the 1920s. Perón, a
soldier for thirty years, was elected
President in 1946 after a campaign
brilliantly stage-managed by his wife
Eva, who was much loved by the
masses of the Argentine working class.
But the glamorous couple presided
over a period of serious economic and
political disorder. Eva died in 1952, and
popular suport for her husband
dwindled with her passing. He was
deposed by the army in 1955 and fled
to Spain. But the military failed to
manage the economy any more
effectively and Peronists continued to
win elections when the generals
permitted. Perón returned in triumph
from Spain in 1973 and died in the
following year.

❦ 8/35 – 1956

Dedans l'entrée de Garonne et Baise
Et la forest non loing de Damazan
Du marsaves gelees, puis gresle et bize
Dordonnois gelle par erreur de mezan.

At the entrance to the Garonne and
    Baise
And the forest, not far from
    Damazan
Frozen discoveries made at sea, then
    hail and northerly winds
Frost in the Dordogne, but in the
    wrong month.

Climate change, a regular
Nostradamian theme. Some interpreters
believe this refers to the uniquely
freakish frosts that struck France in
1956.

❦ 2/90 – 1956

Par vie et mort changé regne d'Ongrie
La loi sera plus aspre que service
Leur grand cité d'hurlements plaincts et
crie
Castor et Pollux ennemis dans la lice.

Through life and death the rule of
Hungary is changed
Law becomes harsher than servitude
Their great city howls and laments
Castor and Pollux confront each
other in the lists.

On 5 November 1956, Hungary's anti-
communist revolution was crushed
under the tracks of Soviet tanks.

❦ 10/87 – 1961–73

Grand roi viendra prendre port pres de
Nisse
Le grand empire de la mort si enfera
Aux Antipolles posera son genisse,
Par mer la Pille tout esvanoira.

A great king will capture a port near
Nice
The terrible empire of death will
come of it
He will place a heifer in Antibes
There will be pillage at sea, all will
vanish.

Like many other quatrains in Century
10, this is seriously oblique. It would
seem to apply to any number of actions
against the southern French coast,
including the Allied landings in 1944, at
Fréjus, just up the coast from Antibes.
However the word heifer is a clue. A
heifer is a young cow yet to give birth to
a calf. It can also be a symbol of
wisdom. The only man who has ever
placed a heifer (in its literal sense) in
Antibes, is Pablo Picasso (1881–1973),

who lived and painted nearby for many
years. Could the empire of death be his
famous painting Guernica, detailing the
terrible bombardment of this Basque
town by a Luftwaffe squadron during
the Spanish Civil War?

❦ 10/65 – 1962

O vaste Romone ta ruine s'approche,
Non de tes murs de ton sang et substance;
L'aspre par lettres fera si horrible coche,
Fer poinctu mis à tous jusques au
manche.

Great Rome, your ruin approaches
Not from your walls, but from your
blood and substance
The harsh man, writing letters, will
cause a horrible rift
Pointed steel will damage everything
as far as the sleeve.

A prophecy of the plague of the
twentieth century, Aids? It is hard to
resist the image of pointed steel
damaging everything up to the sleeve.
The virus attacks not from outside (your
walls) but from within (your blood and
substance). Nostradamus links the
virus to the demise of the Catholic
Church. He could of course simply be
referring to a letter or edict that causes
a rift within the Church, and not to Aids.
This would point to Pope John XXIII's
Second Vatican Council in 1962, in
which the Church attempted to
modernise itself. This caused a horrible
rift. French Archbishop Marcel Lefebvre
and his traditionalist allies immediately
constituted an alternative grouping,
called the Priestly Fraternity of St Pius
X, which damned the council as
heretical. This was not well received in
the Vatican, which suspended Lefebvre
from his priestly duties in 1972.

❦ 2/57 –1962

Avant conflict le grand mur tombera
Le grand à mort, mort, trop subite et
*   plainte*
Nay imparfaict: la plus part nagera
Aupres du fleuve de sang la terre tainte.

The great wall will fall before the
   battle
The great one dies suddenly and
   much lamented
Born imperfect, he will swim most of
   the way
Near the river, the ground is stained
   with blood.

An allusion in all likelihood to President
John F Kennedy. The great wall seems
to be the edifice of American infallibility
so dangerously challenged by Soviet
premier Nikita Kruschev in October
1962 during the brinkmanship over the
USSR's missile bases in Cuba.
Kennedy, a man born far from perfect if
his legion of biographers are to be
believed, was assassinated in
November of the following year.

❦ 10/66 – 1962

Le chef de Londres par regne l'Americh,
L'isle de l'Escosse tempiera par gellee
Roi Reb auront un si faux antechrist
Que les mettra trestous dans la meslee.

London's leader, through the rule of
   America
Will burden the Scottish island with
   an ice cold thing
King Reb will have so false an
   Antichrist
That they will all be brought into
   conflict.

Harold Macmillan (1894–1986), British
Prime Minister from 1957 to 1963 and a
friend of the United States, was
instrumental in having the first ice cold
Polaris missiles stationed in Scotland
during the late 1950s. The yiddish word
Reb, in line 3, is a term of respect for a
man, and stems from the Hebrew word
Rabbi. In this context it implies that a
respected leader may have his
judgement impaired by a false mentor.
This leads us to John F Kennedy and
the Cuban Missile Crisis of 1962, which
may have been triggered by a
misconceived CIA/Mafia assassination
plan to take out Fidel Castro.

2/13 – 1962

Le corps sans ame plus n'estre en sacrifice
Jour de la mort mis en nativité
L'esprit divin fera l'ame felice
Voyant le verbe en son eternité.

The soulless body will no longer be
   sacrificed
It will be born on the day of death
The divine spirit will make the soul
   rejoice
Seeing the word in all its eternity.

One interpretation envisions this
spiritual transformation as the adoption
of the vernacular Mass in place of Latin
at the Second Vatican Council in 1962.

❦ 4/14 – 1963

La mort subite du premier personnage.
Aura changé et mis un autre au regne
Tost, tard venu à si haut et bas aage,
Que terre et mer faudre que on la
*   craigne.*

The sudden death of the leading man
Will cause change, making another
    man leader
Soon, but too late, the young man
    will attain high office
By land and sea he will be feared.

John F Kennedy (1917–63) was, at just
43 years old, the youngest ever elected
President of the United States. When he
was assassinated, in Dallas, on 22
November 1963, he was succeeded by
Vice President Lyndon Johnson (1908–
73). Kennedy had shown his mettle
during the Cuban missile crisis of 1962,
but his untimely death nipped his
longer-term potential in the bud.

❦ 5/56 – 1963

Par le trespas du tres vieillart pontif,
Sera esleu Romain de bon aage
Qu'il sera dict que la siege debisse,
Et long tiendra et de picquant ouvrage.

On the death of the aged Pope
A Roman, in the prime of life, will be
    elected
He will be accused of weakening the
    Pontificate
He will last long, and cause great
    damage.

When Pope John XXIII died, in 1963, he
was replaced by another Roman Pope,
Paul VI, who reigned until 1978.
Achieving much, he was nevertheless
criticised for his conservative policies,
and for allowing Michele Sindona, a

Sicilian banker with Mafia links, to take
over advising the Vatican Bank. This
caused great and lasting damage to
the Church, culminating in the financial
scandals of the 1980s.

❦ 6/37 – 1963

L'oeuvre ancienne se parachevera,
Du toict cherra sur la grand mal ruyne,
Innocent faict mort on accusera,
Nocent cache, taillis à la bruyne.

The ancient task will be
    accomplished
From the roof, evil will fall on the
    great man
They accuse a dead innocent of the
    deed
The guilty one is hidden in the mist.

The assassination of President John F
Kennedy on 22 November, 1963. Some
of the gunshots undoubtedly came from
roof level, and the accused assassin
did not live long enough to stand trial.
Even today, the true identity of the killer
is as hidden in the mist as ever it was.

❦ 6/26 – 1963

Quatre ans le siege quelque bien peu
*   tiendra,*
Un surviendra libidineux de vie
Ravenne et Pise, Veronne soustiendront,
Pour eslever la croix de Pape envie.

The seat will be held, to some good
    purpose, for four years
A sensuous man will take it over
Ravenna, Pisa and Verona will
    support him
Wishing to raise the Papal cross.

Pope John XXIII (1881–1963) reigned
for a little over four years, and presided
over the Second Vatican Council which

began the process of modernising the Catholic Church. He was replaced by Pope Paul VI (1897–1978), a more worldly, sensuous man, who was at one time reputed to have had a homosexual lover.

1/85 – 1963

Par la response de dame, roy trouble,
Ambassadeurs mespriseront leur vie,
Les grand ses frères contrefera double,
Par deux mourront ire, hain envie.

A king troubled by a lady's reaction
Ambassadors have contempt for their
  lives
His brothers go twice against him
They die twice in anger, hatred,
  envy.

This quatrain is popularly linked to the assassination of President Kennedy in 1963 and the subsequent killing of his brother Robert, followed by the disgrace of a third brother, Edward. The Kennedy family would certainly equate to a royal dynasty in the United States. As to the lady whose reaction troubled the President, many sinister allegations have been made about John Kennedy's relationship with his mistresses.

6/36 – 1966

Ne bien ne mal par bataille terrestre
Ne parviendra aux confins de Perousse
Rebeller Pise, Florence voir mal estre
Roi nuict blessé sur mulet à noire house.

Neither good nor evil, by earthly
  battle
Will come to the borders of Perugia
Pisa will rebel, Florence will be hard
  struck
The King, on a mule, is injured
  under cover of night.

Earthly battle speaks not of war but of the struggle against the elements. Flooding springs to mind. The floods which struck Florence in 1966 were the worst for 700 years. Many priceless paintings, including great Renaissance religious works (no doubt including depictions of Christ's Palm Sunday entry into Jerusalem) were damaged or destroyed.

3/28 – 1966

De terre faible et pauvre parentele
Par bout et paix parviendra dans
  l'Empire
Long temps regner une jeune femelle
Qu'oncques en regne n'en survint un
  pire.

Possessing little land and poor
  parentage
The Empire will be gained by effort
  and peace
A young woman will reign long
Never was there such a bad influence
  in the kingdom.

Some interpreters believe this describes Indira Gandhi (1917–84), who served as prime minister of India for several periods from 1966 until her assassination at the hands of her own Sikh bodyguards. Her influence on India was mixed at best, including as it did her imprisonment for electoral fraud, the declaration of several national emergencies, and the notorious storming of the Sikh temple at Amritsar. But she was not of poor parentage. Her father was Jawaharial Nehru (1889–1964) who became independent India's first premier in 1947. But he had hard formative years to his political career. Nehru was imprisoned by the British for sedition for a total of 18 years – and spent five years at Harrow.

❦ 3/22 – 1967

Six jours l'assaut devant cité donné
Livree sera forte et aspre bataille
Trois la rendront et à eux pardonné
Le reste à feu et sang tranche traille.

The city is besieged for six days
It is handed over after a long and
    bitter fight
Three surrender it, and they are
    pardoned
For the rest fire, bloody slashing and
    slaughter.

The city is Jerusalem and the siege the
Six Day War of 5–10 June 1967, in
which Israel was victorious over an
alliance of Arab states. Of course
Jerusalem was not surrendered in
military terms, but a process was
begun in which, one day, peace
between Jews and Palestinians may
break out. In the meantime, the killing
continues.

❦ 3/47 – 1967

Le vieux monarque dechassé de son regne
Aux Orients son secours ira querre
Pour peur des croix ployera son enseigne
En Mitylene ira par port et par terre.

The old king, chased from his realm
Will go to seek help from the
    Orientals
Fearing the crosses, he will fold up
    his banner
Travelling to Mitylene by port and
    by land.

Said to refer to the seizure of power by
a military junta in Greece in 1967. The
reigning monarch, King Constantine
(born 1940) was formally deposed in
1973 and sought help for a return to
power from many sources. Resumption
of democracy in Greece has not been
attended by a restoration of the
monarchy.

❦ 4/43 – 1967

Seront ouys au ciel les armes battre
Celuy an mesme les divins ennemis,
Voudront Loix Sainctes injustement
   debatre,
Par foudre et guerre bien croyants a
   mort mis.

Weapons of war will be heard in the
    sky
The same year will make holy men
    enemies
They will unjustly suppress Sacred
    Law
True believers will be put to death.

Holy war, and battles in the skies. The
prediction of combat in the air is
uncanny. In the light of Nostradamus's
Jewish ancestry, can he be anticipating
the Arab-Israeli wars from 1967 in
which air power has played such a
decisive role? A conflict between two
states dominated by religious leaders is
certainly indicated. Leaders who are
prepared to set aside the teachings of
their own holy laws in the quest for
victory. Leaders who consider the
massacre of innocents – true believers
– an acceptable price.

☙ 10/26 – 1968

Le successeur vengera son beau frere,
Occupera regne souz umbre de vengeance,
Occis ostacle son sang mort vitupere,
Long temps Bretaigne tiendra avec la
France.

The successor will avenge his
handsome brother
He will occupy the realm under
shadow of vengeance
The obstacle slain, his dead blood
seethes in anger
Britain and France will hold together
for a long time.

Robert Kennedy (1925–1968) almost
had it within his power to avenge his
'handsome brother' John F. Kennedy's
1963 assassination, when he agreed to
campaign as Democratic candidate for
the Presidency against Richard Nixon.
The CIA has, allegedly, always privately
accepted that JFK was killed by the
Mafia, and the younger Kennedy had
made it an article of faith to curtail the
power of organised crime in the US. He
was assassinated, before he could fulfil
his pledge, on 5 June 1968, in a Los
Angeles hotel.

☙ 3/83 – 1968

Les longs cheveux de la Gaule Celtique,
Accompagnez d'estranges nations
Mettront captif la gent Aquitanique,
Pour succomber à internitions.

The long-haired ones of Celtic
France
Together with others from foreign
countries
Will imprison the people of
Aquitaine
And force them into line.

In May 1968, riots erupted in the streets
of Paris, Mexico and San Francisco, all
related, in one way or another, to the
Vietnam war. US involvement had
reached its height by that time, with
550,000 military personnel involved, of
whom more than 30,000 had already
died. The long-haired ones wanted US
involvement to end, and their remit was
to change public opinion – to imprison
the government and force them into
line. Aquitaine means England, or a
colony of England. The US is arguably
England's most famous former colony.

☙ 9/65 – 1969

Dedans le coing de Luna viendra rendre,
Ou sera prins and mis en terre étrange.
Les fruits immeurs seront à grand
esclandre,
Grand vitupère a l'un grande louange.

Within, he will bring himself to the
corner of the moon
Where he will be taken out and put
into a strange land
The fruits of the endeavour will be as
a great stairway
From great mockery to great praise.

A clear prediction of man's flight within
a machine to the moon, and Neil
Armstrong's first steps on its surface on
21 July 1979. Nostradamus foresees
that this endeavour will meet with a
mixed reception back on Earth.

9/65 – 1969

Dedans le coing de luna viendra rendre
Ou sera prins et mis en terre estrange
Les fruitz immeurs seront à la grand
esclandre
Grand vitupere à l'un grande louange.

He will wish to go to the far corner
of the Moon
He will be taken and sent to a strange
land
The unripe fruits will cause great
scandal
Great blame, great praise to one.

It is tempting to see this as an uncanny
foretelling of the first manned flight to
the moon of 20 July 1969, and to the
consequent falling away of interest in
the US Space Programme. This
culminated in the Challenger disaster of
28 January 1986, caused by a faulty O-
ring in one of the fuel pods, or unripe
fruits, the Challenger was carrying.

8/17 – 1969

Les bien aisez subit seront desmis
Par les trois freres le monde mis en
trouble,
Cité marine saisiront ennemis,
Faim, feu, sang, peste et de tous maux le
double.

The comfortably-off will lose
everything
Three brothers cause the world's
trouble
The naval city will be seized by its
enemies
Hunger, fire, blood, plague; of each
evil, the double.

Nostradamus often mentions three
brothers in his quatrains, and many
commentators have taken these to be
the Kennedys, John, Robert and
Edward. This now seems unlikely, since
Edward's aspirations to power
effectively ended on Chappaquidick
island in 1969. Both Robert and John
were assassinated before they could
reach their full potential.

3/60 – 1969

Par toute Asie grande proscription
Mesme en Mysie, Lysie, et Pamphyilie
Sang versera par absolution
D'un jeune noir rempli de felonnie.

Orders will travel throughout Asia
Reaching even Mysia, Lycia and
Pamphilia
Blood will flow in absolution
Because of a young and evil black
man.

Muammar Gadaffi was only 27 when he
overthrew the regime of King Idris of
Libya in 1969 and promoted himself to
the highest rank in the revolutionary
army – Colonel. Gadaffi has since been
a principal perpetrator of what is now
called state-sponsored terrorism,
causing outrages throughout the world.

5/40 – 1960s

Le sang royal sera si tresmeslé,
Contrainct seront Gaulois de l'Hesperie
On attendra que terme soit coulé,
Et que memoire de la voix soit perie.

Royal blood will be diluted
The French will be restrained by the
West
They will wait for some time
Until the memory of what was said
has perished.

Royal blood is predicted, correctly, to
thin in France. French global influence

has been steadily retreating during the course of the twentieth century in the face of the tide of Americanisation. The French are so wary of this effect that the Academie Française (established 1629) has since the 1960s taken several steps to protect French language and culture from dilution.

❦ 3/89 – 1974

En ce temps là sera frustree Cypres,
De son secours de ceux de mer Egee
Vieux trucidez, mais par mesles et
*   lypbres*
Seduict leur Roy, Royne plus outragee.

Cyprus, at that time, will be deprived
Of aid by those from the Aegean sea
The old will die, by cannon and grief
Their king will be seduced, their
    queen further outraged.

On 15 July 1974 Greek Cypriot troops overthrew the government of Archbishop Makarios (1913–1977) on the island of Cyprus. Five days later the Turks invaded the island, vowing to restore Makarios. They've been there ever since. In the same year, the Greek monarchy was formally abolished. Makarios was never reinstated.

❦ 8/46 – 1978

Pol mensolee mourra trois lieus du Rosne
Fuis les deux prochains tarasc destrois
Car Mars fera le plus horrible trosne
De coq et d'aigle de France, freres trois.

Celibate Paul will die three leagues
    from Rome
The next two flee the oppressive
    Tarascon
Because Mars will reign horribly
Three brothers, from the cock and
    eagle of France.

Pope Paul VI, the first pontiff to take the name since Paul V (1552–1621), was elected in 1963. He died in 1978 in the Vatican – but had been the most widely travelled pope in history. Paul VI's election fell in the same year as the assassination of President John Kennedy (of the three brothers – acknowledged to be John, Robert and Edward Kennedy) and the horrible reign of Mars concerns the wars in Southeast Asia in which France and then the United States were so desructively embroiled.

❦ 5/46 – 1978

Par chapeaux rouges querelles et
*   nouveaux schismes*
Quand on aura esleu le Sabinois
On produira contre lui grans sophismes,
Et sera Rome lesse par Albanois.

The cardinals will quarrel, finding
    new differences
Once the Sabine has been elected
Lies will be brought against him
And Rome will be humbled by the
    Albanians.

Possibly relating to Pope John Paul I, a 'Sabine', who only reigned for 34 days and died in mysterious circumstances, in 1978, after clashing with his cardinals. The reference to Albania may concern that benighted country's indifferent treatment by the outside world.

❦ 4/11 – 1978

Celui qu'aura gouvert de la grand cappe,
Sera induict à quelques cas patrer
Les douzes rouges viendront fouiller la
* nappe.*
Soubz meutre, meutre se viendra
* perpetrer.*

He who is elected Pope
Will have to act
The twelve red-handed men disturb
  his table
Under cover of murder, murder will
  be done.

Could this apply to Pope John Paul I
(1912–1978) whose death occurred on
the very eve of the day he intended to
shake up the Catholic hierarchy? There
followed a string of murders and
suicides of prominent Vatican bankers,
culminating in the death by hanging of
Roberto Calvi (1925–1982) of Banco
Ambrosiano fame, beneath London's
Blackfriars Bridge. John Paul I reigned
for only 34 days.

❦ 10/12 – 1978

Esleu en Pape, d'esleu sera mocqué
Subit soudain esmeu prompt et timide
Par trop bon doulz à mourir provocqué
Crainte estainte la nuit de sa mort
* guide.*

Elected Pope, he will be mocked by
  his electors
All of a sudden moved, prompt and
  timid
He meets his end through being too
  good
He will fear the death of his guide,
  on the night he dies.

Son of a glass-blower from Murano,
Albino Luciani was elected Pope

number 263 in 1978. Taking the name
John Paul I, he vowed to reform the
existing Catholic bureaucracy, and, in
particular, the notorious Vatican Bank.
34 days after his election, on the very
eve of the morning on which he was
going to publish his proposals, he was
found dead in his bed, with the papers
delineating the radical changes he
intended to make scattered all about
him. The papers were later misplaced.

❦ 1/96 – 1978–2002

Celui qu'aura la charge de destruire
Templus et sectes, changez par fantaisie
Plus aux rochiers qu'aux vivans viendra
* nuire,*
Par langue ornee d'oreilles resasie.

The man charged with destroying
Errant temples and sects
Will confine himself to inanimate
  things
And to those whose ears are filled
  with braggadocio.

John Paul II, Pope at the turn of the
Millennium, has taken it upon himself to
redirect the energies of the Catholic
church back towards its fundamental
doctrines. He has endeavoured to
control schismatic movements within
the church, and to slow down the
sometimes brutish effects of
modernisation. Confining himself
largely to inanimate things, however,
and to those of his people who are
influenced by prevailing tendencies
rather than long-term fundamentals, he
has, perhaps, overlooked the
paganising power of popular science.

☙ 3/64 – 1979

Le chef de Perse remplira grande
Olchade
Classe Frireme contre gent
Mahometique
De Parthe, et Mede, et piller les Cyclades
Repos long temps aux grand port
Ionique.

The Persian leader will replenish
  merchant ships
A trireme fleet will confront the
  Mahommedans
He will pillage the Cyclades from
  Parthia and Medea
There will be a long wait in the main
  Ionian port.

War and the interruption of trade in the
Middle East. The Persian leader is
Ayatollah Ruhollah Khomeini (1900–89)
who returned from exile in 1979 after
the collapse of the previous regime.
Khomeini declared holy war on America
and the West as well as waging a long
conflict with his neighbour Iraq,
causing economic chaos and killing a
million Iranian and Iraqi combatants.

☙ 3/61 – 1980

La grand band et secte crucigere
Se dressera en Mesopotamie
Du proche fleuve compagnie legiere
Que telle loi tiendra pour ennemie.

The numerous followers of the sect
  of the cross
Will mass in Mesopotamia
A lighter company, from a nearby
  river
Will find this law inimical.

Mesopotamia, site of the first cities in
civilisation, built on the shores of the
rivers Tigris and Euphrates, is now

divided between modern Iran and Iraq,
two of the most belligerent Muslim
powers, divided both internally and
externally by the laws of religious
doctrine. The two nations fought a bitter
and inconclusive war from 1980–88, in
which a million lost their lives.

☙ 6/44 – 1980s

De nuict par Nantes L'Iris apparoistra,
Des artz marins susciteront la pluie
Arabique goulfre grand classe parfoudra,
Un monstre en Saxe naistra d'ours et
truie.

The rainbow will appear, by night,
  near Nantes
Rain will fall through the sea's
  artifice
A great army of men will perish in
  the Arabian gulf
In Saxony, a monster will be born of
  a bear and a sow.

Written in symbolical terms, this
quatrain is almost impossible for
modern minds to fathom. A rainbow
indicates hopes or aspirations. Rain
refreshes, but can also wash away. The
army of men may refer to the millions
killed during the Iran-Iraq wars of the
1980s. The bear traditionally refers to
Russia, while a sow denotes fecundity.

☙ 2/5 – 1980s

Quand dans poisson fer et lettre enfermée
Hors sortira qui pis fera la guerre
Aura par mer sa classe bien ramée,
Apparoissant près de Latin terre.

When in an iron fish with a letter
  enclosed
The man who can make war goes out
To sea with a well-equipped fleet
Appearing by the Latin land.

A thoroughly convincing vision of the submarines of the twentieth century, and in particular of the boats now beneath the seas, bearing their orders (letter enclosed) for mass destruction in the event of hostilities. Trident submarines operated by both the United States and the United Kingdom are perpetually on patrol.

❦ 10/21 – 1980

Par le despit du Roi soustenant moindre,
Sera meurdri lui presentant les bagues,
Le pere au filz voulant noblesse poindre
Fait comme à Perse jadis feirent les
    Mague:

A lesser one is sustained, through
    spite of the king
He will be murdered, while offering
    him jewels
The father, wishing to prod his son
    towards noble actions
Does what the Maguses once did in
    Persia.

What didn't the Maguses once do in Persia? One interpretation attributes this to Reza Pahlavi, Shah of Iran (1919–1980).

❦ 3/58 – 1980

Aupres du Rhin des Montaignes
    Noriques
Naistra un grand de gens trop tard venu
Qui defendra Saurome et Pannoniques
Qu'on ne sçaura qu'il sera devenu.

Near the Rhine, in the Austrian
    mountains
A great man of the people will be
    born, too late
He will defend Poland and Hungary
They will never find out what
    became of him.

Who is this shadowy champion? Some modern interpretations believe it could be Lech Walesa (born 1943) whose founding of the Solidarity movement in his native Poland in 1980 triggered resistance in several Warsaw Pact states against Soviet imperialism – thus ultimately liberating Hungary as well as Poland itself. Walesa, formerly President of Poland (1990–1995) has returned to political obscurity, but he was born not in Austria but in Popowo, Poland.

❦ 6/12 – 1980s

Dresser copies pour monter à l'Empire
Du Vatican le sang Royal tiendra
Flamans, Anglois, Espaigne avec Aspire
Contre l'Italie et France contendra.

Armies will be readied to ascend to
    the Empire
Of the Vatican, Royal blood will
    stand firm
Flemish, English, Spain with Aspire
He will fight against France and
    Italy.

Fascinating to see the word *Italie* in a manuscript written in the 1550s, because the nation of Italy was then more than 300 years short of existing. This quatrain is yet another of Nostradamus's inspired future views of Europe, listing the names of most of the key members of the European Union (could Aspire, rhyming with Empire, be a crude anagram for Prussia?). He rightly predicts that conflicts between the nations will continue and wrongly assumes royalties will last the distance. The Empire referred to, linked with the Vatican, is probably the Holy Roman Empire, which lost sway due to the Thirty Years War (1618–48).

❦ 9/36 – 1981

Un grand Roi prins entre les mains d'un
* Joine,*
Non loing de Pasque confusion coup
* coultre*
Perpet. Captifs temps que fouldre en la
* husne,*
Lorsque trois freres se blesseront et
* meutre.*

A great king in the hands of a
  stripling
Near Easter there will be confusion,
  and the cut of a knife
Time's captives, other times when
  lightning is on top
In an era when three brothers are
  wounded and killed.

US President Ronald Reagan was shot
by a stripling, William Hinkley Jr, on 30
March 1981. Only surgery (the cut of a
knife) could save him. This was indeed
an era of assassinations. The two
Kennedy brothers, Robert and John,
had both been killed by gunmen, and
Edward Kennedy, the third brother,
probably only avoided a similar fate by
prohibiting himself from high office by
his behaviour at Chappaquiddick, 19
July 1969, when he failed to report the
death, by drowning, of his date, Mary
Jo Kopechne.

❦ 9/73 – 1981

Dans Foix entrez Roi ceiulee Turbao
Et regnera moins revolu Saturne
Roi Turban blanc Bisance coeur ban
Sol, Mars, Mercure pres de la hurne.

The azure-turbaned king enters Foix
He will reign for less than one of
  Saturn's revolutions
The heart of the white-turbaned king
  is banished to Byzantium
The Sun, Mars and Mercury are near
  Aquarius.

The dating for this quatrain is askew, as
it would appear to imply that an Arabic
leader entered Foix – or France – on 18
February 1981. Perhaps a terrorist
incursion that has not come to light.

❦ 9/8 – 1981

Puisnay Roi fait son pere mettre à mort,
Apres conflit de mort tres inhoneste
Escrit trouvé soubson donra remort,
Quand loup chassé pose sus la couchette.

The last born king will kill his father
After a terrible and dishonest war
Writings are found, suspicion brings
  remorse
When the hunted wolf settles on the
  coverlet.

Killing, in this context, may be intended
symbolically, since it deals with thrones
and kingship. Juan Carlos I of Spain
symbolically took the place of his father
when he was anointed King of Spain, in
1975, following the death of dictator
Francisco Franco, who himself came to
power on the back of a terrible and
dishonest war. Initial suspicion that he
was a stooge of Franco turned to relief
when Juan Carlos proved his
democratic worth by standing up to a
right-wing coup attempt, in 1981. He
has been immensely popular ever
since.

❦ 2/14 – 1982

*A Tours, Gien, gardé seront yeux
   penetrans
Descouvriront de loing la grand seraine
Elle et sa suitte au port seront entrans
Combat, poussez, puissance souveraine.*

At Tours and Gien watchful eyes will
   be on guard
They will espy the serene one from
   afar
She and her retinue will enter the
   harbour
Combat, putsches, sovereign power.

An ingenious, if contrived, interpretation
is that Tours and Gien combine
anagrammatically to indicate Argentina,
making this a prophecy of the seizure
of the Falkland Islands by that nation in
1982. The serene one from afar, whose
retinue entered the islands' waters with
a considerable force, is either the
premier of the day, Margaret Thatcher,
or Queen Elizabeth II.

❦ 10/78 – 1985

*Subite joie en subite tristesse
Sera à Romme aux graces embrassees
Deuil, cris, pleurs, larm. sang excellent
   liesse
Contraires bandes surprinses et troussees.*

Sudden joy becomes sudden sadness
This will be at Rome, kissed with
   grace
Mourning, cries, tears, weeping,
   good blood mocked
Opposing groups surprised and
   trussed up.

During 1985 a number of terrorist
atrocities occurred near Rome,
including bombings, grenade attacks,
the hijacking of a TWA airliner on a
flight from Athens to Rome, and the
attack of Rome airport itself on 27
December, when more than a dozen
people were killed, including some of
the terrorists.

❦ 9/83 – 1985

*Sol vingt de Taurus si fort terre trembler
Le grand theatre rempli ruinera
L'air ciel et terre obscurcir et troubler
Lors l'infidelle Dieu et sainctz voguera.*

With the sun in Taurus, 20°, a great
   earthquake occurs
The grand theatre, crowded with
   people, is destroyed
The earth, land and air are darkened
   and troubled
When the Infidel calls on God and
   the saints.

The sun moves into Taurus around the
19 or 20 April every year and a
measurement of twenty degrees of
latitude takes us to Guadalajara,
Mexico City, or to Santiago de Cuba, all
situated near notoriously shifting
tectonic plates. Although no year is
given for the momentous earthquake
mentioned in line 1, it seems possible
Nostradamus meant the 1985 Mexico
City earthquake, which killed thousands
of people.

❦ 4/59 – 1985–86

*Deux assiegez en ardente ferveur,
De soif estaincts pour deux plaines tasses
Le fort lime, et un vieillart resveur,
Au Genevois de Nira monstra trasse.*

Two find themselves besieged, with
   ardent fury
Two full cups quench their thirst
The fort is burnt, and an old dreamer
Will show the Genevans the road to
   Nira.

Taking Nira as an anagram of Iran, arrives at the Iran–Iraq wars of the 1980s. Some would see the old dreamer as President Ronald Reagan, who swore he would never barter arms for the lives of US hostages held in Lebanon, but was found later, during the Iran-Contra investigation, to have sent emissaries to Geneva for just that purpose.

❧ 6/5 – 1986

Si grand famine par une pestifère,
Par pluye longue le long du Pole Artique;
Samarobyn cent lieux de l'hemisphere,
Vivront sans loy, exempt de politique.

Such a great famine and plague
Will rain down the length of the
    North Pole;
Samarobyn a hundred leagues from
    the hemisphere
Will live beyond the law or politics.

The clue is in the name Samarobyn, which is clearly Russian – though not in any gazetteer. The allusion fits uncomfortably with the nuclear disaster at Chernobyl in the Ukraine on 25 April 1986. Agricultural land for hundreds of miles around the destroyed reactor remains contaminated and radiation sickness has killed uncountable numbers. The explosion sent radioactive material into the upper atmosphere (100 leagues is about 300 miles) and the cloud spread over most of the northern hemisphere. The Chernobyl disaster would never have happened if the local management had been answerable to an elected government or to the courts. In the Soviet Union, electricity generators were a law unto themselves. Historians now agree that the attempted cover-up of the Chernobyl disaster was a major contributing factor in the collapse of communist power in 1990.

❧ 8/15 – 1989

Vers Aquilon grans efforts par hommasse
Presque l'Europe et l'univers vexer,
Les deux eclipses mettra en tel chasse,
Et aux Pannons vie et mort renforcer.

The iron woman will exert herself to
    the North
Nearly all of Europe and the world is
    harassed
She will rout the two failed leaders
Life and death will strengthen
    Hungary.

The mere mention of an Iron Woman is enough to conjure up images of UK Prime Minister Margaret Thatcher, whose joint efforts with US President Ronald Reagan resulted in the cessation of the Cold War in 1989–90, and the temporary side-lining of the European Community. Hungary, which had suffered bitterly under the Russians during the 1956 uprising, finally became an independent state. The two failed leaders could apply to General Galtieri, of Argentina, and to Mikhail Gorbachev of the Soviet Union.

❧ 10/77 – 1989

Trente adherens de l'ordre des quiretres
Bannis leurs biens donnez ses adversaires
Tous leurs bienfais seront pour
    desmerites
Classe espargie delivrez aux consaires.

Thirty members of the Quirite order
Are banished, their goods are given
    to their enemies
All their good actions will be wrongly
    understood
Their fleet will be scattered and
    delivered to the Corsairs.

Quirites may be seen as people's warriors, in which case this quatrain refers to the break-up of the Soviet Union which began in 1989. The fleet in question is the Soviet Baltic fleet, much of which has since been sold off.

❦ 2/89 – 1989

Un jour seront demis les deux grands maistres,
Leur grand pouvoir se verra augmenter
La terre neufue sera en ses hauts estres,
Au sanguinaire le nombre racompté.

One day, two great leaders will become friends
Their already great power will grow further
The new world will be at the height of its influence
To the bloody one, the number shall be reported.

UK Prime Minister Margaret Thatcher (born 1925) and US President Ronald Reagan (born 1911) became great friends during their respective terms in office during the 1980s. It is arguable that the New World, otherwise known as the US, reached the height of its power with the disintegration of the Warsaw Pact in 1989. The bloody one is Satan, a name that became synonymous with the US, in the vengeful outpourings of Iranian leader Ayatollah Khomeini (1900–1989).

❦ 7/7 – 1990

Sur le combat des grans cheveux, legiers
On criera le grand croissant confond
De nuict tuer monts, habits de bergiers
Abismes rouges dans le fossé profond.

Because of the fighting of the mighty light-haired ones
It will be claimed that the great crescent is confounded
At night, on the mountains, those dressed as shepherds will kill
There will be red gulleys in the deep ditches.

The great crescent might equally symbolise the sickle insignium of the former Soviet Union or that of Islam. Any claims that the sickle has been confounded certainly came true with the demise of the USSR in 1990 – a collapse of empire significantly accelerated, it should be said, by Soviet humiliation at the hands of Muslim warriors in Afghanistan.

❦ 9/60 – 1990s

Conflict barbare, en la cornere noire,
Sang espandu trembler la Dalmatie,
Grand Ismael mettra son promontoire
Rangs trembler secours Lusitanie.

A barbaric conflict in the black horn
Blood will be shed, shaking Dalmatia
Great Ishmael will make inroads
Shaking the ranks of Portuguese rescuers.

Dalmatia – Yugoslavia – is the clue. Nostradamus foresees the bitter conflict involving Muslims (Ishmael was regarded by Muhammad as the ancestor of the Arabs) in the Balkans. The seemingly irrelevant Portuguese represent peacekeeping UN forces.

❦ 1/87 – 1990

Ennosigée, feu du centre de terre,
Fera trembler autour de Cité Neufue;
Deux grands rocher long temps ferot la
*   guerre,*
Puis Arethusa rougira nouveau Fleuve.

Erupting, the fire at the earth's
    centre
Will shake the New City.
Two great powers for long at war
Then Arethusa will redden the river
    anew.

A mysterious quatrain clearly
delineating an earthquake and
mentioning Arethusa, one of the Naiads
or water nymphs of mythology credited
with the power of prophecy. The Cold
War, defined as ending with the
collapse of the Soviet Empire in 1990,
is indicated, but the allegories of
earthquake and the renewal of
hostilities remain a disquieting riddle.

❦ 6/27 – 1991

Dedans les isles de cinq fleuves à un,
Par le croissant du grand Chyren Selin
Par les bruines de l'aer fureur de l'un,
Six eschapés, cachés fardeaux de lin.

In the islands, where five rivers
    become one
By the crescent of great Chyren Selin
One man's fury will drift on the mists
Six will escape, hidden in bales of
    flax.

A difficult quatrain, possibly relating to
the long-term struggle of the Kurds for
independence. In 1991, immediately
after the Gulf War, the Kurds rose
against the government of Saddam
Hussein. Hussein used chemical
warfare – fury drifting on the mists –
against the defenceless Kurdish

villages. In all, over a million people
were driven into exile, with untold
numbers killed.

❦ 9/60 – 1991

Conflict Barbar en la Cornere noire
Sang espandu trembler la d'Almatie
Grand Ismaël mettra son promontoire
Ranes trembler secours Lusitanie.

Barbarian conflict in the black corner
Blood is shed, Dalmatia trembles
Great Ismaël will set up his vanguard
The frogs tremble; aid from
    Portugal.

Cornere in line 1 is probably a
misspelling of *cornier*, meaning the
corner of a column, or pilaster. Black
corner almost certainly refers to the
black Balkans, scene of many wars
since the twelfth century. Dalmatia was
incorporated into Yugoslavia in 1918
and corresponds geographically to
modern-day Croatia. The quatrain
seems likely to apply to Slobodan
Milosevic and his pre-Kosovan
brutalities during the Croatian civil war
in 1991.

❦ 1/55 – 1991

Soubs l'opposite climat Babylonique,
Grand sera de sang effusion
Que terre et mer, air, ciel sera inique,
Sectes, faim, regnes, pestes, confusion.

In a non-Babylonian climate
There will be much bloodshed
Land, sea, heaven and air will seem
    unjust
Sects, hunger, new kingdoms,
    plagues and confusion will follow.

The Gulf War, in 1991, took place under
a new, non-Iraqi climate, namely the
clouds of acrid smoke released when

Saddam Hussein torched the Kuwaiti oil fields. Nostradamus foretells air warfare here, as well as the chaos following Operation Desert Storm. The word 'plagues' relates to Saddam's use of chemical warfare, most notably against the Kurds. The hunger is that of his own people, caused by the sanctions that followed his refusal to allow the United Nations to inspect his chemical weapons sites.

❦ 8/70 – 1992

Il entrera vilain, mechant, infame
Tyrannisant la Mesopotamie,
Tous amis fait d'adulterine d'ame,
Terre horrible, noir de phisonomie.

He will enter, wicked, bad, evil
Tyrannising Mesopotamia
The adulterous lady makes many
   friends
The land is horrible, and black of
   aspect

When Saddam Hussein destroyed the Kuwaiti oil wells in February 1992, he left the Persian Gulf covered in a dense, black aspected cloud. To combat him, the adulterous lady (the Statue of Liberty, representing the US) needed many friends.

❦ 10/49 – 1993

Jardin du monde au pres du cité neufve,
Dans le chemin des montaignes cavees,
Sera saisi et plongé dans la Cuve,
Beuvant par force eaux soulfre envenimees.

The world's garden will be near the
   new city
In the roadway, between the hollow
   mountains
It will be seized, and plunged into the
   tank
Drinking, in desperation, the
   sulphur-poisoned waters.

A fascinating quatrain in which Nostradamus appears to envision the skyscrapers of modern day New York, describing them as hollow mountains. The world's garden is an apt description of the World Trade Centre, which was devastatingly bombed in February 1993. If all had gone according to plan, the twin towers would have collided and fallen in the Hudson River (plunging into the tank). Those trapped inside would have drowned in the sulphur-poisoned waters.

❦ 2/32 – 1995

Laict, sang grenouilles escoudre en
   Dalmatie
Conflict donné, peste pres de Balennes
Cri sera grand par toute Esclavonie
Lors naistra monstre pres et dedans
   Ravenne.

Milk and the blood of frogs is
   hatched in Dalmatia
War, pestilence near Balennes
Great will be the cry throughout
   enslaved Slovenia
When a monster is born in and near
   Ravenna.

A dark presage of the tragic events in the Balkans in the 1990s. The identity of the monster born both in and near Ravenna is an unsolved enigma. Ravenna is an Italian city and episcopal see much used in Nostradamian allegory. Could it be a code Pozarevac in Serbia, birthplace in 1941 of one of the great monsters of the century, Slobodan Milosevic?

❦ 10/57 – 1995

Le soublevé ne cognoistra son sceptre
Les enfants jeunes des plus grands
  honnira
Oncques ne fut un plus ord cruel estre
Pour leurs espouses mort noir bannira.

The one raised high will not know
  his own sceptre
The young children of the great ones
  are disgraced
Never was there a filthier nor more
  cruel being
The black one will banish their
  spouses to death.

The problem here lies in line 4. If the
spouses are male, then it fits in very
well with Saddam Hussein's murder of
his two sons-in-law in 1995. They had
previously fled to Jordan with their
wives, but were prevailed on to return
to Iraq after failing in their negotiations
with the Americans. They were
purported to be killed by angry
members of their tribe, incensed by
their treachery to the state and to its
black-hearted leader.

❦ 9/12 – 1997

Le tant d'argent de Diane et Mercure
Les simulacres au lac seront trouvez,
Le figulier cherchant argille neufve
Lui et les siens d'or seront abbrevez.

Despite all the silver of Diana and
  Mercury
Their images will be found on the
  lake
For the sculptor looking for new clay
He and his people will be flooded
  with gold.

This an extraordinary quatrain,
predicting the death of Diana, Princess
of Wales, and of her lover, Dodi Fayed.
Also foreseen is Diana's final resting
place on a lake island on her brother
Earl Spencer's Althorp estate. Mercury
was the Roman god of travel (she and
Dodi were travelling in a Mercedes
limousine at the time of their death),
but, more importantly, he was also the
god of trading and commerce. Dodi's
father, Mohamed al-Fayed, is the owner
of London's Harrods, the most famous
department store in the world. This
makes him, in Nostradamian terms, the
god of trading and commerce. His son
and heir, Dodi, is, therefore, the
Mercury of the first line, making the
quatrain uncannily prescient. In spite of
their great wealth, they will die, and
their images will be found on the lake.
The last two lines refer to the paparazzi,
who, looking for new icons, discovered
Diana on 4 February 1981, when her
engagement to Prince Charles was
announced. They and their newspapers
were, indeed, flooded with gold.

❦ 10/55 –1997

Les malheureuses nopces celebreront
En grand joye mais la fin malheureuse
Mary et mere nore desdaigneront
Le Phybe mort et nore plus piteuse.

They will joyfully celebrate the
  unhappy wedding
It will have an unfortunate end
Husband and mother will scorn the
  new bride
With Phoebus dead, the daughter-in-
  law has an even worse fate.

Prince Charles and Lady Diana
Spencer were married in 1981, in a
ceremony that was televised around the
world. Princess Diana was killed in a
car accident in August 1997, effectively
ending the disastrous marriage that
had made both parties deeply

unhappy. There was said to be little love lost between Queen Elizabeth II and her daughter-in-law. Phoebus, in this context, must mean Dodi Fayed, Diana's Apollo. In the car crash that took both their lives, Dodi was killed on impact, while Diana suffered massive internal injuries and lived for some time before finally succumbing.

✾ 2/28 – 1997

Le penultiesme du surnom du prophete,
Prendra Diane pour son jour et repos
Loing vaguera par frenetique teste,
Et delivrant un grand peuple d'impos.

The penultimate holder of the
  prophet's name
Will take Diana's day for his sabbath
He will wander far in his frenzy
Delivering a great race from
  subjection.

This strange verse links the names of Diana, princess of Wales, and of Emad Mohammed 'Dodi' al-Fayed once again. Mohammed is, of course, the name of the prophet. If Dodi was the penultimate, then the last holder of the name must be his father, Mohamed al-Fayed, who has, indeed, wandered far in his frenzy to discover conspiracies concerning his son's death. Whether he will ever deliver a great race from subjection is an open question. It would be ungallant to interpret this passively, implying that the great British race crave deliverance from Mr al-Fayed.

✾ 9/48 – 1998

La grand cité d'occean maritime
Environnee de maretz en cristal
Dans le solstice hyemal et la prime
Sera tempté de vent espouvantal.

The great maritime city
Surrounded by a crystal marsh
Will be tested by a fearful wind
In the spring and the winter solstice.

The solstice date in line 4 rules out the atomic bombing of the port of Nagasaki, which took place during August 1945. The image of the crystal marsh is a powerful one, and may imply a nest of skyscrapers surrounding a great oceanic port. This brings either Hong Kong or Jakarta to mind, and in particular the 1998 Indonesian riots.

✾ 6/97 – 1999

Cinq et quarante degrés ciel bruslera,
Feu approcher de la grand cité neufve,
Instant grand flamme esparse sautera,
Quand on voudra des Normans faire
  preuve.

The sky will burn at 45 degrees
Fire approaches the great new city
Immediately a huge and scattered
  flame leaps up
When they want proof from the
  Northerners.

In the light of recent events this verse must qualify among Nostradamus's most successful quatrains, including those predicting the rise and fall of Hitler, Franco and Napoleon. The only major city on a 45° latitude is 'New' Belgrade in former Yugoslavia, Serbian capital city since the early twelfth century. Nostradamus brilliantly describes the Nato bombing which began in March 1999, including the huge and scattered flames emanating from the cruise missile targets scattered throughout the embattled city. The Northerners are of course Nato (North Atlantic Treaty Organisation), who took the action following the failure of the Rambouillet Peace Talks, when Slobodan Milosevic wanted proof that Nato really meant what it said in threatening intervention to protect the ethnic Albanians in Kosovo.

❦ 10/75 – 1999

Tant attendu ne reviendra jamais
Dedans l'Europe, en Asie apparoistra
Un de la ligue issu du grand Hermes
Et sur tous rois des orientz croistra.

Eagerly awaited, he will never go
  back
To Europe, but will reappear in Asia
One of the many descendants of
  great Hermes
He will rise above all other kings of
  the Orient.

Hermes is Hermes Trismegistus, otherwise known as the Egyptian god Thoth, author of numerous works on alchemy, magic and astrology. A new spiritual leader or Messiah, to follow on from Jesus Christ, will appear in the East. Elsewhere Nostradamus tells us that this new Messiah will be born at the exact moment in which the sun is blotted out from the earth during the eclipse of 11 August 1999. He will come into his own twenty-seven years later, and will be instrumental in bringing to an end the long-running global conflict that will have started around the time of his birth.

❦ 10/72 – 1999

L'an mil neuf cens nonante neuf sept
  mois,
Du ciel viendra un grand Roy
  d'effrayeur,
Resusciter le grand Roy d'Angolmois,
Avant après, Mars regner par bon heur.

In the year 1999 and seven months
From the sky will come a great and
  frightening King
To revive the great King of the
  Mongolians
Before and after, Mars reigns in good
  time.

There's no doubt about the date, but the great and frightening king reviving a fellow sovereign among the Mongolians remains cryptic. Is Genghis Khan to be reincarnated as a new threat from the East? It need not be military – possibilities which may yet arise include industrial competition from booming China, a new flu epidemic similar to the catastrophic pandemic of 1918 which originated in China and killed 100 million worldwide, or revolution against the Communist regime.

❦ 6/6 – 1999

Apparoistra vers le Septentrion,
Non loin de Cancer l'estoille chevelue
Suze, Sienne, Boece, Eretrion,
Mourra de Rome grand, la nuict
  disparue.

There will appear, towards the North
Not far from Cancer, a long-tailed
  comet
Susa, Siena, Boetia, Eretria
When the Catholic church dies,
  daylight will return.

A total eclipse of the sun is correctly predicted over Europe on 11 August 1999, crossing Susa and Siena in Italy, and also Boetia and Eretria in Greece, as well as the Western counties of England. The immense disaster waiting to happen to us was foretold, according to Nostradamus, by the appearance of the Hale-Bopp comet in the spring of 1997. This quatrain is number 6 and 6; traditional numbers of the devil. The number 666, according to Biblical Revelation, indicates mankind's descent into a condition of sin and loss of faith. Only when the Catholic church dies, will daylight return. Watch the skies.

❦ 3/34 – 1999

Quand le deffaut du Soleil lors sera.
Sur le plain jour le monstre sera veu
Tout autrement on l'interpretera,
Cherté n'a garde mil n'y aura pourveu.

At the eclipse of the sun
The monster will appear in broad
  daylight
Interpretations will differ
None will have forecast the great
  cost.

The total eclipse of 11 August 1999 is foretold as the precursor to the appearance of a monster in broad daylight. It seems that the monstrous one will not at first be taken as seriously as it should be, but that the consequences of its manifestation will be greater than anyone, including (presumably) Nostradamus himself, has predicted.

❦ 4/29 – 1999

Le Sol caché eclipse par Mercure,
Ne sera mis que pour le ciel second
De Vulcan Hermes sera faicte pasture,
Sol sera veu pur, rutilant et blond.

The hidden sun, eclipsed by Mercury
Will take second place in the heavens
Hermes will be Vulcan's food
The sun will reappear, shining, pure
  and golden.

Further implications for the total eclipse of 11 August 1999 in which a monster or monstrous form will appear. Hermes/Mercury was the Herald of the Gods, but Hermes Trismegistus was the Egyptian god Thoth, author of treatises on alchemy and magic. Vulcan was the Roman god of volcanic fire, implying that esoteric learning, in the form of Trismegistus, may be swallowed by a terrible conflagration and will eventually give place to a return of the natural order and the triumph of the sun god, Apollo.

❦ 5/41 – 1999

Nay souz les umbres et journée nocturne
Sera en rege et bonté souveraine
Fera renaistre son sang de l'antique
* urne,*
Renouvellant siecle d'or pour l'aerain.

Born on the day of an eclipse, in the
  shadows
He will be supreme in rule and
  goodness
He will renew his blood in the
  ancient urn
Causing the golden age to turn to
  brass.

An important quatrain, relating to the expected eclipse of 11 August 1999. On that day a new saviour will be born, at the exact moment in which the sun is blotted from view. He will lead the world towards a new, more spiritual path, exemplified by the changing of the gold of the twentieth century into the brass of the Aquarian age. The great urn refers to the wisdom of the Greeks, implying that this new messiah will tend towards the rational rather than the superstitious.

❦ 5/53 – 1999

La loi du Sol, et Venus contendens,
Appropriant l'esprit de prophetie
Ne l'un ne l'autre ne seront entendus,
Par Sol tiendra la loy du grand Messie.

The Sun's law will contend with
   Venus
Appropriating the spirit of the
   prophecy
Neither one nor the other will be
   understood
The Messiah's law will prevail
   through the Sun.

Another foretelling of a new Messiah. Little more can be gleaned with any certainty.

❦ 8/77 – 1999–2002

L'antechrist trois bien tost anniehilez,
Vingt et sept ans sang durera sa guerre.
Les heretiques mortz, captifs, exilez.
Sang corps humain eau rougi gresler
terre.

The Antichrist soon annihilates the
   three
His war will last for twenty-seven
   years
The heretics are dead, made captive,
   or exiled
The water is thick with blood, red
   hail covers the earth.

If the first line is read as 'the third antichrist is soon annihilated' the quatrain is seen to describe a terrible war, lasting twenty-seven years, followed by a return to religion. The red hail in line 4 would be an accurate description of radioactive fallout. Another quatrain 6/24 (see page 204) implies a starting date for the war of somewhere between July 1999 and June 2002.

❦ 2/100 – 1999

Dedans les isles si horrible tumulte
Bien on n'orra qu'une bellique brigue
Tant grand sera des predateurs l'insulte
Qu'on se viendra ranger à la grand ligne.

Such a terrible uproar in the islands
Soon only the warlike party will be
   heard
So severe will be the plunderer's
   violation
That a great alliance will be made
   against them.

The islands are likely to be the British Isles, and the uproar that between the mainland and the divided island of Ireland. Is the warlike party/plunderer the IRA? Revulsion at the bomb outrages during the 30 years of the troubles have recently produced a welcome alliance of the forces of reason against those of terrorist violence, and a happy consummation of the Good Friday Agreement of 1998, granting local power-sharing to the nationalist and loyalist factions of Northern Ireland is awaited.

❦ 6/34 – 1999

Du feu volant la machination
Viendra troubler au grand chef assiegez
Dedans sera telle sedition
Qu'en desespoir seront les profligez.

The besieged leader will be troubled
Because of the flying fire
There will be so much sedition inside
That those abandoned will despair.

Slobodan Milosevic, President of Yugoslavia, finds his Serbian nation under fire from Nato forces – the first European war to be begun exclusively in the air. Factions within Serbia make conflicting demands – that Milosevic should end the bombing by meeting Nato demands (to withdraw his murderous forces from the ethnically-cleansed province of Kosovo), or to hold out in the hope that Russia will enter the war on Serbia's behalf, threatening nuclear war. Meanwhile, the abandoned ones – the million Albanian Kosovans driven from the country – have every cause for despair, whichever route the Serbians take.

10/10 – 1900s

Tasche de murdre enormes adulteres
Grand ennemi de tout le genre humain
Que sera pire qu'ayeulx, oncles ne peres
En fer, feu, eau, sanguin et inhumain.

Stained with murder and terrible
    adulteries
A great enemy of all mankind
He will be worse than any of his male
    forbears
In steel, fire, water, bloody and
    inhuman.

This could apply to any one of the three Antichrists suggested by Nostradamus during the course of his quatrains; Napoleon, Hitler, or the third, but as yet unidentified, mystery man or woman. Given Adolf Hitler's lamentable record, he would seem, at first glance, to be the most obvious candidate. However Joseph Stalin (1879–1953) must also be in consideration, as he was directly responsible for the deaths of nearly twenty million of his own countrymen.

2000–7000

❦ 9/91 – 2000

L'horrible peste Perynte et Nicopolle,
Le Chersonnez tiendra et Marceloyne,
La Thessalie vastera l'Amphipolle,
Mal incogneu et le refus d'Anthoine.

The terrible plague at Perinthus and
    Nicopolis
Will strike both the peninsular and
    Macedonia
It will devastate Thessaly and
    Amphipolis
An unknown evil; a refusal by
    Anthony.

This quatrain has immediate
significance in the light of Serbian
nationalist ambitions in the Balkans. All
the places mentioned are either in
Greece or in the former Yugoslavian
republic of Macedonia. A key player on
the Nato side is British Prime Minister
Anthony Blair. Could world peace hinge
on his refusal in line 4?

❦ 1/16 – 2000

Faulx à l'estang joint vers le Sagitaire,
En son hault Auge de l'exaltation,
Peste, famine, mort de main militaire,
La siecle approche de renouvation.

Saturn, joined with Aquarius,
    aspecting Sagittarius
In its highest ascendant
Foretells plague, famine and death
    through war
As the century approaches its end.

Saturn moved into Sagittarius on 17
November 1985, not long before
Halley's comet made its predicted
appearance. More recently, thanks to
the El Niño current, the world has been
experiencing an unprecedented
number of natural disasters,
culminating in the recent tragedy in
Guatemala and avalanches in France
and Switzerland. Nostradamus makes
repeated reference, throughout his
quatrains, to an apocalypse occurring
around the end of the Millennium –
which correctly concludes on 31
December 2000.

❦ 1/17 – 2000

Par quarante ans l'Iris n'apparoistra,
Par quarante ans tous les jours sera veu
La terre aride en siccité croistra,
Et grans deluges quand sera aperceu.

For forty years no rainbow will
    appear
For a further forty, it shall be seen
    each day
The arid earth will grow more
    parched
Followed by floods, when the
    rainbow is seen again.

A nuclear winter – which could arise
even without an interncontintenal war or
meteorite impact. The Greenhouse
Effect, if allowed to accelerate
unchecked, will produce similar
climatic catastrophe.

❦ 4/28 – 2000

Lors que Venus du Sol sera couvert,
Soubs l'esplendeur sera forme occulte
Mercure au feu les aura descouvert,
Par bruit bellique sera mis à l'insulte.

When Venus is covered by the sun
A mystic form will be concealed
　beneath its splendour
Mercury will have exposed them, by
　fire
They will be violated in the rattle of
　war.

The next complete masking of Venus by
the sun is due to occur on the 9–10
June 2000, with Mercury rising.
Nostradamus foretells a calamity
occurring near this date, leading to war.

❦ 3/3 – 2000

Mars et Mercure et l'argent joint
　ensemble,
Vers le midi extreme siccité
Au fond d'Asie on dira terre tremble,
Corinthe, Ephese lors en perplexité.

Mars, Mercury and the Moon will
　join forces
Causing a terrible drought in the
　south
It will seem as if the earth trembles in
　Asia
And both Corinth and Ephesus will
　be troubled.

The next conjunction indicated in line 1
will take place between 2 July and 1
August 2000. Nostradamus implies that
there will be a terrible drought in Africa,
followed by a possible nuclear incident
in Asia. The nuclear arms race between
India and Pakistan is a clear threat. The
last line indicates a possible altercation
between Greece and Turkey.

❦ 6/24 – 2002

Mars et le sceptre se trouvera conjoinct,
Dessoubz Cancer calamiteuse guerre
Un peu apres sera nouveau Roi oingt,
Qui par long temps pacifiera la terre.

Mars and the sceptre will join
There will be a calamitous war under
　Cancer
Soon afterwards, a new king will be
　anointed
Who will bring long term peace to
　the earth.

Nostradamus warns elsewhere of a
major war around the turn of the
Millennium, possibly in July of either
1999 or 2000, or in August 1999,
around the time of the eclipse. Here he
depicts a configuration that will occur
on 21 June 2002. Nowhere does he
suggest that the war will be short, and
it's possible that he is demarcating the
length of the conflict with these dates.
He does imply, on more than one
occasion, that we will come through the
war, thanks to the emergence of a new
king, or Messiah, who will be born
during the eclipse.

❦ 9/55 – 2004

L'horrible guerre qu'en l'occident s'apreste
L'an ensuivant viendra la pestilence,
Si fort horribles que jeune, vieux, ne
　beste,
Sang, feu, Mercure, Mars, Jupiter en
　France.

The terrible war being prepared in
　the West
Will be followed, one year later, by a
　plague
Of such virulence it spares neither
　young, old, nor animal
Blood, fire, Mercury, Mars, Jupiter in
　France.

A war followed a year later by a terrible virus. The conjunction in line 4 could indicate either July 2002 or, more likely, September 2004. Scientists researching the flu virus which followed the First World War of 1918, killing as many as 100 million people worldwide, are warning that a similarly untreatable pandemic could break out again at any time.

❦ 4/84 – 2006

*Un grand d'Auxerre mourra bien
   miserable,
Chassé de ceux qui soubs lui ont esté
Serré de chaines, apres d'un rude cable,
En l'an que Mars, Venus, et Sol, mis en
   esté.*

A great man from Auxerre will die in
   poverty
Driven out by his own underlings
Bound in chains, at the end of a
   rough rope
In the year in which Mars, Venus and
   the Sun conjoin in summer.

The next window for this particular conjunction is from June to July 2006. As a result, the rest of the quatrain can only be looked at speculatively.

❦ 8/30 – 2007

*Dedans Tholoze non loing de Beluzer
Faisant un puis long, palais d'espectacle
Tresor trouvé un chacun ira vexer
Et en deux locz et pres del vasacle.*

In Toulouse, not far from Beluzer
Making a deep pit, a palace of
   spectacle
A found treasure will upset everyone
Both in two locations and near the
   Basacle.

The famous Latin proverb *habet aurum Tolosanum*, literally 'he has the gold of Toulouse' and signifying ill-gotten gains, has for 1500 years fostered the belief that in this great city of southern France lies a vast treasure waiting to be discovered. Nostradamus's treasure map is as cryptic as might be expected. The palace of spectacle seems likely to be the Roman amphitheatre or circus, but the most important archaeological site lies six miles to the east of the modern city centre in Old Toulouse, where large caches of Roman coins have already been discovered. A local tradition has it that the treasure comprises the royal gold and jewels looted by Clovis, conqueror of Roman Gaul, from Toulouse in 507. The unravelling of this picturesque mystery is keenly awaited.

❦ 1/90 – early 2000s

*Bourdeaux, Poitiers au son de la
   campane,
A grand classe ira jusques à l'Angon
Contre Gaulois sera leur tramontane,
Quand monstre hideux naistra pres de
   Orgon.*

Bordeaux and Poitiers, at the sound
   of the bell
Will go in great force to Langon
The wind will be against the French
And a hideous monster will be born
   near Orgon.

Commentators have never before picked up that one of the largest French nuclear power plants stands only 20 miles upriver from Bordeaux, at the mouth of the Gironde, at Blaye. Langon itself is only 30 miles down river from Bordeaux, while Poitiers is situated just a hundred miles north-west of the E.D.F. Centrale Nucléaire du Blayais. With this information in hand, the quatrain becomes much clearer.

The sound of bells is that of sirens, indicating a major nuclear disaster. The wind will be blowing from the north – the wrong direction for the French – causing the cloud of nuclear radiation to drift across the mainland rather than out to sea, where it would otherwise have dispersed over the Atlantic ocean. Langon would be one of the first towns to be hit by the cloud, necessitating emergency help from Poitiers, relatively untouched, and Bordeaux, in the thick of it. Orgon, only ten miles north of Salon (home of Nostradamus) would undoubtedly suffer fall-out, being directly in the path of the nuclear cloud. Birth malformations (a hideous monster) would become commonplace in the years following the disaster.

❦   6/98 – early 2000s

Ruine aux Volsques de peur si fort terribles,
Leur grand cité taincte, faict pestilent
Piller Sol, Lune et violer leurs temples
Et les deux fleuves rougir de sang coulant.

Ruin, for those of the Languedoc, and terrible fear
Their great city stained, a pestilent deed
The sun and moon are plundered, their temples violated
The two rivers will redden with flowing blood.

This certainly refers back to the same nuclear reactor disaster Nostradamus predicts for the Mediterranean region in the previous quatrain, 1/90. With the wind from the North, the nuclear cloud would drift over the Languedoc to be caught and held by the mountains of the Pyrenees. The two bloody rivers Aude and Ariège flow through the region, and Nostradamus anticipates serious looting, in which many banks, the temples of gold ('sun') and silver ('moon'), are looted.

❦   8/21 – early 2000s

Au port d'Agde trois fustes entreront
Portant d'infect non foi et pestilence
Passant le pont mil milles embleront,
Et le pont rompre à tierce resistance.

Three barrels enter the port of Agde
Carrying malicious plagues and infections
Crossing the sea, they will kill a million souls
The bridge will break at the third attack.

This is an obvious reference back to the nuclear reactor disaster at Blaye, predicted in the two previous quatrains, 1/90 and 6/98. The three barrels are the cooling towers of the reactor. The polluted waters of the Gironde will leak into the Golfe du Lion, causing a million casualties. They will be carried by the waters of the Garonne, the Aude, and the Canal du Midi, whose outlet is a bare ten miles south of the small port of Agde. Line 4 could imply that the reactor disaster follows terrorist action.

❦   5/62 – early 2000s

Sur les rochers sang on les verra plouvoir,
Sol Orient, Saturne Occidental
Pres d'Orgon guerre, à Rome grand mal voir,
Nefs parfondrees et prins le Tridental.

Blood will rain on the rocks
The Sun in the East, Saturn in the West
War will occur near Orgon, and great evil near Rome
Ships will be broached, and the land of the Trident taken.

Nostradamus mentions Orgon many times during the course of his quatrains, but unfortunately the Sun's opposition to Saturn occurs every year, so we do not have an effective dating for this disaster. But if Orgon is a link to the nuclear disaster in France predicted in the last three quatrains above the Trident could refer to Poseidon, who wielded one, and was renowned for sending earthquakes and plagues against his enemies. His festival used to be celebrated on 23 July. It is an odd coincidence that both Trident and Poseidon are names taken by nuclear-powered submarines.

❦ 2/2 – early 2000s

La teste bleu fera la teste blanche
Autant de mal que France a faict leur
bien
Mort à l'anthene grand pendu sus la
branche
Quand prins des siens le Roy dira
combien.

The blue leader will inflict on the white leader
The equivalent in evil that France has done them good
Death will come from the large antenna hanging on the branch
When seized by his own men, the king will say how much.

A vision, perhaps, of the age of telecommunications and the fierce competition for supremacy on the airwaves now breaking out worldwide.

❦ 1/99 – early 2000s

Le grand monarque que fera compagnie,
Avec deux rois unis par amitié
O quel soupir fera la grand mesgnie,
Enfans Narbon à l'entour quel pitié.

The great monarch who will join
With two kings, united in friendship
O how his people will moan
What sadness for the Narbonnais.

The European union brought together France's president and the 'kings' of Luxembourg and Monaco, both of whom France supplies with nuclear generated electricity from the Rhône valley. Narbonne, on the Mediterranean coast opposite the mouth of the Rhône river, would be one of the worst sufferers in any ensuing nuclear disaster.

❦ 3/75 – early 2000s

Pau, Verone, Vicence, Sarragousse,
De glaives loings terroirs de sang
humides.
Peste si grande viendra à la grand gousse,
Proche secours, et bien loing les remedes.

Pau, Verona, Vicenza and Saragossa
Their swords damp with the blood of distant lands
Will suffer an evil plague, borne by a shell
Relief may be near, but the remedies are far away.

France, Italy and Spain will be struck by a terrible virus borne by a shell. This is one of a number of quatrains that appear to foretell the onset of a chemical war in the near future. The relief in question may be death, as the remedy is still far away. Saddam Hussein has long been experimenting with rocket-propelled canisters in an effort to extend the range of his chemical warheads. All three countries mentioned fought in the Alliance against him during the January–February 1991 Gulf War and would figure high on his reprisal list, given the distant geographical locations of his two principal antagonists, the United States and Great Britain.

☙ 1/91 – early 2000s

Les dieux feront aux humains apparance,
Ce qu'ils seront auteurs de grand conflict
Avant ciel veu serein espee et lance,
Que vers main gauche sera plus grand
afflit.

The gods will fool mankind, making
out
That they are the authors of a great
war
Once, the sky was free of hardware
But now, on the left, there will be
great damage.

This foretells a future nuclear war
between the West and China. The
United States lies on the left of the
world map, China on the right. The US
will suffer grievous casualties. Echoing
the themes of other quatrains, the sky,
once free from military hardware, is now
full of danger and menace. The gods
fool mankind into over-populating the
earth, triggering Chinese military
aggression.

☙ 1/67 – 2020

La grande famine que je sens approcher,
Souvent tourner, puis estre universelle
Si grand et long qu'un viendra arracher,
Du bois racine et l'enfant de mamelle.

The great famine which I see
approaching
Will start sporadically, slowly
becoming universal
It will be so great, and last so long,
that roots
Will be torn from the earth, and
babies from their mother's breast.

A quarter of a million people are born
on the planet every day. If this birth rate
continues, the population of the world
will reach eight billion by 2020.
Sporadic famine is already occurring.
China's population, crowded into the
increasingly unstable flood plains of
rivers such as the Yellow and Yangtse,
is fast reaching insupportable numbers.
The only solution will be to expand –
with the inevitable consequences for
neighbouring nations.

☙ 2/34 – 2042

L'ire insensee du combat furieux
Fera à table par freres le fer luire
Les despartir, blessée, curieux
Le fier duelle viendra en France nuire.

The senseless rage of a furious war
Will cause brothers to unsheathe
their swords at table
They are separated, wounded,
curiously cured
The proud duel will cause harm to
France.

The break-up of the European Union.
Turkey's successful application for
membership prompts Greece,
supported by Italy, to threaten
withdrawal. Uproar in the European
Parliament leads to refusals by several
net-contributor nations to continue to
subsidise any more net-recipient
nations, of which there are 17 among
only 22 member states. The war is an
economic one, and by harm to France
Nostradamus means harm to Europe.

☙ 2/65 – 2044

Le parc enclin grande calamité.
Par l'Hesperie et Insubre fera
Le feu en nef peste et captivité,
Mercure en l'Arc Saturne fenera.

The park, through great calamity, will slope

This will be done throughout the West, and Italy

A fire on board ship, plague and captivity

Mercury in Sagittarius will ruin Saturn.

Hesperie can be taken to mean either the West as a whole, or America. The sloping park implies a major earthquake, set to take place on 7 December 2044, the year of the next full conjunction of Saturn and Mercury entering Sagittarius.

2/95 – 2050

Les lieux peuplez seront inhabitables
Pour champs avoir grand division
Regnes livrez à prudents incapables
Lors les grands freres mort et dissention.

Inhabited lands will become uninhabitable

Land will cause division

Power will be given to imprudent men

Death and dissension for the great brothers.

An uncomfortable prediction of the destruction of the environment, and a time in which inhabitable land will be in short supply. In the 1550s, the world's population was under 500 million, and the processes of deforestation and poisoning of farmland by nitrates and agrochemicals had not yet begun. By the 2050s, global population is projected by the United Nations to be 10 billion, and vast tracts of the planet will be beyond both cultivation and settlement.

2/39 – 2051

Un an devant le conflict Italique
Germains, Gaulois, Hespaignols pour le fort
Cherra l'escole maison de republique
Ou, hors mis peu, seront suffoque mors.

One year before the Italian war

Germans, French and Spanish will support the strongest

The republic's house of learning will fall

Where all but a few will suffocate to death.

Future conflict in Europe – with economic origins. Italy, irredeemably mired in debt, faces partition. The wealthy, productive North proposes separation from the corrupt and aid-dependent South. Germany, France and Spain vote in the European Parliament to recognise a northern-Italian state, and to grant it EU membership. But the United Kingdom and other powerful EU states oppose the proposition. Amidst the wrangling, Nostradamus foresees a terrible attack on the Italian Parliament, perhaps by terrorists or even the Mafia.

6/88 – 2055

Un regne grand demourra desolé
Aupres del Hebro se feront assemblees
Monts Pyrenees le rendront consolé
Lors que dans Mai seront terres tremblees.

A great kingdom is desolated

They will gather near the Ebro

The Pyrenees will console him

For the May earthquakes.

The Ebro river runs parallel to and a hundred miles south of the Pyrenees through northeast Spain. This quatrain is believed to augur a great disaster in the region, possibly the earthquakes mentioned, but just as likely a politically earth-shaking event connected with, say, Spain's participation in the European federal experiment or Basque nationalism. The month of May has been interpreted as code for the number 5 and thus possibly a prediction of five centuries forward to around 2055.

❧ 4/77 – 2059

Selin monarque l'Italie pacifique
Regnes unis Roi chrestien du monde
Mourrant voudra coucher en terre blesique
Apres pirates avoir chassé de l'onde.

With a Selin king, Italy is peaceful
Kingdoms are united by the
   terrestrial Christian King
When he dies, he will wish to be
   buried in Blois
Having chased the pirates from the
   high seas.

Blois in the Loire Valley of France is the seat of the dukes of Orléans and thus, of the French kings of Nostradamus's own time. The beautiful château of the Renaissance is still standing. He visualises this dynasty, symbolised by Selin (from the Greek for Moon – an heraldic device of Henri II) producing a king who will scatter the pirates (meaning the heathen, as exemplified by north African corsairs) and unite Europe under a Christian banner. A happy, if optimistic, prospect for the 500th anniversary of the untimely death of Henri II.

❧ 2/43 – 2062

Durant l'estoille chevelue apparente,
Les trois grans princes seront faits enemis
Frappés du ciel paix terre tremulante,
Pau, Timbre undans, serpent sus le bort mis.

When the bearded star appears
The three princes will argue
The world's fragile peace will be
   struck at from the skies
And a serpent will be placed on the
   shores of the winding Tiber and
   the Po.

The bearded star is undoubtedly Halley's Comet, which last appeared in 1986. Once believed to presage wars and upsets, the comet's next appearance is due in 2062. Edmund Halley (1656–1742) witnessed the comet's passage in 1682 but did not live to see the manifestation of his prediction that these 'bearded stars' (so-known from the ice trails, thousands of miles long, in their wakes) orbit around the solar system. But the Astronomer Royal's calculations of the orbit were strikingly vindicated in 1759 when his now-eponymous comet appeared in the sky, exactly as foretold.

❧ 2/46 – 2062

Apres grand troche humaine plus grand s'appreste,
Le grand moteur des Siecles renouvelle
Pluie, sang, laict, famine, fer et peste,
Au ciel veu feu, courant long estincelle.

Following one misery, a further
   misery lies in wait for mankind
The great cycle of the centuries
   brings renewal
Rain, blood, milk, hunger, cold steel
   and plague
Fire will light up the sky, dragging a
   trail of sparks behind it.

This is one of Nostradamus's many foretellings of Armageddon, to be sign-posted by the flaming tail of a comet. Halley's Comet, one of the most frequent visitors, is next due in 2062.

❦ 2/3 – 2000–2100

Pour la chaleur solaire sus la mer
De Negrepont les poissons demi cuits
Les habitans les viendront entamer
Quand Rhod, et Gennes leur faudra le biscuit.

Because of the sun's heat on the sea
The fish from Negrepont will be par-boiled
The inhabitants will come and eat them
When those in Rhodes and Genoa are starving.

Global warming. As carbon dioxide and other greenhouse gases accumulate in the Earth's atmosphere, the oceans heat up. Nostradamus foresees with uncanny acuity the destruction of marine life – already upon us as coral reefs die and shallow-water fish cook in unsheltered, starving seas.

❦ 2/96 – 2000–2100

Flambeau ardent au ciel soir sera veu
Pres de la fin et principe du Rosne
Famine, glaive: tard le secours pourveu
La Perse tourne envahir Macedoine.

A burning flame will appear in the night sky
Near both the source and the estuary of the Rhône
Famine, swords: help will come late
Persia turns and invades Macedonia.

No doubt about the last line. Persia, now Iran, reverses history by avenging

its destruction by the Macedonian giant of history, Alexander the Great, who burnt Persepolis in a drunken fit in 330 BC. Macedonia is now an unstable former republic of the Yugoslav federation. Nostradamus predicts that the country will submit itself to the Muslim faith, and that conflicts elsewhere in Europe will deny aid against the invader.

❦ 4/99 – 2000–2100

L'aisné vaillant de la fille du Roy
Repoussera si profond les Celtiques
Qu'il mettra foudres, combien en tel arroi
Peu et loing puis profond és Hesperiques.

The brave eldest son of the king's daughter
Will drive the Celts a long way back
He will panic them by using thunderbolts
Few and far between, then deep into the West.

The West in the final line refers to America, and the thunderbolts speak of modern firepower. The Celts of ancient time are identified with the pre-Roman peoples of the Low Countries who migrated to the British Isles and elsewhere in Europe. But in the Nostradamian code Celtiques has also been known to refer to the French. A vision of future intercontinental war, but tantalisingly oblique.

1/83 – 2000–2100

La gent estrange divisera butins
Saturne et Mars son regard furieux,
Horrible estrange aux Toscans et Latins
Grec qui seront a frapper curieux.

The alien race will divide the spoils
Saturn and Mars will have an angry
    aspect
Horrible and strange to the Tuscans
    and Romans
Greeks will wonder whether to
    strike.

Nostradamus envisions a time when
war between nations – exemplified by
Greece and Italy – will be interrupted
by the appearance of a common
enemy, an alien race. Perhaps from
another continent, possibly from a
distant world.

1/84 – 2000–2100

Lune obscure cie aux profondes tenebres,
Son frère passe de couleur ferrigine;
Le grand cache long temps soubs les
    tenebres,
Tiendra fer dans la pluie sanguine.

The moon hidden in deep darkness
Her brother changes to a reddish
    colour
The great one hides for long in
    darkness
He will take up arms in a rain of
    blood.

The sun the colour of blood; the moon
unseen; raining blood. A vision of war
in which, the world is, quite literally,
darkened. An uncomfortable portent of
the nuclear winter.

1/46 – 2000–2100

Tout aupres d'Auch, de Lectoure et
    Mirande,
Grande feu du ciel en trois nuits
    tombera,
Chose adviendra bien stupende et
    mirande,
Bien peu après al terre tremblera.

All around Auch, Lectoure and
    Mirande
A great fire will fall from the sky for
    three nights
A stupendous, marvellous thing will
    happen
Soon after, the ground will shake.

Nostradamus describes these
convulsing events as wonderful rather
than terrifying, so a celestial upheaval
rather than an earthly bombardment is
presaged. Auch is a city of southwest
France famed for its immense Gothic
cathedral, founded in 1489. It remained
staunchly Catholic throughout the
religious wars of the sixteenth century.
Perhaps the seer believed it would be a
just reward for the city to witness a
great heavenly happening, when it
comes.

2/30 – 2000–2100

Un qui des dieux d'Annibal infernaux
Fera renaistre, effrayeur des humains
Oncq' plus d'horreur ne plus dire
    journaulx
Qu'avint viendra Babel aux Romains.

One who calls up the infernal gods
Of Hannibal, terror of mankind
Even more horror, more than the
    papers tell
Then the Romans come, through
    Babel.

Hannibal (247–183 BC) was the Carthaginian soldier who came very close indeed to conquering Rome by marching on Italy through France and across the Alps in 218 BC. Nostradamus foresees an imperial invader similarly able to win unexpected victories, who comes through Babel – an allegory for a place of diverse foreign tongues. Alludes to an invasion of Europe from a future Asian superpower.

🐝 5/54 – 2000–2100

Du pont Euxine, et la grand Tartarie,
Un roi sera qui viendra voir la Gaule
Transpercera Alane et l'Armenie,
Et dans Bisance lairra sanglante Gaule.

From the Black Sea and great
   Tartary
A king will come, to France
He will cross Russia and Armenia
And raise his bloody standard in
   Byzantium.

The third Anti-Christ is due to come from the East. Could he be the new Messiah predicted elsewhere by Nostradamus, or will he be evil, bringing terror to the Earth? The fact that he raises a 'bloody standard' does not bode well.

🐝 5/90 – 2000–2100

Dans les cyclades, en perinthe et larisse
Dedans Sparte tout le Pelloponesse
Si grand famine, peste par faux connisse
Neuf mois tiendra et tout le chevronesse.

In the Cyclades, in Perinthus and
   Larissa
In Sparta, and throughout the
   Peloponnese
There will be a great famine, caused
   by a false dust
It will last for nine months in the
   whole peninsular.

Greece faces famine for a whole season, caused by a false dust. The word false implies a synthetic, manufactured material – rather than, say, ash from a volcanic eruption. It could symbolise biological warfare. A horrible harbinger of future warfare.

🐝 2/74 – 2000–2100

De Sens, D'Autun viendront jusques au
   Rosne,
Pour passer outre vers les monts Pyrenées
La gent sortir de la Marque d'Anconne,
Par terre et mer suivra à grans trainées.

From Sens, the Autunois will reach
   the Rhône
To pass from there across the
   Pyrenees
Those born in the Ancona marshes
Will follow, in great numbers, by
   land and sea.

One commentator, taking *trainées* to mean tracks, reads this as a foretelling of the laying of fast TGV train tracks right across Europe! This is extrapolated to include superconductive train lines laid across the floors of oceans. The reader may judge.

🐝 2/75 – 2000–2100

La voix ouie de l'insolite oiseau,
Sur le canon du respiral estage
Si hault viendra du froment le boisseau,
Que l'homme de l'homme fera
   Antropophage.

The cry of a strange bird
Will be heard through the chimney
   shafts
The cost of wheat will rise so high
That men will become cannibals.

Owls, and other avian spiritual messengers, are often accepted as harbingers of doom. Another interpretation could have strange bird describing an aircraft dropping bombs. Following the nuclear war, the cost of wheat would become so punitive that mankind would revert to cannibalism in an effort to ward off extinction.

☙ 2/45 – 2000–2100

Trop le ciel pleure l'Androgyn procrée,
Pres de ciel sang humain respondu
Par mort trop tard grand peuple recrée,
Tard et tost vient le secours attendu.

The heavens weep too much when the Hermaphrodite breeds
High in the sky, human blood is shed
Through death, a great race can no longer be recreated
Sooner or later the expected help will come.

This can now be seen as a reference to human cloning, leading to possible warfare later on. It seems certain that many nations are already experimenting, in deepest secret, with the possibilities of genetic morphology. The expected help is likely to be scientific, allowing the 'great race' to recreate itself after the gradual failure of human fertility due to pollution and hormone poisoning.

☙ 2/84 – 2000–2100

Entre Campaigne, Sienne, Flora, Tustie,
Six mois neuf jours ne ploura une goutte
L'estrange langue en terre Dalmatie,
Courira sus: vastant la terre toute.

Between Campania, Siena, Florence and Tuscany
Not a drop of rain will fall for six months and nine days
A foreign tongue will be heard in Dalmatia
And the country will be overrun and devastated.

Yet another quatrain foretelling the effects of a global drought, this time on Italy, with a warning that Dalmatia (Yugoslavia) will be invaded, perhaps for a connected reason.

☙ 2/86 – 2000–2100

Naufrage à classe pres d'onde Hadriatique,
La terre tremble esmeüe sus l'air en terre mis
Egypte tremble augment Mahometique,
L'Herault soi rendre à crier est commis.

A fleet is wrecked near Adriatic waters
The earth trembles, erupts, and falls on land
Egypt quakes, augmenting Islam
The Herald surrenders, and is forcibly evangelised.

Customarily taken to describe Napoleon's Egyptian campaign of 1799, this quatrain can also be used to foretell a future resurgence of Islamic fundamentalism in Egypt, possibly stemming from an earthquake or the destruction of a ship in the Adriatic.

2/22 – 2000–2100

Le camp Ascap d'Europe partira,
S'adjoignant proche de l'isle submergée
D'Arton classe phalange pliera,
Nombril du monde plus grand voix
*   subrogée.*

The aimless army will leave Europe
Meeting once more near the
    submerged island
The ranks of the d'Arton fleet will
    collapse
And a new world centre, with a
    greater voice, will be substituted.

This could foretell the end of Nato, or
Otan (d'Arton) as it is known in France.
Russia is already putting pressure on
the members of Nato to disband, and
create a new alliance that better
reflects the makeup of the post-Cold
War world.

2/5 – 2000–2100

Qu'en dans poisson, fer et lettres enfermée
Hors sortira qui puis fera la guerre
Aura par mer sa classe bien ramée
Apparoissant pres de Latine terre.

When weapons and letters are sealed
    in a fish
A war-maker will come
His fleet will have travelled far
They will appear near the Latin
    shore.

Military orders carried in a submarine.
The present generation of nuclear-
powered submarine can
circumnavigate the globe, and carry
sealed orders to be opened when
signals are received from on-shore
commanders. The reference to the
Latin shore suggests the Adriatic sea –
within range of that Millennial theatre of
war, the Balkans.

5/25 – 2000–2100

Le prince Arabe Mars, Sol, Venus, Lyon
Regne d'Eglise par mer succombera
Devers la Perse bien pres d'un million
Bisance, Egypte, ver. serp. invadera.

The Arab prince, Mars, the Sun,
    Venus and Leo
The church's realm will succumb by
    sea
Nearly a million men will invade
    Egypt and Byzantium
Followers of the true serpent, from
    the direction of Persia.

Trouble afoot in the Middle East. From
the direction of Persia (Iran) comes an
invasion of Turkey and Egypt and the
extinction of Christianity in the region.
The incursion would appear to be
doctrinal rather than military. The
astrological information is insufficient to
plot a date.

2/62 – 2000–2100

Mabus puis tost alors mourra, viendra,
De gens et bestes une horrible defaite
Puis tout à coup la vengeance on verra,
Cent, main, soif, faim, quand courra la
*   comete.*

Soon Mabus will die, and then will
    come
A terrible undoing of animals and
    people
Then, suddenly, vengeance will
    appear
In the form of a comet; hunger,
    thirst, a hundred hands.

The only illness which kills both animals
and humans indiscriminately is
radiation poisoning. The name Mabus
probably refers to a future world leader,
whose death precipitates the coming

nuclear war. Nostradamus reiterates his belief that a comet will arrive to presage disaster. *M'abus*, written with an apostrophe, means self-abuse.

☙ 2/60 – 2000–2100

La foi Punicque en Orient rompue
Grand Jud. et Rosne, Loire et Tag
changeront.
Quand du mulet la faim sera repue,
Classe espargie, sang et corps nageront.

Libyan treachery breaks out in the east
The river Jordan, the Rhône, the Loire and the Tagus will deviate
Hunger will be sated by a mule
The fleet scattered, bodies and blood floating on the waters.

Some commentators interpret this as a future Muslim invasion of Europe. This seems unlikely at the present time. Instead, bodies and blood floating on the waters conjures up a horrifying image of a downed civilian airliner. With Libya deemed to be responsible for the Pan Am airliner which exploded over Lockerbie, such a reading, implying further atrocities along the same lines, would seem more logical.

☙ 2/4 – 2000–2100

Depuis Monach jusque aupres de Sicile
Toute la plage demourra desolée
Il n'y aura fauxbourg, cité ne ville
Que par Barbares pillé soit et volée.

From Monaco, to near Sicily
The entire coast will be desolated
There will be neither suburb, town nor city
That has not been pillaged and robbed by the Barbarians.

Nostradamus was known to refer to Muslims as Barbarians. He foresees a time when Islam invades all of Italy.

☙ 5/78 – 2000–2100

Les deux unis ne tiendront longuement
Et dans treize ans au Barbare Satrappe
Au deux costez seront tel perdement
Qu'un benira le Barque et sa cappe.

The two will not remain united for long
In thirteen years to the Barbarian Satrap
There will be such loss, on both sides
That one man will bless the Papal ship and cape.

The satraps were the provincial governors of the ancient Persian empire. Here a new empire is perceived in decline because an alliance is breaking up. Perhaps the future disintegration of relations between Russia and the former client states of the Soviet Union. There is every likelihood of the Catholic faith filling the spiritual gap as Marxist dogma retreats.

☙ 1/50 – 2000–2100

De l'aquatique triplicité naistra.
D'un qui fera le jeudi pour sa feste
Son bruit, loz, regne, sa puissance
croistra,
Par terre et mer aux Oriens tempeste.

A triumvirate will be born from the water
One of whom will take Thursday for his feast day
His renown, praises, reign and power will grow
Bringing the East unrest, from land and sea.

This is a reference to the Third Antichrist, who will have the water signs of Aries, Cancer and Aquarius dominant in his birth sign. The fact that he will take Thursday for his feast day implies, in Nostradamus's strict dogmatic interpretation of the scriptures, that he will be a pagan being, causing others to worship him.

☙ 1/53 – 2000–2100

Las qu'on verra grand peuple tourmenté,
Et la loi saincte en totale ruine
Par autres loix toute la Christienté,
Quand d'or, d'argent trouve nouvelle
*   mine.*

Alas, we will see a great nation in
    turmoil
And Holy law in utter ruin
Christianity will be governed by new
    laws
Following the discovery of a new
    source of riches.

Could this be a reference to the ordination of women, a concept which would have been unthinkable to Nostradamus? The Catholic church will almost certainly take this route in the future, causing Christianity to be governed by new laws and throwing the great Vatican nation state into turmoil. The election of women to the prelacy could indeed come to be regarded as the 'discovery of a new source of riches'.

☙ 6/21 – 2000–2100

Quant ceux du polle artiq unis ensemble,
En Orient grand effrayeur et crainte
Esleu nouveau, soustenu le grand
*   tremble,*
Rhodes, Bisance de sang Barbare taincte.

When those of the Arctic pole unite
There will great fear and dread in the
    East
The newly elected man will find
    support, the mighty one trembles
Rhodes and Byzantium will be
    stained with Barbarian blood.

Anticipating a time when Russia and the US will be allies, Nostradamus presages the fear and dread this alliance will provoke in China. Taking advantage of the power stand-off, Turkey and Greece will go to war again, precipitating an Arab invasion.

☙ 2/91 – 2000–2100

Soleil levant un grand feu l'on verra
Bruit et clarté vers Aquilon tendants
Dedans le rond mort et cris l'on orra
Par glaive, feu, faim, mort las attedants.

A great fire will be seen at sunrise
Its noise and light extending to the
    North
Death and cries shall be heard inside
    the circle
Death awaits them through sword,
    fire and famine.

This is a fire that comes suddenly, an ominous picture of a great explosion presaging not just war, but famine. It is now known that the aftermath of an atomic war would include a 'nuclear winter' in which the dust and ash from detonations and conflagrations would settle in the atmosphere, excluding sunlight and trapping the world in a darkness that would make food production impossible.

❦ 2/41 – 2000–2100

La grand estoille par sept jours brulera,
Nuée fera deux soleils apparoir
Le gros mastin fera toute nuict hurlera,
Quand grand pontife changera de
    terroir.

The bright star will burn for seven
    days
The smoke therefrom will cause two
    suns to appear
All night the great hound will howl
When the pope changes his abode.

Taken by many to refer to the 'double
sun' effect of a nuclear explosion, it
could just as easily pertain to the
aftermath of a meteorite striking the
Earth. The impact site might well burn
for seven days, throwing dense clouds
of ash and dust into the atmosphere
from which the sun would reflect,
producing, in effect, 'two suns'. The
hound could be Cerberus, guardian of
Hell's gate, calling the dead down to
Hades with each of his three heads in
turn. Either way, the Pope would
certainly do well, under these
circumstances, to move house.

❦ 5/27 – 2000–2100

Par feu et armes non loing de la
    marnegro
Viendra de Perse occuper Trebisonde
Trembler Phatos Methelin, Sol alegro
De sang Arabe d'Adrie couvert onde.

By fire and armaments, not far from
    the Black Sea
He will come from Persia to occupy
    Trebizond
Pharos and Mitylene will tremble,
    the Sun is quick
The Adriatic waves are covered with
    Arab blood.

The Black Sea city of Trebizond, the
eternally romantic last fragment of
Byzantium, was swallowed up by
Mehmet II (1432–61), 'the Conqueror'
and founder of the Ottoman Empire, in
1461. Mehmet went on to invade the
Balkans and the Mediterranean islands
(of which Pharos off Alexandria and
Mitylene are two) and was in the
process of attacking Persia when he
died. Why does Nostradamus present
this historical item as a prophecy of the
future? He must have expected it all to
happen again. In the context of today's
Asia Minor, it seems all too possible.

❦ 8/16 – 2000–2100

Au lieu que Hieron feit sa nef fabriquer,
Si grand deluge sera et si subite,
Qu'on n'aura lieu ne terres s'atacquer
L'onde monter Fesulan Olympique.

Where Jason built his ship
Will come a great and sudden flood
There will be no land left to cling to
The waves will rise over Mount
    Olympus.

A return to meteor strike predictions,
this one set to occur somewhere in the
Aegean. Mount Olympus (Olympia) is
9,570 feet above sea level, so the
tsunami (sea waves arising from violent
seismic actions) are expected to be
overwhelming.

❦ 1/64 – 2000–2100

De nuict soleil penseront avoir veu,
Quand le pourceau demi-homme on
verra
Bruict, chant, bataille, au ciel battre
aperceu:
Et bestes brutes à parler lon orra.

They will dream they have seen the
sun by night
When the half-man, half-pig appears
Noise, song, battles, combats in the
sky
Brute beasts will be heard to speak.

The Russians have already built and
tested great mirrors that can light up
the sky from space, turning night into
day. The creation of these mirrors eerily
coincides with the cloning of animals
and of human beings. Is it too much to
suppose that one day very soon
humans will be cloned to animals? Pigs'
livers have already been used in
transplant operations. Modern day Dr
Frankensteins will very soon be
capable of turning the magic powers of
Homer's Circe into reality, by cloning
men into pigs, possibly with a view to
creating a less emotionally unstable
fighting machine. At this point,
Nostradamus's prediction of battles
fought in the skies, and of a time when
brute beasts will be heard to speak,
rings horribly true.

❦ 6/20 – 2000 onwards

L'union faincte sera peu de durée,
Des uns changés reformés la pluspart
Dans les vaissaux sera gent endurée,
Lors aura Rome un nouveau liepart.

The pretend union will not last long
Of the ones that are changed, most
will reform
In the ships will be an enduring
people
And Rome will have a new leopard.

A remarkable quatrain that foretells the
downfall of the 1998 Northern Ireland
peace agreement and of the union that
was engineered between North and
South under its auspices. Occurring
around the time a new Pope is elected
in Rome, it details the back-tracking of
those who seemed most in favour of the
agreement. The reference to enduring
people and ships reinforces the Irish
theme, alluding to the fact that many
Irish, over the years, have left their
country in despair, travelling by ship to
the New World. This is a superb
example of Nostradamus incorporating
both the past history and the near
future of an event into one quatrain.

❦ 3/48 – 2000 onwards

Sept cens captifs estachez rudement
Pour la moitié meurtrir, donné le sort
Le proche espoir viendra si promptement
Mais non si tost qu'une quinziesme
mort.

Seven hundred captives, roughly
bound
Lots are drawn, half are murdered
The expected aid comes quickly
But too late to save fifteen of them.

A presage of the hostage crises that
became routine during the outbreak of
terrorist activities that began in the
1970s, including outrages such as the
murder of athletes at the Munich
Olympics and the raid on Entebbe. But
this quatrain is precise in its details,
and no hostage massacre on this scale
has yet taken place. This ghastly event
lies in the future.

❧ 4/98 – 2000 onwards

Les Albanois, passeront dedans Rome
Moyennant Langres demipler affublés
Marquis et Duc ne pardonnes à l'homme
Feu, sang, morbilles point d'eau, failli les
*   bleds.*

The Albanians will enter Rome
Because of Langres, the multitude
   are weakened
The Marquis and the Duke will spare
   no man
Fire, blood, smallpox, no water, the
   crops will fail.

Italy is now all-too familiar with refugees
from Albania and Kosovo, fleeing war,
starvation and disease. But there are
elements of this quatrain which remain
mysterious. Future events may reveal
more.

❧ 5/49 – 2000 onwards

Nul de l'Espaigne mais de l'antique
*   France*
Ne sera esleu pour le tremblant nacelle,
A l'ennemi sera faicte fiance,
Qui dans son regne sera peste cruelle.

Not from Spain, but rather from
   ancient France
He will be elected; the ship will
   tremble
He will make promises to the enemy
Which will cause a great plague to
   trouble his reign.

Could a future Pope be French?
Nostradamus appears to imply that if
this transpires, the pontiff's reign will be
greatly troubled.

❧ 7/17 – 2000 onwards

Le prince rare de pitié et clemence,
Viendra changer par mort grand
*   cognoissance*
Par grand repos le regne travaillé,
Lors que le grand tost sera estrillé.

A prince of rare pity and clemency
Will change and gain great
   knowledge through death
The kingdom will thrive in
   tranquillity
However the great man will soon be
   fleeced.

When Charles, Prince of Wales,
becomes King of Great Britain, he is
likely to be in his sixties, or older. He
has already shown signs of a high
sensibility, and the sudden loss of his
estranged wife, Diana, 36, in a car
crash on 31 August 1997, appears to
have exaggerated this trait.
Nostradamus predicts that the kingdom
will thrive under Charles III, but that his
weak point may be a certain gullibility.

❧ 4/38 – 2000 onwards

Pendant que Duc, Roi, Royne occupera
Chef Bisant du captif en Samothrace
Avant l'assault l'un l'autre mangera
Rebours ferré suivra du sang la trace.

While the Duke occupies the King
   and Queen
The Byzantine chief is captive in
   Greece
Before the assault one will eat the
   other
The armoured retreat will follow the
   trail of blood.

A presage of a future conflict between
Turkey and Greece amidst talks
between major powers. The
cannibalistic phrase is surely
metaphorical.

❦ 5/22 – 2000 onwards

Avant qu'à Rome grand aie rendu l'ame
Effrayeur grande à l'armée estrangere
Par Esquadrons, l'embusche pres de
  Parme
Puis les deux rouges ensemble feront chere.

Before the great man dies at Rome
There will be much terror for the
  foreign army
An ambush, by squadrons, near
  Parma
Then the two red ones will hold a
  joint celebration.

The Pope is dying, and northern Italy
(signified by Parma) is in a state of
conflict. This is good news to two
rebels. A harbinger of a north-south
split in Italy, plotted by factions in both
halves of the country, soon after the
death of the present Pope? The next
quatrain reinforces the suggestion.

❦ 5/23 – 2000 onwards

Les deux contens seront unis ensemble
Quand la pluspart à Mars seront conjoinct
Le grand d'Affrique en effrayeur et
  tremble
Duumvirat par la classe desjoinct.

The two contented men will unite
When most of the others are united
  with Mars
The African leader trembles in terror
The dual alliance is broken by the
  fleet.

The two celebrants find common cause
as the combatants – likely to be rioters
demonstrating either for or against
national unity – fight impotently on. The
African leader is code for an external
party who stands to lose much by the
fall of the Italian national government.
Candidates include the European
Union.

❦ 4/39 – 2000 onwards

Les Rhodians demanderont secours
Par le neglect de ses hors delaissée
L'Empire Arabe revalera son secours
Par Hesperies la cause redressée.

The people of Rhodes will ask for
  help
Abandoned, through the neglect of
  their heirs
The Arab Empire will re-arm
Its cause revived by the West.

It comes as a surprise to tourists
visiting the Aegean islands to discover
that armed Greek troops are stationed
there in a constant state of alert against
invasion from Turkey (the Ottoman and
Arab empires are as one Muslim unit).
Nostradamus correctly predicts the
tension of centuries.

❦ 5/98 – 2100

A quarante huict degré climaterique
A fin de Cancer si grande seicheresse
Poisson en mer, fleuve, lac cuit hectique
Bearn, Bigorre par feu ciel en destresse.

At the 48th climacteric degree
At the end of July, there will be a
  great drought
The fish of the sea, rivers and lakes
  will be boiled alive
Bearn and Bigorre will suffer from
  fire from the sky.

A clear prediction of global warming
and its disastrous implications. If
forecasts by climatologists are to be
believed. World temperatures will
increase by as much as three degrees
centigrade during the twenty-first
century. That's six times the rise of the
twentieth. Extrapolating, the sea will
boil well before the fourth millennium of
the Christian era.

🐝 6/10 – 2100 onwards

Un peu de temps les temples de couleurs
De blanc et noir des deux entremeslee
Rouges et jaunes leur embleront les leurs
Sang, terre, peste, faim, feu, d'eau
*   affollee.*

Soon the temple of colours
Black and white intermixed
Reds and yellows will take theirs
    away
Blood, earth, plague, hunger, fire,
    maddened by thirst.

A vision of a multi-racial society bound
together by the elements of the last
line. It suggests that when these
boundary-crossing troubles afflict the
whole world, as surely they will, we will
at last put nationalism aside and live
together as one race – with our
humanity in common. An optimistic
outlook for the third millennium.

🐝 3/12 – 2100

Par la tumeur de Heb, Po, Tag, Timbre
*   et Rome*
Et par l'estsange leman et Arentin
Les deux grands chefs et citez de
*   Garonne*
Prins mors noyez. Partir humain butin.

Because of the flooding of the Ebro,
    Po, Tagus, Tiber and Rhône
And also of the lakes of Leman and
    Arezzo
The two main chiefs and their cities
    of the Garonne
Are taken, dead, drowned. The
    people divide the booty.

Global warming threatens a substantial
rise in sea levels, through the thermal
expansion of the oceans, attended by
the additional risk of major thaw in the
polar ice caps, during the third
millennium. One well-supported
projection has sea levels rising five
metres by the end of the twenty-first
century.

🐝 8/9 – 2126

Pendant que l'aigle et le coq à Savone
Seront unis Mer Levant et Ongrie
L'armee à Naples, Palerne, Marque
*   d'Ancone*
Rome, Venise par Barb' horrible crie.

While the cock and the eagle are at
    Savona
The Eastern and Hungarian seas will
    be united
The army is at Naples, Palermo, the
    marches of Ancona
Rome, Venice, great cries from the
    barbarian.

The cock signifies France, and there is
the chance that the eagle here
represents America – forming a western
alliance against a threat from the East.
Barbarian can be taken to mean a
Muslim invasion and the route is clearly
through the Mediterranean.

🐝 3/20 – 2192

Par les contrees du grand fleuve
*   Bethique*
Loing d'Ibere au royaume de Grenade
Croix repoussees par gens Mahometiques
Un de Cordube trahira la contrade.

Through the lands either side of the
    Guadalquivir
Far from Spain, to the kingdom of
    Granada
The cross is pushed back by the
    Mahommedans
A Cordoban man will betray his
    country.

Granada, the last Moorish stronghold in Spain, fell to the armies of Ferdinand and Isabella, on 2 January 1492. It is one of the great dates in history – the end of centuries of Mohammedan influence in Europe. But it marked a bleak time for the Jews in Spain. Muslim rulers had always been tolerant, but now that the power of the Catholic Church was absolute, all Jews in the country – about 150,000 of them – were summarily expelled. Some of Nostradamus's own forbears were undoubtedly among them. The seer, brought up a Catholic in spite of his Jewish birth, must have had mixed feelings about the prospect of a Muslim re-invasion of Spain, but predicted it just the same. It hasn't happened yet, but the rise of Islam makes the prospect of the prophecy that Moors will return to Andalucia after 700 years look a legitimate possibility.

🐦 2/48 – 2193

La grand copie qui passera les monts,
Saturne en l'Arq tournant du poisson
Mars
Venins caches soubs testes de saulmons,
Leur chef pendu à fil de polemars.

The great army, which crosses the high passes
Saturn in Sagittarius aspects Mars in Pisces
Hidden poison in salmon-heads
Their war chief will be hanged by a cord.

The conjunction of the planets mentioned in the quatrain last occurred on 7 July 1751. It will occur again on 13 July 2193. The poison hidden in salmon-heads seems a likely rendering of salmonella.

🐦 6/80 – 2570

De Fez le regne parviendra à ceux
d'Europe
Feu leur cité et lame trenchera
Le grand d'Asie terre et mer à grand
troupe
Que bleux, pers, croix, à mort dechassera.

From Fez the kingdom will reach Europe
Their city blazes and the sword slashes
The great Asian leader will cross land and sea with a large army
He will drive out and kill the blues, the Persians and those of the cross.

Nostradamus visualises a Muslim invasion of Europe from the Persian Gulf, aided by a power base in north Africa. Not necessarily a military takeover but quite possibly a doctrinal ingress as the Christian faith retreats. Some traditions date this transcending event to the year 2570, the start of the third Mohammedan millennium.

🐦 8/48 – 2769

Saturne en Cancer, Jupiter avec Mars
Dedans Feurier Chaldondon salvaterre
Sault Castalon affailli de trois pars
Pres de Verbiesque conflit mortelle guerre.

Saturn in Cancer, Jupiter with Mars
In February a soothsayer saves the earth
Sierra Morena is besieged on three sides
Near Verbier there is war and mortal conflict.

Astrologers date this event at 1 February 2769. It appears that a warning about a war will be heeded, and the world saved.

☙ 1/49 – 3255

Beaucoup, beaucoup avant telles menées,
Ceux d'Orient par la vertu Lunaire,
L'An mil sept cens feront grands
*   emmenées,*
Subjugant presque le coin Aquilonaire.

Long, long before such events
The people of the Orient by stealth
In 1700 years' time will expel great
    numbers
Subjugating nearly all the north.

The events referred to in the first lines
are the consuming of the earth by the
sun and the end of humanity in the year
7000. But before this happens, the
Chinese will take over most of the
northern hemisphere (Aquile is an old
word for the North).

☙ 10/67 – 3797

Le tremblement si fort au mois de Mai,
Saturne, Caper, Jupiter, Mercure au
*   beuf*
Venus aussi Cancer, Mars en Nonnay,
Tombera gresse lors plus grosse qu'un euf.

A mighty earthquake, in the month
    of May
Saturn, Capricorn, Jupiter and
    Mercury in Taurus
Venus also in Cancer, Mars in Virgo
Hailstones, larger than eggs, will
    then fall.

The conjunction suggested here next
occurs in May 3797.

☙ 1/48 – 7000

Vingt ans du regne de la lune passez,
Sept mil ans autre tiendra sa monarchie,
Quand le soleil prendra ses jours laissez,
Lors accomplit a fine ma Prophecie.

After 20 years of the moon's reign
Another monarch will take hold for
    7,000 years
When the sun takes the remaining
    days
Then my prophecy is finally
    accomplished.

Armageddon: the sun will consume the
Earth, around the year 7000. In fact,
this is not Nostradamus's own
prediction. He has adapted it from the
pre-Christian Book of Enoch.

☙ 10/74 – 7000

Au revolu du grand nombre septiesme,
Apparoistra au temps jeux d'Hecatombe,
Non esloigné de grand d'age milliesme,
Que les entrez sortiront de leur tombe.

When the great number seven rolls
    around
Will come the time of games at the
    Hecatomb
Not far from the great Millennium
    age
When the interred will depart from
    their tomb.

In the seventh millennium, the dead will
have their day, walking on the Earth
once more. Perhaps a vision not of the
fall of man, but of the ultimate triumph
of medicine. Either way, a ghoulish
prospect.

Prophecies Yet To Be Dated

The quatrains in this section are those for which no firm date has been established with any real certainty. They appear in the sequence in which they were originally published.

Century One

1/4

Par l'Univers sera fair un Monarque
Qu'en paix et vie ne sera longuement.
Lors se perdra la Pisacture Barque,
Sera régie en plus detriment.

The world will make a monarch
Who will not enjoy peace or life for
  long
The Fishing Boat will then be lost
The reign will be even more
  destructive.

An ominous prospect of a short-lived global ruler who threatens the Fishing Boat – possibly a reference to the Church. Nostradamus may be looking ahead to the rise, and fall, of communism – or even consumerism.

1/15

Mars nous menace par la force bellique,
Septante fois fera le sang espandre
Auge et ruine de l'Ecclesiastique,
Et plus ceux qui d'eux rien voudront
  entendre.

Mars threatens us with war
Blood will be spilled seventy times
The clergy will rise, then be reviled
By those unwilling to listen.

This is a general quatrain, foretelling the loss of influence of the churches. In any given year since the Second World War there have been between 20 and 40 wars being fought somewhere on the planet. Nostradamus implies that when this number rises to 70, the Catholic church will reach its lowest ebb.

1/27

Dessous le chesne Guyen du ciel frappé
Non loin de la est cacher le thresor
Qui par long siècles avoit este grappé
Trouvé mourra, l'oeil creve de ressort.

Beneath the mistletoe oak struck by
  lightning
Not far away is the treasure hidden
Which has been hidden and sought
  over many years
The finder will die, his eye pierced
  by a spring.

The treasure is, perhaps, the key that will break the code to all Nostradamus's predictions. Over the centuries, investigators have searched for evidence that the seer wrote a separate document revealing all his secrets, and buried it. If this quatrain is to be believed, it lies at the foot of an oak tree struck by lightning and in which mistletoe grows. But the last line is a warning – the treasure is booby-trapped.

1/30

La nef estrange par le tourment marin,
Abourdera pres de port incogneu
Nonobstant signes de rameau palmerin,
Apres mort pille bon avis tard venu.

Because of a storm, the foreign ship
Will approach an unknown harbour
Despite friendly protestations
    Good advice comes too late to
      prevent death and pillage.

A very general quatrain that could be
applied to almost any exodus, including
that of the Jews to Palestine, after the
Second World War.

1/40

La tourbe fausse dissimilant folie
Fera Bizance un changement de loix
Istra d'Egypt qui veus que l'on deslie,
Edict, changant monnoys et alloys.

The paid mob feigning madness
Will force a change in Byzantine laws
Freeing exiles from Egypt
Changing money and standards by
    edict.

A vision of power changing hands as a
result of 'rentamob' pressure. Byzantine
laws hardly pin this down to any
individual nation – none has ever been
without them. Exiles from Egypt may
suggest an Israeli connection.

1/42

Les dix Calendes d'Avril de fait
    Gothique
Rescuscité encor par gens malins,
Le feu estaint, assemblée diabolique
Cherchand les os du Damant et Psellin.

The tenth of the Calends of April,
    Gothic style,
Raised again by sorcerers.
The light extinguished, a diabolical
    gathering,
Seeking the bones of the demon
    Psellus.

Michael Constantine Psellus (1018–78)
was a great figure of the Byzantine
Empire, a statesman and an important
writer on politics, philosophy and
medicine. He revived an interest in
Plato – at the expense of Aristotle – and
his enthusiasm for the paganism of
ancient Greece raised doubts about his
orthodoxy. Nostradamus will thus have
associated his name with the worst
aspects of the fall of Byzantium.

1/43

Avant qu'avien le changement
    d'Empire,
Il adviendra un cas bien merveilleux,
Le champ mué, le pilier de Porphyre,
Mis, translate sur le Rocher Noileux.

Before the Empire changes
A marvellous event will occur
A field transforms and a pillar of
    Porphyry
Built there will turn into a mound of
    woolscraps.

An opaque quatrain in which the pillar
of Porphyry could equally be a
monument to the third-century Greek
neoplatonist Porphyrius (author of the
celebrated treatise *Against the*
Christians), or any pillar made from
porphyry, the red volcanic stone much
treasured in the ancient world. Noil is a
sixteenth-century word for knots
combed out of raw wool.

1/69

La grand montaigne ronde de sept stades,
Apres paix, guerre, faim, innondation
Roulera loin abismant grands contrades,
Mesmes antiques, et grand fondation.

A great mountain, with a
  circumference of seven stadiums
Will appear after peace, war, hunger
  and flood
Its effect will be far-reaching,
  drowning great countries
Ancient institutions, and their mighty
  foundations.

This almost certainly alludes to an
asteroid strike, similar to the one
believed to have caused the extinction
of the dinosaurs 65 million years ago. It
is a mathematical certainty that a large
asteroid will eventually hit Earth,
causing seismic waves and devastation
on an epic scale. If such an event were
to occur, Nostradamus's prediction of
the destruction of ancient institutions
would undoubtedly come true.

1/71

La tour marin trois fois prinse et reprinse
Par Espagnols, Barbares, Ligurins,
Marseille et Aix, Arles par ceux de Pise
Vast, feu, fer, pille, Avignon des Thurins.

Shore defences taken and retaken
  three times
By Spanish, Barbarians, Ligurians.
Marseilles and Aix, Arles by the
  Pisans.
Avignon laid waste, burnt, put to the
  sword and pillaged by Turin.

Provence attacked from Spain and Italy.
A regular occurrence before, during
and after Nostradamus's own time.

1/74

Après séjourne vogueront en Epire
Le grand secours viendra vers Antioche,
Le noir poil crespe tendra fort à
* l'Empire,*
Barbe d'airain le rostira en broche.

After a respite they will sail on
  Epirus,
Rescue will come towards Antioch.
He of the black curly hair will strive
  hard for the Empire,
Singeing the beard of the brazen one.

The references to Epirus point to that
turning point in the history of Rome
when Julius Caesar landed at the
Macedonian port-city in 48 BC to
destroy the armies of his rival Pompey.
But how this ancient allegory relates to
forthcoming events remains
unexplained.

1/79

Bazax, Lectore, Condon, Ausch, Agine,
Esmeus par loix, querelles et monopole,
Car Bourd, Tholouse, Bay mettra en
* ruyne,*
Remouveller voulant leur tauropole.

Bazax, Lectore, Condon, Auch,
  Agine
Stirred up by legal and trade disputes
Will try to ruin Bordeaux, Toulouse
  and Bayonne
Wishing to renew their bullfight over
  money.

Possibly an account of trade rivalries
between regions of France. Impossible
to pin down.

1/80

De la sixième claire splendeur celeste,
Viendra tonner si fort eu la Bourgogne,
Puis naistra monstre de très hydeuse
*   beste,*
Mars, Avril, Juin grand charpin et
*   ronge.*

From the sixth splendid light in the
    sky
Will come a great storm in
    Burgundy.
After will be born a hideous beast,
March, April, May, June great
    arguments.

The sixth planet from the Sun is Saturn,
but this casts little light on this
astrological enigma.

1/81

D'humain troupeau neuf seront mis a
*   part;*
De jugement et consel separées,
Leur sort sera divise en départ,
Kappa, Theta, Lamda, morts, bannis,
egarez.

From the human throng, nine will
    stand apart;
Separated by judgement and advice
Their depature will cause division
Kappa, Theta, Lamda, dead,
    banished, led astray.

Courts, set apart to judge their peers,
commonly consist of nine members.
The United States Supreme Court is
one. The puzzle is, what do the Greek
letters K, T and L signify?

Century Two

2/6

Aupres des portes et dedans deux cités
Seront deux fléaux et oncques n'apperceu
*   un tel*
Faim, dedans peste, de fer hors gens
*   boutés*
Crier secours au grand Dieu immortel.

Near ports, and in two cities
There will be two, never before seen,
    scourges
Hunger, pestilence within, people
    exiled by the sword
They will cry for help from Immortal
    God.

The cruelty of war, aptly describing any
one of a thousand tragedies.

2/18

Nouvelle et pluie subite impeteuse
Empechera subit deux excercites
Pierre ciel, feux faire la mere pierreuse
La mort de sept terre et marin subites.

News and rain both flow impetuously
They will stop two armies
Stones and fire from the sky will
    make even the sea stony
The sudden death of the seven, by
    land and sea.

A curious pairing of the forces of both
nature and war. Foreseeing some future
conflict in which weaponry becomes
uncontrollably destructive.

2/19

Nouveau venus lieu basti sans defence
Occuper la place par lors inhabitable
Pres, maisons, champs, villes prendre à
plaisance
Faim, Peste, guerre arpen long
labourable.

Newcomers will build a place with no
defences
Occupying somewhere deemed
uninhabitable
Meadows, houses and fields, towns
taken with ease
Hunger, plague, war, much arable
land.

The sense of this quatrain appears to
follow on from the previous one.

2/21

L'ambassadeur envoyé par biremes,
A mi-chemin d'incogneus repoulsez
De sel renfort viendront quatre triremes,
Cordes et chaines en Negre pont troussez.

The ambassador sent by bireme
Is repulsed, half way, by unknown
men
Four triremes will appear, with salt
Cords and chains, bound for Euboia.

Biremes and triremes are, respectively,
two-tiered and three-tiered oar-
powered ships. Salt was a euphemism,
in mediaeval France, for taxation.
Euboia is a large island off the Greek
mainland, in the Aegean sea, also
known as Negreponte to the Venetians.
It belonged to the Turks until 1831,
when it became part of Greece.

2/27

Le devin verbe sera du ciel frappé,
Qui ne pourra proceder plus avant
Du reserant, le secret estoupé
Qu'on marchera par dessus et devant.

The divine word will be struck from
the sky
No further progress can be made
The secret of the revelation will be
hidden
And the populace will step over it,
unwittingly.

The implication here is that a great
secret will be buried – possibly in a
grave – and that people will step over it
unwittingly, missing the revelation
contained within. This quatrain could
easily be manipulated (and has been)
to fit any number of fallen new
'Messiahs', from Osho (Bhagwan Shree
Rajneesh) to David Koresh, late of the
Branch Davidians.

2/47

L'ennemi grand vieil dueil meurt de
poison,
Les souverains par infiniz subjugez
Pierres plouvoir, cachez soubz la foison,
Par mort articles en vain sont alleguez.

The old enemy grieves his death
from poison
Kings are overcome by the infinite
Rocks rain down, hidden by the
fleece
Vain protestations are made by the
dead man.

This alludes to another meteor shower,
possible foretelling Armageddon. The
fleece may be either the Milky Way, or
the cloud curtain. Could the dead man
be Atlas, burden-bearer of our stricken
planet?

2/49

Les conseilleurs du premier monopole,
Les conquerants seduits par la Melite
Rodes, Bisance pour leurs exposant pole,
Terre faudra les poursuivans de suite.

Advisers of the first monopoly
Conquerors, seduced by the Maltese
The towns of Rhodes and of
  Byzantium are exposed
Those who follow will have need of
  land.

This almost certainly refers to an
incident during the time of the Ottoman
Empire, possibly the loss of of the
island of Rhodes. An alternative
reading indicates the Second World
War and England, which awarded the
island of Malta its George Cross medal
for gallantry.

2/52

Dans plusieurs nuicts la terre tremblera
Sur le printemps deux effors suite
Corinthe, Ephere aux deux mers nagera
Guerre s'esmeut par deux vaillans de
  luit.

For several nights the earth will
  tremble
Two pushes will be made in the
  spring
Corinth and Ephesus will swim in
  both seas
War will stir because of two brave
  warriors.

The classical allusions do a thorough
job of shrouding this quatrain.

2/58

Sans pied ne main dent aiguë et forte
Par Globe au fort de port et lainé nay
Pres du portail desloyal transporte
Silene luit, petit grand emmené.

Without feet or hands, but with
  sharp, strong teeth
He passes through the crowd to
  reach the firstborn, at the fortified
  port
He crosses near the treacherous gates
The crescent moon shines, the little
  great one is taken.

The allusion to a snake, in this case a
metaphorical one, is obvious enough,
but the identity of the young victim of
the reptilian kidnapper's nocturnal
mission is far from clear.

2/80

Apres le conflict du lesé l'eloquence,
Par peu de temps se trame faint repas
Point l'on n'admet les grands à
  delivrance,
Des ennemis sont remis à propos.

After the conflict, the eloquence of
  the injured party
Brings a brief, unearned respite
However those leaders responsible
  will not be freed
But will be delivered to their enemies
  at the proper time.

This is all-embracing, and could apply
to a dozen different wars and conflicts.

2/81

Par feu du ciel la cité presque aduste,
L'urne menace encor Ceucalion,
Vexée Sardaigne par la Punique fuste,
Apres que Libra lairra son Phaeton.

The city is as good as destroyed by
fire from the sky
However the urn still threatens
Deucalion
Sardinia is harried by a Punic vessel
Following Libra's abandonment of
her Phaeton.

A meteor strike or full-scale nuclear
bombardment will almost completely
destroy a great city, causing floods
(Deucalion, in Greek mythology,
equates to the biblical Noah). Sardinia
is attacked by a vessel, when Libra,
otherwise Austria, abandons her
shining sun. This last line could narrow
the date to a time in Europe after the
fall of the Austro-Hungarian Empire.

2/92

Feu couleur d'or du ciel en terre veu
Frappé du haut nay, faict cas merveilleux
Grand meutre humain; prinse du grand
nepveu
Morte d'expectacles eschappe l'orgueilleux.

From the earth, sky-borne fire the
colour of gold is seen
Struck by the noble one, a marvel
happens
Much human slaughter; the great
man's nephew is taken
The proud one escapes a spectacular
death.

A vision of the weaponry of the distant
future.

2/98

Celui de sang reperse le visage
De la victime proche sacrifiée
Tonant en Leo augure par presage
Mis estra à mort lors pour la fiancée.

He whose face is spattered with the
blood
Of the newly-sacrificed victim
Is forewarned by Jupiter in Leo
He is put to death for his broken
promises.

An astrological riddle of an ill fate, and
an injunction not to break promises.

Century Three

3/11

Les armes battre au ciel longue saison
L'arbre au milieu de la cité tombé
Verbine, rongne, glaive en face, Tison
Lors le monarque d'Hadrie succombé.

For a long time there is combat in
the skies
The tree has fallen inside the city
The great branch, cut, facing a
sword, Tison
Then the King of Hadrie falls.

A prediction of air battles, 350 years
before the first aircraft took to the skies.

3/18

Apres la pluie laict assez longuette
En plusieurs lieux de Reims le ciel touché
O quel conflict de sang pres d'eux
s'appreste
Peres et fils Rois n'oseront approcher.

After the rather long milky
downpour
Numerous parts of Reims will be
struck from the sky
Oh what a bloody conflict is being
prepared near them
Even Kings, father and son, daren't
approach.

The Champagne region of France may
be the source of everyone's favourite
sparkling wine, but it has been one of
the world's battlefields for very much
longer. The great cathedral at Reims
was for centuries the place of
coronation for French kings. The
allusion to air war presages a conflict
yet to come, and the mention of a milky
downpour rings of some unfathomable
weapon of the future.

3/21

Au Crustamin par mer Hadriatique
Apparoistra un horrible poisson
De face humaine et la fin aquatique
Qui se prendra dehors l'amaçon.

At the river Conca, near the Adriatic
A horrible fish will appear
It will have a human face, but a fishy
end
It will be caught by other than a
hook.

Something between a sea monster and
a mermaid, neither of which have yet to
be recorded in the Adriatic. The
metaphor remains unexplained.

3/26

Des Rois et Pinces dresseront simulacres
Augures, cruez eslueuz aruspices
Corne, victime dorée, et d'azur, d'acre
Interpretez seront les extipices.

Kings and Princes will be worshipped
Seers and soothsaying priests will be
elevated
Horn of plenty, a dazzling, azured,
golden victim
Its entrails will be read.

Nostradamus looks forward to
vindication for his calling as a seer,
anticipating a material world in which
wealth itself is sacrificed in order to
foretell the future. An abstract concept,
or simply wishful thinking, in which
knowledge is averred to be of greater
value than money.

3/36

Enseveli non mort apopletique,
Sera trouvé avoir les mains mangees
Quand la cité damnera l'heretique,
Qu'avoit leurs loix se leur sembloit
  changees.

Angry at being buried alive
He will be found with part-eaten hands
The city will turn on the heretic
Who, as it seemed to them, changed
  their laws.

This can be read as referring to
Rasputin, Richard Nixon or even
Marshal Pétain.

3/41

Bossu sera esleu par le conseil
Plus hideux monstre en terre n'apperceu
Le coup voulant crevera l'oeil
Le traitre au Roi pour fidelle reçu.

A hunchback will be elected by the
  council
A more hideous monster has never
  lived
A shot will be aimed at his eye
The king had thought the traitor
  faithful.

Distinctly reminiscent of the plot of a
nineteenth century romantic novel – 300
years before any such novels were
written.

3/42

L'enfant naistra à deux dents en la gorge
Pierres en Tuscie par pluie tomberont
Peu d'ans apres ne sera bled ni orge
Pour saouler ceux qui de faim failliront.

The child will be born with two teeth
  in its mouth
Stones will fall from the sky in
  Tuscany
A few years later there will be neither
  wheat nor barley
To fill the hungry stomachs of the
  starving.

Nostradamus witnessed famine in Italy,
and rightly expected it to persist.

3/44

Quand l'animal à l'homme domestique
Apres grands peines et sauts viendra
  parler
De fouldre à vierge sera si malefique
De terre prinse et suspendue en l'air.

When domestic animals, after much
  effort
And travail, are able to speak
The lightning will be so harmful to
  the rod
That it will be taken from the earth
  and suspended in the sky.

A prediction that in its literal sense
seems as unlikely now as it must have
done when Nostradamus made it.
Talking dogs, pigs and chickens are an
enduring theme for fairy tales and – it is
to be fervently hoped – will remain so
for ever.

3/46

Le ciel (de Plancus la cité) nous presage
Par clers insignes et par estoilles fixes
Que de son change subit s'aproche l'aage
Ne pour son bien ne pour ses malefices.

The heavens foretell (concerning
    Lyons)
By clear signs and fixed stars
That a time of sudden change is
    approaching
Neither for good fortune, nor for
    evil.

An equivocal quatrain, apparently
parochial in its import.

3/56

Montauban, Nismes, Avignon et Besier
Peste tonnere et gresle à fin de Mars
De Paris pont, Lyon mur, Montpellier
Depuis six cens et sept vingts trois pars.

Montauban, Nîmes, Avignon and
    Beziers
Plague, lightning and hail at the end
    of March
The Paris bridge, the walls of Lyons
    and Montpellier
Twenty-three pairs of six hundred
    and seven.

Numerically specific but shrouded in
mystery. The sum multiplies to 27,922.

3/65

Quand le sepulchre du grand Romain
    trouvé
Le jour apres sera esleu Pontife
Du Senat gueres il ne sera prouvé
Empoisonné son sang au sacré scyphe.

One day after the tomb of the Great
    Roman
Is found, a Pope will be elected

The Senate won't approve of him
His blood will poison the sacred
    chalice.

Archaeological excavation never
ceases in Rome, and the tomb of the
great Roman – perhaps Julius Caesar
(110–44 BC) – may yet be found. Any
Cardinal seeking election may care to
consider his candidacy in the light of
this prophecy.

3/69

Grand excercite conduict par jouvenceau
Se viendra rendre aux mains des ennemis
Mais le vieillard nay au demi-porceau
Fera Chalon et Mascon estre amis.

A great army, led by a youth
Will give itself up to the enemy
But the old man, born at the half-pig
Will make Chalon and Macon
    friends.

Two districts of southern Burgundy
make peace at the behest of an elder
born at what must be a sign at a
butcher's shop. Fascinatingly cryptic,
but thus far unsolved.

3/74

Naples, Florence, Favence et Imole,
Seront en termes de telle fascherie
Que pour complaire aux malheureux de
    Nolle
Plainct d'avoir faict à son chef moquerie.

Naples, Florence, Faenza and Imola
Will be on such bad terms, one with
    another
That, in order to please the wretches
    of Nola
Complaints will be made that they
    mocked its chief.

An obscure quatrain, possibly relating
to the Punic Wars.

3/76

En Germanie naistront diverses sectes,
S'approchant fort de l'heureux paganisme,
Le coeur captif et petites receptes,
Feront retour à payer le vrai disme.

Various sects will originate in
 Germany
Strongly resembling naïve paganism
The heart being captive, and the
 revenues small
They will return to the fold, that the
 true tithe may be paid.

Wishful thinking on the part of
Nostradamus, who was a fanatical
opponent of Calvinism. He imagines
that Germany will return to the Catholic
fold, which has not so far proved to be
the case. There was certainly something
akin to a 'new paganism' abroad during
the 1920s Weimar and 1930s Nazi eras.
Germany, despite being largely
Protestant, still insisted until very
recently on a religious tax or tithe, in
which a proportion of all incomes went
to the Church. The only way to avoid it
was to disclaim, formally, affiliation to
the Christian caucus.

3/78

Le chef d'Escosse avec six d'Alemaigne,
Par gens de mer Orienteaux captif
Traverseront le Calptre et Espaigne,
Present en Perse au nouveau Roy
 craintif.

The Scottish leader, with six
 Germans
Will be captured by Eastern seamen
They will pass by Spain and Gibraltar
And be presented to the cowardly
 new Persian king.

Too far-ranging to locate in place or
time.

3/85

La cité prinse par tromperie et fraude,
Par le moyen d'un beau jeune attrappé
Assaut donne Raubine pres de Laude,
Lui et tous morts pour avoir bien trompé.

The city is taken by deception and
 fraud
It will be tricked by means of a
 handsome young man
Raubine attempts an assault near
 Laude
He and his men all die, for having
 deceived so well.

The river Robine is actually a tributary
of the Aude. No-one has yet discovered
the name of the city taken by trickery,
nor of the handsome young man. If
Nostradamus was looking ahead to the
poet W. H. Auden (1907–73), the
attempted assault by Raubine takes on
an entirely different connotation.

3/90

Le grand Satyre et Tigre d'Hyrcanie,
Don presenté à ceux de l'Occean
Un chef de classe istra de Carmanie,
Qui prendra terre au Tyrren Phocean.

The great Satyr, and tiger of
 Hyrcania
A gift, presented to the people of the
 Ocean
An admiral will come from Carmania
Making landfall at Tyrren Phocea.

Hyrcania and Carmania were provinces
of Persia, which may indicate a
connection with modern-day Iran.
Phocea is normally Marseilles, and
Tyrren may be a euphemism for trading,
as Marseilles is nowhere near Tyre.

3/92

Le monde proche du dernier periode,
Saturne encor tard sera de retour
Translat empire devers nation Brodde,
L'oeil arraché à Narbon par Autour.

The world is near its end
Saturn, late as ever, will return
The empire becomes decadent
Its eye will be ripped out, to no good
    purpose, by others.

Saturn was the god of agriculture, but
he is also associated with the Greek
god Cronus, who ruled over a
purported Golden Age. According to
this reading, the world will be near its
end when it reaches a golden age of
technology and plenty – possibly now.
Heir to a surfeit of good things is
decadence. The final line is a double
pun. When applied to the earth, eye
probably means 'inner eye', or soul. We
are enjoined either to make hay while
the sun shines, or to learn to live more
ascetically.

3/94

De cinq cent ans plus compte l'on tiendra
Celui qu'estoit l'adornement de son
    temps
Puis à un coup grand clarté donra,
Que par ce siecle les rendra tres contens.

For five hundred more years they will
    remember him
The ornament of his age
Then, in one fell swoop, sense will
    prevail
Pleasing that century's people.

Nostradamus expects to be
remembered. The question most often
asked is 'when he says 500 years, does
he mean 500 years?' Numerous
theories have been applied, quoting
lunar years, solar years, and even leap
years.

3/98

Deux royals freres si fort guerroierent,
Qu'entre eux sera la guerre si mortelle
Qu'un chacun places fortes occuperont,
De regne et vie sera leur grand querelle.

Two royal brothers will fight each
    other so fiercely
The war between them will be so
    deadly
That each will live in a fortified place
Quarrelling over kingdom, and life
    itself.

Throughout the centuries there have
been untold occasions when brothers
have fought each other – Henri III and
the Duke of Alençon, Louis XIII and
the Duke of Orléans, the sons of Suleiman
the Magnificent.

Century Four

4/6

D'habits nouveaux apres faicte la treuve
Malice tramme et machination
Premier mourra qui en fera la preuve
Couleur venise insidation.

New clothes will be worn after the
   truce
There will be malice, plots and
   conspiracies
The man who proves it will die first
Venice is the colour of the trap.

A sartorial aftermath of peace. The
metaphor seems unbreakable.

4/7

Le mineur filz du grand et hai Prince
De lepre aura à vingt ans grande tache
De deuil sa mere mourra bien triste et
   mince
Et il mourra là où tombe cher lache.

The youngest son of the high and
   hated Prince
Will be marked by leprosy before he
   is twenty
His sad, thin mother will die of grief
He will die a coward, where his flesh
   falls.

Leprosy was widespread in Europe
during the Middle Ages, and
Nostradamus will certainly have treated
many sufferers. This quatrain rings of a
curse. The identity and fate of the
prince concerned is unknown.

4/10

Le jeune prince accusé faulsement,
Mettra en trouble le camp et en querelles
Meutri le chf pour le soustenement,
Sceptre appaiser: puis guerir escrouelles.

The falsely accused young prince
Will cause trouble and quarrels in
   the camp
The leader will be murdered because
   of his support
To appease the crown; the king's evil
   will be cured.

The king's evil is scrofula, which French
and English kings could apparently
cure by the laying on of their hands.
The rest of the quatrain is too
generalised to be easily ascribed.

4/12

Le camp plus grand de route mis en
   fuite,
Guaires plus outre ne sera pourchassé
Ost recampé, et legion reduicte,
Puis hors des Gaules du tout sera chassé.

The larger army is put to flight
But is unlikely to be chased
The force is reassembled, the legion
   reduced
They will then be driven out of
   France completely.

This could apply to either the First or
the Second World Wars, in which
numerically superior German forces
were finally driven from the battlefield,
and later, from France itself. Then
again, maybe not.

4/18

Des plus lettrés dessus les faits celestes
Seront par princes ignorans reprouvés
Punis d'Edit, chassez comme scelestes,
Et mis à mort là où seront trouvés.

The most erudite astronomers
Will be criticized by ignorant princes
Punished by edicts, they will be
    driven out, like scoundrels
And put to death, wherever they are
    found.

Astronomers and astrologers were
interchangeable in Nostradamus's
Europe, and here he predicts further
witch-hunts against them, continuing on
from those of the Inquisition in the
century before his death.

4/19

Devant Rouen d'Insubres mis le siege,
Par terre et mer enfermés les passages
D'Haynault, et Flandres, de Gand et
    ceux de Liege,
Par dons laenées raviront les rivages.

The Italians lay siege to Rouen
Both sea and land passages are closed
By the people of Hainaut and
    Flanders, Ghent and Lièges
Under a veil of gifts, they will ravish
    the shoreline.

Rouen was captured in 1592 by the
Duke of Parma. Since then it has been
captured by the Germans and the
Americans, during the Second World
War. The Duke of Parma, however, did
not lay siege to it, and was only acting
on behalf of his ally, the Duke of Guise,
against Henri of Navarre. The Italian
connection therefore remains nebulous.

4/22

La grand copie qui sera deschasée,
Dans un moment fera besoing au Roi,
La foi promise de loing sera faulsée
Nud se verra en piteux desarroi.

The great army will be driven away
A time will come when they are
    needed by the king
The faith, promised from afar, will
    be tarnished
And he will be left with nothing, and
    pitiable disorder.

Another general quatrain which could
be manipulated, and often has been, to
apply to any number of military
disasters. Henri II at St Quentin springs
to mind, as does Napoleon at Moscow,
and Hitler at Stalingrad.

4/25

Corps sublimes sans fin à l'oeil visibles
Obnubiler viendront par ses raisons
Corps, front comprins, sens chief et
    invisibles.
Diminuant les sacrees oraisons.

Heavenly bodies, eternally visible
Cloud my conscious mind
My body, my brain and my senses,
    are annulled
Diminish my sacred prayers.

This relates back to other quatrains in
which Nostradamus muses on his gift,
and tries to explain it.

4/27

Salon, Mansol, Tarascon de Sex, L'arc,
Ou est debout encor la piramide
Viendront livrer le Prince Dannemarc,
Rachat honni au temple d'Artemide.

Salon, Mausole, Tarascon and St
  Rémy
Where the pyramid still stands
Will come to save the prince of
  Annemarc
His ransom will not be honoured at
  the temple of Artemis.

St Rémy was the birthplace of
Nostradamus and Salon is where he
lived for much of his life. Mausole is a
nearby priory. He is referring, in line 2,
to a mausoleum near St Rémy, with
which he was well acquainted.
Annemarc, however, presents
problems, but could have some link
with the inscription on the mausoleum.
A simple reversal of the syllables,
however, would give us Mark Anthony,
Cleopatra's lover, and would explain
the presence of the pyramid image in
line 2, and also the reference to
Artemis, who was linked both to Astarte
and to Aphrodite, the goddess who
signified the female principle in all its
aspects.

4/30

Plus onze fois Luna Sol ne voudra
Tous augmenté et baissez de degré
Et si bas mis que peu or on cendra
Qu'apres faim, peste, descouvert le secret.

For eleven more times the moon will
  spurn the sun
Both raised and lessened in degree
Placed so low that no gold will be
  sewn
Only after famine and plague will the
  secret be discovered.

A splendidly cryptic verse, worthy of a
treasure-hunt clue.

4/31

La Lune au plain de nuict sur le haut
  mont
Le nouveau sophe d'un seul cerveau l'a
  veu
Par ses disciples estre immortel semond
Yeux au midi, en seins mains, corps au
  feu.

The moon is seen at midnight, over
  the high mountain
The solitary, pensive young sage has
  seen it
His disciples encourage him to
  become immortal
Looking south, hands on his chest,
  his body is on fire.

Nostradamus seems to be musing over
a young successor to himself, a sage
whose powers are great enough to earn
him immortality.

4/33

Jupiter joinct plus Venus qu'à la Lune
Apparoissant de plenitude blanche
Venus cachée souz la blancheur Neptune
De Mars frappée par la gravée branche.

Jupiter closer to Venus than the
  Moon
Appearing in white fulness
Venus hidden in the glare of
  Neptune
Struck by Mars with a carved stick.

An astrological enigma readable only in
the stars.

4/36

Les jeux nouveau en Gaule redressés
Après victoire de l'insubre champaigne
Monts d'Esperie, les grands liés, troussés
De peur trembler la Romaigne et
l'Espaigne.

New games are set up in Gaul
Following the Insubrian campaign
victory
Great ones are bound in the
Hesperian mountains
Romania and Spain will tremble with
fear.

An opaque view of French military
manoeuvres.

4/42

Geneve et Langres par ceux de Chartres
et Dole
Et par Grenoble captif au Montlimard
Seysett, Losanne par fraudulente dole
Les trahiront par or soixante marc.

Geneva and Langres are captured at
Montelimar
By men from Chartres, Dole and
Grenoble
Seysel and Lausanne, by a crooked
trick
Betray them for sixty gold marks.

Geographically convoluted, but
probably referring to religious wars in
Switzerland.

4/44

Deux gros de Mende, de Rondés et
Milhau
Cahours, Limoges, Castres malo sepmano
De nuech l'intrado de Bourdeaux un
cailhau
Par Perigort au toc de la campano.

Two fat men from Mende, Rodez
and Milau
Cahors, Limoges, Castres have a bad
week
The entrance made by night, an
insult from Bordeaux
Through Perigord, to the tolling of a
bell.

Curiously, the original is written half in
Provençal, though none of the places
mentioned are in Provence. But the
sense is obscure.

4/49

Devant le peuple, sang sera respandu
Que de haut ciel ne viendra esloigner
Mais d'un long temps ne sera entendu
L'esprit d'un seul le viendra tesmoigner.

Blood will be spilled in front of the
people
It won't be far from the high heavens
The news of it won't arrive for a long
time
The spirit of one man will bear
witness to it.

No clues link this to places, times or
events.

4/50

Libra verra regner les Hesperies,
De ciel et terre tenir la monarchie
D'Asie forces nul ne verra paries,
Que sept ne tiennent par rang le
hierarchie.

Libra will reign in the West
Ruling over the earth and skies
The forces of Asia will not lose
Until seven, in succession, hold the
hierarchy.

The seven, in the last line, may refer to the seven great Western economic powers, or, then again, it may refer to a year ending in 77. When Libra, the Balance, rules over the US, there will be a war with Asia, which the West won't win until each of the powers takes over the allied command in succession. This already happens to some extent in Nato, which may imply a connection to the D'Arton of other quatrains.

4/53

Les fugitifs et bannis revoquez,
Peres et fils grand garnissant les hauts
*   puits*
Le cruel pere et les siens suffoquez,
Son fils plus pire submergé dans le puits.

Both fugitives and the banished are
    recalled
Fathers and their sons re-point the
    deep wells
The cruel father and his family are
    suffocated
His even wickeder son is drowned in
    the well.

Variously ascribed either to Tsar Nicholas II and his family and the secreting of their bodies down a mine-shaft; the Indian Mutiny of 1857–59; or to the Black Hole of Calcutta.

4/55

Quant la corneille sur tout de brique
*   joincte,*
Durant sept heures ne fera que crier
Mort presagee de sang statue taincte,
Tyran meutri, aux Dieu peuple prier.

When the crow on the brick tower
Cries, non-stop, for seven hours
A death is foretold, a statue will be
    stained with blood
The tyrant is murdered and the
    people pray to their Gods.

The crow is a well-known harbinger of doom. The brick tower may indicate the Tower of London, where many a traitor and innocent man has heard the call of the famous ravens on his last morning on earth.

4/58

Soleil ardent dans le gosier coller,
De sang humain arrouser terre Etrusque
Chef seille d'eaue, mener son fils filer,
Captive dame conduicte en terre Turque.

The scalding sun will dry the throat
Tuscany will be soaked by human
    blood
A chief, carrying water, will show his
    son how to escape
The captive lady will be taken to
    Turkey.

A general prophecy, hard to ascribe, although possibly pertaining to future global warming.

4/60

Les sept enfans en hostage laissés,
Le tiers viendra son enfant trucider
Deux par son filz seront d'estoc percés,
Gennes, Florence, los viendra encunder.

Seven children will be left as hostages
The third will come to kill his child
Two will be pierced through because
    of his son
Genoa and Florence will arrive to
    harry them.

Some commentators have tried to tailor this quatrain to fit the seven Valois children, but it doesn't hold water. The fact is, no-one knows what it means.

4/63

L'armée Celtique contre les
montaignars,
Qui seront sceus et prins à la lipee
Paysans frais pousseront tost faugnars,
Precipitez tous au fil de l'espee.

The French army will fight the men
from the mountains
They will be caught out, and taken in
an ambush
The peasants, despite making more
wine
Will all be spitted on the point of the
sword.

This could apply either to Marshal
Villar's campaign against the Camisard
rebels of 1702–4, or to Henri de La
Rochejaquelein's ambush and murder
during the White Terror of 1794. In both
examples French armies fought against
Montagnard guerillas, as was indeed
the case in Vietnam, during the French
Indochina War of 1946–54. In that event
the wine in line 4 would be of the rice
variety.

4/64

Le deffaillant en habit de bourgeois,
Viendra le Roi tempter de son offence
Quinze souldartz la plupart Ustagois,
Vie derniere et chef de sa chevance.

The defaulter, in bourgeois dress
Will come to tempt the king with his
offence
Fifteen soldiers, outlaws for the most
part
Take his life, and the greater part of
his estate.

A very general quatrain which has had
numerous unconvincing interpretations.

4/66

Soubz couleur faincte de sept testes rasées
Seront semés divers esplorateurs
Puys et fontaines de poions arrousées,
Au fort de Gennes humains devorateurs.

Seven slap-heads, under false colours
Will be spied on by different powers
Wells and fountains will be poisoned
There will be cannibalism at the fort
of Genoa

The slap-heads could apply either to
Oliver Cromwell's Roundheads, or to
the close-cropped Cardinals of the
Vatican. Either way, the cannibalism in
Genoa is hard to pin down, even
metaphorically. It could equally well
apply to the skin-headed fascists of the
1970s and 80s.

4/67

L'an que Saturne et Mars esgaux
combuste,
L'air fort seiché longue trajection
Par feux secrets, d'ardeur grand lieu adust
Peu pluie, vent chault, guerres, incursions.

The same year that Saturn and Mars
show equal fire
The air is dried out, a long-tailed
comet is seen
A great place is scorched by secret
fires
There is little rain, a hot wind, wars
and incursions.

This conjunction happens frequently,
and has often accompanied war and
conflict; Ypres, Passchendaele, the
battles of Isonzo and Caporetto, not to
mention the Soviet/Finnish War of 1939–
40 have all taken place within its effect.
The North Vietnamese Tet offensive of
1968, and the 'human wave' Iranian

assault of 1987, during the Iran–Iraq War, also fall into the same category. Any one of them could be taken to fit Nostradamus's vision.

4/71

En lieu d'espouse les filles trucidées
Meurtre à grand faulte ne sera superstile
Dedans le puys vestules inondées
L'espouse estraincte par hauste d'Aconite.

Instead of marrying, the daughters are killed
Such a terrible murder that there are no survivors
The virgins are drowned in the wells
The bride-to-be killed by poison.

It sounds like one of the darker tales from the Arabian Nights, but appears not yet to have had any manifestation in the histories of public lives.

4/74

Du lac liman et ceux de Brannonices
Tous assemblez contre ceux d'Aquitaine
Germains beaucoup, encor plus Souisses
Seront defaictz avec ceux d'Humaine.

The people of Lake Geneva and the Macon
Will join against those of Aquitaine
Many Germans, even more Swiss
Will be routed by those from Maine.

Franco–German–Swiss conflict of uncertain period.

4/83

Combat nocturne le vaillant capitaine,
Vaincu fuira peu de gens profligé
Son peuple esmeu, sedition non vaine,
Son propre filz le tiendra assiegé.

In a night-time battle the valiant captain
Is defeated; he flees, betrayed by the few
His people are moved, their sedition is not in vain
His own son will lay siege to his position.

Impossible to pin down, as an innumerable number of night-time battles have been fought in the course of the last five centuries.

4/88

Le grand Antoine du nom de faicte sordide
De Phthiriase à son dernier rongé
Un qui de plomb voudra estre cupide,
Passant le port d'esleu sera plongé.

Anthony, great by name, and foul by deed
Will, at the last, be consumed by lice
Desirous of the coup de grace
He will be drowned, near the harbour, by his successor.

This quatrain should probably be taken metaphorically, even though phthiriatic lice infestation, or pediculosis as it is now known, was quite common in the sixteenth century, when personal hygiene was less rigorous than now. The last two lines, if taken literally, may imply that the reeking Anthony drowned while bathing in the sea. *Coup de Grace* could also be taken to mean 'taking a shot at Grace', a euphemism for sexual congress in mediaeval times. The implication is that Grace was Anthony's wife, his successor, and that she drowned him while washing him in preparation for a congress. An unsolved domestic murder mystery.

4/90

Les deux copies aux murs ne pourront
　　joindre
Dans cest instant trembler Milan, Ticin
Faim, soif doubtance si fort les viendra
　　poindre
Chair, pain, ne vivres n'auront un seul
　　boucin.

The two armies cannot join at the
　　walls
Just then Milan and Pavia tremble
Hunger, thirst and doubt will weigh
　　heavily on them
They won't even have a scrap of meat
　　or bread.

Conflict in Italy, but impossible to place
in time.

4/92

Teste tranchee du vaillant capitaine
Sera gettee devant son adversaire
Son corps pendu de la chasse à l'antenne
Confus fuira par rames à vent contraire.

The severed head of the gallant
　　captain
Will be thrown in front of his
　　adversary
His body will be hung from the mast
Upset, they will flee, rowing against
　　the wind.

This has been interpreted as an
awesomely perceptive preview of the
age of radio, because Nostradamus
uses the word antenne for a ship's
mast. It seems likelier the description of
the capture of a murderous pirate who
is confronted with his capital crimes
and then hanged from the yardarm as
his crew flee.

Century Five

5/17

De nuict passant le roi pres d'une
　　Andronne
Celui de Cypres et principal guette
Le roi failli la main fuict long du Rosne
Les conjurés l'iront à mort mettre.

The king, passing at night through a
　　narrow way
The Cypriot is the main guard
With the king dead, the guilty hand
　　flees along the Rhône
The conspirators will kill him.

The Cypriot is the key, but his or her
identity remains unknown.

5/18

De deuil mourra l'infelix proflige
Celebrera son vitrix l'hecatombe
Pristine loi franc edict redigé
Le mur et Prince au septiesme jour tombe.

The wretched, broken man will die
　　of grief
His triumphant consort will bury him
Good laws and free edicts will be
　　rewritten
Prince and wall will fall on the
　　seventh day.

A clear enough fable of a prince who
dies regretting his own actions and
leaves behind him a wife who undoes
his oppressive deeds. But who was – or
will be – the prince in question?

5/19

Le grand Royal d'or, d'aerain augmenté
Rompu la pache, par jeune ouverte
* guerre*
Peuple affligé par un chef lamenté
De sang barbare sera converre terre.

The great Royal, augmented by gold
  and brass
Breaks the treaty, war is started by a
  young man
The afflicted people lament their
  leader
The land will be covered with
  barbarian blood.

Another gilded royal causing mayhem,
but doing so anonymously.

5/24

Le regne et lois souz Venus esleué
Saturne aura sus Jupiter empire
La loi et regne par le Soleil leué
Par Saturnins endurera le pire.

The kingdom and the law thrive
  under Venus
Saturn will govern beneath Jupiter
The kingdom and the law rise
  because of the Sun
Those of Saturn will cause the most
  trouble.

An astrological puzzle of unsolvable
mysticism.

5/31

Par terre Attique chef de la sapience,
Qui de present est la rose du monde
Pont ruiné et sa grand preeminece,
Sera subdite et naufrage des undes.

The source of wisdom from the Attic
  lands
Otherwise known as the world's rose
Will ruin the pope, his pre-eminence
Will be downgraded, and lost in the
  waves.

The Attic lands refer to Greece, and in
particular the south-eastern corner,
north of the Peloponnesus. Socrates
(470–399 BC), Plato (427–347 BC) and
Aristotle (384–322 BC) were all born in
Attica. Their rational approach to the
world was encapsulated in the
foundation of Plato's Academy, in 387
BC, in honour of Socrates, and of which
Aristotle was the most famous pupil.
The Academy was eventually closed in
529 AD by the Emperor Justinian I, who
objected to its pagan teachings.
Nostradamus is implying here that
rational thought and argument, learned
from the ancient Greeks, may one day
cause the downfall of the Roman
Catholic Church.

5/36

De soeur le frere par simulte faintise,
Viendra mesler rosee en mineral
Sur la placente donne à vielle tardifue,
Meurt, le goustant sera simple et rural.

The girl's brother, pretending
  weakness
Will come to mix poison with her
  water
Her placenta given to the old midwife
She dies; her wake will be simple and
  rustic.

An extraordinary quatrain never
successfully interpreted. Perhaps this
new translation will help. Mineral, in this
context, means water, an accepted use
of the word since mediaeval times. *La
placente* is just that; a placenta. Former
commentators have tended to translate

these words as rock and cake respectively, making a nonsense of what is actually a straightforward parturition. Instinct would indicate a case of incest and poisoning, both of which, by their very nature, involve secrecy.

5/47

Le grand Arabe marchera bien avant,
Trahi sera par les Bisantinois
L'Antique Rodes lui viendra au devant,
Et plus grand mal par autre Pannonois.

The mighty Arab leader will march at
  the front
He will be betrayed by the
  Byzantines
Ancient Rhodes will come to meet
  him
Even worse evil will come through
  other Hungarians.

Some commentators plump for the Gulf War of 1991, seeing the mighty Arab leader as Saddam Hussein, and the Byzantines as the Turks, who made up part of his United Nations opponents. In this case Rhodes would have to stand for Greece, scuppering the interpretation.

5/48

Apres la grand affliction du sceptre,
Deux ennemis par eux seront defaictz
Classe d'Afrique aux Pannons viendra
  naistre,
Par mer et terre seont horribles faictz.

After the insult to the crown
Two enemies will be defeated by them
A fleet from Africa will rise in front
  of the Hungarians
Dreadful acts will happen on land
  and sea.

Possibly continuing on from the last quatrain, and equally indecipherable.

5/52

Un Roi sera qui donra l'opposite,
Les exilez esleuez sur le regne
De sang nager la gent caste hyppolite,
Et florira long temps soubs telle enseigne.

A king will come who will oppose
The exiles who govern the kingdom
The poverty-stricken people will
  swim in blood
He will flourish for a long time under
  such a flag.

A very general quatrain, with numerous interpretations possible. There seems little point in adding to the meretricious versions already available.

5/55

De la felice Arabie contrade,
Naistra puissant de loi Mahometique
Vexer l'Espaigne conquester la Grenade,
Et plus par mer à la gent Ligustique.

In Arabia Felix
A powerful Mahomedan will be born
He will harry Spain, and conquer
  Granada
Assailing, by sea, the people of
  Genoa.

The Moors had already lost Granada in 1492, sixty years before Nostradamus wrote this quatrain. Here he predicts that the Moors, under a mighty new leader, will retake their lost possessions. This quatrain remains to be fulfilled.

5/59

Au chef Anglois á Nimes trop sejour,
Devers l'Espaigne au secours Aenobarbe
Plusieurs mourrant par Mars ouvert ce
  jour,
Quand an Artois faillir estoille en barbe.

The English chief remains too long
  at Nîmes
Aenobarbus comes to the rescue of
  Spain
Many will die due to that day's
  declaration of war
At Artois, a comet will crash to the
  ground.

Open to many interpretations, all
spurious. The best bet for Aenobarbus
and the English Chief would be the
Duke of Wellington, but what was he
doing at Nîmes?

5/60

Par teste rase viendra bien mal eslire,
Plus qu sa charge ne porte passera
Si grand fureur et raige fera dire,
Qu'à feu et sang tout sexe trenchera.

A bad choice will be made by the
  shaven-headed ones
He will be burdened with a load he
  cannot manage
In great rage and fury he will declare
That everyone will die in fire and
  blood.

This may refer either to Cromwell,
Napoleon, or Hitler. All apply about
equally.

5/63

De vaine emprise l'honneur indue
  plaincte,
Galiotz errans par Latins froit, faim,
  vagues
Non loing du Timbre de sang la terre
  taincte.
Et sur humains seront diverses plagues.

Complaints will stem from honour's
  failed endeavour
Cold, hunger, waves; the boat will
  drift near Italy
Not far from Rome, the land will be
  stained with blood
A number of plagues will torment
  mankind.

Following on from the last quatrain, one
is forced to wonder whether
Nostradamus is not here referring to
another nuclear accident, this time
involving a submarine.

5/64

Les assemblés par repos du grand nombre,
Par terre et mer conseil contremandé
Pres de l'Autonne Gennes, Nice de
  l'ombre
Par champs et villes le chef contrebandé.

Those brought together for the peace
  of the many
Will have their advice
  countermanded, both by land and
  sea
Near Autonne, Genoa, and in the
  shadow of Nice
There will be revolts, in field and
  village, against their leader

Autonne is a still unsolved anagram or
piece of word play, and has sometimes
been taken to mean Nato, the twentieth-
century alliance of western powers, but

with little basis. In line 1, it more likely refers to the United Nations, or even, quite simply, Autumn, being the phonetic equivalent in French.

5/65

Subit venu l'effrayeur sera grande,
Des principaux de l'affaire cachés
Et dame en braise plus ne sera en veue
Ce peu à peu seront les grans fachés.

Appearing suddenly, great will be the terror
The principal movers in the affair are hidden
The witch will no longer be visible
Little by little the great ones will be angered.

The witch, and the rest of the verse, present a perpetual enigma.

5/66

Soubs les antiques edifices vestaulx,
Non esloignez d'aqueduct ruine
De Sol et Lune sont les luisans metaulx,
Ardante lampe Traian d'or burine.

Under the ancient buildings of the Vestal Virgins
Not far from the ruined aqueduct
Gold and silver glitter
The fiery lamp of Trajan is engraved with gold.

Taken by many to refer to the convent of St Sauveur-de-la-Fontaine at Nîmes, which was built on the site of a Temple of Diana near the famous Roman aqueduct, the gold and silver lamp (the Holy Grail?) has still to be uncovered.

5/68

Dans le Danube et du Rhin viendra boire,
Le grand Chameau ne s'en repentira
Trembler du Rosne et plus fort ceux de Loire,
Et pres des Alpes coq le ruinera.

The great Camel will not regret Drinking from the Rhine and the Danube
Those of the Rhône will tremble, though less than those of the Loire
Near to the Alps the cockerel will ruin him.

Much speculation has muddied the waters of this prophecy, but it probably refers to an Islamic leader who conquers Germany, at some time in the future, but is finally stopped in France.

5/73

Persecutee sera de Dieu l'eglise
Et les sainctz temples seront expoliez
L'enfant la mere mettra nud en chemise
Seront Arabes aux Polons raliez.

The church of God will be persecuted
And the holy temples pillaged
The child will drive out his own half-naked mother
The Arabs and the Poles will become allies.

Nostradamus looks gloomily ahead to the retreat of the Christian church. But he need not have worried that Poland, now Europe's most devoutly Catholic nation, would convert to Islam.

5/74

De sang Troyen naistra coeur
    Germanique
Qu'il deviendra en si haute puissance
Hors chassera gent estrange Arabique
Tournant l'Eglise en pristine
    preeminence.

A German heart will be born, of
    Trojan blood
He will rise to great power
He will drive out the Arab foreigners
Restoring the church to her former
    glory.

The world awaits a German who will
restore the glories of the Catholic
Church. None in sight.

5/76

En lieu libere tendra son pavillon
Et ne voudra en citez prendre place
Aix, Carpens l'isle volce, mont Cavaillon
Par tous ses lieux abolira sa trasse.

He will pitch his tent in a free place
Refusing to stay in cities
Aix, Carpentras, Vaucluse, Cavaillon
There will be no trace of him in
    these places.

No trace indeed.

5/77

Tous les degrez d'honneur Ecclesiastique
Seront changez en dial quirinal
En Martial quirinal flaminique
Puis un Roi de France le rendre vulcanal.

All degrees of Ecclesiastical honour
Will be changed by Jupiter and Mars
A Quirinal priest, in martial guise
A king of France will make him like
    Vulcan.

Vulcan, god of fire, may be a date clue,
as the Roman festival of Vulcanalia falls
on 23 August. But the ecclesiastical
and astrological elements here are too
much of a riddle.

5/80

Logmion grande Bisance approchera,
Chassé sera la barbarique ligne
Des deux loix l'une l'estinique lachera,
Barbare et franche en perpetuelle brique.

Ogmios will approach great
    Byzantium
The barbarian league will be driven
    out
Of the two existing laws, the pagan
    one will fall
Barbarian and Frank will always be at
    each other's throats.

Ogmios was the Celtic Hercules, adept
at honeyed speech. Nostradamus
seems to be predicting further
crusades against the Moslems, led by a
charismatic leader, with the Catholic
French emerging on top.

5/84

Naistra du gouphre et cité immesuree,
Nay de parents obscure et tenebreux
Qui la puissance du grand roi reveree,
Voudra destruire par Rouen et Evereux.

He will be born of the gulf, and of
    the immeasurable city
Born of obscure and shadowy parents
He who revered the power of the
    great king
Will wish to destroy Rouen and
    Evreux.

This could be about the third Antichrist,
believed unchivalrously by some
commentators to be the Ayatollah

Khomeini (1900–1989). It is hard to find any justification for this. There seems no motive for him to have wished destruction on Normandy, especially after enjoying French hospitality during much of the fifteen-year exile that preceded his triumphal return to Tehran in 1979.

5/89

Dedans Hongrie par Boheme, Navarre,
Et par banniere fainctes seditions
Par fleurs de lys pays portant la barre,
Contre Orléans sera emotions.

Into Hungary, through Bohemia and
   Navarre
Under a banner of false sedition
With the flag carrying a bar
They will cause problems for Orléans.

The *fleur de lys* of the Bourbons was barred at both ends, but the arms of the more junior Vendômes and Condés sported a single diagonal bar through the centre. Bohemia and Navarre were both hotbeds of Protestantism during the sixteenth and seventeenth centuries. Beyond this point, speculation reigns.

5/91

Au grand marché qu'on dict des
   mensongiers
Du tout Torrent et champ Athenien
Seront surprins par les chevaux legiers
Par Albanois Mars, Leo, Sat. un versien.

In the great market, where the men
   are known as liars
And throughout Torrent and the
   Athenian plain
They will be surprised by the light
   cavalry
War from Albania, Leo and Saturn in
   Aquarius.

War in the Balkans – which accounts for much of that region's history from Nostradamus's time to our own.

5/95

Nautique rame invitera les umbres
Du grand Empire lors viendra conciter
La mer Aegee des lignes les encombres
Empeschant l'onde Tirreme defflotez.

The nautical wing will invite the
   shadows
Then come to provoke the great
   Empire
Lines slow them down in the Aegean
Impeding the galleons from moving.

Sea battles in the Mediterranean, but few clues as to whether past, present or future.

5/97

Le nay defforme par horreur suffoqué
Dans la cité du grand Roi habitable
L'edict severe des captifs revoqué
Gresle et tonnere, Condon inestimable.

Born deformed, he is suffocated in
   horror
In the city of the great king
The tough edict of the captives is
   revoked
Hail and thunder, great Condom.

Condom is an old and very pleasant market town in Gascony with a name now irrevocably associated with contraception. (The word condom dates from the eighteenth century but is of unknown origin). The connection with the deformed birth of the first line is an uncomfortable one, but surely any link is improbable.

Century Six

6/1

Autour des monts Pyrenees grans amas,
De gent estrange secourir roi nouveau
Pres de Garonne du grand temple du
* Mas,*
Un Romain chef le craindra dedans
* l'eau.*

Near the Pyrenees, a large number
  Of foreigners will mass to help the
  new king
Near the Garonne, in the great
  church of Le Mas
A Roman leader will fear him, in the
  water.

Beyond the fact that Nostradamus
would have been aware of the famous
Roman antiquities of Le Mas d'Agenais,
near Agen, little more can be deduced
from this quatrain.

6/8

Ceux qui estoient en regne pour scavoir,
Au Royal change deviendront apouvris
Uns exilez sans appui, or, n'avoir,
Lettrez et lettres ne seront à grand pris.

Those who visited the kingdom to
  study
Will be impoverished, thanks to a
  change in the monarchy
Some will be exiled without support
  or funds
Neither learning, nor the learned,
  will be highly valued.

Nostradamus was convinced that
higher learning would deteriorate in the
centuries after his death. This has
proved, continually, to be the case.

6/16

Ce qui ravi sera du jeune Milve
Par les Normans de France et Picardie
Les noirs du temple du lieu de Negrisilve
Feront aulberge et feu de Lombardie.

That which will have been stolen by
  the young Hawk
By the Normans of France and
  Picardy
The black ones of the Black Forest
  temple
Will use Lombardy as their inn,
  firing it.

The diverse locations are clear enough,
but the characters remain in the
shadows.

6/18

Par les phisiques le grand Roy delaissé
Par sort non art de l'Ebrieu est en vie
Lui et son genre au regne hault poussé
Grace donnee à gent qui Christ envie.

The great King is deserted by his
  physicians
By chance and not art he is saved by
  the Jew
He and his people are placed high in
  the realm
Grace is given to the people who
  deny Christ.

A king attended by a Jewish doctor
who saves the sovereign by luck rather
than skill and is rewarded, along with
other members of his race. It sounds
much like an Old Testament story, and
there has surely never been a shortage
of world leaders receiving treatment
from Jewish physicians. Perhaps it is an
autobiographical note by Nostradamus,
but further prognostications would be
futile.

6/22

Dedans la terre du grand temple celique,
Neveu à Londres par paix faincte meutri
La barque alors deviendra scismatique,
Liberté faincte sera au corn et cri.

In the precincts of the great temple
   of the heavens
Someone's nephew is murdered, in
   London, through a feigned peace
The papacy will consequently split
False liberty will be noised abroad.

There is no doubt that a Roman Temple
of Apollo once existed where
Westminster Abbey now stands.
Beyond that, the quatrain makes very
little sense unless it is seen to apply to
the future.

6/28

Le grand Celtique entrera dedans Rome,
Menant amas d'exilés et bannis
Le grand pasteur mettra à mort tout
homme,
Qui pour le coq estoient aux Alpes unis.

The great Frenchman will enter
   Rome
Leading a crowd of banished and
   exiled men
The Pope will put any man to death
Who crossed the Alps to join the
   French.

The last two lines present problems
here, and scupper suggestions that the
quatrain refers either to Napoleon and
Pius VI, the Guises, or to Henri II's heir,
the Duke of Alençon.

6/32

Par trahison de verges à mort battu
Prins surmonté sera par son desordre
Conseil frivole au grand captif sentu
Nez par fureur quant Berich viendra
mordre.

He is beaten to death for treason
He was captured and overcome
   because of disorder
Frivolous advice is given to the great
   captive
Berich bites his nose off in rage.

Berich, the only palpable clue, remains
elusive.

6/33

Sa main derniere par Alus sanguinaire
Ne se pourra par la mer guarantir
Entre deux fleuves craindre main
militaire
Le noir l'ireux le fera repentir.

Finally powerful, thanks to bloody
   Alus
He cannot protect himself by sea
He fears a military putsch between
   two rivers
The black and angry man will make
   him repent.

Is Alus an anagram of Saul? The first
elected king of the Israelities in the
eleventh century BC was certainly a
warrior – he was killed by the Philistines
at Mount Gilboa – but is best
remembered for the fact that he was
deposed from power by his son-in-law,
King David. Nostradamus is no doubt
looking ahead to a parallel life lived by
some future victim of a *putsch*, but the
identity of the victim is obscure.

6/35

Pres de Rion et proche à la blanche laine
Aries, Taurus, Cancer, Leo, la Vierge
Mars, Jupiter, le sol ardra grand plaine
Bois et citez, lettres cachez au cierge.

Near the Bear constellation, close to
    the Milky Way
Aries, Taurus, Cancer, Leo and
    Virgo
Mars and Jupiter, the sun will fry the
    great plains
The woods and cities, letters hidden
    in a candle.

A picturesque astrogolical quatrain with
the theme of drought.

6/39

L'enfant du regne par paternelle prinse
Expolié sera pour delivrer
Apres du lac Trasimen l'azur prinse
La troupe hostaige pour trop fort
s'enivrer.

The king's child, with his father
    captured
Will find himself plundered to free
    him
Near the lake of Perugia the blue
    captive
The troop is taken hostage through
    excess of drink.

An impenetrable verse in spite of the
Perugian location.

6/42

A lomygon sera laissé le regne,
Du grand Selin qui plus fera de faict
Par les Italies estendra son enseigne,
Regi sera par prudent contrefaict.

To Ogmios will go the kingdom
Of great Selin, who will achieve more
He will extend his rule throughout
    Italy
Which will be governed by careful
    forgery.

An uncertain quatrain which has never
been satisfactorily explained.

6/50

Dedans le puys seront trouvés les oz
Sera l'incest conmis par la maratre
L'estat changé on querra bruict et loz
Et aura Mars attendant pour son astre.

The bones will be found inside the
    well
Incest will have been committed by
    the step-mother
Once the state is changed, renown
    and fame will be sought
Mars will be his guiding star.

A grim fable of Oedipal proportions, but
the participants' names have yet to
emerge from the mist.

6/59

Dame en fureur par rage d'adultere
Viendra à son Prince conjurer non de dire
Mais bref cogneu sera le vitupere
Que seront mis dix sept à martyre.

The furious lady, in her adulterous
    rage
Will approach her Prince to
    conspire, and not to tell
But the culprit will soon be known
Seventeen will be martyred.

One interpreter of this quatrain blithely
reports that it refers to Sarah Ferguson
– Duchess of York (born 1959), a semi-
detached member of the British royal
family. It would be ungallant to pass
comment.

6/61

Le grand tappis plié ne monstrera
Fois qu'a demi la pluspart de l'histoire
Chassé du regne loing aspre apparoistra
Qu'au faict bellique chascun le viendra
croire.

The great folded tapestry
Will only show half the story
Driven far from the kingdom, he will
appear so bitter
That everyone will believe his
warlike stance.

Picturesque, but obscure.

6/62

Trop tard tous deux les fleurs seront
perdues
Contre la loi serpent ne voudra faire
Des ligueurs forces par gallots confondues
Savone, Albinque par monech grand
martyre.

Too late the flowers of both will be
lost
The serpent will not wish to act
against the law
The power of the League will be
confounded by the French
Savona, Albenga, great martyrdom
through Monaco.

Reference to the League would
normally be expected to signify the
Catholic or Holy League in the France
of Nostradamus's own time, led by the
fanatical Duke of Guise (1550–88). The
League was later rendered obsolete by
the religiously pragmatic Henri IV. But
much of the meaning of this verse is
unclear.

6/65

Gris et bureau demie ouverte guerre
De nuict seront assaillis et pillez
Le bureau prins passera par la serre
Son temple ouvert, deux au plastre
grillez.

The greys and browns in a half-
declared war
At night they will be besieged and
pillaged
The captured brown will pass
through prison
His temple opened, two put behind
bars.

Modern military uniforms come in
varying shades of grey (such as those
of German forces in the two world wars)
and brown (for example the khaki of the
British army) but the half-declared war
could be any one of a number of
conflicts.

6/66

Au fondement de la nouvelle secte
Seront les os du grand Romain trouvés
Sepulchre en marbre apparoistra couverte
Terre trembler en Avril, mal enfouetz.

At the founding of the new sect
The bones of the great Roman will
be found
A marble-covered sepulchre will
appear
In April, an earthquake; badly buried.

In Nostradamian terms, the new sect is
that of the Lutheran church. Italy has
suffered many earthquakes, but Rome
has yet to be struck by anything violent
enough to reveal long-lost tombs.

6/71

Quand on viendra le grand roi parenter
Avant qu'il ait du tout l'ame rendue,
Celui qui moins le viendra lamenter,
Par Lions, d'aigles, croix, couronne
vendue.

When they give the last rites to the
king
Before he is completely dead
The lesser man will come to mourn
him
The crown will be sold out by lions,
eagles, and the cross.

This could apply to so many kings that
it would be invidious to choose just
one. Shakespeare has written about
most of them.

6/73

En cité grande un moine et artisan,
Pres de la porte logés et aux murailles
Contre Modene secret, cave distant,
Trahis pour faire souz couleur
d'espousailles.

In a great city, a monk and an artisan
Will find lodgings near the gate and
walls
From a distant cellar, against secret
Modena
They will be betrayed, during a
wedding feast.

Modena is an ancient city of the Emilia
in Italy, but there are insufficient other
clues to locate this verse in time.

6/78

Crier victoire du grand Selin croissant,
Par les Romains sera l'Aigle clamé,
Ticcin, Milan, et Gennes n'y consent,
Puis par eux mesmes Basil grand
reclame.

To proclaim the victory of the great
crescent moon
The Romans will clamour for the
Eagle
Pavia, Milan and Geneva will not
agree
The great lord will then be claimed
by them.

The crescent moon symbolises the
Ottoman Empire, and the Eagle, the
Holy Roman Empire. This quatrain
never came true, as no leader of the
Ottomans has been captured since the
fifteenth century.

6/81

Pleurs, cris et plaincts, hurlement
effrayeur
Coeur inhumain, cruel, noir et transi
Leman, les isles de Gennes les majeurs
Sang epancher, frofaim à nul merci.

Tears, cries and plaints, howls of
terror
An inhuman heart, cruel, black and
benumbed
Lake Geneva, the islands and most of
the Genoans
Blood is shed, bread is needed, no
mercy is given.

One of many mentions of Lake Geneva
and the Genoans, and one of the most
inscrutable.

6/82

Par les desers de lieu, libre et farouche
Viendra errer nepveu du grand Pontife
Assommé à sept avecques lourde souche
Par ceux, qu'apres occuperont le cyphe.

Through the wild and deserted places
Comes the nephew of the great
    Pontiff
Beaten by seven club-carrying men
By those who will later occupy the
    Chalice.

Although it mentions a pope's nephew,
the subject of this quatrain has yet to
be identified. Papal elections were
more frequent in the past than now –
there were 12 different incumbents in
Nostradamus's lifetime alone.

6/86

Le grand Prelat un jour apres son songe
Interpreté au rebours de son sens
De la Gascogne lui surviendra un monge
Qui fera eslire le grand Prelat de sens.

The great Prelate, one day after his
    dream
Is falsely interpreted
A monk will come to him from
    Gascony
He will cause the grand prelate of
    Sens to be elected.

An enduring papal mystery.

6/89

Entre deux cymbes piedz et mains
    estachés
De miel face oingt et de laict substanté
Guespes et mouches, fitine amour fachés
Poccilateur faucer, Cyphe tempté.

His feet and hands tied between two
    boats
His face is anointed with honey, he is
    given milk
Wasps and flies, a father's love turns
    to anger
The cup-bearer lies, the Chalice is
    tempted.

The anointing suggests a coronation, but
the remainder of the verse is obscure.

6/93

Prelat avare d'ambition trompé.
Rien ne sera que trop viendra cuider
Ses messagiers, et lui bien attrapé,
Tout au rebours voir, qui le bois fendroit.

A greedy priest, spited in his
    ambitions
Believing that nothing is too good for
    him
He and his messengers will be
    surrounded
The woodcutter sees the other side
    of the coin.

Perhaps a reference to the churchly
power-brokers of seventeenth-century
France, Cardinals Richelieu and
Mazarin.

6/94

Un Roi iré sera aux sedifragues,
Quant interdicts seront harnois de guerre
La poison taincte au succre par les fragues
Par eaux meutris, mors, disant serre serre.

A king will be angry at the heretics
When war is prohibited
Poison will taint the strawberry's sugar
Murdered by water, he will die saying
    'land, land.'

Very obscure, beyond the fact that
Nostradamus is referring, once again,
to perfidious Protestants.

6/95

Par detracteur calumnie à puis nay.
Quant istront faicts enormes et martiaux
La moindre part dubieuse à l'aisney
Et tost au regne seront faicts partiaux.

The youngest will be calumniated
When great and warlike deeds occur
The smallest things will worry the
  oldest
Soon, in the kingdom, there will be
  partisan actions.

This, again, is so general a quatrain
that its application to any specific event
would entail accusations of vainglory to
be aimed at your commentator.

6/96

Grande cité à soldatz abandonné,
Onques n'y eut mortel tumulte si proche,
O quel hideuse calamité s'approche,
Fors une offense n'y sera pardonnée.

A great city, abandoned to the
  soldiers
Never was mortal tumult so near
Oh, what hideous calamity
  approaches
One offence only will be forgiven.

See the previous quatrain, 6/95.

Century Seven

7/2

Par Mars ouvert Arles ne donra guerre
De nuict seront les soldartz estonnés
Noir, blanc à l'inde dissimulés en terre
Sous la faincte umbre traistres verez et
  sonnés.

Arles, thrown open by war, refuses to
  fight
The soldiers will be taken by surprise
  at night
Black, white, concealing indigo by
  land
Traitors will be spotted under the
  faint shadow and the alarm given.

Arles in Provence is, as it was in
Nostradmus's day, one of the best-
preserved Roman towns in France,
complete with a magnificent
amphitheatre with seating for 25,000.
The seer visualises fighting there, but
the conflict described does not tally with
anything in the town's history to date.

7/8

Flora fuis, fuis le plus proche Romain
Au Fesulan sera conflict donné
Sang espandu les plus grands prins à mains
Temple ne sexe ne sera pardonné.

Fly, Florence, flee from the nearest
  Roman
The battle will be at Fiesole
Blood will be shed, the greatest
  captured by hand
Neither church nor sex will be spared.

The great battle for Florence, in which
the city stoutly but unsuccessfully
defended its independence against
Pope Clement and the Holy Roman
Empire, took place in 1529–30 and
brought the Medicis back to power –
until 1737. Fiesole, the hilltop town that
overlooks Florence from three miles to
the northeast, was the scene of much of
the fighting. Nostradamus seems to
believe that Florence will one day face
such a siege again.

7/25

Par guerre longue tout l'exercite expuiser
Que pour souldartz ne trouveront pecune
Lieu d'or d'argent, cuir on viendra cuser
Gaulois aerain, signe croissant de Lune.

The army is exhausted after a long war
Money is not found for the soldiers
Instead of gold and silver, they will
    mint leather
French brass, the moon's crescent sign.

The history of unpaid armies is an
uninterrupted one right up to the
chronically underfunded Russian forces
of the present day. Leather coinage as
a substitute for gold and silver is a
novelty not yet tried by military
paymasters.

7/27

Au cainct de Vast la grand cavalerie
Proche à Ferrage empeschee au bagaige
Prompt à Turin feront tel volerie
Que dans le fort raviront leur hostaige.

The mighty cavalry encircle Vasto
They impede the baggage train near
    Ferrara
Arriving speedily, they plunder Turin
    to such an extent
That they even ravish their hostage
    in the fort.

Italian wars. Vasto, on the Adriatic
coast of the Abruzzi, is the mediaeval
name for the ancient town of Histonium.

7/28

Le capitaine conduira grande proie
Sur la montaigne des ennemis plus proche
Environné, par feu fera tel voie
Tous eschappez or trente mis en broche.

The captain makes great prey
Of his nearby enemies on the
    mountain
Surrounded, he cuts such a fiery path
That all escape, save thirty, who are
    roasted.

No clues whatsoever to place or time,
although there is an implication of the
terrible weapons of the twentieth
century.

7/30

Le sac s'approche, feu, grand sang
    espandu,
Po, grand fleuves, aux bouviers
    l'entreprinse,
De Gennes, Nice, apres long attendu,
Foussan, Turin, à Savillon la prinse.

The sack approaches, with fire, and
    great shedding of blood
The fools will win Po, and the great
    rivers
Genoa and Nice, after a long wait
Fossano, Turin, the capture will be
    made at Savigliano.

This could apply either to the French
war against the Vatican States of 1555–
7, or to the closing stages of the Battle
for Italy, in the Second World War,
during April 1945.

7/31

De Languedoc, et Guienne plus de dix,
Mille voudront les Alpes repasser
Grans Allobroges marcher contre Brundis
Aquin et Bresse les viendront recasser.

More than ten will come from
    Languedoc and Guyenne
A thousand will wish to cross the
    Alps again

The great Savoyards will march
against Brindisi
Aquino and Bresse will drive them
back.

A geographically and numerically
muddled quatrain, which has been
variously ascribed to Garibaldi, and to
the ceding of Savoy in 1601.

7/36

Dieu, le ciel tout le divin verbe à l'unde,
Porté par rouges sept razes à Bisance
Contre les oingtz trois cens de
  Trebisconde,
Deus loix mettront, et l'horreur, puis
  credence.

God, heaven, and the divine doctrine
will cross the seas
To Byzantium, carried by seven red
crop-heads
Three hundred from Trebizond will
oppose the anointed
There will be two laws, first horror,
then trust.

The seven red crop-heads are, as
usual, cardinals, but why they should
be crossing to Constantinople remains
a mystery. Did Nostradamus foresee
yet another crusade, in which Muslim
forces from Trebizond (the Black Sea
port) would oppose the Christian
fanatics?

7/37

Dix envoyés, chef de nef mettre à mort,
D'un adverti, en classe guerre ouverte
Confusion chef, l'un se picque et mord,
Lerin, stecades nefz cap dedans la nerte.

Ten are sent to put the ship's captain
to death
Forewarned by one man, war erupts
inside the fleet
Confusion reigns, one kills himself
The isles of Lerins and Hyères, ships
beneath them.

The image of ships beneath the islands
of Lerins and Hyères conjures up
heady visions of submarines, imagined
by Nostradamus over three centuries
before their existence. The rest of the
quatrain appears so specific that one
feels it must apply to a discoverable
event, but no-one has yet found it.
There is, of course, no law which says
that the events of which Nostradamus
speaks must be historically recorded.

7/40

Dedans tonneaux hors oingz d'huile et
  gresse
Seront vingt un devant le port fermés
Au second guet par mort feront prouesse
Gaigner les portes et du guet assommés.

Twenty-one people will be covered
in oil and grease
And sealed inside some casks
On the second watch they will die
proudly
Winning the gates, killed by the
guards.

Concealed in casks, soldiers manage
to get inside a closed city. They
manage to open the gates but die in
the effort. A specific anecdote, but time
and place are unknown.

7/41

Les oz des piedz et des main enserrés
Par bruit maison long temps inhabitee
Seront par songes concavent deterrés
Maison salubre et sans bruit habitee.

The bones of hands and feet are
    imprisoned
Because of the noise, the house is not
    lived in
They are unearthed because of
    dreams
The now peaceful house is lived in
    again.

A rare reference to a haunting, in this
case a house in which bones have
been found, apparently after the
occupier saw them in a dream. Once
removed, the spirit is exorcized. This
sounds like an account of an actual
event. Perhaps Nostradamus himself
was involved?

7/42

Deux de poison saisiz nouveau venuz
Dans la cuisine du grand Prince verser
Par le souillard tous deux au faicts
    congneuz
Prins que cuidoit de mort l'aisné vexer.

Two newcomers collect poison
And pour it in the kitchen of the
    great Prince
They are caught in the act by the
    scullion
He who thought to kill his elder is
    captured.

An attempted poisoning is discovered
by a kitchen servant.

7/72

Grand oeuvre sera trop pour un seul;
Le comète tombera sans secours,
Un Lirant vieux entendra son gueule,
Travail ensemble prenont quarante
    jours.

A great work will be too much for
    one
The comet will fall without help
An old Reading will hear his crying
The combined labour will take 40
    days.

An enduring mystery. The cryptic 'old
Reading' has confounded scholars for
centuries.

Century Eight

8/2

Condon et Aux et autour de Mirande
Je voi du ciel feu qui les environne
Sol Mars conjoint au Lion puis marmande
Fouldre, grand gresle, mur tombe dans
  Garonne.

Condom, Auch, and around Mirande
I see fire from the sky surrounding
  them
The Sun and Mars joined to Leo,
  then Marmande
Lightning, enormous hail, a wall falls
  into the Garonne.

A violent storm in southwest France,
expected to do structural damage.

8/8

Pres de Linterne dans les tonnes fermez
Chivaz fera pour l'aigle la menee
L'esleu cassé lui ses gens enfermez
Dedans Turin rapt espouse emmenee.

Near Focia, enclosed in wooden
  vessels
Chivasso will plot for the eagle
The elected one broken, he and his
  people confined
Rape in Turin, the bride stolen away.

The eagle tends to represent Napoleon
Bonaparte, and the elected one the
Pope. But the remaining pieces of this
jigsaw have not yet been made to fit.

8/20

Le faux messaige par election fainte
Courir par urban rompu pache arreste,
Voix acheptees, de sang chappelle tainte,
Et à un autre l'empire contraicte.

The false news of the rigged election
Will reach the city, stopping the
  broken pact
Bribed speakers, the chapel stained
  with blood
The empire is contracted to another.

This is too generalised a quatrain to
allow for an accurate interpretation, but
possibly refers to an event during the
time of the Holy Roman Empire.

8/26

De Caton es trouves en Barcellone,
Mis descouvers lieu retrouvers et ruine,
Le grand qui tient ne tient vouldra
  Pamplonne.
Par l'abbaye de Montferrat bruine.

The bones of Cato are found in
  Barcelona
Now uncovered, the place is found
  and destroyed
The nobleman who thinks he holds
  them, wants Pamplona
Drizzle falls near the Abbey of
  Montserrat.

Much speculation and little fact
surrounds this quatrain. Cato the Elder
(234–149 BC) did not die in Barcelona,
but he deserved an early death for
prompting the Third Punic War – which
destroyed Carthage.

8/27

La voye auxelle l'une sur l'autre forniz
Du muy desert hor mis brave et genest
L'escript d'empereur le fenix
Veu en celui ce qu'à nul autre n'est.

The way in which one fornicates with
    the other
Le Muy is deserted, save for our hero
    and his horse
The writing of the re-arisen emperor
Will mean to him what it means to
    no other.

Obscure in spite of a faint echo of the
Shakespearean 'beast with two backs'
in Hamlet. A careful reading could
suggest an enaction of Tomasso
Magister's version of 'animal
husbandry' on the part of the
eponymous hero, who happens to find
himself alone with his horse, in a 're-
arisen' state, in a deserted Provençal
town. The whole thing is pregnant with
hidden meaning.

8/29

Au quart pillier l'on sacre à Saturne.
Par tremblant terre et deluge fendu
Soubz l'edifice Saturnin trouvee urne,
D'or Capion ravi et puis rendu.

The fourth pillar, dedicated to
    Saturn
Is demolished by earthquake and
    flood
Under Saturn's place an urn is found
Gold, stolen by Caepio, is then
    returned.

This could be the clue to a hidden
treasure, looted and hidden by Caepio,
the Roman consul, who plundered
Toulouse in 106 BC. When the
Toulousais Church of St Saturnin is
struck by an earthquake, an urn will be
found, containing all Caepio's gold.

8/32

Garde toi roi Gaulois de ton nepveu
Qui fera tant que ton unique fils
Sera meutri à Venus faisant voeu
Accompaigné de nuit que trois et six.

Beware, French king, of your nephew
Who will do so much harm that your
    only son
Will be murdered, while making his
    vows to Venus
Accompanied at night by three and
    six.

A firm prophecy yet to be fulfilled.

8/34

Apres victoire du Lyon au Lyon
Sur la montaigne de Jura Secatombe
Delues et brodes septieme million
Lyon, Ulme a Mausol mort et tombe.

After the victory of the lion at Lyons
There will be great slaughter in the
    mountains of Jura
Floods, 143,000 dark-skinned people
Lyons, Ulm; death and tombs at the
    mausoleum.

The lion is Great Britain in
Nostradamian code, and by the sound
of this quatrain, an unwelcome visitor in
France. The high casualty figure
suggests the twentieth century, or later.

8/39

Qu'aura esté par prince Bizantin
Sera tollu par prince de Tholoze
La foi de Foix par le chef Tholentin
Lui faillira ne refusant l'espouse.

He who was for the Byzantine prince
Will be taken away by the prince of
   Toulouse
The faith of Foix, through the
   Tolentine leader
Will fail him, not refusing the bride.

A quatrain camouflaged too far for
interpretation.

8/44

Le procreé naturel dogmion
De sept à neuf du Chemin destorner
A roi de longue et ami au mi-hom
Doit à Navarre fort de Pau prosterner.

The natural offspring of Ogmion
Will turn seven to nine off the Road
To the king of tongues, and friend to
   the half-man
He must destroy the fort of Pau at
   Navarre.

Ogmion is the Hercules of Celtic myth,
but here is not a substantial clue to the
significance of this verse.

8/51

Le Bizantin faisant oblation
Apres avoir Cordube à soi reprinse
Son chemin long repos pamplation
Mer passant proi par la Colongna prinse.

The Byzantine makes an offering
After having taken back Cordoba
His road is long, he rests, cutting
   down the vines
Passing by sea, the prey is taken near
   Gibraltar.

Nostradamus foresees that Islam will
regain Spain. The end of wine
production is one implication.

8/55

Entre deux fleuves se verra enserré
Tonneaux et caques unis à passer outre
Huict poutz rompus chef à tant enferré
Enfans parfaictz sont jugetez en coultre.

He will find himself shut in between
   two rivers
Casks and barrels are tied together as
   a bridge
Eight bridges are broken, the chief is
   badly run through
Sweet children have their throats cut.

The number of bridges implies a
conflict in a city, but there are no further
clues.

8/62

Lors qu'on verra expiler le saint temple,
Plus grand du rosne leurs sacrez profaner
Par eux naistra pestilence si ample.
Roi fuit injuste ne fera condamner.

When we see the holy temple
   plundered
And the greatest of the Rhône
   profaning the sacred
Because of them a great plague will
   arise
The king flees injustice, and will not
   condemn them.

This could be applied either to the
French Revolution or Italy after Mussolini.

8/63

Quand l'adultere blessé sans coup aura
Merdri la femme et le filz par despit,
Femme assoumee l'enfant estranglera
Huit captifz prins, s'estouffer sans respit.

When the adulterer, wounded
without a blow
Will have murdered his wife and son,
in spite
His wife struck down, the child
strangled
Eight taken captive, garrotted to
death.

This seems specific, but actually says
very little. An angry cuckold takes
revenge on his unfaithful wife. Did she
take eight lovers? Or has all news of
this deed been stifled?

8/66

Quand l'escriture D.M. trouvee,
En cave antique à lampe descouverte,
Loi, Roi, et Prince Ulpian esprouvee
Pavillon Royne et Duc sous la couverte.

When the signature D. M. is found
Lit by a lamp, in an age-old cave
The Law, the King and the Prince
Ulpian will be tested
In the pavilion, the Queen and the
Duke share one blanket.

The initials D. M. have provided an
Aladdin's Cave of possible meanings
for eager commentators. The most
obvious is Diis Manibus, a common
inscription on tombstones meaning
'Here Lieth'. Ulpian was a Roman
given name.

8/67

Par. Car, Nersaf, à ruine grand
discorde,
Ne l'un ne l'autre n'aura election,
Nersaf du peuple aura amour et
concorde.
Ferrare, Callonne grande protection.

Paris, Carcassone, and France, ruined
disharmoniously
Neither one nor the other will have
any say in the matter
Peaceful France will be loved by its
people
Ferrara and Colonna will be well
protected.

A perplexing quatrain that probably
hinges on the meaning of Nersaf, which
is usually taken as an anagram for
France. Even then, the quatrain is
obscure.

8/83

Le plus grand voile hors de port de Zara,
Pres de Bisance fera son entreprinse,
D'ennemi parte et l'ami ne sera,
Le Tiers à deux fera grand pille et prinse.

The greatest sail, outside the port of
Zara
He will follow his course near
Byzantium
Enemy and friend will not part
A third will pillage, and capture them
both.

Numerous Nostradamian interpreters
consider this to be a simple matter of
record – of the atrocities of the Fourth
Crusade of 1202. But it is a warning,
too, that tragedies of history repeat
themselves.

8/90

Quand des croisez un trouvé de sens
trouble
En lieu du sacre verra un boeuf cornu
Par vierge porc son lieu lors sera comble
Par roi plus ordre ne sera soustenu.

When one of the crusaders is
troubled by his conscience
He will see a horned bull in the
church
Thanks to the virgin, the pig's place
will be filled
By the king; there will be disorder.

A symbolical quatrain, and
consequently hard to pin down. The
horned bull represents the power of
Islam, the implication being that a
crusader receives a vision of an Islamic
threat while attending Mass. The 'pig' is
traditionally seen as evil, therefore,
thanks to the Virgin Mary, he is
supplanted by the 'king', a
representation of Jesus Christ.

8/93

Sept mois sans plus obtiendra prelature
Par son deces grand scisme fera naistre
Sept mois tiendra un autre la preture
Pres de Venise paix union renaistre.

He will be prelate for less than seven
months
A great schism will occur on his
death
Another will hold the prelacy for
seven months
There will be peace near Venice, and
union again.

Although many popes have reigned for
less than seven months, none of them
fit the configuration suggested in lines
2 and 3.

8/95

Le seducteur sera mis en la fosse
Et estaché jusques à quelque temps,
Le clerc uni le chef avec sa crosse
Picante droite attraira les contens.

The seducer will be placed in the
ditch
And kept prisoner, for quite some
time
The scholar unites the leader with his
abbey
The right wing will attract the
bourgeoisie.

This convoluted verse has never been
successfully disentangled.

8/99

Par la puissance des trois rois tempoulz,
En autre lieu sera mis le saint siege
Où la substance et de l'esprit corporel,
Sera remis et receu pour vrai siege.

Through the power of three
temporal kings
The papal seat will be moved
The substance of the spirit and the
body
Will be restored, and acknowledged
as true.

A further quatrain dealing with the
Catholic Apocalypse. The Papal seat
has only once been removed, to date,
and that was to Valence, during the
illness of Pope Pius VI. It was
transferred back to Rome on his death.

8/100

Pour l'abondance de larme respandue
Du hault en bas par le bas au plus hault.
Trop grande foir par jeu vie perdue
De soif mourir par habondant deffault.

By the great number of tears shed
From high to low, from lowest to
   highest
By too great faith, in sport, a life is
   lost
He dies in water, without drinking.

A possible link has been suggested
here to the Grimaldis, the ruling family
of Monaco. Princess Caroline lost her
husband in a power-boat accident. The
theory, however, seems far-fetched.

Century Nine

9/4

L'an ensuivant descouvertz par deluge,
Deux chefs esluez le premier ne tiendra
De fuir ombre à l'un d'eux le refuge,
Saccager case qui premier maintiendra.

The following year begins with
   floods
Two leaders are elected; one does not
   hold power
One of them takes refuge in the
   shadows
Plundering the house which at first
   he maintained.

Too general a quatrain to make an
accurate reading likely.

9/6

Par la Guienne infinité d'Anglais.
Occuperont par nom d'Anglaquitaine
Du Languedoc Ispalme Bourdelois.
Qu'ils nommeront apres Barboxitaine.

A vast number of Englishmen will
   occupy Guyenne
In the name of Anglaquitaine
From the Languedoc, Ispalme and
   Bordelais
Which they will later call
   Barboxitaine.

A failed quatrain which predicts the re-
invasion of the Guienne, Languedoc
and Bordelais regions by the English,
following their expulsion from the region
in the fifteenth century.

9/9

*Quand lampe ardente de feu
    inextinguible,
Sera trouvé au temple des Vestales,
Enfant trouvé feue, eau passant par
    trible
Perir eau Nimes, Tholose cheoir les
    halles.*

When the burning and eternal lamp
Is found in the temple of the Vestals
A child will be found in the fire, like
    water through a sieve
Nîmes will perish, flooded; in
    Toulouse, the markets will
    collapse.

This prophecy has still not been
fulfilled, despite a sporadic history of
flooding in the area during the last 450
years.

9/10

*Moine moinesse d'enfant mort exposé,
Mourrir par ourse et ravi par verrier
Par Foix et Pamyes le camp sera posé.
Contre Tholose Carcas, dresser forrier.*

The child of a monk and a nun will
    be left out to die
To be killed by a bear, or carried off
    by a boar
The army will camp near Foix and
    Pamiers
Carcassonne will besiege Toulouse.

This, again, is a prophecy waiting for
fulfilment. All the towns mentioned are
in south-western France. A few bears
do still eke out an existence in the
foothills of the Pyrenees, and the boar
is widespread throughout the region.
But nuns and monks are growing
scarcer.

9/13

*Les exilez autour de la Soulonge
Condus de nuit pour marcher à Leuxois,
Deux de Modene truculent de Boulogne,
Mis descouvers par feu de Burancois.*

Around Sologne, the exiles
Will be led, by night, on a march to
    Auxois
Two men from Modena, cruel
    against Bologna
They are uncovered by the fires of
    the Buzançais.

A complicated and obscure quatrain
never satisfactorily interpreted.

9/14

*Mis en planure chaulderone d'infecteurs,
Vin, miel et l'huile, et bastis sur forneaulx
Seront plongez sans mal dit mal facteurs
Sept. fum extaint au canon des
    borneaux.*

The dyer's cauldron is laid flat
Wine, honey and oil laid over the
    fires
Innocent men will be immersed
Seven shots are fired by the fanatic's
    cannon.

Many times throughout history men
have been tied to the mouths of
cannons and consigned, in pieces, to
the great hereafter. Burning, too, was
commonplace. To which of the many
victims this refers, however, remains a
mystery.

9/21

Au temple hault de Blois sacre Solonne
Nuict pont de Loire, prelat, roi pernicant
Curseur victoire aux marestz de la lone
Don prelature de blancs à borméant.

To the high temple of Saint Solenne
    at Blois
By night, a bridge over the Loire, a
    priest, a sick king
A messenger, victory for the marshes
    over the stagnant pool
Destruction for the prelacy of the
    whites.

Nostradamus believed that Blois would
one day provide a French king. Royalist
commentators see this as the future
King Henri V of France, whose
accession would represent a victory by
the virile monarchist marshes over the
stagnant pool of Republicanism.

9/28

Voille Simacle port Massiliolique
Dans Venice port marcher aux Panons
Partir du goulfre et Sinus Illirique
Vast à Socile, Ligures coups de canons.

The auxiliary fleet from the port of
    Marseilles
Will arrive in Venice, to go against
    the Hungarians
It will leave from the gulf and bay of
    Illyria
Sicily and Genoa are devastated by
    cannon shot.

Impossible to date, as the variety of
place names could imply a Second
World War connection or an invasion
from an earlier period.

9/30

Au port de Puola et de saint Nicolas,
Perir Normande au goulfre phanatique,
Cap. De Bizance raues crier helas,
Secours de Gaddez et du grand
    Philipique.

At the ports of Pola and San Nicolo
A Norman will perish in the Gulf of
    Quarnero
The Pope cries 'Alas' in the streets of
    Byzantium
Help comes from Cadiz, and Philip
    the Great.

All the towns mentioned in the first two
lines are in former Yugoslavia. None of
the events indicated, however, appear
to have taken place.

9/31

Le tremblement de terre à Montara,
Cassich saint George à demi perfondrez,
Paix assoupie, la guerre esveillera,
Dans temple à Pasques abismes enfondrez.

An earthquake at Mortara
Will half-sink the English isles of tin
Lulled with peace, a war begins
In the temple, at Easter, chasms will
    open.

St Columba predicted, in the year 592,
that Ireland would sink beneath the
waters of a great flood seven years
before judgement day. Presumably the
flood would affect England as well,
especially if it was connected to an
earthquake. Mortara, however, is
situated more than 1000 miles from the
British Isles. An alternative translation of
line 2 would allow for an existing statue
of St George, in Mortara, partially made
of Cornish tin, to suffer instead.

9/37

Pont et moulins en Decembre versez,
En si haut lieu montera la Garonne
Murs, edifices, Tholose renversez,
Qu'on ne scaura son lieu avant
matronne.

Bridges and mills cast down in
    December
Because the Garonne rises so high
Walls, buildings, Toulouse
    overturned
None will know where they came
    from.

This continues the theme of an earlier
quatrain that a great flood destroys
Toulouse.

9/39

En Arbissel à Veront et Carcari,
De nuict conduitz pour Savonne
attrapper,
Le vifz Gascon Turbi, et la Scerry
Derrier mur vieux et neuf palais
gripper.

In Albisola, Varano and Carrara
They are taken, by night, to catch
    Savona
The lively Gascon, La Turbie and
    L'Escarène
Are set upon behind the old wall of
    the new palace.

Veront, until now assumed to be
Vorazzo or Voragine, is more probably
Varano, near Carrara, which puts all the
towns mentioned within hailing distance
of Savona. But this does not further
clarify this rather obscure quatrain.
L'Esacarène and La Turbie are both
near Monaco. The lively Gascon evokes
Cyrano de Bergerac, or possibly even
D'Artagnan.

9/43

Proche à descendre l'armee Crucigere
Sera guettez par les Ismaëlites
De tous cottez batus par nef Raviere
Prompt assaillis de dix galeres eslites.

The Crusader Army, on the point of
    landing
Will be ambushed by the Ismaelis
Struck from all sides by the red-
    blossoming ship
The attack is followed up by ten elite
    galleys.

Raviere means a radish bed in Old
French, and from there comes the
image of a fire-ship, blossoming red.
Beyond that, the quatrain would appear
to refer to the consistent Nostradamian
topic of the Battle of Lepanto.

9/61

La pille faite à la coste marine,
Incite nova et parens amenez,
Plusieurs de Malte par le fair de
*   Messine,*
Estroit serres seront mal guerdonnez.

The looting done on the coast,
Incites newcomers to bring kinsmen.
Several from Malta by virtue of
    Messina.
Closely gathered at table will do
    badly.

A prediction of an ill-fated peace
conference between the islands of
Malta and Sicily.

9/62

Au grand de Cheramon agora
Seront croisez par ranc tous attachez
Le pertinax Oppie, et Mandragora
Rougon d'Octobre le tiers seront laschez.

To the great man of Cheramon agora
Crosses will be attached, by rank
Long-lasting opium and mandrake
    root
Those of Rougon will be released on
    the 3 October

Ceramon-agora is the name of an
ancient town in Asia minor, now part of
Turkey. There is a village called
Rougon situated high above Fréjus, in
the Provencal Alps, about 60 miles from
Salon, where Nostradamus lived.
Opium and mandrake root were both
used in occult practices and alchemy.

9/63

Plainctes et pleurs, cris et grands
    hurlements,
Près de Narbon à Bayonne et en Foix,
O quel horribles, calamités, changements,
Aant que Mars revolu quelquefois.

Pleas and tears, cries and great howls
Near Narbonne, Bayonne and in
    Foix
O what horrors, calamities and
    changes
Before Mars turns some times.

The reference to Mars signifies the wars
that brought such troubles to southern
France for much of Nostradamus's life.

9/66

Paix, union sera et changement,
Etats, Offices, bas haut, et haut bien bas
Dresser voyage, le fruict premier,
    torment,
Guerre cesser, civils proces, debats.

There will be peace, unity and change
Land, positions, low to high and high
    very low
To prepare a voyage whose first fruit
    is pain
To end war, civil proceedings and
    debates.

A vision of a fairer, more peaceful
future, but with a warning that the
journey towards it will not be painless.

9/67

Du hault des monts à l'entour de Dizere,
Port à la roche Valent, cent assemblé,
De Château-Neuf, Pierrelate, en
    Douzere,
Contre le Crest, Romains for assemblés.

From the mountain peaks around
    Dizere
A hundred gathered at Valent Rock.
From Châteauneuf, Pierrelate, in
    Douzere.
Against the Crest, Romains a strong
    assembly.

A gazetteer of place names in the Midi,
and seemingly little more.

9/69

Sur le mont de Bailly & la Bresse,
Seront caché de Grenoble les fiers,
Outre Lyon, Vien, eux si grand gresle,
Langoult en terre n'en restera un tiers.

On Mount Bailly and Bresse
The proud ones will be hidden at
 Grenoble
Outside Lyons, Vienna such hail will
 fall
Not even a third of those languishing
 on the ground will be left.

It seems to presage a terrible
bombardment, extending from Bresse
(the Jura of eastern France) all the way
south to Lyons and east to Austria.

9/71

Au lieux sacrez animaux veu à trixe
Avec celui qui n'osera le jour
A Carcassonne pour disgrace propice
Sera posé pour plus ample sejour.

Wool-producing animals are seen at
 the sacred place
With one who dares not face the day
Carcassonne is ready for well-earned
 disgrace
He is well set for a longer stay.

Can Nostradamus be dealing with
vampires, renowned for not being able
to bear sunlight? Sheep as well as
people were prey for the vampires
believed to be abroad in sixteenth
century France. Many stories of the
time persist, most notably the one
concerning Joan of Arc's erstwhile
protector, Gilles de Rais (1404–1440),
the French Bluebeard. He was hanged
for the brutal and anthropophagous
murder of 140 young boys, after
confessing all under threat of torture
and excommunication.

9/74

Dans la cité de Fersod homicide
Fait et fait multe beuf arant ne macer
Retour encores aux honneurs d'Artemide
Et à Vulcan corps morts sepultures.

A homicide, in the city of Fersod
Act and act, many cattle used for
 ploughing rather than sacrifice
A further return to the honours of
 Artemis
Vulcan must bury the bodies.

Ferté Sodom, the stronghold of Sodom,
would seem a reasonable definition for
Fersod. Artemis is the protector of
young women, as well as being the
Greek counterpart to Diana, goddess of
hunting and the moon. Vulcan is the
God of fire. This, together with the lack
of sacrifice in line 2, provides an
unnerving picture of a city gone to the
bad, in which faith and human life are
held cheap. God, or nature, destroys
this city, leaving Vulcan to mop up the
dead with his volcanic fire.

9/78

La dame Greque de beauté laydique
Heureuse faicts de procs innumerable
Hors translater au regne Hispanique
Captive prinse mourir mort miserable.

The belle-laide Greek woman
Is made happy by numerous suitors
If translated to the kingdom of Spain
She will be taken, and die a wretched
 death.

The belle-laide Greek woman may refer
to Helen of Troy, who was certainly
beautiful, but also caused ugly deeds
to be done in her name. But the
equation could apply to many other
temptresses through the ages.

9/79

Le chef de la classe par fraude stratageme
Fera timides sortir de leurs galleres
Sortis meutris chef renieur de cresme
Puis par l'embusche lui rendront les saleres.

The admiral of the fleet, through a deceitful stratagem
Will force the scared ones from their galleys
Once out, they are killed by the recusant leader
Then, through ambush, they give him what he deserves.

Some commentators manipulate this quatrain in the direction of Admiral de Coligny – but unconvincingly. It probably applies, once again, to the Battle of Lepanto.

9/82

Par le deluge et pestilence forte
La cité grande de long temps assiegee
La sentinelle et garde de main morte
Subite prinse, mais de nul oultragee.

The great city is assailed for a long time
By floods and terrible pestilence
The sentinel and guard are killed by bare hand
Suddenly taken, yet no-one perpetrates outrages.

Paris is usually understood as the great city, but in this case the clue leaves us none the wiser. The city has been the victim of both flood and plague during the course of its history, and has fallen numerous times into the hands of outside invaders. None, if any, have failed to commit outrages on the population.

9/84

Roi exposé parfaira l'hecatombe
Apres avoir trouvé son origine
Torrent ouvrir de marbre et plomb la tombe
D'un grand Romain d'enseigne Medusine.

The exposed king will complete the slaughter
Once he has found his origin
A flood will open the marble and lead tomb
Of a great Roman, with a Medusan sign.

Medusine is an anagram of Deus In Me, which implies that the discovered tomb will be that of St Peter, the great Roman, whose motto it was. The present tomb of St Peter is obviously a fake.

9/92

Le roi vouldra dans cité neuf entrer
Par ennemis expugner lon viendra
Captif libere faulx dire et perpetrer
Roi dehors estre, loin d'ennemis tiendra.

The king will wish to enter the new city
Enemies will come to subdue it
A freed captive will speak and act falsely
The king will be outside, and remain far from his enemies.

The new city could apply to New York, built on land bought by the Dutchman Peter Minuit from the Canarsie chiefs on 6 May 1626. Line 2 predicts that the city will be attacked in a bid to free a captive held there. The king, in this case the US President, might wish to be there in command, but decides to stay (no doubt on advice from his aides) at a safe distance from the fighting.

Century Ten

10/3

En apres cinq troupeau ne mettra hors un
Fuytif pour Penelon l'aschera,
Faulx murmurer secours venir par lors,
Le chief le siege lois habandonnera.

Five are lost from the flock, no more
    are put out
A fugitive from Penelon is turned
    loose
False rumours that help is close at
    hand
The leader will then abandon the
    siege.

An obscure quatrain that relies on the
correct interpretation of Penelon. Could
it be Poland?

10/9

De Castillion figuires jour de brune,
De fame infame naistra souverain
    prince.
Surnon de chausses perhume lui
    posthume,
Onc Roi ne faut si pire en sa province.

On a misty day, in the castle of
    Figueras
A shameless woman will give birth to
    a sovereign prince
After his death he will be known as
    'stick in the mud'
Never was any king so destructive of
    his province.

There has never been a convicing
interpretation of this. The Spanish
connection is obviously paramount.

10/14

Urnel Vaucile sans conseil de soi mesmes
Hardit timide par crainte prins vaincu
Accompaigné de plusieurs putains blesmes
A Barcellonne aux chartreux convaincu.

Urnel Vaucile, lacking a plan
Bold but beaten, made hesitant
    through fear of kidnap
Accompanied by a few pale whores
He'll be converted at the Carthusian
    convent in Barcelona.

A *vaurien* is a good-for-nothing, and an
imbecile needs no explanation. A
portmanteau of the two words is
Vaucile. Nostradamus was fond of
word-games, and would often change a
single letter to make his meaning less
obvious. This is the case with Urnel,
which now becomes the Catalonian
town of Urgel. The Carthusian
monastery is Monte Allegro, near
Barcelona.

10/15

Pere duc vieux d'ans et de soif chargé
Au jour extreme filz desniant les guiere
Dedans le puis vif mort viendra plongé
Senat au fil la mort longue et legiere.

The Duke and father, old and thirsty
On his last day his son will deny him
    a drink
He'll be plunged alive into the well,
    emerging dead
The Senate will give his son a long
    and light death.

A long and light death would imply
hanging by the neck as the end
enjoyed by this fickle and cruel son. No
suitable candidate has yet been found
for the unfortunate Duke.

10/25

Par Nebro ouvrir de Brisanne passage,
Bien eslongez el tago fara muestra,
Dans Pelligauxe sera commis l'outrage
De la grand dame assise sur l'orchestre.

A passage to Brisanne is opened
    through the Nebro
Far away, the Tagus will complain
An outrage will be committed in
    Pelligoux
By the great lady, in the orchestra
    seat.

The outrage committed by the great
lady in an orchestra seat has
fascinated commentators for many
years, but no harmonious explanation
has emerged.

10/27

Par le cinquieme et un grand Hercules
Viendront le temple ouvrir de main
    bellique,
Un Clement, Iule et Ascans recules,
Lespe, clef, aigle n'eurent onc si grand
    picque.

By the fifth, and a great Hercules
They will come, warlike, to open the
    temple
A Clement, a Julius and an Ascanius
    step back
The sword, the key and the eagle are
    more angered than ever.

An unsuccessful quatrain, that is open
to much misinterpretation. It could
apply to any number of events.

10/28

Second et tiers qui font prime musicque
Sera par Roi en honneur sublimee,
Par grasse et maigre presque demi eticque
Rapport de Venus faulx rendra deprimee.

The second and third who make fine
    music
Will be sublimely honoured by the
    king
Through good times, and bad, nearly
    half consumptive
The account of a false Venus will
    depress them.

This, and the quatrains either side of it,
10/27 and 10/29, constitute a rather
poor run for Nostradamus, who may
well have been feeling tired by this
time. Johann Sebastian Bach (1735–
1782) was the father of between twenty
and thirty children, most of whom, if
they survived infancy, became
musicians. This could apply to any of
them. Carl Philipp Emmanuel and
Johann Christian are the most likely
contenders.

10/31

Le saint Empire viendra en Germanie
Ismaelites trouveront lieux ouverts
Anes vouldront aussi la Carmanie
Les soustenens de terre tous converts.

The Holy Empire will come to
  Germany
The Arabs will find everything open
Carmania will also wish for asses
The supporters will be covered with
  earth.

This would appear to be one of
Nostradamus's rare failures, as the
events described have neither
happened in the past, nor seem likely
to happen in the foreseeable future.

10/33

La faction cruelle à robbe longue
Viendra cacher souz les pointus poignars
Saisir Florence le duc et lieu diphlongue
Sa descouverte par immeurs et
  flaugnards.

The cruel long-robed faction
Will hide daggers beneath their hats
The Duke will seize Florence and the
  hyphenated place
Youths and flatterers will discover it.

Reminiscent of Romeo and Juliet, this
quatrain is impossible to interpret with
any degree of certainty. The
hyphenated, or two-syllabled place,
may conceivably be Fiesole.

10/52

Au lieu où Laye et Scelde se marient
Seront les nopces de longtemps maniees
Au lieu d'Anvers où la crappe charient
Jeune vieillesse consorte intaminee.

In the place where the Lys and the
  Scelde meet
Nuptials will have been long
  prepared
At the place in Anvers where the
  chaff is spread
A young virgin will become consort
  to a dotard.

The place must be Ghent, but the
marriage referred to is obscure.

10/54

Nee en ce monde par concubine fertive
A deux hault mise par les tristes
  nouvelles
Entre ennemis sera prinse captive
Et amené à Malings et Bruxelles.

The child of a furtive concubine
At two, raised high by sad tidings
She will be captured by enemies
And taken to Malines and Brussels.

This is too vague for any definite
reading. Diane de Poitiers had two
daughters by Henri II, but neither was
taken to Malines or to Brussels.

10/70

L'oeil par object ferra telle excroissance
Tant et ardente que tumbera la neige
Champ arrousé viendra en descroissance
Que le primat succumbera à Rege.

Because of a foreign object, the eye
will swell terribly
As much and as vigorously as the
snow falls
The watered fields begin to shrink
When the Primate dies at Reggio.

The foreign object in the eye leads
inexorably back to Henri II's death in a
joust. Who the primate is who died in
Reggio remains a mystery. The quatrain
must consequently remain undated.

10/73

Le temps present avecques le passé
Sera jugé par grand Jovialiste
Le monde tard lui sera lassé
Et desloyal par le clergé juriste.

Time present with time past
Judgement by the great and cheerful
Jove
Only later will the world tire of him
Turning disloyal through the oath-
taking clergy.

The first line here is echoed in the
opening line of T. S. Eliot's poem Burnt
Norton: 'Time present and time past/Are
both perhaps present in time future/And
time future contained in time past.' Eliot
was a student of Nostradamus, and was
certainly aware of this quatrain when
writing the Four Quartets. Eliot's
implication, and, by definition,
Nostradamus's, is that hope is ultimately
meaningless, as time itself is
unredeemable. Nostradamus uses the

image of the pagan Gods, epitomised by
Jove, their King, to put his point across
about the fundamental fatuity inherent in
wishing to influence future events.

10/81

Mis tresor temple citadins Hesperiques
Dans icelui retiré en secret lieu,
Le temple ouvrir les liens fameliques.
Reprens ravis proie horrible au milieu.

Western citizens put their treasure in
a temple
Once inside, it is taken to a secret
place
The temple's locks are opened by the
famished
Retaken, plundered, something
terrible inside.

Nostradamus seems to anticipate a
universal Western loss of faith, caused
by the bottling-up of beliefs. Once the
locks are opened, the contents are
seen as putrid.

10/93

La barque neufve recevra les voyages
Là et aupres transferont l'empire
Beaucaire, Arles retiendront les hostages
Pres deux colomnes trouvees de paphite.

The new ship will make a few voyages
The empire will move there and away
Beaucaire and Arles will keep the
hostages
Near a place containing two columns
of porphyry.

This is about the Papal See, and its
hoped-for eventual move back to
France, although why to Beaucaire, a
small town 15 miles south of the former
Papal city of Avignon, remains a
mystery.

10/94

De Nismes, d'Arles, et Vienne contemner
N'obei tant à l'edict Hespericque
Aux labouriez pour le grand condamner
Six eschappez en habit seraphicque.

Scorn from Nîmes, Arles and Vienne
They will refuse to obey the Western
edict
It is hard work to condemn the great
man
Six escape in Franciscan garb.

This is both detailed and obscure, at
one and the same time. The last line
spoils any real chance of an accurate
commentary. It may refer once again to
Marshal Pétain. Could the mock monks
be escaped prisoners-of-war?

10/96

Religion du nom des mers vaincra
Contre le secte fils Adaluncatif
Secte obstinee deploree craindra
Des deux blessez par Aleph et Aleph.

A religion, named for the seas, will
triumph
Against the sect of the caitiff son of
Adam
This obstinate, deplorable sect will
fear
The two wounded by Aleph and
Aleph.

Aleph is the first letter of the Hebrew
alphabet. Adam is the first man created
of God. His caitiff (or cowardly) son
was Cain, who slew his brother Abel
through jealousy. Where Abel was a
shepherd and nomad, Cain was a
farmer. Cain is therefore the forerunner
of all historical land-grabbing and
enclosure, and the effective forefather
of our nation states. The new religion
that takes over from its war-like and
invasive predecessor will be named for
the seas. Will its new Messiah be the
one born on 11 August 1999, at the
time of the eclipse?

Index

Abbé Torné 129, 160
Abbey of Vermandois 8
Abdh-Allah IV 46
Abel 277
Aboukir Bay 98
Abyssinia 145, 146
Abyssinia, Emperor of 148
Academie Française 187
Act of Union with Northern Ireland (1800) 101
Adalbert, Crown Prince of Germany, 139
Adam 277
Adda river 95
Aemathion 62, 70
Agde 206
agrochemical 209
Aids 180
Alamo 123
Alaska 130
Alba 5
Alba (Spain), Duke of 5
Albanian Kosovans 202
Alcazar-Qivir, battle of 25
Alençon, Duke of 236, 252
Alexander the Great 211
Alexandria 98
Alexandra, Empress 140
Alfonso XIII, King 146
al-Fayed, Mohamed & Dodi 197, 198
Algeria 122, 123
Algiers 122
Ali Pasha 20
Alice in Wonderland 100

Allenby, General 139
Ambel 171
Amboise 13
Amboise, conspiracy of 13
Amboise, Edict of 23
Ambrosiano, Banco 188
Amritsar 183
Ancona 4
Andelot 7
Anet, château at 18
Angers 27
Angoulême, Duke of 86, 88, 95
Anjou, Duke of 31
Anne of Austria 54
Anne, Queen 55, 72
Anschluss Day in Austria 148
Antananarivo 120
Antibes 111
Antin, Bishop of 82
Antonio, José 147
Antwerp 26
Appian Way 135
Aqualeia 44
Aquitaine 170
Arab-Israeli wars 184
Araxum 20
Arcis-sur-Aube 112
Ardennes, forest of 160
Ariège 206
Aristotle 245
Arles (Provence) 54, 257
Armageddon 211, 224, 229
Armstrong, Neil 185
Arno river 120
Arras 13
Aryans 153
asteroid strike 227
Auch 212
Aude 35, 206, 235
Auden, W. H. 235

August Wilhelm, Crown Prince of Germany, 139
Aumale, Duke of 120
Aurora 31
Auschwitz 167
Australia 121
Austro-Turkish War 65
Avignon 83
Axis 165, 168
Ayatollah Khomeini 189, 194, 249

Babylon 38
Bach, Carl Philip Emmanuel 275
Bach, Johann Christian 275
Bach, Johann Sebastian 275
Badoglio, Pietro 166
Balagny 32
Banking Secrecy Law (1934) 156
Bantry Bay 67
Barbaris 35
Barcelona 9, 262
Barée 81
Barry, Madame du 73, 87
Bavaria 51, 52
Bayonne 111
Bazaine, General 132
Beachy Head 67
Beard, Thomas 62
Beaucaire 277
Beauharnais, Eugène de 105
Beauharnais, Joséphine de 95
Belgrade 198
Bellerophon 102, 114
Bengal 77
Benso, Camillo , Count of Cavour 127
Berich 252

Berlin 172, 173, 176
Berlin Wall 126
Berry, Duchess de 88,
  118, 119, 124
Bèze, Théodore de 16
Béziers 62
Bigorre 40
Biremes 229
Black Prince (1330–76)
  41
Black Sea 104
Blackfriars Bridge 188
Blair, Anthony 203
Blaye 205, 206
Bleterans 63
Blitzkrieg 58, 150,
  160, 162
Blois 27, 28, 29, 210,
  268
Blücher 114, 115, 116
Bluebeard 271
Boetia 200
Boétie, Etienne de la
  44
Bohemia 250
Bonaparte, Caroline
  78, 112
Bonaparte, Elisa, 78
Bonaparte, Empress
  Joséphine 78, 103,
  105, 108
Bonaparte, Joseph 110
Bonaparte, Napoleon
  78, 79, 81, 82, 88,
  91, 94, 95, 96, 97,
  98, 99, 100, 101,
  102, 103, 105, 107,
  108, 109, 110, 111,
  112, 113, 114, 115,
  116, 117, 119, 124,
  126, 198, 202, 238,
  247, 252, 261
Bonaparte, Pauline 78
Booth, John Wilkes
  130
Bouillon, Cardinal de
  71
Bordeaux 112, 157,
  170, 205
Bordeaux, Duke of 88,
  119
Bordelais 267

Borodino, battle of
  (1812) 109
Bothwell, Earl of 27
Bouches du Rhône 60
Boulogne 102
Bourbaki, General 133
Bourbons 13, 72, 82,
  84, 87, 91, 100, 117,
  118, 119, 146, 250
Bourbon, Cardinal de
  35
Bourbon, Charles of
  75
Bourbon-Condés 120
Bourg 44
Bourg-la-Reine 117
Bowie, Colonel
  William 123
Boyne, battle of the
  66, 67
Brabant, dukes of 59
Braunau am Inn 146
Bresse 271
Britain's General
  Election (1945) 172
British Empire 30
Brumaire 89
Brunswick-
  Wolfenbüttel, Duke
  Christian of 49
Brussels 52, 276
Buccleuch, Anne
  Countess of 65
Buffalora 96
Burgos 147
Burgundy 234
Burlamacchi, Francesco
  51
Burnt Norton 276
Butcher of Drogheda
  58
Buxar 77
Byron, Lord 119

Cadiz 36
Caepio 262
Cain 277
Cairo 144
Calabria 112
Calais 8
Calcutta, Black Hole of
  241

Calvi, Roberto 188
Campanella, Tommaso
  30
Campania 135
Canal du Midi 206
Canary Islands 147
Capets 66
Caporetto, battle of
  242
Cappe 93
Capture of Calais (6
  January 1558) 9
Capua 135
Capuchin monks 2
Capulet 93
Carcas 35
Carcassonne 35, 107
Carlos I 137
Carmania 235
Carter, Howard 144
Casket Letters 18
Castro, Fidel 181
Cateau-Cambrésis,
  Treaty of 12
Catherine the Great of
  Russia 72
Catholic Emancipation
  Bill 112
Catholic League 27,
  29, 30, 33, 34
Cato the Elder 262
Centrale Nucléaire du
  Blayais 205
Ceramon-agora 270
Cevennes 65
Challenger disaster (28
  January 1986) 186
Chamberlain, Neville
  (1869–1940) 149
Chambéry 36
Chambord, Count of
  124
Chanignon 42
Chappaquiddick 186,
  191
Casau, Charles de 36
Charles Emmanuel IV
  98
Charles I, King of
  England 44, 46, 50,
  55, 56, 57, 58, 61,
  62, 63

Charles II, King of
  England 55, 60, 62,
  65, 69, 70
Charles V, Emperor of
  Spain 4, 5, 9, 11, 17,
  22, 25, 39, 49, 53
Charles IX, King of
  France 15, 21, 23,
  24, 28
Charles X, King of
  France 19, 35, 88,
  118, 121, 124, 126
Charles XII, King of
  Sweden 108
Charles, Prince of
  Wales 197, 220
Chartres 117, 170
Chateau d'If, island of
  36
chemical war 207
Cherbourg 169
Chernobyl 193
Chios 104
Chislehurst 133
Chol, Nivière, mayor
  90
Christ's Passion 93
Churchill, Winston
  150, 172
Cinq-Mars 54
Ciudadela 10
Civil Constitution of
  the Clergy 83
Civil Rights Act 129
Civila Castellana 123
Clement V, Pope, 92
Clement VII, Pope, 9
Clerepeyne, Monsieur
  52
Clovis, conqueror of
  Roman Gaul 205
Cold War 176, 193,
  195
Coligny, Admiral
  Gaspard de 7, 19,
  22, 42, 55, 272
Committee of Public
  Safety 93
Common Market 178
Commonwealth 58
Commune 87
Concini Concino 47

Condés 250
Condé, Prince de 7,
  14, 15
Condom 250
Conservative Party 172
Constantine, King 184
Constantinople 3, 106
Convention of the
  Revolution 87
Corsica 6, 61, 77, 78
Cortes, Hernan 43
Cosimo 4
Courier de Paris à
  Versailles 90
Cranmer, Thomas 44
Crete 57, 98
Cristeros, Rebellion 82
Croatia, civil war
  (1991) 195
Crockett, Davy 123
Cromwell, Oliver 54,
  55, 56, 58, 59, 60,
  61, 62, 242, 247
Cromwell, Thomas 62
Crusader Wars 21
Cuban Missile Crisis
  (1962) 181
Culloden 76
Cyprus 39, 187
Cyrano de Bergerac
  269

D-Day landings see
  Normandy
Dachau 159
Dallas 182
Damscus 139
Danton 80
Danube 110, 175
Dardanelles 106
Darlan, Admiral 165
Darnley, Lord 18
Dauphin Francis 33
Dauphin of France in
  1558 26
Davout, Marshal 109
de Châtillon see
  Coligny
de Gaulle, Charles
  146, 154, 156, 160,
  165, 178

deforestation 209
Derby 76
d'Este, Cardinal Ipolito
  120
destruction of the
  environment 209
Diana, Princess of
  Wales 197, 198,
  220
Diane de Poitiers 4,
  12, 18, 37, 276
Diderot, Denis 72
Dien Bien Phu 178
Dieppe 4
Diocletian 103
Dolgorolkoff, Prince
  141
Don Carlos 26
Don John of Austria
  19, 20, 22, 23
Douro, Baron 107
Drake, Sir Francis 23,
  29
Duchy of Brunswick 49
Duckworth, Admiral
  Sir John Thomas
  106
Dubois, Guillaume 74
Dumas, Alexandre 55
Dunbar 59
Dunes, battle (1657)
  56
Dunkirk 157

E. H. Baily 105
Ebro river 209
Ebro, battle of 152
eclipse of the sun (11
  August 1999) 200,
  204, 277
Edinburgh 59, 76
Edward VIII 146, 147
Egyptian campaign of
  1799 112
El Niño current 203
Elba 5, 114, 115, 117
Elbe 174, 175
Elector of Mainz 105
Eliot, T. S. 276
Elizabeth I, Queen of
  England 9, 10, 18,
  27, 40, 45

Elizabeth II, Queen of England 178, 192, 198
Elizabeth of Austria 15
Emathios 31
Emiglia 127
Engels 126
English Civil Wars 60
Entebbe 219
Essex, Captain 36
Essonne 37
Étampes 37
ethnic-cleansing 202
Eugenie, Empress 127, 128
Euphrates 100, 189
Exposition Universelle 134

Falkland Islands 192
Farnese, Duke Alessandro 26
Fawkes, Guy 112
Ferdinand 39, 40, 47
Ferdinand I 10
Ferdinand II, Holy Roman Emperor 47, 48
Ferdinand, King of Bulgaria 142
Ferdinand Philippe 124
Ferdinand of Bohemia 48
Ferdinand, Archduke 137, 138, 139
Ferretti, Mastoi Count of Senigallia 127
Fieschi , Giuseppe Maria 123
Fiesole 257
First World War I (1914–18) 137, 138, 139, 141, 142, 143, 151, 237
Fleurus, battle of (1794) 79
Florence 3, 31, 47, 52, 76, 174, 183, 257
flu epidemic 199
flu virus 205
Foix, Gaston de 43

Ford's Theatre in Washington 130
Formentara 147
Fougères 31
Four Quartets 276
Fourth Crusade (1202) 265
France, fall of 163
France, occupation of 158
France's Revolutionary Constituent Assembly 84
Francis, duke of Lorraine 76
Francis II, King of France 11, 13, 15, 27
Francis IV, Duke of Florence 124
Franco, General Francisco 146, 147, 148, 192, 198
Franco-Prussian War 125, 131, 132, 133, 134
Franco-Spanish war of 1595–98 36
Franco-Spanish wars in Italy 6
François, Duc d'Alençon 24
Francus 94
Frederick the Great of Prussia 72
Frederick William III, King of Prussia 109
Fréjus, Allied landings at 174, 180
French Indochina War (1946–54) 242
French National Committee 156
French nuclear power plants 205
French Resistance during World War II 153
French Revolution (1789–99) 79, 80, 81, 82, 83, 88, 89, 93, 94, 100, 264

Friesland 67
Frondes 54

Gabriel de Lorge, Count Montgomery 11
Gabrielle d'Estrées 34, 37
Gadaffi, Colonel 55, 104, 186
Galtieri, General of Argentina 193
Gandhi, Indira 183
Ganges 77
Gard 51
Gardon river 6
Giuseppe Garibaldi 127, 130, 131, 133,259
Garonne 206
Gascony 35
Geneva 38, 65, 71, 175
Genghis Khan 199
Genoa 52, 77, 101, 102, 106, 115, 159, 167, 242
Gensoul, Admiral 154
George Cross medal 230
George Herbert, 5th Earl of Carnarvon 144
George I, King of England 72, 73
George V, King of England 142, 178
George VI, King of England 146
Ghent 276
Gibraltar 105
Gien 192
Gilboa, mount 252
Gironde river 112, 205, 206
global drought 214
global warming 211, 222
Glorious Revolution of 1688–9 66, 67
Goebbels 175
Golfe du Lion 206

Good Friday Agree-
    ment of 1998 201
Gorbachev, Mikhail,
    Soviet Union 193
Gorsas, Anoine Joseph
    90
Governor of Provence
    39
Goyon Grimaldi family
    53, 92, 266
Graham Greene 82
Granada 223, 246
Grand Banks of
    Newfoundland 138
Grassini, Guiseppina
    78
Gravelotte 132
Great Fire of London
    63
Great Plague of
    London 61, 63
greenhouse effect 203
Greenville, treaty of
    (1795) 94
Grenoble 115, 171
Grey, Lady Jane 44
Grimaldi see Goyon
    Grimaldi
Grouchy 114
Guadalajara, Mexico
    City 192
Guatemala 203
Guernica 180
Guienne 267
Guise 27
Guise, Cardinal of 30
Guise, Claude de 12
Guise, Duke of 5, 7, 8,
    9, 13, 27, 29, 30, 34,
    35, 238, 254
Guises 252
Gulf of Genoa 97
Gulf War (1991) 195,
    196, 207, 246
Gustavus Adolphus 52
Guyenne 148

Habsburg Spanish king
    4
Habsburg/Valois
    Italian Wars
    (1555–6) 3, 5

Habsburg/Valois War
    of 1547–59 41
Habsburgs 57, 105
Hague, Cap La , battle
    of (1692) 66
Haiti 78
Hale-Bopp comet
    (spring 1997) 200
Halley's comet 137,
    203, 210, 211
Halley, Edmund 210
Hannibal 213
Hanover 72
Hari, Mata 140
Harlay, Achille de 47
Harmand, Dr 93
Harrods 197
Helen of Troy 272
Henri 33
Henri Charles, Comte
    de Chambord 119
Henri II, King of
    France 5, 6, 7, 8, 11,
    12, 13, 15, 24, 28,
    34, 37, 41, 42, 210,
    238, 276
Henri III, King of
    France 15, 19, 23,
    25, 27, 28, 29, 30,
    31, 32, 34, 37, 236
Henri IV of Navarre,
    King of France 21,
    30, 31, 32, 33, 34,
    35, 36, 254
Henri V, King of
    France 268
Henry VII, King of
    France 27
Henrietta Maria 50
Henry, Bishop
    Maximilian of
    Bavaria 59
Henry VIII, King of
    England 40, 62, 80
Heraklion 57
Herne 84
Herodotus 38
Hinkley, William , Jr
    191
Hiroshima 176
Hitler, Adolf 133, 146,
    150, 151, 155, 157,

158, 159, 164, 165,
    166, 167, 170, 171,
    172, 173, 174, 175,
    198, 202, 238, 247
Hofkirche 53
Hohenzollern 132
Holy League of Italy,
    circa 1576 24
Hong Kong 198
Honoré II 53
Hôtel de Ville, Paris
    52
Houses of Parliament
    113
Houston, Sam 123
Howard, Captain 36
Hudson River 196
Huguenot/Catholic
    wars 19
Huguenots 5, 7, 8, 12,
    14
human cloning 214
Hundred Years War
    170
Hussein, Saddam 195,
    196, 197, 207, 246
Hyrcania 235
I
Ibiza 147
Idris, King of Libya
    186
Indian Mutiny (1857–
    59) 241
Indonesian riots (1998)
    198
Invalides 124
IRA 201
Iran–Iraq war (1980–
    88) 189, 190, 193,
    243
Iran-Contra
    investigation 193
Isabella 35
Isonzo, battle of 242
Israel 178
Italian wars 97
Italy, Allied invasion of
    166
Ivan IV, the Terrible,
    first Tsar of Russia
    14
Ivry, battle of 34

Jacques Clément 24, 32
Jakarta 198
James I *see* James VI
James II, King of
  England 63, 65, 66
James VI, King of
  Scotland (later also
  James I of England)
  18, 27, 45, 72, 113
Jarnac, battle of 14
Jawaharial Nehru 183
Jean Baptiste Amar 91
Jerome Groslot 15
Jerusalem 39
Jesus Christ 199, 265
Joachim, Crown Prince
  of Germany 139
John XXIII, Pope 180,
  182
John Calvin 16, 17, 38,
  42, 65, 71
John Paul I, Pope 187,
  188
John Paul II, Pope 188
Johnson, Vice-President
  Lyndon 182
Journée des Barricades
  27
Juan Carlos I, King of
  Spain 191
Juan Carlos, Prince
  146
Juan Negrín 152
Jules Mazarin 54
Julius Caesar 91, 227,
  234
Justinian I, Emperor
  245

Wilhelm I, Kaiser of
  Germany 132
Wilhelm II, Kaiser of
  Germany 139, 141,
  142, 143
Karlowitz, Treaty of
  64
Kennedy, Edward 183,
  186, 187, 191
Kennedy, John F., US
  President 181, 182,
  183, 185, 186, 187,
  191

Kennedy, Robert 183,
  185, 186, 187, 191
King Darius 38
King David 252
King of Fossano 118
King of Naples 75, 109
Kirk, Captain 98
Knights of Rhodes 97
Kopechne, Mary Jo
  191
Koresh, David 229
Kristallnacht 149
Kruschev, Nikita 181
Kutuzov, Marshal 109

La Fère-Champenoise
  112
La Ferté-Vedame 15
La Reine Margot 47
La Rochelle 50, 51, 64
La Turbie 269
Labour Party 172
Lake Geneva 255
Langon 205
Langres 27
Languedoc 206, 267
Lattre, General de 170
Laud, William,
  Archbishop of
  Canterbury 44, 56
Lausanne 16
Laval, Pierre 155, 172
Lawrence, T. E. 139
Le Désiré 117
Le Havre 16
Le Mans 12
Le Mans, battle of 91
Le Mas d'Agenais 251
League of Nations 175
Lebanon 193
Leda and the Swan 39
Lefebvre, Archbishop
  Marcel 180
Leganés 150
Legislative Assembly
  85
Leipzig 110
Leon 133
Leopold II, Grand
  Duke of Tuscany
  128
Lepanto 19

Les Arcs 167
Les Rosiers 62
L'Esacarène 269
Lepanto, battle of (7
  October 1571) 20,
  21, 23, 105, 269, 272
Lesbos 28, 218
Libertat, Pierre 36
Libya 104
Liége 59
Ligorio, Pirro 120
Ligurian sea 159
Limousin 148
Lincoln, Abraham 128,
  130, 131
Linz 175
Lisbon 77, 153
Lockerbie 216
Lodi, battle of (10
  May 1796) 95
Loire 88, 89, 110, 210
London 63, 156, 188
London Bridge 58
London, Great Fire of
  63
London, Tower of 58,
  241
Lorraine 35
Lorraine, House of 28,
  38
Lorraine, Nicolas de
  15
Los Angeles 185
Louis, Cardinal 28
Louis Napoleon later
  Napoleon III 118,
  123, 125, 126
Louis-Philippe, King
  of France 120, 121,
  122, 123, 124, 125,
  126, 137
Louis Phillippe of
  Portugal 137
Louis XIII, King of
  France 45, 47, 50,
  51, 52, 54, 206
Louis XIV, King of
  France 26, 53, 54,
  55, 56, 62, 64, 65,
  67, 68, 69, 70, 71,
  73, 74, 81

Louis XV, King of France 73, 74, 75, 78, 81, 87
Louis XVI, King of France 78, 80, 81, 83, 84, 85, 86, 87, 88, 89, 90, 91, 93, 94, 95, 117
Louis XVIII, King of France 88, 111, 115, 117, 119
Louvel 118
Louvre palace 21, 47
Lubéron 153
Lucca 51, 174
Lucerne 53
Luciani, Albino 188
Luciano, Lucky 177
Lunigiana, valley of 96
Lusignan family of crusader knights 39
Luther, Martin 48
Luxembourg 207
Lygustian sea 97
Lyons 87, 89, 90, 91, 92, 99, 159, 171, 271

Macedonia 142
Macmillan, Harold 181
Madame Guillotine 87, 88
Madrid 147, 150
Mafi 209
Mafia 185
Maginot, André-Louis-René 160
Maginot Line 34, 160
Magister, Tomasso 262
Magnavacca 130
Mahomet IX 46
Mainz 57
Makale 145
Makarios, Archbishop 187
Malines 276
Malines, Council of 46
Malta 17, 76, 97, 98, 159, 230, 270
Man in the Iron Mask 55

Mandosus 35
Mantor and Albe, Duke of 85
Mantua 152
Mao Tse Tung 108
Marengo, battle of 102
Margot, Reine 38
Marie-Antoinette, Queen of France 81, 84, 85, 86, 87, 91, 93
Marie Louise, Archduchess of Austria 108
Marie Thérèse Charlotte 86, 95
Maria Theresa, Empress of Austria 85
Marlborough, Duke of 67, 71
Marne river 113
Marne, battle of 138
Marseilles 36, 62, 90, 169, 235
Marx 126
Mary, Princess 63
Mary, Portuguese infanta 26
Mary, Queen of Scots 15, 18, 26
Mary Tudor, Queen of England 8, 10, 36
Masle 35
Massena 102
Matteoti, Deputy 144
Mausole 239
Mayenne, Duc de 28, 30, 34, 35
Mayenne, forest of 31
Mazarin, Cardinal 54, 55, 68, 256
Mechelen, near Maastricht 52
Medici, Catherine de 3, 4, 7, 11, 15, 17, 21, 22, 23, 24, 29, 30, 31, 33, 34, 47
Medici, Cosimo de, Duke of Florence 6
Medici, Giulio de 9
Medici, Queen Marie de 47, 50, 51

Medina Sidona, Duke of 29
Mehmet II 218
Melas, Baron von 102
Melilla 146
Memphis 53
Mendosus 33
Mers-el-Kebir 154
Mesopotamia 100, 153
Messiah 78, 199, 201, 204, 229, 277
Messina 76
meteor 218, 229, 231
Metternich 112
Metz 57, 132
Meuse 138
Mexico 82
Mexico City earthquake 193
Mexico, conquest of (1519) 43
Milan 96, 101, 102, 173, 174
Milosevic, Slobodan 195, 196, 199, 202
Mimnermia 127
Minorca 10
Minuit, Peter 273
Mir Kasim, Nawab of Bengal 77
Missolonghi 119
Mitylene 28
Modena 255
Monaco 53, 92, 101, 168, 207, 266, 269
Monségur 100
Montagnard guerillas 242
Montaigne 44, 134
Monte Allegro 274
Monte Cassino 167, 169
Montélimar Gap 171
Montezuma, Emperor of the Aztecs 43
Montferrand 79
Montferrat 79
Montgolfier 79
Montgomery, Count 12, 24
Montlhéry 37
Montmartre 112

Montmélain 36
Montmorency, Anne de 6, 7, 16, 44
Montmorency, Henri de 52
Moreau, General 91
Mortara 268
Moscow 109, 111, 238
Muhammad 195
Munich Olympics 219
Munich Pact (1938) 149
Munro, Sir Hector 77
Murano 188
Murat, Joachim 109, 110, 112
Muscadet 69
Mussolini, Benito, Il Duce 133, 143, 144, 145, 146, 148, 149, 150, 152, 159, 165, 166, 171, 173, 174, 175, 179, 264

Nagasaki 198
Nancy 52, 57, 75
Nantes 69
Nantes, Edict of (1598) 32, 33, 65
Naples 166,
Napoleon see Bonaparte
Napoleon III 120, 127, 128, 129, 131, 132
Napoleonic Wars 101, 109, 110, 111
Narbon 84
Narbonne 35, 207
Narbonne, Count Louis de 90
National Assembly 80
National Convention 88, 90, 92
Nato (North Atlantic Treaty Organisation) 199, 202, 203, 215, 241
Nato bombing (March 1999) 198
Navarre 21, 32, 34, 40, 250
Nelson, Admiral Lord Horatio 104, 105

New York 196, 273
Ney, Marshal 109, 116
Nice 71, 114
Nicholas II, Tsar 140, 141, 241
Nîmes 6, 51, 247
Nixon, Richard 185, 233
Nolaris 35
Normandy, Allied invasion of (6 June 1944) 158, 168, 170
Normandy, Duke of 85, 88
North Vietnamese Tet offensive (1968) 242
Northern Ireland peace agreement 219
Noyades at Nantes 88
nuclear war 208
nuclear winter 212, 217
nuclear-powered submarines 207
Nuremberg 52

Ogmiom 122
Ogmion 263
Olympus, mount 218
Operation Desert Storm 196
Oporto 107
Oradour sur Glane 168
Orange 72
ordination of women 217
Orgon 206, 207
Orléans 27, 119, 170
Orléans, Duke of 74, 119, 122, 125, 236
Orsini, Felice 127
Osho (Bhagwan Shree Rajneesh) 229

Palermo 166
Pan Am airliner 216
Panama, isthmus of 23
Papa, Cape 20
Paris 21, 27, 30, 33, 34, 35, 37, 54, 68, 81, 84, 85, 86, 88,

90, 105, 112, 113, 114, 115, 121, 122, 131, 140, 157, 158, 160, 185, 272
Parma 42, 44, 75
Parma, Duke of 26, 33, 34, 238
Parme 34
Pasha, Yusuf Karamanli 104
Pasteur, Louis 131
Passchendaele 242
Patrice Chereau 47
Paul IV, Pope, 10
Paul V, Pope 46, 187
Paul VI, Pope 79, 108, 182, 183, 187, 252
Pavia, battle of 41
Pearl Harbour 163, 164
pediculosis 243
Peninsular War 107
Peron, Eva 179
Perón, Juan Domingo 179
Perugia 42
Petacci, Clara 173, 174
Pétain, Marshal Henri Philippe 154, 155, 156, 157, 158, 159, 166, 170, 171, 233, 277
Pharos 161, 218
Philip II, King of Spain 5, 11, 13, 17, 20, 25, 26, 29, 33, 35, 36, 39, 49, 62, 70
Philippe, Duke of Orléans 73
Philistines 252
Philosophes 72
phthiriatic lice infestation 243
Piazza Colonna 174
Piazza San Michele 51
Picardy 36
Picasso, Pablo 180
Piombino 5, 114
Pisa 42, 52
Pisseleu, Anne de 37
Pius IV, Pope, 40
Pius VI, Pope 79, 97, 98, 99, 100, 108, 252

Pius VII, Pope, 82, 97, 98, 99, 103, 106, 107, 108
Pius VIII, Pope, 88
Pius IX, Pope, 127
Pius XII, Pope 150
Place de la Concorde 93
Place de la Revolution 81, 87, 93
Plato 245
Po river 97, 173
Poitiers 205
Poitiers, Edict of 25
Poitou 51
Pompey 227
Pont d'Antony 117
Pompadour, Madame de 73, 74
Popowo, Poland 190
population of the world 208
Porceau, Cap de 61
Porto de Garibaldi 130
Potosi mines of New Castile 23
Potsdam 139
Pozarevac in Serbia 196
Pradelles 79
Prague 47
Prato 144
Priam, King of Troy 39, 94
Prince Imperial, son of Napoleon III 133
Provençal Alps 171
Provence 119
Ptolemaic Dynasty of 323–30 BC 53
Punic Wars 234
Pyrenees 31, 36, 107, 110, 111, 120, 206, 209, 267

Radama I 120
Rais, Gilles de 271
Raleigh, Captain 36
Rambouillet Peace Talks 199
Ranavalona I 120
Rasputin, Grigori 140, 233

Ratonneau, islands of 36
Ravenna 43, 127, 130, 196
Reagan, Ronald, US President 176, 191, 193
Reformation (1525) 52
Reggio 276
Reich 157
Reign of Terror 91, 92, 93
Reims 69, 232
Religious Wars 41
Revocation of the Edict of Nantes in 1685 64
Révolution de Juillet 121
Revolutionary Wars 80
Reza Pahlavi, Shah of Iran 190
Rhine 68
Rhodes 162, 173, 230
Rhône 87, 91, 92, 99, 100, 207
Rian , Jean de 61
Richelieu, Cardinal 45, 50, 51, 54, 256
Rimini 144
Risorgimento 128, 131
Rivera, Primo de 147
Riviera 176
Robespierre, Maximilian 80, 87, 93
Robine river 235
Roche, Cape 105
Rochejaquelein, Henri de la 242
Romagna 133
Romania 47
Romanoffs, Olga, Tatiana, Marie and Anastasia 14, 141
Rome 79, 98, 99, 106, 107, 108, 130, 131, 135, 146, 174, 192, 234
Romeo and Juliet 275
Roosevelt, Franklin D. 119

Rouen 131, 170, 238
Rougon 270
Rousseau, Jean-Jacques 72, 100
Route Napoleon 114
Rump Parliament 61
Rundstedt, Field Marshal Gerd von 170
Russian Revolution 140, 142

Sabine mountains 120
Saint Catherine 3
Saint Catherine of Siena 22
Saint-Cloud 31
St Bartholemew's Day massacre (24 August 1572) 21, 22, 23, 34, 38, 42
St Columba 268
St George 269
St Helena 108, 111, 114, 115, 116, 119, 124
St Jean de Luz 111
St Jean-de-Maurienne 36
St Julien 36
St Lucy's day 91
Saint Napoleon 103
St Paul 50
St Paul's cathedral 63
St Peter 273
St Peter's, Rome 28
St Pius X 180
St Privat 132
St Quentin, battle of (1557) 7, 8, 13, 238
St Rémy 2, 239
St Sauveur-de-la-Fontaine at Nîmes 248
Salerno 159
Salò 173
Salon 1, 3, 206, 239
Salonika 3
Saluces, Monsieur 84
San Francisco 185
San Sebastiani, Jacopo 44

Sanson 88
Santa Anna 123
Santiago de Cuba 192
Saône 87, 91, 92, 99, 100
Sarajevo 137, 139
Sardinia 61, 231
Saturn 64
Saul 252
Savona 4, 115
Savoy 129, 259
Savoy, Duke of 7, 11, 17, 36
Savoy, House of 115
Scheldt river 17
Scott, James, Duke of Monmouth 65
Second Vatican Council (1962) 180, 181, 182
Second World War (1939–45) 34, 139, 146, 150, 151, 152, 153, 154, 155, 156, 157, 158, 162, 163, 164, 165, 167, 168, 169, 174, 175, 176, 177, 178, 230, 237, 238, 268
Sebastian, King of Portugal 25
Seine 110, 113
Selim II, son of Great Suleiman 19, 20
Selim III of Turkey 106
Senger und Etterlin, General Frido von 167
Senta, battle of (1697) 67
Seventh War of Religion 26
Seward, William 130
Shaefer, Major General 170
Shakespeare, William 262
Si-Hamza of the Walid-sidi-Sheikh family 122
Sicily 39, 76, 166, 177, 270

Siena 3, 4, 6, 200
Sigmariggen 170
Simon the Shoemaker 93
Simpson, Wallis 146, 147
Sindona, Michele 182
Six Day War (5–10 June 1967) 184
Smolensk 109
Socrates 245
Sodom, Ferté 271
Solidarity movement 190
Solway Firth 27
Sopron 64
Soult, Marshal 107, 111, 113
Soviet Baltic fleet 194
Soviet-German Non-aggression Pact (1939) 151
Soviet/Finnish War (1939–40) 242
Spanish Armada 28, 30
Spanish Civil War (1936–39) 147, 148, 150, 152, 165
Spanish Republic, formation in 1923 175
Spencer, Earl 197
Stalin, Joseph 202
Stalingrad 175, 164, 238
Stanislas Leczinski, last Duke of Lorraine 75
Stewart, Henry, Cardinal of York 106
Stuart, Charles Edward (Bonnie Prince Charlie), the Young Pretender 76
Stuart, James (the Old Pretender) 72
Sudetenland 149
Suleiman II, Sultan 66, 67
Suleiman the Magnificent, Sultan of Turkey 3, 5, 19

Susa 200

Talleyrand-Périgord, Charles de 82
Tarpean Rock 118
Tarsus 50
Temple 94, 95
Temple prison 93
Tende, Count of 39
Thames 67
Thatcher, Margaret, UK Prime Minister 192, 193, 194
The Power and the Glory 82
Thessaly 98
Third Estate 123
Third Punic War 262
Third Reich 151, 172
Third Republic of Thiers and MacMahon 120
Thirty Years' War (1618–48) 47, 48, 49, 50, 52, 57, 191
Tibur river 120
Ticino river 173
Tigris river 100, 189
Titanic 137
Tithonus 31
Tivoli 120
Tolentino, Treaty of (1797) 79
Torfou 37
Toulon 90, 91
Toulouse 64, 92, 113, 205, 262, 269
Touraine, rosé of 69
Tours 69, 157, 192
Trafalgar, battle of 104, 105
Trafalgar Square 105
Trebizond 104, 218, 259
Tripoli 104
triremes 229
Trojan Wars 39
Troyes 27
Tuileries Palace 81, 84, 99, 131
Tunis 22, 23
Turin 75, 115, 127

Tuscany 152

United Nations 175, 248
Urban VII, Pope 50
Urban VIII, Pope 50
Urgel 274
US Fifth Army 159
US hostages 193
US Seventh Army 174
US Space Programme 186
Utrecht, Treaty of 69, 70
Uzès 51

V-1 rockets 169
V-2 rockets 169
Valence 99, 100
Valois 34
Valois, Marguerite de 38
vampires 271
Var river 129
Varano 269
Varennes 84, 86, 89, 90
Vasto 258
Vatican 33, 107
Vatican Bank 182, 188
Vendôme 33, 35
Vendômes 250
Venice 19, 44, 96, 124, 127, 133, 164
Vercors Plateau 171
Verona 44, 52, 96
Versailles 53
Versailles, treaty of (1919) 134, 142, 143, 151
Vervins, treaty of 36
Vicenza 96
Viceroy of Italy 105
Vichy Government of 1940–44 159, 166

Vichy Milice 166
Victor Emmanuel I 98
Victor Emmanuel II 127, 129, 130, 148
Victor Emmanuel III 143, 165
Vienna 148
Vienna, Congress of (1815) 59
Vienna, relief of 64
Vienne 171
Vietnam war 185
Villa d'Este 120
Villar, Marshal 242
Villeneuve, Admiral 105
Villmergen 71
Vitry-le-François 80
Vittoria 110
Vo Nguyen Giap, General 178
Voltaire 72

Walesa, Lech 190
Walewska, Maria 78
Walpole, Robert 72
Walter, Lucy 65
War of Independence 101
War of Independence (1821–32) 119
Wars of Religion (1562) 15, 28
War of the Spanish Succession (1701–14) 26, 69, 70
War of the Malcontents 24
Wars of Religion 16, 32, 38, 40
Warsaw Pact 194
Waterloo, battle of

(1815) 94, 112, 113, 114, 115, 116, 117
Wellesley, Arthur, later Duke of Wellington 106, 107, 111, 112, 113, 115, 116, 247
Wellington see above
Wesley, John 75
Westminster Abbey 62, 252
Westphalia, treaty of 50,57
White Star Line 138
White Terror of 1794 242
Whitehall Palace 58
Wilhelm, Crown Prince of Germany 139
William III of Orange 56, 63, 66, 67
Windsor Castle 58
Wittgenstein, Ludwig 159
Woolwich 133
Worcester 60
Worcester, battle of (1651) 60
World Trade Centre 196

Yangtse river 208
Yekaterinberg 141
Yellow river 208
York, Duchess of, Sarah Ferguson 253
York, Duke of 147
Ypres, battle of 242

Zeus 39
Zidan 46
Zopyrus 38